SHAKESPEARE AND REPUBLICANISM

Shakespeare and Republicanism is a groundbreaking work by a leading scholar of the Renaissance. Andrew Hadfield reveals for the first time exactly how Shakespeare was influenced by contemporary strands in political thought that were critical of the English crown and constitution. Shakespeare has often been seen as a conservative political thinker characterized by an overriding fear of the 'mob'. Hadfield argues instead that Shakespeare's writing emerged out of an intellectual milieu fascinated by republican ideas. From the 1590s onwards, he explored republican themes in his poetry and plays: political assassination, elected government, alternative constitutions, and, perhaps most importantly of all, the problem of power without responsibility. Beginning with Shakespeare's apocalyptic representation of civil war in the *Henry VI* plays, Hadfield provides a series of powerful new readings of Shakespeare and his time. For anyone interested in Shakespeare and Renaissance culture, this book is required reading.

ANDREW HADFIELD is Professor of English at the University of Sussex. He is the author of *Spenser's Irish Experience* (1997), *Literature, Travel and Colonial Writing* (1998) and *Shakespeare and Renaissance Politics* (2003). He is also the editor of *Representing Ireland* (with Willy Maley and Brendan Bradshaw, 1993), *The Cambridge Companion to Spenser* (2001) and *Shakespeare and Renaissance Europe* (with Paul Hammond, 2004).

SHAKESPEARE AND REPUBLICANISM

ANDREW HADFIELD

CAMBRIDGE
UNIVERSITY PRESS

CAMBRIDGE UNIVERSITY PRESS
Cambridge, New York, Melbourne, Madrid, Cape Town, Singapore, São Paulo

Cambridge University Press
The Edinburgh Building, Cambridge CB2 2RU, UK

Published in the United States of America by Cambridge University Press, New York

www.cambridge.org
Information on this title: www.cambridge.org/9780521816076

First published 2005

Printed in the United Kingdom at the University Press, Cambridge

A catalogue record for this book is available from the British Library

ISBN-13 978-0-521-81607-6 hardback
ISBN-10 0-521-81607-6   hardback

For Lucy Eleanor Hadfield

Contents

Preface

This book has had something of a complex history, one that fanciful observers might suggest actually mirrors its subject. I was able to write it only because I was awarded a Leverhulme Major Research Fellowship (2001–4). I am extremely grateful to the Trust, whose members have been most generous in supporting my research, and I hope that the finished product is what they envisaged. Nearly all of the book was written in the Department of English at the University of Sussex, a truly republican institution, where friendship is valued alongside intellectual endeavour, and (relative) equality is the order of the day. The research was carried out at two rather more tyrannically inclined centres of learning, an obscure outpost near a Black Sea, the name of which escapes me for now, and one right in the heart of the new Rome, overseen by a modern Tiberius. Nevertheless, I had the benefit of some splendid republican allies, most notably my friends David Scott Kastan, Tom Paulin and Jim Shapiro, who helped shape the book through an extensive series of conversations, also reading and correcting extracts, as well as providing useful leads and references. I will miss their company. I also enjoyed working with and learnt much from Julie Crawford, Cathy Eden, Jean E. Howard and Bruce Robbins. My students, too, were a great source of inspiration, especially those who took my Shakespeare lecture course and Spenser graduate course.

Many other friends and colleagues have helped make this book see the light of day. It has been a pleasure, as always, to work with Ray Ryan at Cambridge University Press, who has believed in the project from the start and made my life easier by allowing me to obtain an advance contract for the book. His advice has always been valuable, as has his friendship. The four anonymous readers who commented on the proposal I submitted to the press gave extremely good advice that helped sharpen and focus my ideas at an early stage. My new early modern colleagues in the English Department at Sussex – Brian Cummings, Matt Dimmock,

Margaret Healy and Alan Sinfield – have all proved splendid to work with, as I always knew they would. I am grateful to David Armitage; Colin Burrow, who has given me the benefit of his vast erudition and sceptical attention; Patrick Cheney, for many stimulating conversations over the years, in person, as well as by telephone and e-mail, and most especially for his comments on Marlowe, which have helped shape this study; Tom Corns, who was most helpful in the early stages of the project; Martin Dzelzainis, who listened patiently and shared some thoughts with me on a longish train journey; Professor Jack Hadfield, always a loyal companion, who has made many long walks seem short; Paul Hammond, for being an important mine of information and source of genial conversation, as well as a trenchant critic of badly expressed ideas; John Kerrigan; Rebecca Lindner for helping me understand the political nature of early modern romance; Nigel Llewellyn, who went well beyond the call of duty in helping me sort out the cover illustration; Willy Maley, who has been a kind and generous reader over the years, as well as a dear friend; Rebecca Nesvett for teaching me a great deal about English perceptions of classical Greece, a subject that informs this study, implicitly, if not always explicitly; David Norbrook; Markku Peltonen; Nicholas Royle, who lent me his thoughts on *Julius Caesar*; Kevin Sharpe, who has always been an encouraging friend and mentor; and my former research assistant, Matt Zarnowiecki, who was a great help with Chapter Three, a pleasure to work with, and very good at making the most of hopelessly vague questions and unreasonable demands. I should also add that this book would not have been possible without the labours of those historians, scholars and literary critics who have done so much to unearth and conceptualize the forms that early modern republicanism took. Although they may not agree with my methods and conclusions, this study has greatly benefited from the work of David Armitage, J. H. Burns, Patrick Collinson, Mark Goldie, David Norbrook, Markku Peltonen, J. G. A. Pocock, Quentin Skinner, Nigel Smith and Blair Worden. Alison Hadfield provided a splendid index at short notice.

I have been grateful to be able to air my views at various venues, and for the discussion and feedback I have received from critical, but invariably helpful audiences. Parts of Chapter Three were presented at the London Renaissance Seminar (November 2003), my thanks to Tom and Margaret Healy for inviting me to speak; parts of the introduction and chapter 5 were presented at the Pennsylvania State University (October 2002), my thanks to Patrick Cheney for inviting me, and at the English Graduate Colloquium, University of Sussex (October 2003), my thanks to Jenny

Bourne Taylor for inviting me; part of Chapter Four was presented at the symposium 'Religion and Politics in English Poetry and Drama, 1520–1640' at the Université of Fribourg, Switzerland (May 2004), my thanks to Anthony Mortimer for inviting me, and as one of the annual Jon Lopategui lectures at Hampton Court, sponsored by the University of Kingston-upon-Thames (December 2004), my thanks to Tom Betteridge for inviting me; and an overview of the book, along with sections of Chapter Six, was presented as a plenary lecture at the Ninth Nordic Conference for English Studies, Aarhus Universitet, 27–29 May 2004, my thanks to Dominic Rainsford for inviting me.

I would like to thank the editors of *Textual Practice* and Routledge for allowing me to reproduce sections of my article 'Shakespeare and Republicanism: History and Cultural Materialism', *Textual Practice* 17 (2003), 461–83, in the Introduction and Chapter Five; and the editors and Manchester University Press for allowing me to reproduce part of my essay, 'Hamlet's Country Matters: The "Scottish Play" within the Play', in Willy Maley and Andrew Murphy, eds., *Shakespeare and Scotland* (Manchester: Manchester University Press, 2004), pp.87–103.

My family have, as ever, made my labours all the more enjoyable and, I hope, I have been able to repay them by getting better at containing my efforts within the working week and becoming more charming and less grumpy at home. My love and thanks, as always, to Alison, Lucy, Patrick and Maud. The book is dedicated to Lucy, even though she may be a royalist at heart.

Note on the text

i/j and u/v have been silently modernized. Elsewhere I have tried to use original texts where possible, but have sometimes used modern editions where it is more convenient to do so, does not affect the argument, and allows readers the chance to explore the material more easily themselves. I have used the Arden Shakespeare as my main Shakespeare text, but referred to other editions when necessary or desirable.

Abbreviations

AHR	*The American Historical Review*
AJLH	*The American Journal of Legal History*
BJRLM	*Bulletin of the John Rylands Library of Manchester*
CD	*Comparative Drama*
CR	*The Centennial Review*
DNB	*Dictionary of National Biography*
EHR	*English Historical Review*
ELH	*English Literary History*
ELR	*English Literary Renaissance*
ES	*English Studies*
HJ	*The Historical Journal*
HLQ	*The Huntington Library Quarterly*
JBS	*Journal of British Studies*
MLQ	*Modern Language Quarterly*
MRDE	*Medieval and Renaissance Drama in England*
MRTS	*Medieval & Renaissance Texts & Studies*
N. & Q.	*Notes and Queries*
P. & P.	*Past and Present*
PHR	*Pacific Historical Review*
PMLA	*Publications of the Modern Language Association of America*
RES	*Review of English Studies*
RHS	*Royal Historical Society*
RQ	*Renaissance Quarterly*
SEL	*Studies in English Literature, 1500–1900*
Sh. St.	*Shakespeare Studies*
Sh. Sur.	*Shakespeare Survey*
SJ	*Sidney Journal*
SP	*Studies in Philology*
SQ	*Shakespeare Quarterly*
TLS	*The Times Literary Supplement*

SHR	*Scottish Historical Review*
SHS	*Scottish History Society*
SP	*Studies in Philology*
Sp. Stud.	*Spenser Studies*
YES	*Yearbook of English Studies*

Introduction I: Was Shakespeare a republican?

Was Shakespeare a republican? Does it matter whether he was? And what do we mean by republicanism? These are the main questions that I want to answer in this book. What I wish to show is that Shakespeare's work emerged out of a culture that was saturated with republican images and arguments, even if these were never clearly defined or properly articulated, as many historians have argued.[1] Shakespeare produced literary works of republican significance at key points in his career: the *Henry VI* plays (late 1580s, early 1590s); *The Rape of Lucrece* (1593); *Titus Andronicus* (1594); *Julius Caesar* (1599); *Hamlet* (1601); *Othello* (1602?); and *Measure for Measure* (1603), to name only the most obvious examples. However, this history has disappeared from view for a variety of reasons, resulting in an impoverished and distorted understanding of the nature of Shakespeare's achievement. My hope is that this book will enable readers to revisit the issues that Shakespeare raises in many of his works, even if they do not agree with my particular interpretations of the plays. It is little short of a scandal that the vigorous and lively political culture of Elizabethan and Jacobean England, one that no writer would have wished to avoid, has become so obscured that debates over Shakespeare's politics have all too often either been concerned with his allegiance and affiliation, or considered a minor question of specialist interest rather than a central issue that, if ignored, will diminish our understanding of English Renaissance culture. Before the central issues that this book seeks to explore can be analysed the reasons for such serious neglect need to be explained and the nature of early modern English political culture outlined. It is my contention that republicanism is not simply one of many subjects we might wish to use to contextualise Shakespeare's work. Rather, it is one of the key problems that defined his working career.

I

HISTORICAL PROBLEMS

Shakespeare's political culture has been seriously misrepresented and misread by a whole variety of critics and historians who are more closely connected to popular, mass perceptions of Shakespeare than they often realize.[2] This symbiotic relationship, amounting to collusion at times, should not surprise us, given Shakespeare's overwhelming, often stifling cultural authority.[3] Shakespeare has become part of our intellectual furniture, so much so that his presence can serve to preclude thought rather than to encourage it.[4] Yet Shakespeare assumed his cultural dominance only after his death. The rise of Shakespeare was only just beginning in the early seventeenth century; he would assume his unassailable position in England after the Restoration, and, in European letters, towards the end of the eighteenth century.[5] As Brian Vickers has recently argued, it is likely that many of his plays were co-written, either with other working dramatists such as George Peele, Thomas Middleton, John Fletcher and George Wilkins, or with various members of his company.[6] However, when his fellow actors Henry Condell and John Heminge collected together plays that Shakespeare had written to cash in on his name with the posthumous publication of the first folio in 1623, they undoubtedly realized that it was the title *Mr. William Shakespeares Comedies, Histories, & Tragedies* that would sell the large, expensive volume, not the scrupulous inclusion of others who had lent a hand.[7]

The point is that if we are seriously interested in recovering the archaeology of Shakespeare, of reconstructing the contexts in which he existed and wrote, and in trying to understand the culture in which his work developed, then we have to put to one side most of Shakespeare's dramatic tradition.[8] The records of early performances of Shakespeare's plays are scanty, as all scholarly editions inform their readers. There is a picture in one of Henry Peacham's surviving manuscripts which may be a scene from *Titus Andronicus*.[9] The Swiss traveller Thomas Platter has left a record of the first run of performances of *Julius Caesar* at the Globe Theatre in 1599.[10] The astrologer and physician Simon Forman has left records of a number of performances, but these often raise as many questions as they answer. His accounts of *Macbeth*, *Cymbeline* and *The Winter's Tale* all diverge significantly from any surviving texts and call into question his reliability as a witness.[11] The first substantial records of performances date from the Restoration, after the reopening of the theatres in 1660 when they had been closed for eighteen years.[12] This hiatus marks the end of one dramatic tradition, separating it from the start of another, characterized by the accepted rule of Shakespeare. In fact, as David Scott Kastan points out, the closure of the theatres resulted in more plays being published, enlarging and changing the dramatic canon.[13] The first age of commercial theatre in England existed from the 1560s until 1642.[14]

Recovering involves forgetting as well as remembering.[15] The very tradition that makes Shakespeare so centrally important to an understanding of our culture, and the reason why more books are written about him than any other writer, paradoxically, only serves to interfere with and distort the writing of the history of the theatre for which he wrote. It is not that we know nothing at all about Shakespeare's theatre, or that attempts to reconstruct it are doomed to failure. The task is by no means impossible, even though it is clearly difficult and problematic. Every effort has gone into making the Globe Theatre as accurate a reconstruction of the original as is humanly possible, with considerable success.[16] And, if the advent of the New Globe has had any effect on the performance of Shakespeare, it has been to ensure that we approach the plays with less reverence and awe than was the case before. The Globe experiment has shown that the common playgoers standing in front of the stage are more important in the dramatic process than most theatre historians had acknowledged. Their ability to move around freely, interject and participate in the action, as well as show approval and disapproval, reveals the Elizabethan and Jacobean theatre to have been a relatively democratic public space, certainly when compared to a modern theatre. If a developing consensus about the relatively wide social composition of the audience for early modern plays is also correct, then we can see that Shakespeare's theatre was a different world, one that we have to reconstruct carefully, always alert to the possibility that what we assume we know about Shakespeare may be false or misleading.[17]

Shakespeare wrote for the theatre at a time of great uncertainty for actors and writers, a state of affairs neatly mirrored by our own shadowy notions of why writers produced literature and drama and what function drama and literature served.[18] The surviving evidence also indicates that writers entered a profession that provided them with an insecure livelihood, as they sought remuneration from aristocratic patrons such as the earl of Leicester or the Sidney family, publication, or through using their skill at writing to persuade great men and women to employ them in the capacity of secretaries and other functionaries within the household.[19] Many writers of Shakespeare's generation who came to London, such as Thomas Lodge (?1557–1625), Robert Greene (c.1558–92), George Peele

(1558–96), Henry Chettle (*c.*1560–*c.*1607), and Christopher Marlowe (1564–93), wrote a variety of works – plays, poetry, prose fiction, romances, pamphlets – and were employed in different ways at different times – printer, spy, physician and sailor among them. The famous reference to Shakespeare as an 'upstart crow' suggests that there was a keen rivalry between such writers as they competed for scarce resources.[20] Shakespeare, as is well known, acquired considerable wealth through becoming a shareholder of the King's Men, and had a hand in other business enterprises.[21] In pointed contrast, Henry Chettle and Robert Greene produced enormous quantities of works, Chettle writing or co-authoring some fifty known plays in fourteen years (1593–1607) compared to Shakespeare's output of about thirty-nine in some twenty-two years (*c.*1590–*c.*1612). Even so, both Greene and Chettle died in poverty.[22]

In such a professional climate, dramatists – and writers in general – had to produce material quickly, take risks and hope that what they wrote appealed to a wide audience (or a few powerful and influential courtiers). One way of doing this was to be topical and to refer to recent events, whether in the main plot or more allusively and occasionally. It is hardly surprising that so much drama produced in the first age of the English commercial theatre is either political in nature, or has topical signifi-cance.[23] There was a long court tradition of drama that was inherently political in seeking to advise the monarch either forcefully, or subtly, a tradition which continued alongside the commercial theatre, either through plays being performed at court, sometimes probably adapted from their public stage productions, or in the form of specific court entertainments such as the masque.[24] One of the most significant court plays, Thomas Norton and Thomas Sackville's *Gorboduc*, first acted in 1561 and published in 1565, which sought to persuade the queen to marry and produce an heir for her subjects, was later adapted for the commercial stage by William Haughton in the 1590s as *Ferrex and Porrex* (now lost), undoubtedly because of its topical relevance.[25] One of the many things that connected the court and the London theatre was an interest in political events and issues.[26]

Exactly how political events, problems and theories are represented in plays is a matter of considerable conjecture and is often impossible to establish with any confident certainty. Some critics argue that the theatre was seen as a powerful social institution that members of the government feared would lead to the development of either some form of opposition to the status quo, or more random subversion and sedition: specifically, rioting. Others counter that the theatre was regarded more as a form of escapist entertainment, possibly a safety valve for excess emotion, but hardly a serious political forum.[27] The issue is a complex one, but probably the truth is that the theatre played both roles at different times, or even, at the same time for different members of the audience (and those watching them). It is little wonder that the authorities would become nervous of the theatre at various times and try to close it down (generally using the excuse of the plague), given that it provided a public space where large numbers of disgruntled and unruly citizens could meet. Barbara Freedman has argued, in an article that deserves to be much more widely known by historians of the theatre, that apprentices would often meet in the theatre, energetic and aggressive young men, conscious of their relative poverty and economic exploitation, more interested in drinking and bear-baiting than watching thoughtful drama.[28] Such evidence cuts both ways. On the one hand, it shows that the authorities were nervous of the theatres because of the sheer number of people assembled in them; but on the other, it suggests that such fear was not generated because an articulate citizenry was being formed through observing subversive, politically astute drama.

However, we need not assume that Freedman's analysis transforms the theatre into a place of endless carnivalesque riot; rather, that it complicates an already complicated picture. Further evidence of the attitudes of powerful courtiers, churchmen and members of the government – specifically those in the Privy Council, the inner circle of the monarch's advisers – is provided by the history of censorship.[29] Once again, the evidence is hotly disputed by scholars. On the one side are those, following in the footsteps of F. S. Siebert, who argue that an authoritarian and nervous government tried to control what was produced on the stage and published as carefully as possible, scrutinizing material sent to it when the play was entered in the Stationers' Register, and then calling in subversive works which had somehow slipped through the net.[30] On the other are scholars who argue that actually very little censorship of literature, drama and historical writing took place during the reigns of Elizabeth and James. The office of Master of the Revels, the overseer of drama in the capital and at court, collaborated with playing companies so that they did not run into any trouble and was not a simple agent of repression.[31] A great deal of comment and criticism was permitted on the stage particularly, and only when a book or a play threatened to create a diplomatic incident, or seriously undermined the stability of the regime – as was the case with the publication of John Stubbs's *The Discoverie of a Gaping Gulf Whereunto England Is Like to be Swallowed* (1579), which attacked Elizabeth's proposed marriage to the French duke François, duke of Alençon, or the scandalous criticisms made of the Spanish ambassador and the proposed match of Prince Charles and the Spanish Infanta in Thomas Middleton's *A Game at Chess* (1624) – was the power of the regime deployed to silence its opponents.[32]

The latter view appears to be gradually establishing itself as the prevailing orthodoxy among scholars.[33] However, we still need to know far more about the impact of censorship and the fear it produced, whether writers felt the need to encode their messages and how far allegorical readings were generated as a result of a few spectacular acts of brutality, such as the severing of John Stubbs's right hand when he was convicted of sedition, or the Privy Council's interrogation of Doctor John Hayward after he dedicated his history of *The Life and Raigne of King Henrie IIII* (1599) to Robert Devereux, second earl of Essex.[34] A 'cat and mouse' game was undoubtedly in progress, but how clear were the rules to each side? And how much did either side want to play by them?[35] Moreover, it is still very hard to know whether omissions of passages from some plays in certain editions, such as the absence of the deposition scene from the first quarto of Shakespeare's *Richard II* (1597), which was restored in the folio, was the work of censorship, fear of censorship, editing or even memory loss.[36] Equally, it is hard to know whether subsequently controversial works such as Edmund Spenser's *A View of the Present State of Ireland*, entered into the Stationers' Register in April 1598, but not published until 1633, were censored or failed to appear in print for other reasons.[37]

It is clear that whatever the truth about the practice of censorship in early modern England, various political opinions and arguments did enter the public sphere, whether by default or design. Evidence also shows that those involved in high-profile cases of censorship often went on to enjoy successful careers and were sometimes generously rewarded by the crown. John Stubbs, his physical mutilation a vivid testimony of his transgression, was an MP for a number of years after his punishment; John Hayward went on to become a successful civil lawyer in James's reign; the tactless Edmund Spenser managed to offend both Elizabeth's chief minister, William Cecil, Lord Burghley, and James VI of Scotland, but was still one of the few poets to secure a pension from the queen.[38] Rebecca Lemon has made the persuasive case that Hayward was a royalist opponent of the crown and that he has been cast as a more significant political transgressor than he really was by subsequent commentators.[39] Yet it is also possible that Hayward simply modified his political views after James assumed the throne in 1603 and became more confident in the process and stability of hereditary monarchy. After all, Shakespeare's first patron, Henry Wriothesley, earl of Southampton, who was quite fortunate not to be executed after the attempted coup of the earl of Essex in 1601, became a steady and unremarkable supporter of the crown's initiatives when he was released from imprisonment by James soon after he took up residence in London.[40] Not everyone shared the fate of Sir Walter Ralegh, who waited some fifteen years before he was finally executed.[41]

English literature – especially drama – emerged as a discipline in the late sixteenth century within a culture of political argument.[42] Sometimes political references were carefully disguised and signalled only obliquely, as is perhaps the case with works such as John Lyly's prose romance *Euphues: The Anatomy of Wit* (1578), or Shakespeare's comedy *Love's Labour's Lost* (*c*.1594).[43] But there was a long tradition of more forceful and direct representation of issues and debates, often in works which reached either the eyes of the monarch or those of his or her nearest councillors and advisers, such as *Gorboduc* and Philip Sidney's *The Lady of May* (1578), an unsubtle pastoral playlet which urged the queen to intervene more vigorously in the war with the Spanish in the Netherlands.[44] It was not simply a case of writers producing political allegories or choosing to incorporate political material into works of imaginative fiction at strategic points – although both of these processes did take place. Rather, literature was an especially important form for advancing political debate, given that the key issue of sixteenth-century England, the succession, could not be discussed easily or straightforwardly. Early on in her reign, Elizabeth effectively banned any mention of who might succeed her and how the matter could be resolved.[45] Eventually the Jesuit Robert Parsons published a lengthy discussion of the candidates, under the pseudonym Robert Doleman, *A Conference about the Next Succession to the Crowne of Ingland* (1594), concluding, hardly surprisingly, in favour of the Spanish Infanta.[46] This work caused a considerable scandal and serious discomfort for the earl of Essex to whom it was dedicated, and it was deemed treason to be caught with a copy.[47] Peter Wentworth, an MP with Puritan leanings who had previously been imprisoned for demanding that parliament preserve its right to freedom of speech, defended the principle of hereditary monarchy and declared his hand in favour of James in a treatise designed to refute Parsons, *A Pithie Exhortation to Her Majestie for Establishing her Successor to the Crowne* (1598).[48] This exchange draws attention to the fact that most discussion of the succession question took place in literary and dramatic texts and not official political discourse.[49]

MODERN CRITICAL ORTHODOXY

An analysis of the political history of sixteenth and seventeenth century England makes little sense if literary texts are ignored, as many historians have realized.[50] The same is true of the history of art and architecture.[51] Much of this will, of course, be familiar to students of early modern literature, and suggesting that literary texts had a political significance, or, going further, proposing that they played an especially important role in the development of political argument, will not strike many readers as a revelation.[52] What is notable is that a tiny canon of political texts, many of them secondary works, dominate and often determine the discussion of political discourse for students of English literature.[53] The diffuse critical movements, New Historicism and Cultural Materialism, have produced many exciting new avenues for literary critics to explore, and helped banish an arid formalism that refused to see literature as inherently political.[54] Furthermore, the notion that we ought to regard culture as an interactive whole, rather than seeing contexts as background information (sometimes) necessary for the proper study of the literary (or artistic) object, has also transformed our understanding of early modern literature. Nevertheless, it ought to be widely acknowledged that such arguments have been won and that new historicist modes of scholarship have more or less triumphed in literary departments, dominating the forms of study in universities and the ways in which the curriculum is decided.[55]

The explosion of theory in the early 1980s happened because numerous intellectuals and academics wanted to mount a challenge to a previous series of moribund, unexamined and unintellectual assumptions that had become enshrined in university and school pedagogy.[56] In Renaissance studies the principal villain was E. M. W. Tillyard, whose 1943 book, *The Elizabethan World Picture*, was still taught as useful contextual material for students in the 1980s.[57] Tillyard claimed that English Renaissance writers had a faith in a static, hierarchical universe, 'some kind of order or degree on earth having its counterpart in heaven', a belief that every educated Elizabethan shared.[58]

Cultural materialists exposed such assumptions as historically false – historians saw a much more contested picture of the age – and politically suspect – a Tillyardian Shakespeare was used to promote a reactionary agenda both inside and outside the classroom.[59] A 'materialist' agenda was proposed to replace this 'idealist' one, seeking to articulate and bring into the open the assumptions and terms of debate that often remained hidden and mystified. Again, the arguments are familiar enough but they are worth revisiting because crucial aspects appear to have become obscured over the course of time.[60]

In their foreword to *Political Shakespeare*, Jonathan Dollimore and Alan Sinfield argued that Cultural Materialism 'insists that culture does not (cannot) transcend the material forces and relations of production. Culture is not simply a reflection of the economic and *political* system, but nor can it be independent of it. Cultural Materialism therefore studies the implications of literary texts in history, (my emphasis).[61] A key aspect of the cultural materialist agenda insists that literary texts need to be read in terms of a 'political system', which must, of course, refer to political structures, events and theories. Dollimore and Sinfield also insist that acts of literary criticism cannot avoid being acts of political thought, and it is the duty of the critic to try to articulate his or her political position: 'cultural materialism does not pretend to political neutrality. It knows that no cultural practice is ever without political significance' (p.viii).

A few years later, in what is probably the best work of cultural materialist criticism, *Faultlines* (1992), Alan Sinfield was open enough to respond to what he felt were inadequately formulated aspects of cultural materialist theory. In seeking to find a space for 'dissident' reading, Sinfield argued, following orthodox Marxist lines, that 'groups with material power will dominate the institutions that deal with ideas' and then posed the question: 'if we come to consciousness within a language that is continuous with the power structures that sustain the social order, how can we conceive, let alone organize, resistance?' He then considered the criticisms of feminist critics who accused 'both new historicism and cultural materialism of theorizing power as an unbreakable system of containment, a system that positions subordinate groups as effects of the dominant, so that female identity, for instance, appears to be something fathered upon women by patriarchy'.[62]

It is at this point that I would argue that Cultural Materialism is in danger of losing a vital aspect of its political significance and, while properly foregrounding the problem of subjectivity, this is at the expense of an analysis of politics. Few would dispute that powerful groups dominate cultural production, but it does not follow from this that they can determine consciousness as straightforwardly. Everyone exists within ideological formations, but there is still room for argument, including political argument. Of course, Sinfield realizes this problem and his book contains numerous references to a variety of sixteenth- and seventeenth-century political theorists: Buchanan, Calvin, Hotman, Languet, Machiavelli, Ponet, and so on. His model of dissident reading is formulated as a means of breaking free from the stultifying limitations of the subversion/containment debate.[63] But even so, there is a danger that the dominant-subordinate model tends to fix political positions as 'pro' or 'anti' the establishment when they may not fit into this binary model so easily.

A brief survey of some rather broad political issues would seem to indicate that we need to consider certain key political realities in terms other than subversion/containment and dominant/dissident binary oppositions. Given the existence of two queens within the British Isles for three-quarters of Elizabeth's reign, Mary Stuart and Elizabeth, how should we reconstruct and analyse the dominant political paradigm, which troubled and confused most people's notions of hierarchy and order? Each had roughly equal claims to the throne and attempts to exclude Mary were made on the basis of her Catholicism. Should we then see her supporters as dissident? Or reactionary followers of an older order? Furthermore, was opposition to a queen always simply and straightforwardly misogynist? Or did the fact that a queen would have to give her nation away to a foreign monarch or a subordinate subject provide more reasons for fear of female rule, especially after the marriage of Mary Tudor to Philip II of Spain? And was opposition to Elizabeth herself in the last years of her reign dissident or simply misogynist?[64]

Questions such as these have most often become the province of historians rather than literary critics writing in the wake of New Historicism and Cultural Materialism. There are, of course, some honourable exceptions, but these are in a minority and are often ignored by theoretically minded critics who discuss political and historical material. In his afterword to the revised edition of his groundbreaking monograph, *Poetry and Politics in the English Renaissance*, David Norbrook noted sadly that that a 'sharp opposition, between a Dark Ages of simple-minded positivism and a Golden Age of theoretical progress – a moment of inexorable "post"ness, whether labelled poststructuralist or postmodern – has become taken for granted in much current discussion'.[65] Such a division, as Norbrook rightly argues, is a disaster for those who are interested in political – and politicized – literary criticism. On the one hand, there is a debate among 'theoretical' critics as to whether Shakespeare is relevant in the present; on the other, there are historically informed literary critics who talk to historians.[66]

Why has this division happened? The most obvious reason is that it is simply hard to do everything, to be genuinely interdisciplinary with all the skills available to read and contextualize texts.[67] But perhaps another reason might be given if we examine the second part of the quotation from Alan Sinfield's essay cited above. There is a swift and seamless move from an analysis of hegemonic culture to the construction of the self, one that owes as much to Foucault and a wide range of feminist criticism and historiography as it does to Marx *per se*.[68] Analysis of the construction of identity has become hegemonic itself, and it dominates the theorized field of Renaissance studies. In so many ways this has been a beneficial and timely development that has transformed the study of Renaissance litera- ture and made it a much more exciting field in which to work than it was twenty-five years ago before the publication of Stephen Greenblatt's *Renaissance Self-Fashioning* (1980). More pertinently still, the study of Renaissance literature has become democratized and its high-cultural focus has given way to a variety of different approaches in the wake of Cultural Materialism, New Historicism, Gender Studies, Queer Theory and Feminism.[69] It is also easy to see why a pedagogy based on the forms and variety of the self would have a wider appeal to undergraduates and graduates alike, constructing a sturdy bridge between present and past. Indeed, the use of the term, 'early modern', preferred by many Cultural Materialists and New Historicists to the high-culturally biased, Italianate term, 'Renaissance', makes the connections and argument explicit because the 'early modern' period marks the emergence of the modern conception of the self for many such critics.[70]

A representative of numerous current critical assumptions is Hugh Grady. Writing in 2002, Grady notes with approval that 'today in early modern literary studies, historicism, new or old, interwoven with femi- nism and psychoanalysis or not, has become virtually an unrivalled paradigm for professional writing'.[71] Showing that he is keen to write within this dominant paradigm, Grady explains that 'In studying the configuration and reconfiguration of the themes of power and subjectivity in central Shakespearean plays, I have come to the conclusion that these plays, in effect, constitute interventions within our own theoretical dis- courses on these topics within late modernity' (pp. 3–4). Grady's logic is perfectly circular: the plays are about power and subjectivity, which is what his methodology has been designed to analyse (and the suppressed premiss is that this is what we are all interested in). As Jean Howard argued in *The Stage and Social Struggle in Early Modern England*, political commitment – in this case, Marxist Feminism – does not necessarily mean 'shoddy criticism', precisely because it does not save its practitioners 'from the labour of constantly rethinking and reshaping the possibilities of that tradition so that it will remain adequate to emergent conditions'.[72] Grady's words suggest that the time is ripe for some form of rethinking.

My point is not to denigrate the body of literary criticism that has developed in the wake of Cultural Materialism and New Historicism, nor to suggest that analysis of literature in terms of categories of self and power is inevitably mistaken. Nevertheless, there does come a time when theory ceases to be radical and even properly theoretical, because it has become hegemonic and inscribed within the academic culture at large, a development that ought to be acknowledged. What might broadly be termed 'Cultural Historicism' has become a method that can be reproduced and repeated, not a sophisticated philosophy that requires significant new thought to lead others to see the world in a different way.[73] 'Theory' as a subject now often occupies the place of practical criticism, both within the university curriculum, and as a commonly understood critical vocabulary.[74] Paradoxically enough, an argument *could* be made that less is more: radical thinking would be better served by more historical analysis and less theory. Simply reading a wide range of early modern books and manuscripts might make for more interesting criticism than work that has to prove its professional status by showing a knowledge of the field in question. It might. . . Certainly there is a diminishing marginal return for a political criticism that turns to a theoretically inflected discourse rather than political thought for inspiration. As a result, I would argue, vital aspects of public political culture disappear from view and distort not just our understanding of the past, but also the forms and varieties of political intervention we might wish to adopt.

Shakespeare studies is a case in point, as it has often been too immersed in its own history as a subdiscipline to ask new questions that might seem more obvious to an outsider.[75] Many books and articles on Shakespeare have appeared which make use of the term 'politics', but relatively little attention has been paid to the sorts of issues which characterized political discussion in late sixteenth-century and early seventeenth-century England: when one could resist a tyrant; whether hereditary monarchy was the best form of government; what were the effects of the rule of queens; who could and who should occupy political offices; how exactly the people at large should be represented by their rulers, and so on.[76] The word 'politics' is ubiquitous in Renaissance literary criticism, but it is clear that there is no consensus that provides the word with a relatively stable definition. The irony is, I think, that a more careful analysis of the political options open to Shakespeare, and his use of them in his plays and poetry, will reveal a highly politicized and radical thinker, interested in republicanism. As Annabel Patterson has pointed out, one should not assume that all canonical authors were necessarily conservative, even though a subsequent critical tradition may well have tried to transform them into reactionaries. We always need to read between the lines.[77]

This book is a work of historical and cultural archaeology. My hope is that I will be able to redraw the map of late sixteenth-century political culture, at least as it has been constructed by literary specialists.[78] The book is divided into two distinct sections. The first attempts to establish what republicanism and republican culture meant in the late sixteenth and early seventeenth centuries, an urgent task, given that one would be hard pushed to identify a republican faction or even party before the Interregnum.[79] I also try to outline the various forms that republican thought and ideology assumed in political and historical discourse, as well as literature. Republicanism, as the writings of two of its most important contemporary historians, John Pocock and Quentin Skinner, have demonstrated, was both a language and a belief system.[80] It might also be regarded as a collection of *topoi* or, in terms of Renaissance rhetorical theory, 'places', examples or triggers that signalled and stood for a larger argument or set of beliefs.[81] Republicanism was a fund of stories and potent images – the rape of Lucrece, the civil war between Julius Caesar and Pompey the Great, the assassination of Caesar, such biblical stories as Judith's killing of the tyrant Holofernes, the 'artificial angel' that was the republican city of Venice – as well as a collection of ideas and a political programme.[82] Given the inchoate and unformed nature of its existence when Shakespeare was writing, we should pay more attention to the importance of this diverse collection of powerful, miscellaneous scraps of literature, history and culture. I have written at length in this section because much of the material may well be unfamiliar to some readers. Those more versed in the history of political thought may wish to skip certain sections and move more quickly towards the second section.

The second part of the book examines how Shakespeare – and some of his contemporaries – interacted with the republican culture I have outlined in the first part. There are, of course, certain problems with the tasks I have set myself. It is unlikely that a 'smoking gun' exists which will prove that Shakespeare read republican works avidly and wished to use his plays and poetry to persuade others of the necessity of implementing his heartfelt convictions. Few of the plays – especially the comedies – would stand up to such a programmatic reading, although political argument in the English Renaissance did often work by using historical examples to persuade an audience or readers that a certain course of action was desirable and/or necessary.[83] My case depends on establishing what political ideas were current in Shakespeare's London and how they might relate to his surviving work. In short, my study is rooted in the most important body of material for modern readers of Shakespeare: his writing. In marked contrast, much of another fascinating area of cultural archaeology, the arguments over Shakespeare's religious persuasion, depend on biographical information that may or may not be true, possibilities, associations and what Shakespeare does not write.[84] And, if it is noted that two of Shakespeare's earliest works, *Titus Andronicus* (*c.*1590?) and *The Rape of Lucrece* (*c.*1594), are based on explicitly republican stories, then it is clear that there is another story that has not been properly told – yet.

PART I

Republican Culture in the 1590s

CHAPTER I

Forms of republican culture in late sixteenth-century England

If republicanism stood for any clear and coherent doctrine in late sixteenth-century England, it was the intellectual conviction that it was necessary to control the powers of the crown by establishing a means of ensuring that a coterie of virtuous advisers and servants would always have the constitutional right to counsel the monarch, and so influence and control his or her actions within the limits of the law. Patrick Collinson has controversially labelled this notion of politics a 'monarchical republic'.[1] Professor Collinson argues that although forms of official propaganda tried to define those living within Elizabeth's realms as 'subjects' of the crown, many cosmopolitan urban intellectuals from the early part of the sixteenth century onwards saw themselves as citizens, akin to the influential figures who dominated the histories of the Roman republic they had all read. Citizens were unfortunately 'concealed within subjects'.[2] For large stretches of time, such a notion was perhaps little more than a severe irritant for important men who felt themselves to be undervalued by the state. However, at many key moments throughout the century political identities and definitions assumed a crucial importance.

The presence of Mary Stuart as second queen within the British Isles alongside Elizabeth, a monarch whose hereditary claim was perhaps as good as that of the English queen, and who was supported by all of Catholic Europe, triggered many of the most dangerous crises of Elizabeth's reign.[3] Soon after Elizabeth was dangerously ill in December 1562, her chief secretary, William Cecil, composed a document which aimed to 'tackle the potential problem of England without a monarch'.[4] Cecil's paper, 'an act for the succession but not passed', was composed in February–March 1563. It contained a clause which enabled parliament to establish a 'conciliar interregnum' and then nominate a successor, thus activating the familiar distinction between the two bodies of the monarch, the office and person of the queen, in order to preserve the realm in a stable state.[5] Elizabeth survived, and nothing came of this document. But similar political issues were raised in 1572, after the discovery of the Ridolfi Plot, when parliament debated the implications of Mary's presence within the realm and tried to force Elizabeth to have her rival executed. Again, such discussions did not lead to any action or a legal change. Rather, they seemed to show that the monarchy was 'not an indelible and sacred anointing but a public and localised office, like any other form of magistracy'.[6] In 1584, after the assassination of William of Orange (the Silent) in Delft, a large group of MPs signed the 'Bond of Association', which was designed to protect the life of the queen, by swearing revenge on anyone who tried to harm her person. Yet in seeking to protect the life of the monarch, the Bond drew attention to the importance of its signatories and emphasized their power within the constitution, not that of the queen.[7]

Other crisis points, which led to political argument and debate, might also be mentioned. There were numerous revolts against the Tudors throughout the sixteenth century, most notably the Pilgrimage of Grace (1536–37), which saw Italian republican history and theory used as a means of countering the demands of the rebels in the treatises of Richard Morison and Thomas Starkey.[8] Thomas Starkey had earlier composed the influential *A Dialogue between Pole and Lupset* (*c.*1533–35), which circulated widely in manuscript at court.[9] The dialogue was an attempt to persuade Henry VIII and his courtiers to pay more attention to a broader political sphere beyond the immediate circle of the monarch, to agree voluntarily to establish the rule of law and so limit the king's powers.[10] Starkey's work reveals the complexity and potentially contradictory nature of republican arguments in England, as well as the important fact that republican thought could be used to defend as well as attack the monarchy. Starkey's writings also show that men who used republican arguments were often just as horrified by rebellion as more conservative thinkers.[11]

The unstable, experimental reign of Edward VI led to a wealth of propaganda, legal treatises and historical and literary works that could perhaps be described as 'republican', most notably, *A Mirror for Magistrates*.[12] The equally short, contrasting reign of Mary Tudor helped inspire a number of 'monarchomach' Protestant treatises, most produced in exile.[13] These claimed that God would sanction the assassination of an evil, Catholic ruler if it were in the interests of the people, a mode of argument that had significant affiliations with republican thought, which also legitimized political killings on occasions.[14] The behaviour and reputation of Mary Stuart probably had the greatest single impact on British political thought in the sixteenth century, a pervasive influence that was both direct and indirect.[15] The theories of George Buchanan, undoubtedly the most important republican theorist to have lived in the British Isles before the Interregnum, were developed in large part in opposition to Mary.[16] His three major works of political theory and history – the dialogue *De Jure Regni Apud Scotos* (1579); his polemical attack on Mary, *Ane detectioun of the duinges of Marie Quene of Scottes* (1571); and his posthumously published magnum opus, *Rerum Scoticarum Historia* (1582) (*The History of Scotland*) – were well known in England.[17] Most relevant to Shakespeare, as has often been pointed out, was the disastrous rebellion of the earl of Essex, which followed the earl's supporters having a version of *Richard II* – quite probably Shakespeare's play – staged before them.[18]

Sixteenth-century English political history reveals that republicanism was ubiquitous. The Latin term '*res publica*' literally meant the 'public thing', but it was most frequently translated as the 'common weal' or 'commonwealth'.[19] This meant that 'republicanism' was either directly or indirectly a ghostly presence in English political life from the early sixteenth century onwards, as many examples demonstrate. Nicholas Udall, better known as the author of what is probably the first English comedy, *Ralph Roister Doister* (*c.*1540–*c.*1553), wrote a Christmas interlude, *Respublica*, which was performed at court in the last year of Edward VI's reign (1553). The play tells the story of the poor widow Respublica, who is led astray by the false advisers, Flattery, Avarice, Insolence and others, falsely posing as virtuous counsellors. The common people are severely affected by their bad government until Veritas exposes their lies and, with Pax and Justia, restores order.[20]

Sir Thomas Smith (1513–77), a prominent humanist scholar and states-man who became a significant political figure during Edward's brief reign, wrote the influential *A Discourse of the Commonweal* in 1549.[21] The work circulated widely in manuscript before it was eventually published in 1581.[22] Smith's series of three dialogues between various estates figures, the knight, doctor, husbandman and merchant, argues the case that the commonweal will function best if it is governed by learned men, skilled in the new knowledges and arts of husbandry, science, scriptures, history, and so on, a familiar humanist refrain, largely derived from the writings of Cicero, who is indeed mentioned early on in the first dialogue by the doctor: 'we be not born only to ourselves but partly to the use of our country, of our parents, of our kinfolk, and partly of our friends and neighbours'.[23] The commonwealth is seen as a body that is external to any of the citizens living within it, which they all have a duty to serve and protect from harm. Such political formulations indicate that many Englishmen regarded the state (commonwealth) as an entity separate from those governing it and did not simply think of their status in terms of the ruling dynasty.²⁴ To cite the doctor once more:

Tell me what counsel can be perfect, what Commonweal can be well ordered or saved upright, where none of the rulers or counsellors have studied any philosophy, specially the part that teaches of manners? . . . What Commonweal can be without either a governor or counsellor that should be expert in this kind of learning? . . . if men expert in this science [husbandry] were consulted and followed, the Commonweal should be so ordered as few should have cause to complain.²⁵

Smith made a more substantial contribution to English political thought a few years later when he provided a political anatomy of England, *De Republica Anglorum: A Discourse on the Commonwealth of England*. As with *A Discourse of the Commonweal*, this work also circulated widely in manuscript and had an important influence before it was actually published in 1583, some eighteen years after it was written.²⁶ Smith's work was also made available in William Harrison's 'Description of England', reproduced in the first edition of Holinshed's *Chronicles of England, Scotland and Ireland* (1577).²⁷ Smith follows Aristotle in classifying types of government in his first few chapters: monarchy, 'where one alone doth governe', oligarchy, 'where the smaller number' (govern), and democracy, 'where the multitude doth rule', as the three basic political forms (Smith, *De Republica Anglorum*, p. 9).²⁸ However, Smith, again following Aristotle, argues that most states do not fit easily into these categories, but are really 'mixed', just as the body is made up of the four elements of fire, air, earth and water (p. 14). In his first book, which outlines the types of government, Smith makes it clear to the reader that a 'mixed' form of constitution is best, being fairest to all citizens, more stable than other types of government, and, most crucially, in harmony with the general principles of politics that he has outlined. Implicitly contrasting contemporary England with ancient prerepublican Rome, Smith argues that

A common wealth is called a society or common doing of a multitude of free men collected together and united by common accord and covenauntes among themselves, for the conservation of themselves aswell in peace as in warre. For properly an host of men is not called a common accord and covenauntes among themselves but abusively, because they are collected but for a time and for a fact: which done, ech divideth himselfe from others as they were before. And if one man had as some of the old Romanes had (if it be true that is written) v. thousande or x. thousande bondmen whom he ruled well, though they dwelled all in one citie, or were distributed into diverse villages, yet that were no common wealth: for the bondman hath no communion with his master, the wealth of the Lord is onely sought for, and not the profit of the slave or bondman. (Smith, *De Republica Anglorum*, p. 20)

De Republica Anglorum shows the reader that it is not simply a piece of dispassionate political analysis, but, like Aristotle's *Politics*, has a definite sense of political value. The term commonwealth does not refer to any form of political union or organization, but only to one that works in the interests of all its members. Ancient Rome, before the advent of the republic, is not a state that can define itself as a commonwealth. Smith is obviously referring to the Rome of its ancient kings, a line which culminated in the tyrannical Tarquins who ruled for their own benefit and pleasure and not for that of the city's inhabitants. Their fate, he implies, is richly deserved; Smith's source was undoubtedly Livy, the historian who chronicled Rome from its origins and who was also notably sympathetic to the overthrow of the Tarquins and the establishment of the Roman republic.[29]

This contrast is an important structuring principle of Smith's treatise: England is implicitly and explicitly compared to the Roman republic and shown to be unlike tyrannies such as the corrupt Roman monarchy. Smith concludes his first book by cataloguing the types of men who make up a commonwealth: gentlemen (the nobility), knights, citizens, yeomen and labourers. He excludes women from the political realm, 'except it be in such cases as the authoritie is annexed to the bloud and progenie' (Smith, *De Republica Anglorum*, p. 30), i.e., queens, duchesses, etc. He also effectively excludes labourers, 'which the olde Romans called *capite censii proletarii* or *operae*' (again showing that the England-Rome comparison is uppermost in his mind), but with an ambiguous formula: 'These have no voice or authoritie in our common wealth, and no account is made of them onelie to be ruled, not to rule other, *and yet they be not altogether neglected*' [my emphasis] (Smith, *De Republica Anglorum*, p. 46). Even here, Smith makes every effort to include the humblest sections of society as a means of emphasizing that the English common-wealth is a collective enterprise.[30] He opens the second book with a discussion of the significance of the English parliament – having already established the continuity and importance of England's legal tradition.[31] Parliament stands as the 'most high and absolute power of the realme of Englande' because it successfully brings together all the different estates of the commonwealth to consult with the king:

so in peace and consultation where the Prince is to give life, and the last and highest commaundement, the Baronie for the nobilitie and higher, the knightes, esquires, gentlemen and commons for the lowest part of the common wealth, the bishoppes for the clergie bee present to advertise, consult and shew what is good and necessarie for the common wealth, and to consult together, and upon mature deliberation everie bill or law being thrise reade and disputed upon in either house . . . *That is the Princes and whole realmes deede*: whereupon no man can complaine, but must accommodate himselfe to finde it good and obey it [my emphasis]. (Smith, *De Republica Anglorum*, p. 48)[32]

Parliament is what makes England like the Roman republic: even if it is a 'mixed' constitution with a monarch, it functions as a commonwealth, including all men within its political sphere, as many as possible, able to take part in the formal process of lawmaking. Just as republican Rome was an indirect democracy in which the people could legitimately petition their rulers and expect to be heard, so is England: 'And to be short, all that ever the people of Rome might do either in *Centuriatis comitiis* or *tributis*, the same may be doone by the parliament of Englande, which representeth and hath the power of the whole realme both the head and bodie' (Smith, *De Republica Anglorum*, p. 49).

But was Smith a bold and innovative political thinker, or simply an unimaginative man who reproduced and codified what was, in fact, commonly agreed political discourse? Can we discern a meaningful notion of republicanism in his two major works, or simply a host of commonplace observations that, in the end, worked to reinforce rather than limit the monarchy's power? Certainly, it is true that the notion of the 'mixed constitution' was an ubiquitous cliché, which very few thinkers tried to challenge, and which dominated much European political thought from the sixteenth to the eighteenth century.[33] In England it could easily be derived from native traditions as well as classical republican thought.[34] The fifteenth-century lawyer Sir John Fortesque, whose *De Laudibus Legum Anglie* (*c.*1470) was translated by Robert Mulcaster as *A Learned Commendation of the Politique Lawes of England* (1567), was as likely a source as Aristotle or Polybius.[35] Fortesque argued a strong case that absolutism was a European phenomenon, alien to an English tradition (fos.129–32). England, by way of contrast, had enjoyed a largely stable tradition of legal development, its laws changing in a piecemeal and orderly fashion case by case (fos.25–27). This common law tradition only functioned because it operated within the context of a secure and flexible constitution in which the monarch was subject to the laws of the land. The king or queen had the right to establish their prerogative, but only through parliament, the highest court of the land, defining the constitution as 'mixed', a combination of regal and politic [i.e., parliamentary] government. It was the duty of the judges, not the sovereign, to establish the law, and wise rulers would leave them to their task (fos.130–31). People could enjoy possession of their property without fear of the interfering whim of a tyrant. Indeed, as all readers of Fortesque would have known, tyranny, following Aristotle's definition, was generally perceived in terms of a monarch's abuse of his or her subject's property and the desire to amass wealth for himself at the expense of his people.[36] Fortesque argues, following Thomas Aquinas, that 'the king is gyen for the kingdome, and not the kingdome for the king' (fo.87).[37]

Another readily available source of the 'mixed' constitution was Polybius's *History*, which narrated the development and spread of the Roman empire after the first Punic War (264–241 BCE) to the third (149–146 BCE).[38] Book VI contains an extended discussion of the 'Roman constitution in its prime'.[39] This book shows Polybius (*c.*200–118 BCE), himself a conquered Greek subject of the imperial power, to be suspicious of the forces that enabled Rome to dominate the known world, and an enthusiastic advocate of the merits of the Roman republic. Polybius signals his discussion as a detour, thus marking it out as the heart of the history. He defines life and virtue in the familiar terms of late Roman Stoicism, values which were to become more significant in the histories of Tacitus (AD *c.*55–*c.*112) and Suetonius (AD *c.*70–*c.*160)[40]:

The test of true virtue in a man surely resides in his capacity to bear with spirit and with dignity the most complete transformation of fortune, and the same principle should apply to our judgment of states. And so, since I could find no greater or more violent changes of fortune in our time than those which befell the Romans, I have reserved this place in my history for my study of their constitution. (p. 302)

Polybius makes it clear that his *History*, dominated as it is by details of military conflict and conquest, is really a lament for the loss of the Roman republic, showing that imperial history often contained its own critique and that a symbiotic relationship existed between the two.[41] Furthermore, his comment opens up the possibility, which he does not explore but leaves unstated, that with the decay of the ideal constitution, the need for citizens to participate in the active political life probably no longer applies. Instead, wise withdrawal into a private space, exactly the sort of retreat from tyranny that later Roman writers advocated as a necessity for survival, had become a more sensible and practical mode of existence. The question that Polybius falls to ask, however, is why the Roman republic decayed if it was such an ideal constitution, as political theory placed so much emphasis on the need for longevity and stability.[42]

Polybius – as usual following the authority of Aristotle, along with Plato and Herodotus – notes that political constitutions are conventionally divided into three kinds: kingship, aristocracy and democracy. He then poses an obvious question and provides the obvious answer: 'We are, I think, entitled to ask them [political theorists] whether they are presenting these three to us as the only types of constitution or as the best, for in either event I believe that they are wrong. It is clear that we should regard as the *best* constitution one which includes elements of all three species' (p. 303). Each form has its own problems and disadvantages: 'Thus in kingship the inbred vice is despotism, in aristocracy it is oligarchy [i.e., the oppressive rule of a few], and in democracy the brutal rule of violence, and it is impossible to prevent each of these kinds of government . . . from degenerating in to the debased form of itself' (p. 310). One of the most successful attempts to offset such decay took place in Sparta through the intervention of their astute lawgiver, Lycurgus. He made sure that Sparta had a written constitution which ensured limited monarchy. The people were 'also given a sufficiently important share in government', but were 'restrained from showing contempt for the kings through their fear of the Senate'. The Senate was the key institution of state and functioned well because its members 'were chosen on grounds of merit, and could be relied upon at all times to take the side of justice unanimously'. The overall happy 'result of the drawing-up of the constitution according to these principles was to preserve liberty for the Spartans over a longer period than for any other people of whom we have records' (p. 311). Polybius argues that the best states promote and employ the natural virtue of their citizens (p. 341). But he makes no effort to deal with the perennial political problem of stability and decay. Aristotle had confronted this issue, arguing that occasionally tyranny could prove to be the best form of government for its citizens. Even if it was not the most desirable political state and did not promote virtue, it did at least provide much-needed stability in times of extreme crisis.[43] Polybius is more whimsical and nostalgic than Aristotle: 'The fact, then, that all existing things are subject to decay is a proposition which scarcely requires proof, since the inexorable course of nature is sufficient to impose it on us' (p. 350).

The constitution of the Roman republic was a perfect balance of its three different elements:

[I]t is . . . the people who bestow offices on those who deserve them, and these are the noblest rewards of virtue the state can provide. Besides this, the people have the power to approve or reject laws, and most important of all, they deliberate and decide on questions of peace or war. Furthermore, on such issues as the making of alliances, the termination of hostilities and the making of treatises, it is the people who ratify or reject all of these. And so from this point of view one could reasonably argue that the people have the greatest share of power in the government, and that the constitution is a democracy. (p. 315)

Polybius clearly approves of this form of political existence, whereby the people are able to determine whether a state starts or ends a war. This democratic emphasis was conspicuously at odds with the Tudor monarchs' understanding of their absolute right to determine foreign policy in the interests of their subjects, who they thought had no reason to know what diplomatic manoeuvres were taking place.[44] The ability of the people to accept or reject laws was more controversial. The king or queen existed as the monarch in parliament, which allowed for a variety of interpretations of the relationship between the ruler and the highest court in the land.[45] A distinction between an 'ascending' interpretation of the relationship between crown and parliament, which placed emphasis on the role of the monarch being bound by laws passed in parliament, and a 'descending' view of the same relationship, which reduced the powers of the elected chambers to advisory bodies and placed clear emphasis on the monarch's prerogative as the determining political will, had often been made by political theorists. The two views of political culture existed more or less side by side for much of the sixteenth century.[46] But in the second half of Elizabeth's reign, there was a sea change and the two views of English political culture were more obviously at odds, leading to such outbursts in parliament as Sir Peter Wentworth's insistence in 1587 that parliament had the right to 'free speech' and so could discuss the problem of the succession. The 'mixed' policy, as expressed by thinkers such as Sir Thomas Smith, was no longer so obviously an establishment view, but could be utilized by disaffected subjects to argue that parliament should play a more central role in governing England.[47]

In the reign of James, such divisions opened up further, surfacing in his first parliament of 1604, and continuing throughout his reign. James was hardly an autocrat, as he has often been caricatured.[48] But he did have a very clear sense that the monarch's word should be law – even though the monarch should not be above the laws that he or she made – and that parliament was there to be summoned when it suited him to act as a sounding-board for his ideas.[49] This approach brought him into conflict with his elected subjects, starting with the dispute over the election of Sir John Fortesque.[50]

Nevertheless, Polybius was seen as a vitally important Roman historian who was widely read in Tudor England. Roger Ascham referred to Polybius as 'that wise writer', and urged schoolmasters to persuade their charges to compare his *Histories* with those of Livy, because Livy declared that he was a follower of Polybius.[51] Along with Tacitus and Sallust – especially recommended by Ascham – Polybius was generally regarded as a 'paragon . . . of narrative style and political judgement'.[52] Humanist works such as Laurentius Grimaldus's *The Counsellor*, anonymously translated into English in 1599, endorsed Polybius's extravagant praise of the Roman republic, arguing that the 'mixed state' which combined monarchy, aristocracy and democracy exactly resembled the parts of a man's mind, making it a natural form of political existence.[53] Polybius's *History* was one of the canonical works of European politics, and had a profound and far-reaching influence, largely among a humanist readership who saw his balanced and careful historical analysis as similar to that of Tacitus, who was emerging as the key historian that everyone had to read in the 1590s.[54] The Huguenot François Hotman cited Polybius as a key plank in his attack on the tyranny of the French monarchy, arguing, yet again, that the 'mixed constitution' was the best form of government.[55] Hotman's analysis reveals the close links many made between religious – in this case, Protestant – political thought and republican texts. And, as Kevin Sharpe's study of the reading habits of Sir William Drake, a seventeenth-century country gentleman with a keen interest in politics, reveals, Polybius was also essential reading for most active educated Englishmen – not just those with republican sympathies.[56]

The only translation made of Polybius in Elizabeth's reign shows how keen historians were to forge links between English and Roman history, suggesting that, as in Europe, the political lessons of the past were seen as easily transferable to the present.[57] Christopher Warton's translation of *The Hystories of the most famous and worthy Cronographer Polybius* (1568) contains only the first of the forty books of the *Universal History*, divided into two discrete sections which catalogue the events of the First Punic War. As the subtitle, *Whereunto is annexed an Abstract, compendiously coarcted out of the life & wothy actes, perpetrate by oure puissant Prince king Henry the fift*, indicates, the real value of this book for an English reader is the connection made between the military success of ancient Rome and England's most celebrated warrior king.[58] Warton includes an interim section that links the two histories, entitled 'To the Questioners. Those which are desirous to know the causes why I joyned this abridgment of king Henry the fift, his life, to this foraine history, let them reade the Epistle folowing' (fo.101). In it he describes the task he has just completed in terms which seem to belong to the genre of dream vision. The model he undoubtedly has in mind is the *Somnium Scipionis*, the vision of Scipio Africanus, who was the most successful Roman general in the Third Punic War, as recounted by Polybius.[59] Scipio was also a republican hero, who helped to defend the republic against its enemies, principally in the form of the terrifying figure of Hannibal, but if the translator is providing a clue as to his political sympathies, it is certainly a very subtle one. Warton describes himself as weary after reading through Aristotle and Plato. He is reminded that 'When thou arte fatigue with studie, recreate and repose thy selfe with revolving worthy Histories' (fo.101). Inspired by this, he then turns to Edward Hall's *Chronicles*, which he happens to have open at the oration of Henry Chickley, archbishop of Canterbury during the reign of Henry V. Chickley describes the achievements of the king and, in response, Lord Rafe, earl of Westmorland, suggests that 'if it had ben in *Greke* and *Latine*, it had ben nothing inferiour, but equivalent with the Orations of *Demosthenes* or *Tully*' (fo.102). Such words inspire Warton to reread Roman history, which he then translates so that others less scholarly than himself can learn from it. He then decides that he needs to attach the oration which originally moved him, because everyone would need to know why the archbishop made such a fine speech, which cannot be done without including the life of Henry V (fo.103).

Warton's stated reasons are eloquent, elegant and a crafted fiction designed to persuade readers that English and Roman history can be read side by side. Henry is shown to be as successful as any Roman emperor, which a purple passage of praise in the archbishop's oration demonstrates:

For all Authors doe agree, that the glorye of Kynges consyysteth not only in high bloud and hautie progenie, not in abundance of riches and superfluous substance, nor in pleasant pastime, nor in joyous solace: but the verie type of the magnificencie in a prince resteth in populous riche regions, subjects, beautiful cities and townes, of the which thanked be God, although you be conveniently furnished bothe within your realmes of England and Irelande, and the princi-palitie of Wales, yet by lineall descent by progenie of bloude, and by very inheritance, not onely the Duchie of *Normandie*, and *Aquitane*, with the Countries of *Anjow*, and *Mayne*, and the country of *Gascoyne*, is to you as true and indubitate beire of the same, laufully devoluted and lineally desended from the high and most noble prince of famous memorie kyng *Edwarde* the thirde, your great grandfather, but also the whole realme of *Fraunce*, wyth all the prerogatives and preheminances to you as heire to your great grandfather is of right belonging, and appertaining. (fo.113)

In short, Henry has it all. He has the right, through his lineal descent, as well as through the burden placed on him as a king, to seize France, which the reader knows he will successfully achieve. The opening lines also draw our attention to the duties that kings have to their people and their nation's place in history, duties which weigh so heavily on Shakespeare's Henry V. Henry is obliged to rule not simply through his bloodline, but also through his acts. The good king rules well through establishing cities and towns, allowing regions to flourish, and making his subjects rich and happy. The argument is not republican, but the implication is that kings who fail to establish a successful and happy state because they indulge themselves with 'riches and superfluous substance' and easy living are not acting as they should. It is a short step to branding them tyrants and arguing that they can be overthrown, showing that quasi-republican arguments were part of the intellectual and political mainstream, shadowing defences of the monarchy.

The ease with which Warton merges Roman and English history is repeated in numerous other works, especially in the 1590s. Many of these are rather more concerned to exploit the tensions between the rights of hereditary monarchy and the need for honourable, virtuous government. A prime case is Richard Beacon's *Solon his Foliie, or a Politique Discourse touching the Reformation of common-weales conquered, declined or corrupted* (1594), which has attracted a great deal of scholarly attention. Interestingly enough, it has been read as a key work of English republicanism, and as a defence of strong monarchical government cast in republicanesque terms.[60] Given that the book was dedicated to Elizabeth yet makes extensive use of Livy and Machiavelli, this is perhaps hardly surprising.[61] The nature of the scholarly dispute itself further reveals how close opposing arguments often were. Just as Catholics and Protestants were frequently forced to adopt each other's styles and forms of devotion, so both arguments supporting the status quo and ones desiring change often employed the same rhetorical manoeuvres and sometimes even the same sets of examples.[62]

Solon his Follie is principally indebted to Machiavelli's *Discourses on the first Ten Books of Titus Livius*, a work as central to a European republican tradition as Polybius's *Universal History*.[63] Beacon's intellectual energies are devoted to the question of the 'Reformation of a declined commonweale', and the dialogue shows how Ireland can be reclaimed and reformed by the English authorities, through the story of Solon, the legendary Athenian lawgiver, who has to explain and justify the reasons for his conquest of the island of Salaminia to Pisistratus and Epimenides.[64] Just as Christopher Warton was able to range easily enough from Roman to English military history, so is Beacon comfortable with his allegorical dialogue linking Greek and Roman political history to events in contemporary England and Ireland.[65] The examples cited range from ancient Sparta and Athens to Machiavelli's Florence and the Desmond Rebellion in Munster (1579–83).[66] In the second chapter, Epimenides argues that all commonwealths that decay can be restored back to their original form, if that first state served its citizens well. He chooses the example of Rome, which was first established by Romulus and Numa, who established good laws that made the city a thriving and happy state. The city enjoyed 'an happy temper and forme of government, compounded of three sortes and kindes of governement, namely the *Monarchia, Aristocratia,* and *Democratia*' (p. 21). The endorsement of the 'mixed constitution' as the best form of government is familiar enough. Beacon is following Machiavelli, who, after dismissing Athens under Solon and then Pisistratus as an unstable state shuttling back and forth between democracy and tyranny, shows how Rome managed to establish a constitution that combined all three elements, which survived for a long time, and was always an ideal that could be recovered.[67] Epimenides draws the same conclusion as Machiavelli:

wee maie conclude, that those common-weales which have their foundation good, though not perfit and complete, *ex iis quae subinde occurrunt, emedari & perfici queant ad exemplum Romae* [for these (states) which withstand these things are able to improve and be perfected according to the example of Rome]: for it is saide, *non prima illa Romanae reipublicae: institutio tantum a recta via aberrabat, ut perfici non posset* [if Rome did not get fortune's first gift, it got its second. For her early institutions, though defective, were not on wrong lines and so might pave the way to perfection]. (p. 21)

The subsequent development of the dialogue, which shows that military conquest and the establishment of colonial outposts are more important in recovering seriously decayed states than the imposition of the law, should not blind us to this early endorsement of the Roman republic's constitution as the ideal form of government. In the context of the 1590s, as the monarchy sought ever more to establish its prerogative and forbade discussion of such contentious and serious issues as the impending succession and the wars in Ireland, Beacon's Machiavellian-inspired enthusiasm for republican values would have assumed an obvious importance. Most significant of all, perhaps, Lucius Junius Brutus, the first republican hero, is singled out as a model for the Irish Lord Deputies, the English magistrates in Ireland, to copy:

the weaknes and facilitie of *Collatinus* the Consull, did much encourage the traitours, in such sorte, as he had never prevailed against the *Tarquines*, nor reformed the state of *Rome*, if the great vertue and severitie of *Brutus* had not governed at that time the helme and sterne . . . Therefore provident were the counsel of *Athens* in committing this action of the reformation of *Salaminia*, sometime into the handes of the L. *Gray*, sometimes into the handes of Sir *William Russell*[.] (p. 65)

The heroic virtue of the first Brutus is seen as the example that English magistrates need to possess in order to govern resolutely and well. The political implications of this link are complicated and certainly far from straightforward. On the one hand, republican virtue does seem to be used to strengthen the power of the monarchy.[68] Yet, on the other, the suggestion is that if the English monarchy fails its magistrates – the principal focus of the work – then it may well find itself under attack.[69] When read alongside Beacon's endorsement of the virtues of the constitution of the Roman republic, the comparison functions as an acknowledgement that the queen simply cannot govern alone.

Solon his Follie is further notable as an eclectic work because it combines discussion of Roman and Greek history with biblical examples and prophecy. A discussion of tributes and impositions as means of raising revenue condemns Nero's foolish and impetuous decision to waive them as a means of restoring his popularity alongside the deposition of Rohoboam for excessively taxing his people (pp. 115–16). In the following chapter, which analyses the problem of the shaky authority of magistrates who are not properly endorsed by their rulers, Epimenides cites the example of Camillus, the Roman governor who was accused 'for stealing part of the spoile of the *Tuscans*', familiar to Beacon's readers in Sir Thomas North's translation of *Plutarch's Lives*.[70] He is then compared to the youthful David struggling against all the odds: 'for with *David*, he is placed to fight with a beare after a lion, with a Giant after a beare, with a King after a Giant, and with the *Philistians* after a King' (p. 119).

The example which stands out most is the second chapter in the third book, 'The times wherein common-weales doe usually fall and decline'. The discussion between Solon and Epimenides is explicitly apocalyptic, based on the Book of Daniel, which was linked to the Revelation by many of the 'hotter' Protestants, most notably in the annotations to the Geneva Bible (1560, 1578).[71] Solon argues that the success of mighty kingdoms is about to be reversed when overpowerful kings come to dominate them:

kingdomes and principalities, being at their highest, doe then decline and fall: for so did this mighty king *Alexander* (whome the Prophet *Daniel* nowe intendeth) sometimes rule great dominions, but even then saieth the Prophet did he perish, even when he commanded at his pleasure, and lastly, even when this king (saith the Prophet) did stand uppe, and was at the highest, even then did he fall with a disease which followed his drunkennes and superfluitie. (p. 94)

Beacon, following the annotations to the Geneva Bible, has in mind the combined power of papacy and the Catholic king of Spain, as well as the powerful lords in Ireland who were starting to look towards Spain for help to free them of English rule.[72] The use of the example of Alexander the Great – also found in Plutarch's *Lives* – again illustrates how easy it was for writers to juxtapose classical and biblical examples.[73] On the next page Solon refers to the destruction of the Roman empire, which, despite Augustus's victories over the Parthians and Judeans, 'came they to their ende, and none was founde that could helpe them'. The Romans once ruled from shore to shore like gods, 'but even then eftsoones they perished as men' (p. 95). Unless we regard Beacon as a careless, eclectic author with no real control over his material, this example must surely have a further republican resonance. The body of the text recommends the constitution, politics and history of the Roman republic as an ideal to be imitated, especially for those states trying to recover and govern their lost territories. The Roman empire, by way of contrast, is compared to the contemporary evil empire of Spain, the rise and imminent fall of which signals that human history is entering its final phase.[74]

Warton's *Polybius* and Beacon's *Solon his Follie* show that republican examples and republican arguments could be used alongside similar religious arguments for the deposition of unjust and tyrannical princes. The history of classical republicanism and the history of 'monarchomach' resistance theory were never mutually exclusive in the sixteenth century. If anything, they reinforced each other. The most widely cited Huguenot treatise advocating the assassination of tyrants who opposed the will of God and the people, *Vindiciae, Contra Tyrannos, or, concerning the legitimate power of a prince over the people, and of the people over a prince* (1579), went out of its way to advertise the link between republicanism and Protestant resistance theory. It was supposedly written by 'Stephanus

Junius Brutus, the Celt', translating the first Brutus to Scotland and
signalling support for those radical Protestants, such as John Knox, who
opposed the imposition of Catholic rule by Mary Stuart.[75] The text ends
with a plea for the tyranny of Iberian Catholicism to be overthrown and
the author stating in block capitals: 'O BRUTUS, YOU WERE MY
TEACHER' (p. 187).

However, if the text is framed by an apparatus and a series of paratexts
that remind readers of the republican history of political assassination, the
text itself argues from a Protestant point of view.[76] Interestingly enough,
Machiavelli is dismissed in the (fake) letter from the printer, Scribonius
Spinter, the Belgian, to the reader, being labelled a 'Poxy Pelt . . . a long-
winded sophist, the gravest pestilence to Christians' (p. 7).[77] Innocent
Gentillet's *Anti-Machiavel* was published in 1576, three years before
Vindiciae, Contra Tyrannos, and so was undoubtedly the source of these
comments. Gentillet's work criticizes Machiavelli not because he was a
radical figure who threatened the status quo, but because Gentillet saw the
cynical advice given to rulers in *The Prince* (written 1513, published 1532) as
a key reason for Catherine de Medici's decision to massacre the Protestants on St Bartholomew's Day, 1572.[78] Gentillet's case against Machiavelli
is based on his lack of respect for the rights of individuals and his support
for the unscrupulous ruling class in Florence, the Medici, who had now
crossed over the Alps with Catherine – as Christopher Marlowe had
recognized in the prologue to *The Jew of Malta* – and destroyed the
Huguenots.[79] Machiavelli is seen as a Catholic enemy of the Protestant
people. Such conflict reminds us that the history of republicanism was
discontinuous, fractious and confused, not a smooth development towards a clearly perceived goal when a full form of the idea was finally
produced. Far from demonstrating that republicanism did not really exist
in the late sixteenth century, these clashes show just how many elements
and strands could be defined as republican.

Vindiciae, Contra Tyrannos poses four questions, the answers to which
make up the four sections of the book: whether subjects have to
obey princes who command them to act against the word of God; whether
princes who make such demands can be resisted; whether princes who
ruin their states can be resisted; and whether neighbouring princes have a
duty to help the subjects of an oppressed people overthrow their prince.
The examples used throughout are predominantly biblical, although there
is some mixture of Roman history, too. In answering the third question,
the text proclaims that 'kings are made by the people' and a whole wealth
of biblical examples from *Kings* and *Chronicles* are given, following on

from Rehoboam, who was made king after the death of Solomon. Israel was, in effect, an elective monarchy:

After Jehoram, Ahaziah was constituted; and after Josiah, Jehoahaz his son, whose father's piety was, all the same, not able to protect him sufficiently. Here what Hushai said to Absalom is relevant: 'I will follow', he said, 'that king whom God, the people, and all together as a whole in Israel will have elected'; that is, the king legitimately and duly constituted. And so, although God had promised His people a perpetual light from the line of David – although, I say, the succession of the kings of Israel was approved by the very word of God – nevertheless, since we see that kings do not rule before they are formally constituted by the people, it is legitimate to conclude that the kingdom of Israel was certainly hereditary if you consider lineage, but was clearly, if you regard persons, entirely elective. (p. 70)

Even the appearance of hereditary monarchy cannot disguise the fact that what is taking place is a quite different constitutional arrangement between monarch and people. The argument continues and our attention is turned to early Rome, which was ruled by one hundred senators after the death of Romulus. This did not suit the people, so the Senate agreed to allow kings to return, but only on terms that would be popular: 'Tarquinus Superbus was therefore considered to be a tyrant because he was created neither by the people nor by the senate, but held command by relying on force and power alone' (p. 71). He could therefore be deposed legitimately as a tyrant on two grounds: as a usurper and as an oppressor. An Aristotelian tradition was careful to distinguish between tyranny as usurpation and tyranny as oppression: here the archetypal tyrant, Tarquin, is shown to be liable to deposition on both grounds[80] There is no difference between the history lessons that classical Rome and biblical Israel can teach modern Europeans.

Vindiciae, Contra Tyrannos certainly had an impact in Shakespeare's England. It was well known to the Sidney circle, having probably been co-written by Sir Philip Sidney's correspondent and mentor, Hubert Languet (with Philippe du Plessis Mornay).[81] More significantly perhaps, a translation of the final part was published in London in 1588, entitled, *A Short Apologie for Christian Souldiours*. The purported author was still called Stephanus Junius Brutus, but the target of the work was clearly altered. In reprinting just the section that dealt with the right of legitimate, neighbouring princes to intervene to help an oppressed prince or people, it is evident that the translator, H. P., was using *Vindiciae, Contra Tyrannos* as a piece of anti-Spanish propaganda, either before or immediately after the attempted invasion of the Armada.[82] English readers would have learnt that princes are allowed to defend those oppressed by tyranny (A2r); that it was the duty of Christian soldiers to liberate souls oppressed by the forces of Satan and that if they ignored such duties they would be punished for their failure to help Christ (A7r–B2r); that true Christians were obliged to help depose tyrants, and any prince who behaved unjustly could be overthrown with the help of a foreign prince (B5r–B6v); and that the Bible, as well as ancient Greek and Roman history, was full of examples of virtuous princes who helped overthrow tyrants, so that modern princes would do well to copy their example (B7v–B8r). While such criticism was aimed at the oppressions of Catholic powers, it is easy to see how it opened the door for other uses and interpretations, and how easily such language could be translated to another context with a very different significance.

Of course, a strain of Catholic resistance theory developed in opposition to a Protestant one, based on identical but inverted assumptions.[83] The most influential exponent of such theories in an English context was the leading English Catholic, Cardinal William Allen (1532–94), who went into exile soon after Elizabeth became queen in 1558, and subsequently founded the seminary at Douai, dedicated to converting his fellow countrymen back to the Catholic faith.[84] Allen was determined to oppose the twin evils of Calvinism and the 'politiques' who had started to dominate government because both groups were eager to suppress the true Catholic faith. In *A Treatise made in Defence of the lawful power and authoritie of Priesthod to remedie sinnes* (Louvain, 1567), Allen argues that rebellion against God's anointed priesthood is the same as rebellion against lawful governors, echoing and reversing the arguments of Calvinist treatises such as *Vindiciae, Contra Tyrannos.*[85] Allen refers to the head of the Catholic Church as the 'supreme governor' (p. 9), deliberately echoing the title that Elizabeth took as head of the Church of England to assert a prior right and reduce the queen's claim to a parody of the truth.[86] Allen also argues that only those who can be seen as public officers of the church, ordained priests, have the right to power because they are governors over people's souls (pp. 76, 103), another inversion of the Huguenot distinction between the legitimate actions of magistrates and the duties of private persons.[87] Allen also describes Catholics as 'Godes electe people' (p. 282), a further parody and inversion of Calvinist language.[88]

Allen argued much more aggressively in *A True, Sincere and Modest Defence, of English Catholiques* (Rouen, 1584), written in the wake of the execution of Edmund Campion (1581), the most celebrated Catholic martyr in Elizabeth's reign, whose trial and death generated an enormous quantity of printed debate.[89] Allen argued that England needed to be saved as there had been a revolt from the true faith, precipitated by the false advisers who had led the queen astray.[90] This was an argument frequently made by English Catholics, as the anonymous *Leicester's Commonwealth*, published in the same year as Allen's work, indicates.[91] Allen makes a plea for 'libertie of conscience' (p. 16), and argues that the queen has been abusing the treason laws, specifically those that forbid 'compassing' (imagining) the king's death, in order to have religious opponents executed on less controversial grounds (pp. 18–19).[92] He contrasts the true martyrs who died for the church with those heretics and traitors celebrated by Foxe (pp. 45, 55–56). Allen sees monarchs who oppose the will of God as liable to deposition and supports Pope Pius V's bull excommunicating Elizabeth and absolving her subjects from their allegiance to her (1570) (pp. 61–68).[93] The core of Allen's argument rests in his effort to contrast Protestant theories of resistance and religious martyrdom with those of Catholics. He acknowledges that both Catholics and Protestants agree that tyrants can be deposed (p. 88), and that kings and queens themselves accept that they have no right to rule if they can be shown to be heretics (p. 73). However, Allen makes the case that whereas Protestants are forced to rely on their own conscience to know what is right, Catholics are supported by the institution of the Church, which is a higher earthly and spiritual authority than any monarch (pp. 84–85).

Allen makes a number of references to Scotland, condemning the Protestant rebels against Mary Stuart, who had been imprisoned in England since she fled in 1568 (preface, p. 83, 184–85).[94] His comments reveal just how central to the English political imagination her northern neighbour was. Scotland was a key nation, not simply in terms of political strategy and the forging of allegiances within Europe, but also as a major intellectual centre of republican thought and theories of resistance to tyranny. This was based in part on the readily available histories by John Major (*A History of Greater Britain* (1521)) and Hector Boece (*Scotorum Historiae* (published 1574)), who both provided extensive catalogues of the poor behaviour of Scottish kings and the people's readiness to depose them when they exceeded their authority, as well as the writings and reputation of the Presbyterian John Knox.[95] But the key figure who dominated the intellectual reputation of Scotland in the late sixteenth century was George Buchanan (1506–82).

Buchanan was well known because he was a genuinely European figure who had taught for a long time in Paris and had also been interrogated by the Inquisition in Portugal.[96] He also played a crucial role in Scottish politics, returning to Scotland in 1561 as a Calvinist convert, ready to play his part in establishing Protestantism in his native land. But he attracted greatest attention as an author, writing a number of tragedies in Latin, the most important being *Jephtha* and *Baptises Sive Calumnia* (*The Baptist*); a treatise on Latin prosody, *De Prosodia Libellius*; a significant collection of Latin poems on various subjects, including an epithalamium for King Francis II of France and Mary Stuart who were married on 24 April 1558; and his three principal political works, *Ane detectioun of the duinges of Marie Quene of Scottes* (1571), *De Jure Regni Apud Scotis* (1579), and *Rerum Scoticarum Historia*, published posthumously (1582).[97] As well as being the most celebrated Scottish humanist in Europe, Buchanan also had a claim to be the leading republican figure in the British Isles.[98]

In the dialogue, *De Jure Regni*, Buchanan expounds his political theories in conversation with Thomas Maitland. Buchanan, needless to say, manages to persuade the cautious Maitland to abandon his belief that custom and law will be enough to resist the onset of tyranny and accept Buchanan's more radical charge that a reasoned resistance to autocracy, one that allows the people to overthrow their ruler if he fails to follow their wishes, is justified.[99] He uses the same range of classical examples and authorities that we find elsewhere in contemporary political treatises – Tiberius, Caligula, Nero, Domitian, Catiline, Cicero, Herodotus, Plato, Aristotle, Xenophon and Alexander – alongside examples from the Old and New Testaments, to show that kings are elected representatives of the people and are there to serve their needs, not vice versa.[100] The people have the power to elect their kings as 'Kings are not ordained for themselves, but for the people' (p. 181). Kings who are not good enough can be deposed if they refuse to stand aside in favour of more suitable candidates (pp. 186–87). Following his reading of Cicero, Buchanan argues that the people educate their rulers and establish the laws and that it is the king's duty to implement them (pp. 195–96, 210). When kings think themselves above the law, they become tyrants and need to be deposed, as Ahab was, as they have ceased to have a common bond of humanity with the people they rule (pp. 269, 304). The law is the key to society's proper functioning (pp. 287, 290). The best sort of monarch was a Stoic: virtuous, constant, modest, eager to serve the people before himself or herself, and keen to uphold the law (pp. 314–15). Buchanan hoped that the marriage of Francis II of France and Mary would lead to this form of Stoic rule, praising Mary for her virtue and prudence, as well as her modesty and beauty, which would guide her husband in a union that would prove fruitful for both France and Scotland.[101] The poem is also notable for its lack of reference to Christianity, and its use of classical examples to celebrate the wedding. Buchanan claims that France was especially receptive to 'The teachings of Greek and Roman wisdom' (line 212). As has frequently been observed, even when Buchanan does make extensive reference to the Bible, or represents a biblical subject, his focus seems to be essentially secular.[102]

Buchanan's *History of Scotland*, a revision of Boece's *History*, shows the Scots establishing a workable constitution and then being forced to overthrow many of their kings, who lapse into tyranny by placing themselves above the law. Scotland exists as an elective monarchy. The ruler has to nominate an heir apparent who is often, but not always, from his on her family, or even the next of kin. The system changes dramatically with the advent of Kenneth III, whose devious practices enable him to settle the succession exclusively within his own family and so establish the alien principle of hereditary kingship.[103] Buchanan argues that this change in the law has no real advantage for the Scots and leads in the end to tyranny, and, ironically enough, the instability that tyranny brings with it, when defences of Kenneth's actions were that the new law would establish order: 'For what is less conducive to Perpetuity, than Tyranny?' (pp. 205–6).[104] A rather more pointed irony results when Mary Stuart, once celebrated by Buchanan as the future of the Scottish monarchy, assumes the role of the apotheosis of tyranny, the culmination of years of suffering on the part of the Scottish people after Kenneth forced through his selfish and unjust law (Books 15–20).

Although she is justly deposed by the Scottish parliament, which recognize that she is a tyrant and so removes her authority (p. 139), Mary continues in power, feeding her own faction at the expense of everyone else (p. 152). In some ways this is learnt behaviour, as she had the misfortune to have been brought up in the corruptest of courts (p. 160). A key point in Buchanan's case against Mary is that she rules without consulting her council, truly wicked behaviour (p. 175). Her disastrous marriage to the earl of Bothwell after her murder of her second husband, Lord Darnley, makes her behave in an even more tyrannous manner, imposing popish practices on a hostile people who take up the general chant, 'Burn the Whore, burn the Parricide' (pp. 189–90, 196, 210). Even after she escapes the Scottish civil war and is granted refuge in England, Mary continues to support her son – James VI, Buchanan's pupil – in inappropriate ways, trying to make him rule alone without the regent, James Douglas, fourth earl of Morton (pp. 226–27).[105] Buchanan includes a

speech by the royalist faction's ambassador, claiming that the acts of
Kenneth III prevented the strife and bloodshed that accompanied elective
monarchy by securing the throne for just one family. Buchanan responds
with his habitual attack on the cruel tyranny of some kings, arguing that
elective monarchy serves to prevent this problem, clearly having in mind
the behaviour of Mary and with the hope that the Protestant faction to
which he belonged would be able to determine the future of Scotland by
making the monarch behave virtuously and so be worthy of his or her
election to the throne.[106]

   Buchanan concludes the *History* by reiterating his main points through
the speech of the regent. Morton argues that throughout history all good
kings have realized that they existed beneath the law, even Roman emperors. Kings could be put to death for their crimes, an understanding of
the law that had been accepted in Athens, Sparta, Rome, Venice and
all other civilized societies (p. 269). Mary has abrogated this fundamental agreement between sovereign and people, and so is now a creature
whose behaviour transgresses both divine and natural law (p. 272). In
short, Buchanan's *History* ends with a plea for Mary to be tried and
executed, making it little wonder that her son eventually had the book
banned and conceived his own defence of the divine right of kings in direct
opposition to Buchanan's notions of kingship.[107] The campaign against
Mary eventually proved too powerful to resist and, after the Throckmorton Plot was discovered in 1586, Mary was executed on 8 February 1587.[108]

   Buchanan was widely read in England. He had a particular influence
on the Sidney circle, who were especially interested in Protestant resistance theory, as articulated in works such as *Vindiciae, Contra Tyrannos*.
Buchanan corresponded with a number of authors close to the Sidneys.[109]
This group included Christopher Goodman, a Marian exile who had
known John Knox in Geneva, and had published the monarchomach
treatise, *How superior powers oght to be obeyd of their subjects* (1558), a work
that adopted a political stance very similar to that of Buchanan.[110] Sir
Philip Sidney's *Arcadia* made extensive use of Protestant theories of
resistance to tyranny, probably derived from Buchanan, as well as *Vindiciae, Contra Tyrannos*.[111] Edmund Spenser, who was connected to the
Sidney circle, made a number of references to Buchanan's *History* at
crucial points in his own dialogue, *A View of the Present State of Ireland*
(*c*.1596).[112] Spenser's work may have also been influenced by *De Jure
Regni*. Both dialogues are Socratic in form. They cast a rational but
ignorant speaker, whose assumptions probably mirror those of the projected readership, confronting a wiser and more masterful speaker. The

latter's views are undoubtedly shocking, but they hold sway and his opponent acknowledges what he has learnt from the debate.[113] Spenser's representation of Mary's trial and execution in *The Faerie Queene* aroused James's ire (see below, pp. 91–92).[114] It is likely that James saw Spenser as a follower of Buchanan, using a hostile image of his mother to blacken the name of the monarchy and arguing that monarchs should be accountable to the people.[115] It is also likely that James was right.[116] Shakespeare, as is well documented, clearly read Spenser.[117]

Buchanan was, of course, condemned by many English readers who took exception to his acerbic political views and style of argument.[118] But even hostile comment is testament to influence and importance, especially in Buchanan's case. Buchanan's attack on the Welsh historian Humphrey Llwyd's acceptance of Geoffrey of Monmouth's evidence for the existence of Arthur resulted in a series of dismissive comments on his own work from Thomas Churchyard, Richard Harvey and others.[119] Most significant of all was the revision of Holinshed's *Chronicle of Scotland,* first published in 1577, which was updated by Francis Thynne for the second edition of 1587.[120] Thynne incorporated Buchanan's *History* into his narrative, and, although he often criticizes Buchanan's conclusions and labels him 'greatlie learned but manie times maliciouslie affected', he relies heavily on his work to revise the history of Scotland for English readers, which, in turn, had been largely derived from Major and Boece.[121] The passage describing the reign of Kenneth III (V, pp. 301–11), for example, a crucial part of Buchanan's argument against the assumption of hereditary monarchy in Scotland, is translated almost verbatim from Buchanan's *History.* Even the extensive narrative of Mary's failings is largely preserved, although Thynne does warn his readers that Buchanan always refers to those who are loyal to Mary as the 'rebellious faction'.[122]

It is hard not to read Buchanan's extensive writings in the context of republican thought and language. Buchanan goes further than virtually all monarchomach writers, arguing throughout his published works that any godly person could dispose of a tyrant, not just magistrates [i.e., government officials].[123] His conception of kingship places power and authority as securely in the hands of the people as is possible within a monarchical framework; his list of political examples is based on Roman history as well as the Bible; his conception of the law is not derived from an English tradition of the sanctity of the common law as represented by Fortesque, but notions of natural law derived from Huguenot theorists, Thomist thought and a study of Roman law.[124] Furthermore, Buchanan was a great admirer of the Venetian republic, one of the key signs of republican enthusiasm, and a phenomenon that was developing swiftly in the 1590s in England.[125]

Buchanan expressed ferrent praise for the Venetian republic in *De Jure Regni*, putting the words into his own mouth within the dialogue. He argues that the Duke of Venice (the Doge) is really a king, but one who is elected, obeys the law and does not occupy the office for life (pp. 189–91). The object of Buchanan's redefinition of the Venetian constitution is clearly so that he can compare other kingdoms unfavourably with Venice – Scotland, as a less successful elective monarchy, being the chief case in point; imperial Rome being another designated target – not so that he can deny the political identity and significance of Venice. When James VI published *The Trew Law of Free Monarchies* in 1598, a work intended to defend his belief that hereditary monarchy which granted the king absolute powers was the best form of government, he very deliberately denied that Venice was a monarchy. James argued that kings, although they had to obey the laws they have established, should have power over the people they ruled, which meant that such 'free Monarchies' could never endure 'elective kings, and much lesse of such sort of governors, as the dukes of *Venice* are, whose Aristocratick and limited government, is nothing like to free Monarchies'.[126] James was trying to scotch the republican snake as he developed his theories of government in direct opposition to those of his former tutor.

Praise of the Venetian republic had been a key feature of English political life since – at least – the reign of Edward VI when William Thomas published his *Historie of Italie* (1549).[127] Thomas praised Venice for its wealth as a trading port; its stability, having lasted more than a thousand years; and its ability to absorb and tolerate a variety of foreign citizens within the body politic. Venice's success was no happy accident but the result of a liberal constitution that put the needs and desires of its citizens first, not those of an aristocratic oligarchy or an overmighty monarch. Venice had an elaborate constitution which promoted and protected the rights of its citizens. All citizens had the right to vote in secret and elected a great assembly which Thomas argued was the equivalent of the English parliament (fo.80). The Council in turn elected six Signori, who were trusted to advise the Duke (Doge), and three of them, the Signor Capi, had greater powers than the Duke, enabling them to control and limit his actions (fos.77–78). None of these offices was tenable for life, but they were regularly rotated so that no one assumed excessive power for themselves. As a result, public service, the preservation of individual and collective liberty, and the promotion of virtue were always political values that all Venetians believed in and were able to enjoy.

Thomas's *History* was evidently designed to force English subjects to think carefully about their political rights and liberties, as a key part of the political changes and experiments that were taking place in the reign of Edward VI.[128] How influential the work was is difficult to judge, especially given that Thomas was executed for his part in Wyatt's Rebellion soon after Mary came to the throne.[129] Nevertheless, it is hard to dispute that Venice was exalted as a beacon of liberty by numerous Englishmen in the latter years of Elizabeth's reign when the future had become perilously uncertain because of the nature of the succession, and many saw Elizabeth as a remote and arbitrary monarch who had little interest in her subjects.[130]

It is surely no coincidence that the work that contained the most sustained and positive representation of Venice, Gaspar Contarini's *De Magistratibus et Republica Venetorum* (1543), should be translated into English in 1599 when criticism of Elizabeth was reaching epidemic proportions, as she herself acknowledged after Essex's coup.[131] It is a pointed irony that Lewis Lewkenor's *The Commonwealth and Government of Venice*, which provided a rosy image of a city-state dedicated to fostering freedom and liberty, appeared in print in the same year that the archbishop of Canterbury and the bishop of London ordered the Master and Wardens of the Stationers' Company to ban the publication of verse satires and epigrams because they had become too scurrilous and critical in nature and tone.[132] Lewkenor's work seems to have been designed as a comprehensive guide to Venice for English readers. It contains not only Contarini's text, which had already become well known throughout Europe as the most important description of the Venetian constitution, but also extracts from the writings of other historians, and a guidebook, *Delle cose notabiliti della citta di Venetia*, showing that Lewkenor intended to write a work with a practical purpose that would serve as the one book any English reader needed to explain the mysteries of Venice.[133] Such supporting material serves to highlight rather than diminish the political importance of the translation.

Contarini places emphasis on Venice as a city-state that can regulate the virtue of its citizens. Venetians are neither more nor less virtuous than people elsewhere, but they live under a regime, an 'artificial angel', that enables them to make the best of themselves and preserve the stability that the Roman republic almost managed.[134] Venice is the perfect 'mixed' constitution, having the correct balance of monarchy, aristocracy and popular assembly (p. 37); citizens are accorded equal status through being eligible for a whole range of offices which are rotated at periodic intervals (p. 33); the laws are impartial and just (p. 25); taxes are moderate and fair (p. 109); and the twin evils of tyranny and popular sedition are avoided (p. 11). More pointedly, Contarini argues that factionalism is absent in Venice, because everyone can become involved in the process of government (p. 8). Given the increased importance of factions at the English court in the late 1590s, with the conflict between the Cecils and the earl of Essex's circle, this point would have assumed an especial significance for many readers in 1599.[135]

Contarini expresses his belief that those who see monarchy as the best form of government are sadly mistaken. Monarchy inevitably declines into tyranny, and government by the greater number is more suited to man's natural disposition: 'the government of the multitude is farre more convenient to the assemblie of citizens . . . because wee have not read that there was among the auncientes any soverainty of a king' (p. 57). The translator does, though, insert marginal notes which undercut the message of the text. Against a passage that speaks of the evils of concentrating power in the hands of one ruler, Lewkenor asserts that in spite of the example of Venice, 'all great philosophers chiefly extoll . . . the monarchy' (p. 56). Nevertheless, as with the use of Buchanan's text in Holinshed's *Chronicles*, or the extensive citation from *The Prince* and *The Discourses* in Gentillet's *Anti-Machiavel*, the subversive material is made available for any reader to see. Contarini uses the ubiquitous analogy of the 'body politic' to claim that the constitution of Venice is natural because it incorporates the city's citizens (not all Venetians are citizens):

Now a unitie cannot well be contayned, unlesse one being placed in authoritie above, not onely the vulgar multitude, but also all the rest of the citizens and officers, have authoritie to combine them together, being scattered & disjoynted, and to bind them (as it were) all into one entire body: which the great philosophers that were the searchers out, and (as it were) divers into the secretes of Nature, did notably marke and observe, as well in the continuation of the whole worlde, as also of this Microcosme or little worlde, which is Man. (p. 38)[136]

Venice, according to Contarini, has established 'an excellent contrived mixture of the best and justest governments', a judicious mixture of nobles and 'popular estate' is contained in the elected great council, so that all elements of the body politic are represented in the political process (pp. 33–34). Citizens are allowed to challenge the authority of the Duke. After an election when the new Duke's name is read out by one of the chief citizens, if anyone thinks that the chosen candidate is 'unfit, or uncapable, or unworthy of so great a dignity, or for any other cause shall not thinke his creation to bee for the good of the common-wealth, he riseth up, and with an honest modestie speaketh his opinion, declaring the cause why he thinketh it unmeet that he should be chosen' (pp. 57–58). The objections are then put to the new Duke, who answers them. If the citizens are satisfied, then he is elected; if not, the debate continues until a solution is reached (by lots if necessary). Indeed, so successful and powerful is the Venetian constitution that the worst forms of government, such as tyranny, cannot be established through the efforts of a tiny minority determined to undermine the social and political fabric of the state (p. 42); it contains the political safety net that Aristotle recommended.[137]

It is, of course, hard to know exactly what late Elizabethan readers made of Contarini's treatise, as no real evidence of readers survives in the form of notes, marginal annotations, or explicit discussions in manuscript or print. However, we do know that *The Commonwealth and Government of Venice* had a significant impact on literature. Sir Philip Sidney sought the work out, probably under the influence of one of his Huguenot mentors, Hubert Languet, and Edmund Spenser wrote one of the dedicatory sonnets to Lewkenor's translation.[138] It was also used as a guide by both Shakespeare and Ben Jonson when they wrote their Venetian plays, *The Merchant of Venice, Othello* and *Volpone*, which indicates that Lewkenor's work did have an important influence on English readers.[139]

But arguably the most significant impact on English intellectual culture in the 1590s was made by the advent of 'Tacitism', the vogue for the histories of Rome by Tacitus, Sallust and Suetonius. Tacitism was a European phenomenon and can be traced back to the efforts to promote the virtues of Tacitus's writing by the Frenchman Marc-Antoine Muret (1526–85) and the Netherlander Justus Lipsius (1547–1606). Lipsius produced a definitive edition of Tacitus's *Annals* and *History of Imperial Rome*, as well as his own work of political thought, *Sixe Bookes of Politickes or Civil Doctrine* (1589), which makes extensive use of Tacitus for examples and analysis. It is a sign of the intellectual dominance of Tacitism in European thought that the *Annals* and *History* went through forty-five editions in the sixteenth century (a further sixty-seven appeared between 1600 and 1649); more than a hundred commentaries on Tacitus were published between 1580 and 1700; and Lipsius's *Six Books* was reproduced fifteen times in Latin in eleven years (it was translated into English in 1594).[140] Editions of Tacitus had become so widespread in the early seventeenth century that Ben Jonson, in his poem 'The New Cry', satirizing the increasingly frenetic vogue for novelty in London, felt able to sneer at both the book trade and the would-be statesmen who carried 'in their pocket Tacitus', believing it to be the key to political wisdom.[141]

Tacitus's two major works of Roman history – he also wrote two accounts of the Roman campaigns in Britain and Gaul, the *Agricola* and *Germania*, in defence of the actions of his father-in-law, the general Agricola – narrate the story of the reigns of the Roman emperors from Augustus to Vespasian (died AD 79).[142] Tacitus appealed to Renaissance readers because he was seen as an eloquent, albeit sometimes wordy, stylist, who analysed his subjects in a detached and dispassionate manner, attempting to understand why they behaved as they did. Given that his histories narrated the events of the reigns of the most tyrannical of Roman empowers, Tiberius, Nero and Caligula, Tacitus was often taken to be the model of historical writing for critics of absolutism eager to survive under the most brutal regimes, preserve their integrity, and point the way towards beneficial change. He was also often coopted for quite different political ends, as a model for those who wished to learn how to behave when in power. Louis XI of France is often quoted as saying, 'who can't feign, can't reign', which demonstrates that Tacitus, like Machiavelli, could be read by some as a republican, challenging received wisdom, and by others as a cynical proponent of *ragioni di stato*.[143] Samuel Daniel could read Tacitus to show that Rome degenerated from the virtue of the republic to the corruption of the period of imperial rule; Edmund Bolton and Peter Heylyn read the same author to prove that monarchy was the best form of government in a flawed world.[144] After the publication of Sir John Hayward's Tacitean history, *The Life and Raigne of King Henrie IIII*, which caused such scandal because it had been dedicated to the earl of Essex and seemed to be comparing Essex to Henry IV and Elizabeth to the deposed monarch, Richard II, Sir Francis Bacon tried to relieve a tense encounter with the queen by attempting a joke. Asked if he found treason in the work, Bacon replied that the history contained many felonies but no treason because 'the author had committed very apparent theft: for he had taken most of the sentences of Cornelius Tacitus, and translated them into English and put them into his text'.[145] Tacitus had become the common currency of political exchange.

It is therefore inaccurate to cite evidence of the widespread study of Tacitus as a sign that republicanism was rife in late Tudor and early Stuart England, not least because Elizabeth herself 'was an avid reader of Tacitus'.[146] But it would be equally problematic not to see the vogue for

Tacitus and Sallust and other detached and Stoical historians as an indication that many intellectuals wished to forge a means of political analysis, both a style and a method, that enabled them to criticize the assumptions of the status quo. Thomas Hobbes, as has often been noted, blamed the English Civil War on the reading of Greek and Roman history:

And as to Rebellion in particular against Monarchy; one of the most frequent causes of it, is the Reading of the books of Policy, and Histories of the ancient Greeks, and Romans; from which, young men, and all others that are unprovided of the Antidote of solid Reason, receiving a strong, and delightfull impression, of the great exploits of warre, achieved by the Conductors of their Armies, receive withall a pleasing Idea, of all they have done besides; and imagine that great prosperity, not to have proceeded from the aemulation of particular men, but from the vertue of their popular forme of government: Not considering the frequent Seditions, and civill warres, produced by the imperfection of their Policy.[147]

Hobbes, who was educated in the 1590s and whose habits of thought and use of rhetoric date from the last decade of Elizabeth's reign, argues that Greek and Roman writers serve an important moral purpose.[148] It is when these lessons are applied to the public sphere and made political that problems arise, allowing second-rate thinkers to exceed the bounds of their limited abilities, because they mistakenly believe that they have the right to challenge higher authorities. Hobbes undoubtedly exaggerated his historical evidence for rhetorical effect.[149] Nevertheless, the case he makes is an important indication of what many felt was the corrosive influence of Tacitus, who provided an easy means of sliding from moral outrage to rebellious action, the simplest form of political critique. Hobbes's angry rhetoric against unsophisticated thinkers shows that he wanted a proper examination of institutions and their effects on the people they served, rather than what he saw as the misconceived moralization of political language and hence action.

A translation of the *Annals* was published in 1591, by Henry Saville (1549–1622), an Oxford scholar, provost of Eton, and perhaps Elizabeth I's tutor in Greek.[150] The work was dedicated to Elizabeth, like *Solon his Follie. The ende of Nero and beginning of Galba Fower bookes of the Histories of Cornelius Tacitus. The life of Agricola* (Oxford, 1591) contains not only Tacitus's surviving, unfinished text, but a continuation of the reign of Galba in Tacitean style by the translator, as well as Tacitus's *Agricola*.[151] Saville's additions show that he reads Tacitus as a political moralist, making astute judgements on the performance of individuals in power, not as a sophisticated analyst of the constitution or political institutions. A. B.'s prefatory letter 'To the Reader' thanks God that he serves Elizabeth, rather than the ferocious tyrants who ruled imperial Rome, and commends Tacitus as the best historian, even though his matter is often harsh. Nevertheless, Saville, describing the reigns of the emperors that Tacitus represents in the *Histories*, asserts that 'Even good Princes are jealous of soveraine points, and that string being touched, have a quick eare' (p. 3). The comment can easily be interpreted as approving, but it also indicates the ambivalence that many writers felt they had to make central to their style under excessively authoritarian government. Given Elizabeth's notorious – but not necessarily unreasonable – sensitivity about the succession, as well as foreign policy, the remark has an obvious contemporary relevance.[152] Even those close to Elizabeth could see parallels between aspects of her reign and those of Roman emperors.[153]

Saville's descriptions and judgements in his history of the reign of Galba imitate those of Tacitus himself. Saville tries to produce an accurate and balanced view of the elderly military man who became emperor by chance, seeing him as old and feeble, promoting his own friends and favourites, even though he was a man of admirable character in other ways.[154] Tacitus sums up the character of Galba after his murder at the hands of Nero's men:

This ende had Scrutius Galba, hauing lived seventy three yeares, and out-lived five Princes in greate prosperity; happier under the Empire of others then in his owne: his house of auncient nobility, and great wealth: himselfe a man of midle disposition, rather vicelesse, then greatly vertuous; neither neglecting his fame, nor yet ambitiously carefull of it: of other mens money not greedy, sparing of his owne, of the common a niggard: bearing with his favorites and freedmen, without reprehension, when they were good; if they were bad, to his owne shame ignoraunt of their ill doings: but his honourable birth, and the dangerous times covered the matter, entitling that wisedome, which in truth was but slouth: in his flourishing age greatly renowned for service in Germanie: Africke he ruled as Proconsull with great moderation: and growing in yeares, the nearer Spaine uprightly & well: serving more than a private man, whilest he was private, and by all mens opinion capable of the Empire, had he never bene Emperour. (pp. 27–8)

The last, rhetorically balanced, phrase is particularly damning. Galba was a man of some virtues, although even these were often less impressive than they seemed to be, but not a man who should ever have been emperor. His limit was the level of provincial governor, responsible to his seniors, as he did not have the imagination or force of personality to rule outright. This shows in his treatment of money and gifts, neither of which he coveted and which he was able to distribute to others. However, he was naive and not able to see that others behaved differently, demanding more and abusing their positions. Galba did not deserve his ignominious end, his head discovered beside the tomb of a freeman he had had executed, although even here there is a neat poetic justice in his fate.

Tacitus's concluding comments on Galba's reign are typical of his historical style. He is concerned to analyse and evaluate the behaviour of rulers, with the clear indication that it is up to his readers to decide whether their examples are applicable to their own rulers. He says nothing about the form and constitution of government, nor about the ways in which government institutions and practices function, in contrast with other Roman historians available to Elizabethan readers, most notably Livy and Polybius.

Tacitean history is not necessarily – or even often – republican in inclination, although it is worth noting that Tacitus's most devoted European follower, Justus Lipsius, places great emphasis on the need for kings to obey the law, serve the people and promote virtue rather than retain power at all costs, in his influential treatise *Sixe Bookes of Politickes or Civil Doctrine*. In his prefatory letter, Lipsius, whose works are studded with maxims, states, 'O rightly is that Prince just, & lawful, who in his greatest felicitie, had not rather heare men say, that he is mightie, then that he is good.'[155] In Lipsius's *Two bookes of constancie*, translated into English in the following year, Lipsius expresses his Stoic belief that reason is vital to order the world and protect mankind against the contingencies of war and other disasters.[156] Tacitean history contributed to a critical discourse that could examine and explain the faults and failings of contemporary government and so has an important affiliation with republican political analysis. Moreover, the interest in Tacitus had a huge impact on the writing of English history as well as literature.[157]

My argument so far might well suggest that republicanism was ubiquitous and that it could not be avoided, even if not every form of political analysis was republican *per se*. This would be wrong. Many writers – not simply James VI and I – were hostile to republican notions of government and argued vigorously against the need to control and limit the power of the monarch, or made the case that hereditary monarchy was the best form of government and that a monarch's powers should be limited as little as possible.[158] There was, of course, 'An Homily against Disobedience and Wilful Rebellion', published in 1574 as part of the reaction to the Northern Rebellion (1569–70), which used to be taken as a statement of orthodox Tudor political belief.[159] This text, designed to be read out periodically in churches throughout the land, does indeed argue that 'subjects must learn obedience both to God and their princes'.[160] But it is unlikely that it had a serious impact on educated citizens, especially those living in London, who were reading other works of political philosophy. The full title of the work in which the Homily appeared shows that its authors recognized who it was intended to influence: *Certaine sermons appoynted by the Queenes Majestie, to be declared and readde, by al parsons, vicars, and curates, every Sunday and holy daye in their churches: and by her graces advice perused and overseene, for the better understanding of the simple people.* The horrifying warnings against rebellion were designed to prevent the uneducated 'simple people' from rioting and rebelling. Aristocratic republicans were also strongly opposed to the 'rude multitude' and had no more patience with rioting and popular rebellion.[161] The work was not seriously designed to express an orthodoxy that all had to espouse.

More serious and sophisticated arguments in favour of hereditary monarchy which placed emphasis on the rights of the crown were available and easy to find. Charles Merbury's *A Briefe Discourse of Royall Monarchie* (1581) argues a reasoned and careful case that, for England, at least, hereditary monarchy is the best form of government, and that England is its 'perfecte paterne'.[162] Merbury ranges through a wealth of examples of political forms, once again carefully considering the Venetian republic as another type of excellent government, appending a series of Italian '*proverbi vulgari*', routinely dismissing both tyranny and democracy (pp. 7–10, 13–14), and concludes that hereditary monarchy is much better for a people than elective monarchy, because it is 'more commendable, more sure, lesse subject to corruption, more capable of perfection' (p. 19). As long as kings are virtuous and exist under the rule of law, then all will be well.

A similar case is made in Thomas Floyd's much more substantial *The Picture of a perfit Common wealth* (1600). In an equally erudite and well-informed work, Floyd also argues that monarchy is the best form of government, using the often favoured political analogy of bees, who 'do create & elect one to be their king and chiefe governour, as experience of the Bees teacheth us, which do make choise of the chiefest Bee, to be a king over all the hieve, by which the whole swarme are ledde and guided, as being more provident and wise than the rest'.[163] Nevertheless, Butler is also able to gloss the Latin 'Respublica' as the English 'commonwealth', and, like Merbury, divide forms of government up into the three basic types: democracy, oligarchy and monarchy (p. 11). He also, like Butler, argues that the happiest commonwealth is one where 'the people in genrall do observe the customes and rightes of law' (p. 10).

Floyd's text shows that many early modern political works employed a shared language, or rather, a shared series of languages. He is able to describe the king as 'a Father over his children' (p. 36), an image that resembles a favourite trope used by James VI and I throughout his descriptions of kingship.[164] Two pages later, Floyd condemns the actions of Julius Caesar for causing civil war: 'What destroyed countries? subdued kingdomes? depopulated Cities? but envie. Julius Caesar waged war with his owne sonne in lawe Pompeius, beying mooved with envie' (p. 38). Attacks on Julius Caesar, especially those which condemned him as an enemy of the state who caused unnecessary bloodshed, were frequently republican in orientation, being derived from a reading of Lucan's *Pharsalia*, a key republican literary text that was to play a vital role in the seventeenth century.[165] Caesar is later praised for his 'regard of equitie and justice' (p. 90), a sign that Floyd was using examples to fit his case, a common habit among Renaissance readers.[166]

Floyd's argument reveals the complex nature of early modern political discourse. Authors did indeed share meanings, examples and modes of analysis, but they also were quite capable of making a clear and distinct case, arguing for or against certain forms of government, even as they used a language and style employed by their opponents.[167] No one could imagine that James VI and George Buchanan had similar political beliefs. Nevertheless, their works overlap in a variety of ways: they use similar analogies, tropes, images, and at times espouse identical values.[168] When Floyd argues that 'A tyrant is a king chosen by popular & ambitious election, on behalf of the communalties, to patronize their cause against the chiefest citizens' (p. 47), he is following Aristotle in comparing tyranny to extreme democracy.[169] He is also selecting the evidence, the received wisdom of the standard canonical texts, to suit his case and place particular emphasis on the link between democracy and tyranny, and show that only hereditary monarchy has the means to offset these twin evils. When Floyd argues that stability and constancy are the most desired assets in a governor, he uses the same language as Lipsius, but whether his political goals are the same is debatable.[170]

Other treatises, such as Henry Cross's *The Schoole of Pollicie* (1605) and Edward Forset's *A Comparative Discourse of the bodies natural and politique* (1606), argue similar cases, even as they acknowledge the viability of other political forms – such as republicanism – and employ republican language and imagery.[171] Such works would seem to support Patrick

Collinson's understanding of Elizabethan England as a 'monarchical republic', if it is acknowledged that different writers would use the general currency of shared meanings to articulate opposing political stances. William Covell's treatise *Polimanteia, or The means lawfull and unlawfull, to judge of the fall of a common-wealth* (1595), a work that bears fruitful comparison with Richard Beacon's *Solon his Follie*, contains a similar mixture of examples from Roman history along with praise of Elizabeth (although she is criticized for being far too lenient towards Irish rebels).[172] However, Covell's work is clearly directed at the looming problem of the succession, devoting considerable energy to reminding readers of the burdens they will suffer under a tyranny, as well as the ongoing war between Spain and the Low Countries.[173] Furthermore, it was dedicated to Robert Devereux, in the wake of his 'exposure' of Dr Lopez's plot to poison the queen, and casts Essex as England's chief defender in a time of crisis.[174] A similar manoeuvre caused severe problems for Dr John Hayward only four years later.

This last example indicates that contingency also plays a part in politics, affording some works significance they might not otherwise have had.[175] Yet this is not a case of the wilful and forced misreading of a text, but, rather, the meaning changing according to contingent historical factors. Late Elizabethan England was a culture of lively intellectual debate, as the works cited in this chapter demonstrate, republicanism being a key element within such political discussions, and one that became more prominent towards the end of the century.

However, not everyone is convinced that the political elements isolated here can be legitimately described as 'republican'. The most sustained and cogent argument against the existence of republicanism before the English Civil War has been made by Blair Worden, who claims that, whether one defines republicanism as a language or a programme, its constituent elements are simply not present in Elizabethan England: 'In pre-civil-war England it was the abuse of monarchy, not the principle, that attracted complaint.'[176] Worden is undoubtedly right to make this claim, but whether it means that we cannot legitimately write about republicanism is another question. Does it really make sense not to describe George Buchanan as a republican thinker; to deny that Lewkenor's translation of Contarini establishes a positive image of the Venetian republic, as a pointed contrast to late Elizabethan England; to see republican elements in such monarchomach treatises as *Vindiciae, Contra Tyrannos*; or to see the profound influence of Polybius and other Roman political thinkers eager to revise and update Aristotle as simply critiques of the abuse of monarchy? Worden further claims that 'pre-war discontent . . . was invariably directed towards the reform, and thus to the strengthening, of the monarchy'.[177] The inserted premise does not necessarily follow from the first. Reforming the monarchy did not always involve strengthening it, but, more often than not, limiting its powers in order to strengthen those of the people under the rule of law.[178] As Markku Peltonen has reminded us, if English humanists took 'the princely context for granted, it did not prevent their adopting a number of "civic" and republican themes in their writings'.[179]

If everyone did believe in the monarchy, there were clearly very different positions taken on its role and purpose, not just on whether it was an institution worth preserving. Political debates in early modern England cannot be reduced to this either/or formula. Worden rightly points out that major writers such as More, Sidney and Bacon did turn to 'non-monarchical models of government for guidance', and even if we can agree that 'constitutional collapse was the dread, not the hope, of the class of lay intellectuals to which these writers belonged', their exploration of alternative political institutions would appear to indicate that they did not necessarily believe that the monarchy had to remain static, and that a change of the constitution would not make society better. There was a long tradition of commonwealth thought, placing emphasis on the needs of the people as well as the monarch, which could easily be mapped on to republican thought, as Smith's *De Republica Anglorum* demonstrates.[180]

Yet, if we are justified in writing about republicanism, we also need to acknowledge its inchoate nature as well as its existence as a series of related, overlapping and sometimes contradictory points. This is, of course, hardly a surprising revelation, given the limited means of expression of republican ideas before the Civil War. As Sean Kelsy has demonstrated, the Rump Parliament which ruled England from 1649 to 1653 after the execution of Charles I had to invent a 'parliamentary republic', assembling a series of images, documents, ideas, ceremonies, and so on, to form a political reality. Interregnum politicians had to make use of the materials they had to hand, which meant that 'This post-revolutionary raiment was essentially conservative. Its strands recast old forms and reinvented traditional pomp in order to restore an edifice of civil governance rocked to its foundations by civil war and revolution.'[181] Advocates of republican thought and ideas could not risk anything as explicit in the 1590s, this was their aim; rather, they had to rely on suggestive hints, references and lavish praise of foreign and historical nations, rarely on outright and sustained expression. This is one reason why republicanism seems to have appealed as much to imaginative writers of literature, who could explore their ideas in their chosen forms, as political theorists and historians (see Chapter Two).

Nevertheless, having surveyed the evidence it is possible to outline what republicanism would have meant for a young writer such as Shakespeare, coming to maturity in the later 1580s.[182] Republicanism was not a monolithic concept indicating the participation of all citizens in the political process. Rather, it was a

Cluster of themes concerning citizenship, public virtue and true nobility . . . Virtue was closely linked with the distinctively *republican* character of classical republicanism: to ensure that the most virtuous men governed the commonwealth and to control corruption, magistracy should be elected rather than inherited. In this sense republicanism (in the narrow sense of a constitution without a king) could be an anti-monarchical goal: civic values required concomitant republican institutions, but monarchical arrangements were said to suppress these. Arrangements usually favoured by classical republicans were those of the mixed constitution, and the term republic was also used in the wider and more general sense of referring to a good and just constitution.[183]

I would suggest that a republican tradition constituted a number of different elements and languages, not all of which were exactly congruent or fitted together perfectly. Furthermore, this cluster of beliefs, ideas and identifiable modes of writing do not necessarily indicate republicanism or republican thought if produced in isolation.[184] First, there is a rhetoric against tyranny, often derived from Tacitus's *Histories* and *Annals*, but which also often stemmed from Protestant resistance theorists such as John Knox, John Ponet and Christopher Goodman, writing in the 1550s.[185] Second, there is a strong commitment to the humanist programme of educational reform and a concentration on the study of the classics. Through the study of Cicero, Aristotle, Plato, Polybius, Thucydides et al. came an interest in the political ideas they espoused, as well as an understanding of the institutions and forms of political organization they advocated. Such study led to a select group of highly educated men possessing the means and the confidence to distinguish between different constitutions in the ancient world and contemporary Europe and so debate alternative forms of government, including varieties of mixed rule made up of elements of monarchy, oligarchy and democracy, as well as republics such as Rome and Venice.[186] Third, there is a stress on the need for virtue in government officials or magistrates, often leading to the suggestion that hereditary monarchy was not the ideal form of government because one could not guarantee that the best would inherit the throne.[187] Often such arguments would praise the constitution of Venice because official positions were not held for life or at the whim of a monarch but rotated every few years. Equally important to note, other arguments, generally derived from Machiavelli, would praise republics as best equipped to pursue wars, and claim that active virtue was best achieved in the trying conditions of battle.[188] Fourth, there is a keen interest in histories of the republic and enthusiasm for Livy, who exhibited nostalgia for the lost republic and portrayed the opponents of and conspirators against Caesar – Brutus, Cassius and Pompey – in a positive light.[189] There is also enthusiasm for Lucan's *Pharsalia*, a key text in the grammar school curriculum, and certainly a work against tyrants and arguably a republican classic (see Chapters Two and Four).[190] The very representation of the founding of the republic, the story of the rape of Lucrece – narrated in Livy's *History of Rome from its Foundation* – can, of course, be read as a republican gesture.[191] Fifth, the language of natural rights is employed, often derived from Huguenot treatises and the opposing arguments made by Catholic monarchomachs such as Francisco Suarez.[192] This language grants citizens rights to relative autonomy and freedom from the oppressions of bad monarchs whom they have the right to oppose if necessary. Sometimes treatises, such as Robert Hitchcock's translation of Francesco Sansovino's long collection of aphorisms (803 in total), *The Quintesence of Wit* (1590), place great emphasis on the need for citizens to enjoy liberty.[193] The final element I would single out is the importance of offices and positions of responsibility held by ordinary citizens/subjects, which can be seen to constitute a public realm developing alongside that of formal political representation in parliament. According to Mark Goldie, such participation in public life constituted

a republican tradition in which the active involvement of the citizen rather than the passive exercise of the franchise was the essential feature of a good polity . . . Early modern England was neither a democracy nor, in our modern sense, a republic. It was monarchical. Yet it could be said to be an unacknowledged republic, or a monarchical republic.[194]

This final aspect of republicanism seems to have had a particular influence on Shakespeare, who, more than any of his contemporary playwrights, was especially interested in how political institutions functioned, who they represented, and how individuals came to occupy offices of state. In turning his attention to issues of republicanism, Shakespeare became the most prominent of a number of English Renaissance writers who wished to explore similar issues in their writing.

CHAPTER 2

Literature and republicanism in the Age of Shakespeare

Republicanism was a literary phenomenon, as well as a matter of constitutional belief and doctrine, because it consisted of a series of stories. These were easy to narrate, repeat, retell and refigure, signalling a republican subject matter, or area, without *necessarily* entailing a commitment to any programme. This particular aspect of republicanism is another reason why it is hard to define and isolate, and why some historians have been sceptical that the scraps and fragments of republican culture that undoubtedly exist in pre-Civil War England can be accorded any substance. But it is a mistake to argue that historical documents and evidence precede literary evidence, as if the latter were simply derived from the former as a supplementary discourse. Brian Cummings has recently made the compelling case that the advent of the Reformation in England was as much a literary as a religious phenomenon, the two being inseparable parts of a whole.[1] Kevin Sharpe has advanced a similar argument, claiming that historians will fail to understand early modern culture if they define their sources narrowly and construct arguments based on the examination of state papers, letters, political treatises, parliamentary records, and so on, because political culture also consisted of literary texts, court performances (including nonverbal activities such as dancing), art works and clothing.[2] The same, of course, is true of early modern republicanism.

The basic stories of republicanism are well known, and are often repeated. These two fundamental narratives dovetail neatly, representing the birth of the republic, and its prolonged death, linked through the name that has perhaps become the most republican of all names, Brutus. The first story is that of the rape of Lucrece, whose abuse at the hands of Tarquinus Sextus, son of the tyrannical king of Rome, Tarquinus Superbus, results in the end of the dynasty of the first kings of Rome, and the founding of the republic when Lucius Junius Brutus leads the revolt that has them banished. The most familiar source for readers in the

English Renaissance was Livy's *The History of Rome from its Foundation*.[3] Of course, the story could be inflected in a variety of ways, often being used as a paradigmatic example of female virtue and chastity, as in Chaucer's *The Legend of Good Women* (reprinted in the complete edition of Chaucer in 1561).[4] More often, however, it possessed a clear political charge, as the example of *Vindiciae, Contra Tyrannos* demonstrates, whereby Lucius Junius Brutus is declared to be the tutor of his modern namesake, Stephanus Junius Brutus, the Celt (see above, pp. 31–32). Exactly the same political connotations are provided, albeit more cautiously, in William Painter's *The Palace of Pleasure*, one of the most popular works of the second half of the sixteenth century, which, like the even more successful *A Mirror for Magistrates*, went through a variety of editions and ever-expanding versions after its initial publication in 1566. Painter's subtitle, *with pleasaunt histories and excellent novelles, selected out of divers good and commendable authors*, makes the work sound innocent enough, but this influential compendium of prose tales started life as what must have been a more politically oriented work entitled *The Cytie of Civilitie*, when it was entered in the Stationers' Register in 1562.[5] Painter derives a number of tales from Livy, as well as contemporary Italian and French collections. The second novel in the collection is 'The Rape of Lucrece', a narrative that may have influenced Shakespeare's poem, especially given the use of Painter's work by other dramatists to provide source material for their plays (most famously, John Webster's *The Duchess of Malfi*).[6] Shakespeare's decision to publish a version of the legend in 1594 was certainly a bold move and would have marked him out as a writer keen to explore political ideas and themes, however he chose to tell the story (see Chapter Five).[7]

The second story is a little more complex and involved, but is easy enough to recognize. The republic ended and imperial Rome began when Octavius Caesar assumed control after defeating the republican forces led by Brutus and Cassius. Just as the republicans had to fight a series of wars with the forces of the Tarquins to retain control of the body politic they wished to control – a section in Livy that is not always reproduced by those who retold the story of Lucrece – Octavius had to defeat his former ally, Antony, now in league with the Egyptian queen, Cleopatra. When he managed this feat, he was left in sole command and assumed the title of Augustus. The Roman empire was born. Augustus's triumphant moment, as all readers of Tacitus, Suetonius and Plutarch would have known, was all too brief, and he was succeeded by a series of horrible tyrants whose names were a byword for cruelty and excess – Tiberius, Caligula, Claudius and Nero – eventually killed off by a popular coup, leading to the rule of the Flavian dynasty. The cyclical nature of Roman history was, as always, apparent.[8]

The events leading up to this political transformation are just as important as other elements of the story in the Renaissance imagination. The decay of the values and morals of the republic led to a bloody civil war between the former allies, Pompey and Julius Caesar, which Caesar won. The story of this struggle was told in Lucan's epic/antiepic poem, *Pharsalia*, their author becoming a republican martyr when he participated in a plot against Nero, and was forced to commit suicide.[9] Caesar then seized control of Rome, and, although he was not actually crowned, he became its sole ruler, following in the footsteps of the dictator Sulla. Caesar was subsequently assassinated in a republican coup by Brutus and Cassius, who hoped to restore the values of the Roman republic, but only succeeded in unleashing a further wave of destructive violence.[10]

A large number of the most significant writings that told the history of Rome narrated these events and their consequences. They encapsulate the common perception that its history was essentially cyclical, with an oscillation back and forth between diametrically opposed forms of government. There were other significant narratives, moments and images, too, and a list might include the attempted coup of Sejanus against the emperor Tiberius, narrated in a variety of Roman histories, including Tacitus and Dio Cassius's *Roman History*, and represented in Ben Jonson's *Sejanus His Fall* (1603);[11] the conspiracy of Catiline, governor of Africa, narrated in Sallust's well-known work, and represented in Jonson's *Catiline His Conspiracy* (1611);[12] the suicides of Lucan and Seneca during the reign of Nero, the first narrated in Tacitus, Cassius Dio and Suetonius's *Twelve Caesars*, the latter also in Suetonius, but more importantly in his letters, and through the profound influence of his tragedies on early modern drama;[13] the murder of Cicero at the hands of Mark Antony's agents in AD 43, as Cicero's work was ubiquitous and impossible to avoid in Elizabethan England, the biography being most readily available in Plutarch's *Lives*.[14]

Taken together, these stories and events represent a general historical picture.[15] The historical lesson given declares that the republic is a far more desirable form of government than the empire, although the latter may be preferable in times of decay and corruption, taking its political cue from Aristotle's belief that tyranny could be a plausible form of government if the world had become bad enough.[16] The republic is thought to be not always strong enough to incline men to virtue and so sometimes be vulnerable to the attack of the wicked, desperate and corrupt, such as Catiline, whose attempt to seize power was thwarted by the republican hero, Cicero. Eventually, if the guardians of the republic are not vigilant enough, an oligarchy will seize power and end the republic, promoting their own interests at the expense of the general citizens. Of course, the danger of imperial government is tyranny, as Rome soon discovered, when the reign of the problematic but essentially public-spirited Augustus was followed by those of Tiberius, Caligula and Nero. And, as the works of Tacitus so frequently demonstrate, secrecy, plotting and conspiracy become the way of life under the rule of a tyrant. Roman history shows that it is better to try to make the republic function properly, and then to defend it against its enemies, than to throw one's lot in with the imperialists. Everybody knows where the assassination of Julius Caesar leads, but it is not clear who is really to blame: the assassins who despatch the putative tyrant, or Caesar and his followers, who have already killed off the republic by promoting their champion at the expense of everything else, including the republic?[17]

Shakespeare narrates more of the republican story than any other dramatist working in Elizabethan and Jacobean England, as well as applying the lessons of a history of the republic to the English crown. He tells the story of the birth of the republic in *The Rape of Lucrece*, and the death of the republic in *Julius Caesar* and *Antony and Cleopatra*, which show the rise of Julius Caesar leading eventually to the assumption of power by the colourless Octavius Caesar, the future Augustus. The play concludes with Octavius arriving in Egypt to find the dead Cleopatra and Antony, announcing that 'Our army shall / In solemn show attend this funeral, / And then to Rome' (5.2.362–64).[18] Octavius's bland lines depend on the audience knowing exactly what has passed and what the future holds in store for Rome. And, perhaps, there is a pointed contrast with the concluding lines of *Hamlet*, a play that contains a king with the name of one of Augustus's successors, Claudius, whose underhand behaviour leads to the end of his family's rule in Denmark. There, Fortinbras, another foreign martial king who arrives on the scene to find a mass of dead bodies, arranges the funeral of Hamlet before assuming power himself in an equally deadpan manner:

> Take up the bodies. Such a sight as this
> Becomes the field, but here shows much amiss.
> Go, bid the soldiers shoot. (5.2.406–8)

The audience cannot possibly have any idea of what the future will hold for Denmark, and whether the burial of the dead will bring peace and political stability, or a renewed cycle of violence.

The comparison between the plays should also alert us to the fact that the influence of Roman history on Shakespeare's imagination was not simply confined to the works he wrote using the relevant source materials. Early in his career, Shakespeare was confident enough a dramatist to produce a play, *Titus Andronicus*, written sometime before 1594, possibly much earlier, that invented a Roman history.[19] *Titus* would appear to be set in very late Rome, as the empire was being overrun by the barbarian Goths, and shows either the last chance of the empire to revitalize itself through the establishment of its republican government, or that it has decayed too much to be saved.[20] Later on, Shakespeare meticulously analyses the electoral process in Rome in *Coriolanus*, relating the Roman constitution to voting practices he may well have observed in London.[21]

But if Shakespeare seems to have exhibited a particular interest in the history and meaning of republican Rome, he was by no stretch of the imagination alone. Many of his contemporary writers, including Christopher Marlowe, Ben Jonson, Edmund Spenser, Sir Philip Sidney, Samuel Daniel, Michael Drayton, George Chapman, William Alexander, John Fletcher and Fulke Greville were also well aware of the importance of republican politics and history, even if some were less than enthusiastic about its viability as a political form. However, it would be a mistake to imagine that only argument and belief are what matters in early modern political debates. The representation of a range of material also played a vital role in making ideas and arguments available to readers. Innocent Gentillet's famous *Anti-Machiavel*, eventually published in 1602 but circulating in manuscript well before that date, contained a series of quotations from Machiavelli's works, as well as lengthy refutations of them. In the same way, readers of Fulke Greville's long poem, *A Treatise of Monarchy* (664 stanzas, 3984 lines), would have learnt of a wide variety of political forms, including the Roman, Dutch and Venetian republics.[22] Such balanced and dramatic treatments of political ideas are, if anything, easier for playwrights to appropriate than other forms of political argument.[23]

Republicanism and early modern literature are interlinked in two fundamental, interrelated ways. Literary texts adopt and adapt stories from republican history and literature. They also contain republican ideas with which they engage. This is especially evident in the case of Shakespeare's most dominant predecessor, Christopher Marlowe, whose work defined late Elizabethan commercial theatre, opening up a series of

possibilities for writers, which had not existed before.[24] Marlowe's plays
launched a series of provocative attacks on traditional ideas of place, belief
and status, as was clear to his contemporaries, and has long been recognized by commentators.[25] Marlowe's first play, *Tamburlaine the Great,
Part One* (1587, published 1590), narrates the story of the Scythian shepherd whose conquest of the known world shows that there is no inherent
relationship between ability and status, a key debate everywhere in Europe
after the advent of humanist education programmes and systems, represented in England most obviously in the vogue for courtesy books, such as
Castiglione's *The Courtyer of Court Baldessar Castilio*, translated in 1561,
and Stefano Guazzo's *Civile Conversation*, translated in 1586.[26] Birth and
rank are shown to have no significance in the brutal world of the play, in
which power holds sway. In the first scene in which he appears, Tamburlaine tears off his shepherd's clothes to reveal a suit of armour underneath
(1.2.42).[27] Given that he is wooing his future wife, Zenocrate, the moment
is simultaneously terrifying and comic for the audience, as she is forced to
realize the true order of things. The gesture is also metatheatrical, suggesting that all clothing is effectively a disguise and that we dress up to
impersonate people we are not, just as actors impersonate characters on
stage before us. The grander the person, the bigger the disguise required
and deception practised.[28] Furthermore, the implication is that if we
believe what we see on stage, then it is the actors who have the power
and not the people who dress up in the world outside the theatre.

Tamburlaine's behaviour throughout the play shows that royal status is
not a birthright, but something that can be earned. Talking to his ally,
Cosroe, brother of the king of Persia, in the next act, Tamburlaine asserts
that 'fates and oracles of heaven have sworn / To royalise the deeds of
Tamburlane' (2.3.7–8), the first recorded instance of this usage of 'royalise' in the *OED*, probably copied by Robert Geeene in *Friar Bacon and
Friar Bungay* (1589).[29] Theridamas explains that he has defected from the
Persian army to join Tamburlaine precisely because 'he is gross and like
the massy earth / That moves not upwards nor by princely deeds / Doth
mean to soar above the highest sort' (2.7.31–33). Time and again the
audience is reminded that Tamburlaine achieves what he does because
he is powerful and is favoured by fortune, not because he is nobly born
and has any hereditary right to rule. Indeed, as Theridamas's words
indicate, Tamburlaine's lowly status seems to guarantee his success. His
protracted humiliation of the Turkish emperor and empress, Bajazeth and
Zabina, shows that even the powerful Ottoman empire, the most potent
threat to Christian Europe in the sixteenth century, cannot resist his

advance.[30] The transfer of Zabina's crown to Zenocrate and then to
Tamburlaine in a play that makes so much capital out of theatrical props
is another key symbolic gesture which clearly also has metatheatrical
significance:

> ZABINA: Injurous villains, thieves, runagates!
>   How dare you thus abuse my majesty?
> THERIDAMAS: Here, madam, you are Empress, she is none.
> TAMBURLAINE: [As *Zenocrate* crowns him]
>   Not now, Theridamas, her time is past:
>   The pillars that have bolstered up those terms
>   Are fall'n in clusters at my conquering feet. (3.3.225–30)

Court plays such as *Respublica* or John Skelton's *Magnificence* (1515–23),
showed majesty abused and led astray by bad advisers, but it was left to
the commercial theatre to show a monarch actually being dethroned on
stage.[31] The words, 'Not now . . . her time is past', would appear to refer
to the execution of Mary Stuart, which took place earlier in the year
(8 February) the play was written and probably first performed. Marlowe's
lines show that Elizabeth's fear that the execution of a monarch would
damage the security of hereditary rulers had been recognized and dis-
seminated among several thousand people.[32] The deposed despots can
only watch in horror from their cages as Tamburlaine and Zenocrate
change places with them, death being the only escape (as it was for the
incarcerated Mary).

  Tamburlaine continually advertises the subversive and blasphemous
nature of its plot, reminding the audience that what they are watching
challenges a whole range of traditional beliefs and values. Tamburlaine
appropriates the power of death, and, worse still, he can get away with this
shocking arrogance. When the four virgins of Damascus, decked in
emblems of peace, try to persuade Tamburlaine not to destroy their city,
he explains that the edge of his sword carries 'imperious Death' (5.1.111)
and so they are doomed. Tamburlaine is able to assume this god-like
power without interruption throughout his triumphant progress in the
play, demonstrating that religious hierarchy is afforded no more respect
than the political and social.[33] Given the tremendous success of *Tamburlaine*, it is clear that aggressive subversion and an assault on received
wisdom was a winning commercial formula, one that helped to define
the nature of the English public stage.[34]

  Tamburlaine the Great, Part Two, undoubtedly written quickly to cash
in on the success of Part One, continues this assault on Christian values.

The alliance of Christian kings is shown to be deceitful and hypocritical and they are justly defeated by Tamburlaine's forces, as the dying Sigismond acknowledges (2.3.1–9). It is unclear which deity actually rules the universe of the play, although by the end we can be fairly certain that it is not the Christian God. Tamburlaine finds that he no longer has control over death as he had in the first part. Zenocrate dies, he kills Calyphas, and Olympia fools Theridamas into fatally stabbing her, before Tamburlaine himself expires from disease after he has publicly burnt the Koran when he seizes Babylon, goading Mahomet into punishing him for his defiance (5.1.185–200). If anyone destroys Tamburlaine, it is the forces of Islam not Christianity.[35]

Tamburlaine is not a work of republican ideology or propaganda. It is, however, a spectacular and relentless assault on received values, in particular hereditary kingship, which is shown time and again to be an illusion that fails to protect the monarch in question from being overthrown. Kings stand and fall through their own might and power, not because of any titles they hold, or any birthright they possess. Religion is shown to be a myth, and one that harms rather than helps rulers, who foolishly believe that it will protect them when their own abilities are what really matter, suggesting that Marlowe was well aware of Machiavelli's famous claim that religion could prove useful to a prince to help keep the people obedient, even as he slyly inverted it.[36] In essence, *Tamburlaine* reveals traditional belief – especially that in hereditary monarchy – to be a confidence trick played on the gullible public, effectively urging people to look elsewhere to find reasonable and politically desirable forms of government.

The Massacre at Paris (*c.*1592) develops the same line of political exploration. Marlowe appears to have been especially interested in the political significance of the Massacre of St Bartholomew's Day and was well versed in the literature produced in its wake.[37] His play, even though it has come down to us in what may be a butchered version that was not what Marlowe wrote or what was performed on stage, shows both the French Protestant faction under Henri IV, and the Catholic faction led by the Duke of Guise, favourite of the notorious Catherine de Medici, behaving in underhand and self-interested ways.[38] After orchestrating the massacre of the Huguenots in Paris, Guise is lured to his death by the king who has him murdered in his private cabinet, a manoeuvre that shows how political possibilities have been reduced to the space of a confined room, the secret preserve of a few actors remote from the people they supposedly represent.[39] Guise is urged to repent by his assassins, but he haughtily declines. When asked to pray for the king's forgiveness, he refuses and his last lines after he has been fatally wounded are a scornful assertion of his own aristocratic worth:

> Trouble me not, I ne'er offended him,
> Nor will I ask forgiveness of the King.
> O that I have not power to stay my life,
> Nor immortality to be revenged!
> To die by peasants, what a grief is this! . . .
> Pope, excommunicate, Philip, depose
> The wicked branch of cursed Valois his line.
> *Vive la messe!* Perish Huguenots!
> Thus Caesar did go forth, and thus he died. (scene 21, lines 81–91)

Guise's contempt for the lower classes does not, of course, save him any more than Tamburlaine's disdain for religion could prevent his death. The comparison of himself to Caesar – following on from the same comparison made in his opening soliloquy (scene 2, lines 95–103) – is simultaneously ironic and appropriate. He invokes Caesar's 'going forth' on the Ides of March, ignoring all intimations of danger, as a sign of his own undoubted courage in the face of imminent danger, proving his worth. But, given that the comparison to Caesar comes in Guise's last line, the image also reveals the destructive futility of his actions. Guise is hardly going anywhere, except to his grave.

Guise's contempt for the common people, whom he dismisses as peasants, is also ironic. Guise is killed because he believes that Henri III is about to hand over his crown to him, acknowledging that he has the power, in the shape of overwhelming Catholic support, to force his hand – once again, a sign that the crown is a piece of property that can be transferred from one king to another as power struggles develop. Yet Guise has shown no sign of suitability for the kingship at any point in the play, other than being adept at plotting behind the scenes, removing his enemies and murder. The Duke of Navarre, the future Henri IV, reveals the cost of the factional struggles, even as he defends his own part in the killing and destruction:

> How many noble men have lost their lives
> In prosecution of these cruel arms,
> Is ruth and almost death to call to mind.
> But God, we know, will always put them down
> That lift themselves against the perfect truth[.] (scene 18, lines 9–13)

Guise, as we have seen, is a much worse – if more heroic – villain. Neither's appeal to divine justice legitimates their actions, or serves any purpose. The bloodshed is caused by the actions of overambitious and selfish men who put their own desires before the needs of a wider public they ostensibly serve. *The Massacre at Paris* shows the dangers of losing sight of the frequently repeated maxim that 'Princes were not first created to benefite themselves . . . but to profit the people.'[40] Guise imagines that comparing himself to Julius Caesar proves his noble virtue, but the play, relying on the audience's knowledge of the basic history of the Roman republic, casts the link in a far more sinister light. Caesar's ambition led to the destructive chaos of civil war, and then to the establishment of the imperial regime ruled by a succession of bloody tyrants. Guise shows that he is a poor reader of historical precedent, copying Caesar as if he were a good role model and so making himself the mainspring behind the Massacre of St Bartholomew's Day. However, the play implicitly invites its audience to see that spectacularly violent event as one of the many destructive battles, most prominent of which was the Pharsalia, that left the Roman republic bereft of leadership and vulnerable to the ruthless ambitions of the many would-be tyrants who subsequently rose to prominence.[41]

Marlowe was the first translator of Lucan's poem, completing his version of the first book before his death. It was posthumously published in 1600, but had undoubtedly circulated in manuscript earlier.[42] Lucan's incomplete poem became one of the key republican literary works of the seventeenth century, a translation of the extant work first appearing in 1614 in a version by Arthur Gorges (1557–1625), friend of Sir Walter Ralegh and Edmund Spenser, who was keen to produce his version to criticize James's suppression of opposition to his attempts to establish a rapprochement with Spain after years of mutual hostility.[43] Marlowe's connection to this later republican tradition seems to have gone largely unnoticed – as does the link between *The Massacre at Paris* and the history narrated in Lucan's poem, which was frequently studied at school and prescribed by both Erasmus and Ascham.[44]

The *Pharsalia*, especially the first book, emphasizes the horrors of civil war, as the opening lines inform the reader:

> Wars worse than civil on Thessalian plains,
> And outrage strangling law, and people strong
> We sing, whose conquering swords their own breasts launch'd,
> Armies allied, the kingdom's league uprooted,
> Th'affrighted world's force bent on public spoil,
> Trumpets and drums like deadly threat'ning other,
> Eagles alike display'd, darts answering darts. (lines 1–7)[45]

Although it is undoubtedly the case that the *Pharsalia* is a 'poem charged
with paradox' that 'at once denounces civil war and incites it', Marlowe's
translation demands to be read in terms of the destruction wrought by
grand and selfish ambition represented in his plays.[46] Rome reveals itself
to be a force for evil rather than good, which first conquers the world and
then turns against itself (lines 23–24). Caesar, like Guise, is shown to be
the architect of terrible destruction and waste, and there can be little
doubt that he is to blame for Rome's shameful legacy, when he is
addressed directly by the poet:

> Pharsalia groan with slaughter,
> And Carthage souls be glutted with our bloods;
> At Munda let the dreadful battles join;
> Add Caesar, to these ills, Perusian famine,
> The Mutin toils, the fleet at Leuca sunk,
> And cruel field near burning Aetna fought. (lines 38–43)

However, the dire sequence of events was not wholly Caesar's fault,
because the people of Rome had chosen him for their king, so the
responsibility is theirs, too:

> Yet Rome is much bound to these civil arms,
> Which made thee emperor, thee (seeing thou, being old,
> Must shine a star) shall heaven (whom thou lovest)
> Receive with shouts, where thou wilt reign as king,
> Or mount the sun's flame-bearing chariot[.] (lines 44–48)

Marlowe, following Lucan, shows that the inability of the republic to
preserve its constitution leads directly to a catastrophic failure of political
virtue, as an ambitious tyrant seizes power and destroys all the institutions
that had characterized republican Rome, the city-state lapsing into a cycle
of violence. It is a narrative that Shakespeare employs to great effect in
Titus Andronicus. Rome is 'bound' to both its ruler, and those who
allowed him to rule. One of the direct products of this process is the
reign of Nero, who forced Lucan to commit suicide when he tried to end
the cycle of violence by taking part in a coup, as Marlowe's double-edged
lines, 'but gladly we bear these evils / For Nero's sake' (lines 37–38),
acknowledge.[47] In the end it is the city that has torn itself apart: 'O Rome,
thyself art cause of all these evils, / Thyself thus shiver'd out to three men's
shares [i.e., Caesar, Pompey and Crassus]' (lines 84–85). The great republican constitution has been reduced to the struggle of three powerful
individuals, just as in *The Massacre at Paris* the body politic of France,
with all its voluminous writings on the constitution and resistance to

tyranny, has been reduced to the king's cabinet where the murder of Guise takes place.[48] The struggle between Catholics and Protestants in Paris is mirrored by the rivalry of Caesar and Pompey: 'Pompey could bide no equal, / Nor Caesar no superior' (lines 125–26). The famous simile whereby Caesar is compared to 'a lion of scorch'd desert Affric', carefully waiting for his moment to strike at the hunters, shows how the republic has degenerated to the bestial precivilized, prepolitical world before the advent of proper society and government when a contract was drawn up between rulers and subjects.[49]

It is hard to see how any monarch or monarchist watching Marlowe's plays or reading his works could have taken any comfort from what they encountered, although exactly how the material might have been related to Elizabeth is an open question.[50] Marlowe's works do not amount to an articulate political theory. Nevertheless, they are relentlessly hostile not just to kings, but to the conception of hereditary kingship, and political power preserved in the hands of a few. The only king represented as personally sympathetic in Marlowe's work, *Edward II*, is shown to be ineffective, weak and vacillating, and unfit to rule, exactly as Shakespeare represents the other famously feeble English monarch, Henry VI.[51] Furthermore, lines from the *Pharsalia* are scattered throughout the play, as editors have often noted.[52] The problem seems to be, as *The Massacre at Paris* and the translation of Lucan reveal, a political culture that restricts power and decision making to a small circle around the monarch, precisely the nature of political complaint throughout the second half of Elizabeth's reign.[53] Marlowe also launched a series of ferocious attacks on the hypocritical ways in which religion was used to keep the mighty in power. Altogether, such interventions indicate that one of his key targets was the restrictive lack of social mobility and access to political institutions and offices characteristic of republican critiques of absolutist government and prevalent in England in the 1580s and 1590s.[54] It is hardly surprising that Marlowe, an ambitious young writer of ability, who had to make a living from his wits, should hold such views of the social order, and he was by no means alone.[55] Equally, his move to London exposed him to a citizen culture of independent ideas, one that had a significant impact on the development of English drama.[56] Marlowe's work, as his immediate successors were not short to acknowledge, shaped the nature and character of the English commercial stage.[57]

Republican themes, ideas and subjects were easy to observe on the English stage in the 1590s and early 1600s. There were a significant number of plays on Roman republican subjects in addition to such familiar examples as Ben Jonson's *Sejanus* and *Catiline.*[58] An early example is Thomas Lodge's *The Wounds of Civil War*, published in 1594, but possibly acted as early as 1586.[59] Lodge's play would undoubtedly have been known to Shakespeare, who later used Lodge's prose fiction, *Rosalynde* (1590), as the principal source for *As You Like It* (1599).[60] *The Wounds of Civil War* tells the story of the conflict between Sulla and Marius which wrought havoc in Rome between 88 and 78 BCE adapted from Appian's *Roman History*, translated in 1578 as *An Auncient Historie and Exquisite Chronicle of the Romanes Warres*, a translation that was probably also consulted by Shakespeare when he wrote *Julius Caesar* and *Antony and Cleopatra.*[61] There are a number of resemblances between *The Wounds of Civil War* and *Tamburlaine*, but it is not clear which play came first.[62] Lodge has often been seen as a minor writer, so his importance as an innovative figure has usually been underrated.[63] If *The Wounds of Civil War* does predate *Tamburlaine*, then it deserves to be far better known for its place in literary history as it clearly had an influence on the political possibilities Marlowe realized could be exploited on the English stage.

The Wounds of Civil War contains a number of key republican features. It represents the destructive struggle between Sulla (Scilla) and Marius as closely resembling that of the *Pharsalia*; a large number of consuls constitute the body politic and discuss the conflict in terms of its effect on Rome in general; there are severe warnings against tyranny and the evils that are corrupting the body politic of Rome; there is a discussion of the responsibilities of those who undertake important state offices; and, most obviously, the play not only anticipates the rise of Caesar and imperial Rome, but looks back to the banishment of the Tarquins. The opening scene takes place in the Capitol, the meeting place of the Senate, thus establishing the play's political focus.[64] The assembled senators and tribunes debate what they should do about the ruthless rise of Sulla, who, as the opening speech by Sulpitius notes, has 'forced murders in a quiet state' (1.1.10), to achieve his goal of being general in Asia to oppose the threat of Mithridates. Sulpitius's support for his rival, Marius, is met scornfully by one of Sulla's chief allies, Pompey, later to be the opponent of Julius Caesar in the civil war which ended with the battle of Pharsalia. Pompey's objection marks him out, at this stage, as an opponent of the republic and a supporter of imperial Rome, something of an irony, given his later role as champion of the people and defender of the republic:

> Believe me noble Romans and grave Senators,
> This strange election and this new-made law
> Will witness our unstable government
> And dispossess Rome of her empery . . .
> Yet may the sunshine of his [Marius's] former deeds
> Nothing eclipse our Scilla's dignity.
> By lot and by election he was made
> Chief General against Mithridates,
> And shall we then abridge him of that rule? (lines 44–54)

Pompey sees the contested election of Marius as a sign of a deteriorating body politic, one which chops and changes its loyalty to its leaders when it needs to support the right person in power, the classic Aristotelian defence of monarchical government.[65]

However, Pompey's argument is then undercut by Junius Brutus, who counterargues:

> Why Pompey, as if the Senate had not power
> To appoint, dispose, and change their generals;
> Rome shall belike be bound to Scilla's rule,
> Whose haughty pride and swelling thoughts puff'd up
> Foreshows the reaching to proud Tarquin's state. (lines 58–62)

It is hard to imagine a more republican speech in a more republican context. The details are largely Lodge's invention: Junius Brutus plays a tiny role in Appian's *History*, and makes no speech at all.[66] The name Junius Brutus provides a neat link between the legendary champion against the Tarquins, Lucius Junius Brutus, and the assassin of Caesar, his son, Marcus Junius Brutus, who was born soon after this scene took place, and whose story is told later in the history of the Roman civil wars.[67] The political debates of the earlier and later events, the two familiar republican moments, are refigured and revisited here. Pompey and Sulla are seen as opponents of the republic, keen to overthrow the power of its central institution, the Senate, for their own gain. Sulla is cast as a potential tyrant, like Tarquinus Superbus. The senators line up one after another to cast their vote for Marius, who accepts the office on their authority. When the Senate does exercise its authority and appoints Marius as general, Sulla stages an armed insurrection and seizes power.

Marius's acceptance speech had singled out his own 'honor' (line 117) as a quality that derived from the Senate, and reveals himself as the military heir of Scipio Africanus, the great general of the republic who

defeated Hannibal.[68] In refusing to accept Marius's election, Sulla asserts
that his own worth and honour count far more than those of his
rival:

> Marius shall lead then, then, if Scilla said not no,
> And I shall be a Consul's shadow, then?
> Trustless Senators and ingratefull Romans,
> For all the honors I have done to Rome,
> For all the spoils I brought within her walls,
> Thereby for to enrich and raise her pride,
> Repay you with ingratitude? (lines 158–64)

While Marius derives his authority from the republican Senate, Sulla
asserts that they should all be loyal to him. His 'honour', in the form of
conquest and loot, should gain him military and political authority.
Marius looks back to the most famous and successful republican general,
who protected Rome from her most terrifying enemy in a dangerous and
protracted war that led to the unchecked rise of Rome as the key power in
the Mediterranean. Sulla, in contrast, places the military first as the
mainspring of imperial Rome, the first step towards tyranny (it was, of
course, no coincidence that so many of the Julio-Claudian and Flavian
emperors had either had military experience, or came to power as successful generals). When the two factions neatly divide on stage at the end of
the scene, the audience knows that civil war has been declared, literally
and figuratively, as the Senate dissolves and political debate is replaced by
military conflict. Mark Antony, father of the ally of Julius Caesar,
throughout much of the play a spokesman for peaceful resolution, joins
Sulla's faction but urges his leader to reconsider his actions. Antony tries
to persuade him to listen to 'The pleading plaints of sad declining Rome'
(line 247), articulating the familiar motif of Rome's republican decline
leading to civil war and eventually tyranny. Antony tries to appeal to
Sulla's understanding of common – republican – values and to suppress
his own selfish ambition so that the waste and destruction of civil war can
be avoided. He poses a series of questions that he then proceeds to answer
himself:

> Tell me, my Scilla, what dost thou take in hand?
> What wars are these thou stirrest up in Rome?
> What fire is this is kindled by thy wrath?
> A fire that must be quench'd by Roman's blood,
> A war that will confound our empery,
> And, last, an act of foul impiety. (lines 254–59)

The later conflict between Pompey and Julius Caesar could be represented as a tragic waste, and it was hard to support one over the other,
given their equally grand self-regard, causing a civil war when they should
have united against Rome's enemies.[69] But here it is impossible to
disagree with Antony's judgement, one made all the more powerful for
being put into the mouth of a supporter of Sulla, a ruler who has already
started to refer to the body politic in imperial terms as the 'empery', that
the rebel general is to blame for all that follows. Sulla has lost sight of the
republic he is supposed to serve and his reaction to Antony's speech shows
just how far his political understanding has fallen:

> Enough Anthony, for thy honied tongue,
> Wash'd in a syrup of sweet conservatives,
> Driveth confused thoughts through Scilla's mind.
> Therefore, suffice thee; I may nor will not hear. (lines 282–85)

Sulla's recognition of his confusion means that he will not be able to
carry through his plans if he pays attention to the sort of reasoned
argument for which Mark Antony was justly famous. Politics has to give
way to war, which will now dominate events in Rome, whereas before
Sulla's actions, military might was controlled by the republic's political
institutions.

The Wounds of Civil War shows that tyranny is the appropriate and
inevitable political form for an overly militarized culture. Events transform Marius into a cruel tyrant, demanding that his followers dispose of
anyone who offends his dignity and able to concentrate only on revenge
for the ills done to him (4.1), before he is killed offstage in the final battle
for mastery of Rome (5.2). His son, young Marius, rather than yield to
Lucretius, Sulla's envoy, stabs himself onstage. Lucretius had appealed to
young Marius to surrender as one who wished him 'An humble heart, and
then a happy peace' (5.3.16), because he had come to realize the courage
and suffering of Sulla's enemies and now wanted to heal the breach
between the factions and establish peace in Rome. But young Marius
refuses to be persuaded as he has already convinced himself of the need for
a dramatic, public end:

> Now unadvised youth must counsel eld,
> For governance is banish'd out of Rome.
> Woe to that bough from whence these blooms are sprung;
> Woe to that Aetna, vomiting this fire;
> Woe to that brand, consuming country's weal;

Woe to that Scilla, careless and secure,
That gapes with murder for a monarchy.
Go, second Brutus with a Roman mind,
And kill the tyrant, and for Marius's sake
Pity the guiltless wives of these your friends,
Preserve their weeping infants from the sword,
Whose fathers seal their honors with their bloods.
Farewell, Lucretius, first I press in place,
  Stab[s himself].
To let thee see a constant Roman die. (lines 69–82)

The speech and the scene are entirely Lodge's invention, as Appian merely tells us that he 'hid himself in an underground tunnel and shortly afterward committed suicide'.[70] Given that his father's faction is about to lose the civil war, it is not clear whether his death is to be taken as a noble gesture, and his desire to see Sulla assassinated one that we should support. If so, then the death of young Marius is keeping alive the flame of a republican tradition in invoking the spirit of Lucius Junius Brutus, founder of the republic, and acting to vindicate the legitimate authority of the Senate which granted his father his official position. Alternatively, the suicide might be read as a futile gesture, one that will only add to the destruction already caused by the civil war, a sign that death and glory have come to mean more than political debate, thought and action when armies rather than elected bodies rule the state. Cicero, in his *De Officis*, had pointed out that military success was not desirable without good government, and argued that the achievements of peace were far greater than those of war.[71] Either way, I would suggest, *The Wounds of Civil War* positions itself as a republican play, one that clearly had a major influence on the development of Shakespeare's early theatrical career. The brutal effects of military dominance when political ideas and institutions are cast aside is a theme explored throughout *Titus Andronicus*, as well as the early history plays; and the dilemma of political assassination and its effects are studied in *Julius Caesar* and *Hamlet*.

The suicide of young Marius casts a shadow over the remainder of the play. Sulla learns of his death just as he is declared dictator by his victorious troops. Lucretius repeats the boy's own evaluation of himself as a 'constant Roman', declaring that he died with 'more constancy than Cato' (5.5.57), an anachronistic reference to the suicide of the younger Cato, who supported the interests of the Senate in the civil war between Caesar and Pompey, and killed himself rather than surrender to Julius Caesar's troops.

He was one of the best known of classical authors, a key hero of the *Pharsalia* who became a symbol of Stoicism, the principal philosophy of the Roman republic and later republicans who resisted tyranny, shaming autocratic oppression with their deaths.[72] Sulla's declaration and this subsequent news transform him into a cruel autocrat such as Caligula or, more likely still, Nero, who forced the Stoic heroes Seneca and Lucan to commit suicide when they plotted against him.[73]

In Appian's *History*, Sulla was made dictator for life and ruled over an exhausted and impoverished Italy for two years, making compromises with the Senate, before he grew weary of political life and retired to his country estate, dying a year later.[74] Lodge telescopes these events, so that Sulla's disillusionment takes place immediately after he receives the news of young Marius's death. His reflections on life, the world's vanity, the pointless pursuit of earthly glory, and preparation for death, transform the would-be military dictator into another 'constant Roman', a Stoic philosopher, who chooses the contemplative life in a time of tyranny.[75] The irony is, of course, that if anyone has been responsible for the destruction of the republic's institutions and the onset of tyranny, it is Sulla himself. He now corrects his errors by simply refusing to govern. When two Roman burghers seek out his justice by asking him to adjudicate in a minor civil suit, in which one has accused the other of seducing his neighbour's daughter and then abandoning her, Sulla seems astonished at their presumption: 'And what of this, my friend? Why seek you me, / Who have resign'd my titles and my state / To live a private life, as you do now?' (lines 216–18) and he passes the case over to his consul Flaccus.[76] Sulla's abrupt abandonment of politics is as culpable as his overweening personal ambition was before his sudden change of mind.[77] Fortunately, the republican institutions have not been completely destroyed so a residual form of government can continue. Sulla's decision to become a Stoic philosopher, desiring 'To dwell content amidst my country cave, / Where no ambitious humors shall approach / The quiet silence of my happy sleep' (266–68), serves only to emphasize that Lodge has granted the moral victory to the republicans.

It is hard to read *The Wounds of Civil War* as a topical allegory of events in the late 1580s, although there have been some rather unconvincing attempts.[78] Nevertheless, the play undoubtedly has a significant political charge, attacking tyranny and the violence it produces, and showing that reasoned argument and the preservation of political institutions that represent the people they were designed to serve is an infinitely superior course of action to that of achieving success through the use of force.

Lodge was the son of a Lord Mayor of London, the grocer Sir Thomas Lodge, who was imprisoned in the Fleet for debts of £2,500 at the end of his term of office, having to borrow the money from London companies in order to be released.[79] It is probable that, like many Londoners, Lodge had great faith in the value of the customs, regulations and institutions of the city, seeing these as vital for the preservation of the public and personal liberty of its citizens, a confidence Shakespeare may well have shared.[80] The anonymous treatise *A Breefe discourse, declaring and approving the necessarie and inviolable customes of London* (1584) praises London for its laudable customs, which have developed alongside the common law of the land, and which preserve the ancient liberties of Londoners.[81] The author concludes that, like Rome, it is the duty of the city to spread its good practices far and wide.[82]

Lodge later co-wrote two ferocious warnings that London was in danger of losing all that it had slowly built up over the previous centuries if its citizens did not try to unite, cease rioting and prevent corruption spreading throughout the land. The first, a morality play written with Robert Greene, *A Looking Glass for London and England* (1594), uses the story of Jonah and compares London to Nineveh in order to persuade their fellow citizens to repent of their numerous sins.[83] It also, tellingly enough, contains a number of serious criticisms of 'Princes plagu'd because they are unjust'.[84] The second, *A Larum for London, or The siedge of Antwerpe With the vertuous actes and valorous deedes of the lame soldier* (1602), was based on George Gascoigne's eyewitness account, *The spoyle of Antwerpe. Faithfully reported, by a true Englishman, who was present at the same* (1576), reproduced to warn Londoners that if they failed in moral and political terms, their city could be overrun and destroyed as Antwerp was by the Spanish in 1576.[85] Clearly, the timing of this work has an eye on the impending succession.

The point to be made is that Lodge characteristically saw political upheavals through the eyes of the citizens of London and it is likely that *The Wounds of Civil War* is no exception. Perhaps, given Lodge's eventual conversion to Catholicism in the early 1600s, his desire for republican reason rather than military action is a response to the laws passed against recusants and Jesuits in the 1580s, and the wave of executions in that decade.[86] Lodge was called before the Privy Council for an unnamed offence in 1591 and later had to go into exile for two periods because of his religious convictions.[87] *Rosalynde* (1590), his prose romance and the principal source for *As You Like It*, can also be read as a plea for toleration and the acceptance of differences, as the usurper Saldyne's banishment of his brother Roasader to the Forest of Arden solves nothing, and the right and better ruler returns at the end.[88]

Whatever the truth of these speculations, it is clear that both Lodge and Marlowe, talented men on the make who did not enjoy the benefits of aristocratic status, helped define the increasingly successful Elizabethan commercial theatre in the late 1580s as a place where republican ideas could flourish.[89] Lodge's work in particular contains many of the characteristics of republicanism: concern for the establishment and maintenance of a civic culture; hatred of tyrannical rule; suspicion of hereditary succession; belief that the ruler is really a servant of the people, whatever he or she might think; interest in political assassination; an awareness of the key features of the history of the Roman republic and a desire to show that they have widespread significance and application. In short, the Elizabethan and Jacobean theatre that came in their wake was often intensely political, frequently much more so than work that entered the public sphere through straightforward political channels.[90]

Later plays also explored the issues and problems raised in the key texts of Roman republican history. The earliest of these is probably the anonymous *The Tragedie of Caesar and Pompey or Caesars Revenge*, published in 1607, but undoubtedly first performed in the early 1590s.[91] The play is based on Appian's *History*, making use of the *Pharsalia*, too, but clearly heavily indebted to *Tamburlaine* and *The Spanish Tragedy*, as well as *The Wounds of Civil War*.[92] It follows the history of the eminent Romans involved in the civil wars from the defeat of Pompey at Pharsalia; his assassination at the hands of the Egyptians; the growth of the republican faction led by Cicero and Brutus; the suicide of Cato; the triumph of Caesar; his assassination by Brutus and Cassius; the regrouping of Caesar's followers and their eventual victory. The action is framed by the figure of Discord, a character derived from Revenge in *The Spanish Tragedy*, who orchestrates and controls the plot. Discord celebrates the defeat of Pompey at the start of the play, recognizing that it will bring chaos to Italy (lines 1–38). He ends the play pleased with his achievements, expressing no remorse for Caesar's death, but glad that his led to so many others. Caesar is rewarded with eternal joy in Elysium.

Caesar, like Sulla in *The Wounds of Civil War*, is the obvious villain, placing his own ambition before the needs of the people he wishes to rule. He is spurred on to tyranny in part through his affair with Cleopatra, whose 'tyrannizing' eyes inspire him (line 506), just as the beauty of

Zenocrate helped fuel the bloodlust of Tamburlaine. Caesar is always shown to be an isolated male figure, either alone or in the company of women (Cleopatra, Calphurnia), his self-regard and inability to cooperate with his fellow citizens becoming more pronounced as the play progresses.[93] In contrast, Brutus and Pompey establish a friendship that is designed to combat tyranny, showing how closely interlinked notions of republican politics and personal ideals of friendship often were (lines 157–70).[94] Their relationship looks forward to the friendship between Brutus and Cassius, which very nearly managed to restore the republic, although it is not represented as problematically as the accord between the republican allies is in Shakespeare's *Julius Caesar*. The personal and public interaction of friends and allies is shown to be infinitely preferable to solitary action. The former leads to cooperation, the exchange of valuable advice and the establishment of a desirable body politic among equals; the latter to solitary, hierarchical rule, which invariably degenerates into tyranny. Even though Caesar refuses to become king of Rome, Brutus and Cassius see him as a second Tarquin (lines 1477, 1551), usurping ancient freedoms in order to establish a rule of personal tyranny (lines 1567–72). The chorus condemns the assassins (4.1), as the republicans have now become the conquerors. This does not, I think, suggest that the play is delicately balanced between support for Caesar and the republicans. Rather, the point is that in times of violent crisis and upheaval it will be virtually impossible to tell the good from the bad, precisely the situation Discord aimed to produce. The world becomes a version of hell (line 2149) and the only viable course of action is to retreat into private life and learn to practise the dictates of Stoic philosophy (lines 2257–59).

The play makes it clear that Caesar is really to blame for unleashing Discord on the Roman world. His ghost gains revenge in the short term, but the ghost that appears to Brutus before his defeat and death tells him that he, too, will gain revenge. Caesar is described as happy in Elysium at the end of the play, but obtaining grace in a pagan universe is not necessarily a secure achievement or an unmixed blessing. Caesar finds happiness because he has helped to implement the plan of Discord, just as the characters in *The Spanish Tragedy* fulfilled the designs of Revenge and so satisfied the bitter ghost of Andrea. But the promise to Brutus at the end of *The Tragedie of Caesar and Pompey* suggests that Caesar may not have the last laugh, although when the revenge of Brutus will take place is left unclear, in itself a chilling message for any European monarch living in a world after the publication of *Vindiciae, Contra Tyrannos*.

In James's reign, it seems that dramatic versions of the story became more contentious.[95] Some emphasized the horror of the assassination of Caesar and adopted a conservative position in favour of monarchy in line with James's views on kingship; others supported the actions of the republican faction, and explored issues of political authority and representation. Sir William Alexander, a courtier who travelled down from Scotland with James I, and who later became secretary of state in the reign of Charles I (1626) and was created earl of Stirling in 1633, collected together many of the plays he had written in the 1590s and published them as *The Monarchick Tragedies* in 1604, as a gift to the king to mark his union of the British nations.[96] The collection contained a number of closet dramas, acted at court and in private and not on the public stage, including *The Tragedy of Croesus, The Tragedy of Darius* and *The Alexandrean Tragedy*, all of which demonstrated that a powerful monarchy was the best form of government and that nations were plunged into chaos when this most desirable political form was undermined, either by the actions of subjects, or by the failings of monarchs.

The *Tragedy of Julius Caesar*, not surprisingly, interpreted the story of the assassination of Caesar rather differently from the version offered in *The Tragedie of Caesar and Pompey or Caesars Revenge*, although the play does not shirk from casting Caesar as a tyrant, or praising the noble motives of Brutus, Cicero and Cassius. Caesar is shown reerecting Tarquin's throne; there are demands for another Brutus to repeat the acts of the founder of the republic; and it is made clear that one can love Rome and hate Caesar.[97] Brutus and Portia are portrayed as equal partners in a Stoic marriage (Portia asks Brutus's pardon when she becomes too passionate in her feelings for her husband, pp. 390, 392), and Brutus expresses his regret that Rome's freedom must be bought with bloodshed, before confirming his commitment to freedom before tyranny (pp. 404–6). *The Tragedy of Julius Caesar* differs from its predecessors in analysing the problem of Roman politics as the monarchy going awry, not the republic losing its bearings.[98] Caesar's initial wish is to help Rome out of its morass of civil wars by becoming its king and so ensuring stability (p. 364). He would really prefer to live as a private man – the revelation that came to Sulla in the last act of *The Wounds of Civil War* – but knows that he needs to serve the state (p. 365). Brutus is shown supporting Caesar, whom he sees as the pilot who will lead Rome out of chaos (p. 367), until he is persuaded by Cicero that the cure for civil war is worse than the disease (pp. 369–70). The tragedy does indeed end on an ambiguous note, with the chorus commenting on Caesar's fall from power to a sad death as illustrative of the vicissitudes of life (pp. 440–42). Nevertheless, it is clear that Alexander's version of the story is told to support James's political ideas – without lapsing into sycophancy – not to open up a space for oppositional political thought.[99]

Rather more critical of monarchy are two other works first performed in James's reign, the anonymous *The Tragedie of Claudius Tiberius Nero, Romes greatest tyrant*, published in 1607 and George Chapman's tragedy, *Caesar and Pompey a Roman tragedy, declaring their warres. Out of whose events is evicted this proposition. Only a just man is a freeman*, not published until 1631 – which, along with the title, may indicate how it was read by contemporaries, or how Chapman feared it might be read – but probably first written in 1605 and then rewritten in 1612–13.[100] *The Tragedie of Tiberius* is relatively easy to analyse. It is an adaptation of material primarily derived from Tacitus, but also Suetonius and other Roman histories.[101] The play represents the Julio-Claudian family as ambitious and cruel individuals, who will stop at nothing to gain power. One scene that takes place in the period of uncertainty after Augustus's death has Tiberius, Caligula, Julia and Sejanus onstage unseen by any of the others, each soliloquizing at length as to why they have the right and ability to rule Rome (D1r-E1r). The play shows a nervous and paranoid court full of powerful, untrustworthy individuals who will obviously become tyrants if they achieve their aims, as two of the four do. After the failure of Sejanus's plans, which end when he is exposed and is killed by a burning crown (L4r), the last scenes see the rise of Caligula, who had already shown his ambition and suitability for rule by poisoning Julia (G4v). Caligula meditates on the nature of justice in the world, coming to the convenient conclusion that there is none so he may as well continue behaving as he has done (M4r-v). He starts to refer to Tiberius as 'Tarquinus', a neat irony as the audience would have known that Caligula's crimes easily exceeded those of the more venial but less cruel Tiberius. Caligula eventually murders the emperor, first poisoning him, and then stabbing him, while Tiberius laments that all the people in the world do not possess one neck he can cut off (N3v), a potent image of the mind of a tyrant. Caligula becomes emperor, listing the crimes of his predecessor and claiming that he will restore Rome's glory.

Events that occurred during the reign of Tiberius were seen by one commentator, at least, as useful parallels to those that occurred in James's reign, a comparison also exploited by Ben Jonson in his tragedy *Sejanus His Fall*.[102] *The Tragedie of Tiberius* shows a world in which there is no obvious way out of the cycle of violence and destruction, representing the aftermath of the decline of the republic as a breeding ground for tyranny, and building on the sense of despair felt by the beaten republican factions after the civil wars had been lost and the assassination of Caesar failed to restore the Roman constitution. The ghost promised Brutus revenge as he was about to meet his death at the conclusion of *The Tragedie of Caesar and Pompey*, but *The Tragedie of Tiberius* shows the apparent future of Rome as one long list of dreadful tyrants.

The Tragedie of Tiberius is an analysis of absolute power and its effects, showing that an unlimited monarchy leads inevitably to tyranny.[103] This message is consistent with republicanism, but it would be naive to classify every such play as a republican work.[104] *Caesar and Pompey* is rather more obviously tilted towards the republican side. Chapman's play retells the story of the civil war between Caesar and Pompey, making use of Lucan, especially in the representation of Caesar as a vainglorious politician. Chapman shows how Pompey could have won the war had he pursued Caesar when he had the upper hand, but allowed his opponent time to recover and then defeat him.[105] Caesar's triumph is, however, tainted by the awareness of the destruction he has caused, and the play concludes that it is better to die honourably than to live as a slave under a tyrant. The opening page bears the maxim, 'Onely a just man is a free man' (p. 541). The last act is Cato's suicide, which Caesar arrives too late to prevent, so he plans to erect a tomb in his honour. Caesar acknowledges Cato's moral and political superiority in the play's concluding speech: 'O Cato, I envy thy death, since thou / Enviest my glory to preserve thy life' (5.2.214–15). Caesar's envy is carefully distinguished from that of Cato. Caesar wishes he could be like Cato, whereas Cato's suicide has besmirched Caesar's glory, acting in accordance with the opening statement and so ensuring that Stoic values, true honour, will triumph over worldly vanity, false honour.[106]

Cato acts as the moral centre of the play.[107] Standing as chorus in the opening scene, he roundly condemns the actions of Caesar and Pompey, whom he sees as 'the two Suns of our Romane Heaven / . . . With their contention, all the clouds assemble / That threaten tempests to our peace and Empire' (1.1.1, 3–4). This is a familiar image, one derived from Lucan's epic similes in the *Pharsalia*. But Cato is quite clear about who is to blame for the dissension that threatens to engulf Rome. He excuses Pompey, whose army is 'brought so neere / By *Romes* consent, for feare of tyrannous Caesar' (lines 9–10), before pouring especial scorn on the despicable sight of Caesar in an extended, epic image:

> And such a flocke of Puttocks follow *Caesar*,
> For fall of his ill-disposed Purse
> (That Never yet spar'd Crosse to Aquiline vertue)
> As well may make all civill spirits suspicious.
> Looke how against great raines, a standing Poole
> Of Paddockes, Todes, and water-Snakes put up
> Their speckl'd throates above the venemous Lake,
> Croking and gasping for some fresh falne drops
> To quench their poisond thirst, being neere to stifle
> With clotterd purgings of their owne foule bane;
> So still, where *Caesar* goes, there thrust up head,
> Imposters, Flatterers, Favourites, and Bawdes,
> Buffons, Intelligencers, select wits,
> Close Murtherers, Montibanckes, and decaied Theeves,
> To gaine their banefull lives reliefes from him. (lines 14–28)

This catalogue of foul beasts, all of them revealing their disgustingly self-interested nature, is an image that drowns the opening comparison of Caesar and Pompey to two mighty Roman suns.[108] It shows where Chapman's real interest lies: less in the achievements of great men, and more in the ability of the few to remain morally upstanding while others are following the powerful, transforming themselves into the worst forms of scavengers. Only in recognizing this truth can one be free, as even Caesar himself realizes at the end of the play.

Cato is especially incensed at the corrupt electoral practices of Caesar and his followers. When the Senate take exception to the two armies coming too close to Rome, Caesar insists that both armies be allowed into the city so that they can help influence the vote that will determine whether they are able to continue their struggle for Rome. Cato objects and is threatened with imprisonment by Caesar, a gesture that helps to crystallize the two factions and makes civil war all the more likely. Pompey, who as the argument prefacing the play acknowledges, assembled his 'more for feare of *Caesars* violence to the State, then mov'd with any affectation of his own greatnesse' (p. 540), agrees that neither he nor Caesar should have brought their armies into Rome: 'there is right in him . . . to send us both to prison' (1.2.218–19).[109] Perhaps the most telling detail is Cato's vociferous opposition to the decision of the corrupt tribune, Metellus, a follower of Caesar, to allow the armies into Rome:

MET: We will have the army,
  Of *Pompey* entred.
CAT: We? which we intend you?
  Have you already bought the peoples voices?
  Or beare our Consuls or our Senate here
  So small love to their Country, that their wills
  Beyond their Countrys right are so perverse,
  To give a Tyrant here entire command? (lines 62–68)[110]

Cato seizes on a key detail, who has the right to speak for whom, which gets right to the heart of political questions.[111] Just as most plays that deal with the assassination of Julius Caesar represent the body politic as too moribund to recover its republican ethos so that violent acts seem to be the only way to escape from tyranny, so does Cato see the republican constitution as already too corrupt to function.[112] The citizens of Rome are incapable of making independent decisions. Their political virtue has been replaced by greed so that they no longer act as republicans, but as slaves. The problem is a circular one: the republic's institutions cannot protect the citizens from themselves, because the citizens are too corrupt to enable the institutions to function. Yet again, this failure is directly connected to the militarization of society. In the end suicide is the only form of resistance to tyranny, and, as the play makes clear in its last lines, Cato's death does shame Caesar.

It is not hard to see why Chapman felt that it might be wiser to leave *Caesar and Pompey* unpublished until the reign of Charles I (assuming that this is the reason for it remaining in manuscript), especially as he did later find himself in serious trouble for his two-part play on the French wars of religion, the *The Conspiracie of Charles Duke of Byron* and *The Tragedie of Charles Duke of Byron*, when the French ambassador saw a performance at the Blackfriars Theatre and took great offence at the representation of the French court.[113] James seems to have objected to literary works only when they related directly to his status as king, or threatened to cause a scandal.[114] *Caesar and Pompey* may simply have reflected rather too carefully on James's notorious attempts to control parliament and parliamentary elections, as well as buy supporters by giving them titles and favours.[115]

Chapman, who was born in *c.*1560, was an almost exact contemporary of Shakespeare and their careers followed similar paths. Both started writing for the theatre in the late 1580s or early 1590s and were well known by the end of the century; both were especially interested in political and historical plays, as well as a range of other dramatic forms;

both wrote poetry as well as drama (although Chapman was a great deal more prolific as a writer of verse than Shakespeare); and both were associated with the Essex faction, as well as the earl of Southampton, and refer to both in their work (Shakespeare dedicated *Venus and Adonis* and *The Rape of Lucrece* to Southampton, and referred to Essex in the chorus to *Henry V*, Act 5; Chapman dedicated the first volume of his translation of the *Iliad* to Essex in 1598, and then included a dedicatory sonnet to Southampton in the 1608 version of the same work).[116] Chapman may have been a rather more bookish writer than Shakespeare – it is not clear whether he had the benefits of a university education – but they would appear to have had much in common. Chapman's books were produced by the same publisher, and he moved in the same circles and knew many of the same people. Chapman completed Marlowe's *Hero and Leander* after his death; he collaborated with Marston and Jonson on *Eastward Ho!* (1605); and Michael Drayton and Jonson contributed commendatory verses to his translation of Hesoid's *Works and Days*.[117] His interest in the history and literature of the Roman republic is something else that they share and indicates what writers of the generation who made an impact in London in the 1590s were often keen to read. Another example is the slightly younger Thomas Heywood (1573–1641), one of the most prolific authors of his generation, who claimed to have contributed to some 220 plays (only about thirty survive).[118] Heywood also produced a translation of Sallust's *The Conspiracy of Catiline and the War of Jugurtha* (1608), and *The Rape of Lucrece: A Roman Tragedy* (published in 1638, but performed *c*.1609).[119]

Literary republicanism cannot be confined to an interest in the Roman republic. Numerous other plays deal with subjects that might legitimately be described as republican, or contain republican themes and issues. John Lyly's comedy *Campaspe* (*c*.1584) is a moral tale which promotes a specifically humanist ideal of freedom.[120] The plot, derived from Plutarch's 'Life of Alexander' and Pliny's *Natural History*, tells how Alexander the Great became so attracted to his Theban prisoner, Campaspe, that he commissioned the painter Apelles to produce her portrait.[121] Apelles falls in love with Campaspe, and ruins his finished portrait so that he has to repeat his labours. When Alexander discovers the trick that has been played on him, he gives Apelles and Campaspe their freedom and returns to war because he recognizes that 'It were a shame Alexander should desire to command the world if he could not command himself' (5.4.168–70).

Plutarch paired his 'Life of Alexander' with that of Julius Caesar, a link which influenced the interpretation of the two men's careers in the early modern period.[122] The play itself works as a series of complicated structured contrasts; between love and war; between philosophy and military action; and between the cynical philosopher, Diogenes, his rival, Anaxarchus, and Alexander, who, despite being taught by Aristotle, chooses the path of conquest rather than contemplation. For all the play's charm and humour, it obviously deals with serious political and social issues central to humanist republicanism.[123] *Campaspe* revisits many of the central themes of Thomas More's *Utopia*, a work with a considerable republican pedigree.[124] In the opening speech of the play, Clitus, a Macedonian officer in Alexander's army, expresses surprise that Alexander has not razed Thebes to the ground and has concluded 'a cruel war in a mild peace' (1.1.6–7). Any reader of Plutarch's 'Life of Alexander' – probably many in the audience – would have known that this was simply not true, and that the city had been destroyed, six thousand of its citizens killed, and thirty thousand sold into slavery.[125] The play conspicuously advertises itself to the reader as a fantasy, a comedy made out of historical material that usually formed tragedies – as was the case with *Tamburlaine*. But we should bear in mind that *Campaspe* was a play written to be performed at court, not on the public stage, and so it had explicit designs on its audience, who were learned enough to read its significance and subtext. Alexander announces that he has 'resolved . . . to have as many philosophers as [he] had in [his] camp soldiers' (1.3.70–72), a reopening of the perennial question of the relationship of learning to action, which the career of Aristotle's most celebrated pupil invariably raised. Giovanni Botero, in his account of Alexander's life, articulated a familiar ambivalence. On the one hand, Alexander was a man of god-like virtue, lucky enough to have been expertly schooled by Aristotle, who always taught him to listen to counsel, and helped make him into a great leader able to inspire his men; but on the other, he betrayed an unseemly lust for glory, could not bear to hear ill spoken of him, and often indulged in excessive, cruel revenge on his defeated enemies.[126]

Campaspe represents a fictional version of Alexander, a great conquering king who can lay aside his arms when the time for military glory is past and establish a court which resembles Athenian democracy at its best. Many in the audience would also have been aware that Athens only became a great centre for philosophy after its time as the democratic beacon of the ancient world had passed, a further indication of the play's self-consciously fantastic nature.[127] Alexander is able to tolerate and argue with Diogenes, the notorious cynic philosopher, who lives apart from society and insists that Alexander seeks him out for advice, rather than being forced to compromise his antisocial ideals by coming to court. Alexander, by now a philosopher-king, finds Diogenes so absurd that he confesses that he 'cannot be angry with him' (5.4.62). It is indeed hard to imagine any European princes committed to worldly glory, such as Henry VIII, acting with such tolerant equanimity. It is possible that Lyly may have had Henry in mind in the play, given his notorious treatment of Sir Thomas Wyatt, Henry's rival for the affection of Anne Boleyn, a story well known in the later sixteenth century.[128] The court that develops in Thebes is based on fostering virtue among an assembly of equals, the central idea of humanist republican political thought, and one cherished by the Protestant humanist intellectuals who formed such a central tradition within English politics in the sixteenth century.[129] In the opening scene, an exchange develops between Parmenio, a Macedonian officer, and Timoclea, his female Theban prisoner, in which it is clear that the loser in the war is the victor in the argument, as Clitus, another of Alexander's troops, implicitly acknowledges:

PARMENIO: Madam, you need not doubt; it is Alexander that is the conqueror.
TIMOCLEA: Alexander hath overcome, not conquered.
PAR: To bring all under his subjection is to conquer.
TIM: He cannot subdue that which is divine.
PAR: Thebes was not.
TIM: Virtue is.
CLITUS: Alexander, as he tendereth virtue, so he will you; he drinketh not blood but thirsteth after honour; he is greedy of victory but never satisfied with mercy. In fight terrible, as becometh a captain; in conquest mild, as beseemeth a king. In all things, than which nothing can be greater, he is Alexander. (1.1.50–62)

Alexander is represented as the courtier-hero, able to lay aside the manly pursuits of war when necessary, recognize female virtues of mercy and cultural sophistication, and so make his court from the best of both worlds, the central argument of Castiglione's *The Book of the Courtier* and the genre of courtesy books it inspired.[130] The newly established court is designed to promote virtue: it is evident that the legitimate fears of Timoclea's fellow prisoner, Campaspe, that her virginity will be threatened by the conquering army, will not be realized (lines 63–68). Military honour gives way to the honour of behaving well at court, and the very fact that such arguments can be made at all shows that Alexander means to be the ruler of a 'monarchical republic', like the dukes and duchesses of Urbino.[131] There the ideal ruler allows the twin virtues of the republic and the monarchy to flourish and citizens can enjoy liberty, a word singled out in the margin as a key feature for readers to note.[132] The life of a good ruler must be 'free and safe & as deere to his subjectes as their owne', an ideal of unity between sovereign and citizens.[133]

Flesh is put on the bones of this ideal in the second act when there is an extended discussion of counsel. Once again, this debate looks back to the ways and means of advising a monarch, through literature as well as other more direct forms of counsel, developed in the first half of the sixteenth century.[134] Alexander starts to confess his passion for Campaspe to his confidant, Hephestion, who, knowing he will be forced to discharge advice that his king will undoubtedly not want to hear, makes a bold plea for free counsel: 'Might my words crave pardon and my counsel credit, I would both discharge the duty of a subject (for so I am) and the office of a friend (for so I will)' (2.2.28–30). Hephestion wishes to combine the relationships of subject and friend to Alexander, just as Castiglione's ideal prince desired to be the equal and the superior of those he rules. When Alexander insists that he wishes to pursue his suit for Campaspe, Hephestion warns his sovereign that he is playing a dangerous game, not just in his course of action, which threatens the ruler's commitment to governing properly and has little hope of flourishing, but also in upsetting the balances he has sought so hard to establish: 'I must needs yield, when neither reason nor counsel can be heard' (lines 110–11). Alexander's final lines in the play are an acknowledgement that he has been a fool and that his counsellors, courtiers and assembled philosophers see matters more clearly than he can. By recognizing this relationship, Alexander shows himself to be an ideal king – albeit a fictional one – who wants to create a perfect state in which the king rules as a citizen, not a tyrant.

As might be expected, the whole range of George Chapman's tragedies demonstrate similar political interests and leanings. His particular fascination with the French wars of religion may have been inspired by Marlowe's provocative *The Massacre at Paris*, especially given his literary relationship with the dead writer. The two *Byron* plays (1608), which follow the ambitions of the late Marshal of France who was executed in 1602, show a corrupt and shady world, very like the imperial court of Rome after the overthrow of the Roman republic. Virtue no longer has a public role, but has come to mean the ability to seize power, as in Machiavelli's discussion of the actions of Agathocles the Sicilian in *The Prince* rather than Cicero's *De Officis*.[135] Byron is a noble and able citizen, but his inability to play a leading role in French political life leads him to conspire against the king, Henri IV. In the first play, he is discovered but pardoned, then in the second he repeats his crime and is duly executed. Byron's attempted coup is incited by Picoté, a French courtier in the service of Albert, archduke of Austria, who provides Byron with a historical precedent for his intended actions by spreading out a history of Catiline's rebellion on the carpet before Byron enters his chambers.[136] The comparison is pointed and appropriate, indicating how Chapman envisaged his play. Sallust had represented Catiline as restless, ambitious and of a depraved nature, and whose plot to seize power, after having planned to assassinate Cicero, resulted from the degeneration of the Roman republic into corruption, vice and tyranny.[137] Jonson used the same source and represented Catiline in a similar way, casting Cicero as the saviour and hero of the republic.[138] Early in *Caesar and Pompey*, Chapman makes the audience aware that the action they are about to witness takes place just after Catiline's conspiracy, as Metellus, immediately before he is admonished by Cato, reminds the assembled citizens. He argues that Pompey's army should be allowed to enter Rome: 'that his forces here, / As well as he, great *Rome* may rest secure / From danger of the yet still smoking fire / Of *Catilines* abhorr'd conspiracy' (1.2.34–37). Rome has lurched from one crisis to another, fearing that the one to come may be as bad as the last, a sign of a decaying body politic in the last days of the republic. Under these circumstances ruthless and ambitious men like Caesar can triumph, even if they – and the people they rule – will pay a heavy price.

Chapman, following Marlowe, clearly sees a similar situation having developed in France. Ruled by ruthless leaders after the murder of the Huguenots in 1572, and divided between implacably opposed religious enemies, the nation bears an uncanny resemblance to Italy during its civil wars. Byron, a Machiavellian antihero, is able to threaten the state because its institutions are simply not strong enough to contain him or to channel his civic virtues into its service. Byron's twisted logic, in the second of the two plays, shows him linking stage Machiavellianism and the history of imperial Rome in an attempt to convince his chief supporter, D'Auvergne, that the best should rule:

> we must not be more true to kings,
> Then Kings are to their subjects; there are schooles,
> Now broken ope in all parts of the world,
> First founded in ingenious *Italy*,
> Where some conclusions of estate are held,
> That for a day preserve a Prince, and ever,
> Destroy him after: from thence men are taught,
> To glyde into degrees of height by crafte[.][139]

The opening two lines of his speech read like a parody of the arguments used in such Huguenot treatises as *Vindiciae, Contra Tyrannos*, perhaps an indication that monarchomach theory stood in relation to French government as republican theory stood to Rome.[140] The subsequent lines are also undoubtedly indebted to another prominent work of Huguenot political philosophy, Innocent Gentillet's *Anti-Machiavel*.[141] The lines reveal the direction of Byron's thought. The next section of the speech ostensibly uses the example of the Julio-Claudians to affirm loyalty to the rightful monarch:

> But God, who knowes kings are not made by art,
> But right of Nature, nor by treachery propt,
> But simple vertue, once let fall from heaven,
> A branch of that greene tree, whose root is yet,
> Fast fixt above the starrs: which sacred branch,
> Wee well may liken to that Lawrell spray,
> That from the heavenly Eagles golden seres,
> Fell in the lap of great *Augustus* wife[.] (3.1.10–17)

The grand image unravels as the speech progresses. The negative statement 'who knowes kings are not made by art', shows that Byron has already realized that this may not be the case and is a point that has to be argued, even if it is not accepted as a final conclusion. Given what the audience sees in the play, and what they would have known of recent French history, the notion that 'simple vertue' will preserve a French monarch threatened by a Guise or a Byron is clearly intended as an irony.[142] The root of the tender green tree being established suggests its fragility as well as its potential growth into a powerful dynasty, a point made evident immediately afterwards: 'And as the armes of that tree did decay, / The race of great *Augustus* wore away; / *Nero* being the last of that imperiall line, / The tree and Emperor together died' (lines 21–24). Dynasties come and go and new trees are grown which flourish and then die in turn. Byron does not mention the fact – although, given the monarchomach opening of his speech it may well be a reference the audience would be expected to detect – that Nero did not die a natural death, but was overthrown and forced to commit suicide, as any reader of Tacitus would have known.[143] Byron's admiration for imperial Rome, an enthusiasm that does not sit well with his other points of reference in the speech, shows that the Roman emperors are his inspiration, not any faith in a divinely ordained nature that preserves kings. It is obvious where his train of thought leads towards the end of the speech:

> the tree that grew from heaven
> Is overrunne with mosse; the cheerful musique,
> That heertofore hath sounded out of it,
> Beginnes to cease; and as she casts her leaves,
> (By small degrees) the kingdomes of the earth
> Decline and wither: and looke, whensoever
> That the pure sap in her, is dried up quite,
> The lamp of all authoritie goes out,
> And all the blaze of Princes is extinct[.] (lines 34–42)

Henri IV is extremely anxious about securing the succession, having no immediate heir, as the opening scene of the *Conspiracie* informs us (1.1.193–218). It is not surprising that we find Byron, shortly after this speech, expressing the belief that he could occupy the throne if the opportunity arose (lines 122–55).

The two plays, especially when read with *Caesar and Pompey* in mind, or the contrastingly noble figure of the Stoical Protestant hero, the Admiral Chabot, are further evidence of a republican literary tradition that developed in the Elizabethan and Jacobean commercial theatre.[144] Byron's rise and fall are possible only because of the degeneration of French political life, which provides no outlet for his restless ambition, or means of controlling and harnessing his energy, and so leads him to become a destructive force. The lessons of the plays are also, of course, designed to be applied to English political life, the purpose of most works of history or descriptions of foreign states produced in the early modern period.[145] The links between England and France are indicated when Byron visits Elizabethan England in Act 4 – as indeed they were at the end of *The Massacre at Paris*. The implication is that England could well be rather more like France than many would like it to be, certainly if the ambitions of the leading character are read in terms of those of the earl of Essex, or Sir Walter Ralegh, as was the case with Jonson's *Sejanus His Fall* (1603) and Samuel Daniel's *The Tragedy of Philotas* (1607).[146] More to the point is the general significance of a play that situates itself within a 'mirrors for princes' literary tradition, or, more feasibly, the equally well-developed tradition of 'mirrors for magistrates', showing the audience – and then readers of the printed text – how the play can be read as a 'speaking picture' analysing government.[147] The plays consider the significance of virtue and its relationship to political action for both princes and mighty subjects, concluding that politics demands ethics if a public culture is to develop, the basic moral of Ciceronian political philosophy.[148] French justice demands the execution of Byron, just as Roman justice demanded the execution of the Catiline conspirators in *Caesar and Pompey*, when Cato urged the corrupt city-state to perform its duty to its citizens (1.2.40–48).

The play ends with the now abject figure of Byron waiting for the traitor's death by hanging on the scaffold, his offence so grave that he is not even afforded the usual courtesy of his rank, death by beheading.[149] The responsibility is partly that of Byron himself, who fails to acknowledge his guilt, and dies lamenting the extinction of his bloodline, displaying a warped notion of personal honour that serves only to undermine the commonwealth.[150] The prologue to the *Conspiracie* had indeed made this link between the 'uncivill, civill warres of France' and the revolt of 'our Conspirator . . . / how honors flood / Ebbes into ayre, when men are Great, not Good' ('Prologus', lines 1, 22–24). Chapman's prefatory poem argues that the self-wounds inflicted by civil war destroy the body politic so that men of talent but no morals such as Byron can inflict substantial damage on their fellow citizens. The wistful republican nature of the plays could hardly have been made more clear.

Republican thought was not simply available on the public stage, but also in privately performed works and, more importantly, in a large number of poems. Sir Philip Sidney's *Arcadia*, the revised form of which was published in 1590, followed soon after by the hybrid of the old and new versions, *The Countess of Pembroke's Arcadia* (1593), made extensive use of French monarchomach theory through Sidney's personal connections with his French mentor, Hubert Languet, co-author of *Vindiciae, Contra Tyrannos*, a work that haunts the romance.[151] Sidney was also influenced by George Buchanan's political ideas.[152] Sidney's long work was read by Shakespeare, who adapted the story of the blind king of Paphlagonia and the good son who saves him, Leonatus, as the subplot for his tragedy of the British King Lear.[153] Shakespeare also showed a keen knowledge of and interest in the French wars of religion and the political literature resulting from them, evident even in seemingly apolitical comedies such as *Love's Labour's Lost* (1594–98), perhaps through reading other writers such as Sidney who were clearly knowledgeable about such affairs early in his career. More important still may have been his connection with the publisher Richard Field, a fellow Stratfordian, who was one of the two main publishers of works relating to the French wars, and who also published works known to have been used extensively by Shakespeare, such as North's translation of Plutarch's *Lives*.[154]

Sidney's political views centre on a severe interpretation of contract theory, derived undoubtedly from Languet, Buchanan et al., which insists that the monarch be responsive to the desires and needs of the people.[155] At the heart of the *Arcadia* there is a beast fable, 'Ister Bank', based on Aesop's fable of 'The Frogs desiring a king', which encapsulates Sidney's thought.[156] The song is sung by the shepherd, Philisides, a figure of Sidney himself. Philisides claims that he has been taught by 'old Languet, the shepherd best swift Ister knew', a biographical detail that resembles those planted throughout the sonnet sequence *Astrophil and Stella*, which encouraged readers to see Astrophil as a version of Sidney and Stella as Penelope Devereux (his intended wife, who instead married Lord Rich).[157] The deliberate link to a prominent Huguenot political theorist surely serves to authenticate the discussion in the fable. Languet's song represents a golden beast world in which the lion lies down with the lamb and the animals 'Like senators a harmless empire had', which would appear to be a reference to the Roman republic before the harmful empire became established.

However, all political forms are subject to change and the animals eventually appeal to Jove, their 'neighing, bleaing, braying, and barking, / Roaring, and howling, for to have a king', the form of address a sign that their perfect body politic has already degenerated. Jove warns them that a king will be demanding, but they think they can offset this problem by endowing the 'naked sprite' that endows them with all their qualities, giving the ass patience, the lion, heart, the sparrow, 'lust to play', and so on. In doing so they create man, who, at first, cooperates with his subjects, 'Not in his sayings, saying "I", but "we"; / As if he meant his lordship common be', but eventually appropriates their common political culture for himself alone, ruling successfully by enfeebling his opponents, managing to divide them up into small self-interested factions. Soon society is based on strict hierarchies, with the stronger enjoying far better lives than the weaker, who are excluded from the business of government that they once helped determine. The fable ends on a suitably ambivalent note:

> But yet, O man, rage not beyond thy need;
> Deem it no glorie to swell in tyranny.
> Thou art of blood; joy not to make things bleed.
> Thou fearest death; think they are loath to die.
> A plaint of guiltless hurt doth pierce the sky.
> And you, poor beasts, in patience bide your hell,
> Or know your strengths, and then you shall do well. (lines 148–54)[158]

The message of the fable is ambiguous, and it would appear to be ending on a note of quietism, making an appeal for toleration from the powerful, and Stoic acceptance of the status quo from the powerless. The fable is also reminiscent of the biblical narrative of the Fall and its attendant curse of work. However, the last line undercuts this conclusion, reminding those in authority that worms can turn, the lynchpin of monarchomach arguments. This verse brings together a cluster of ideas. We are reminded that politics does not stop with the right to exercise power, but, given the contractual origins of kingship, thoughtful and considerate treatment of one's fellow creatures is equally important. Tyranny is, of course, to be avoided at all costs, and Sidney leaves us in no doubt that the responsibility for this rests with the potential tyrant in power. The fable demonstrates the familiar cyclical pattern of political history, the change from democracy to monarchy, to a form of oligarchy or aristocracy, and, finally to tyranny, in itself a quasi-republican message, cemented by the earlier reference to the animals as 'senators' of a benign empire. The last line reminds us that tyrannical monarchy is no more secure a form of government and that things can easily change back again. Sidney's search, in common with virtually all early modern European political theorists, is for government that is both stable and just. 'On Ister Bank', especially when read in terms of the rest of the *Arcadia*, makes the case that only a form of government that satisfies the desires and needs of the people, one that includes them in some level of the decision-making process, will function effectively and fairly. And this means a republic, like the Dutch republic that Sidney fought and died for, or a monarchical republic, the form of government that the animals first enjoyed before they foolishly relinquished it for a tyrant.[159]

The circle of writers who developed in the wake of Sidney's example, gravitating towards his family and network of patrons, also tended to share his political concerns.[160] The most prominent was Edmund Spenser (1552?–99), who had two frantic bursts of poetic output, the first when he arrogantly announced his arrival as the great new English poet with the publication of *The Shepheardes Calender* (1579–80), and the second more sustained period of publication (1590–96), when he produced an astonishing array of poetry, including the six books of *The Faerie Queene*. Spenser was well known to Shakespeare for his part in the acrimonious feud between his friend Gabriel Harvey and Thomas Nashe in the early 1590s, but also as a poet whose work he read and used.[161] Spenser may well have represented Shakespeare allegorically in *The Tears of the Muses* (1591) and *Colin Clouts come home againe* (1595).[162] *The Shepheardes Calender* contains a series of attacks on the hierarchical nature of the Church of

England, which have been construed as 'republican' in nature.[163] The 'May' eclogue consists of a debate between the two shepherds, Piers and Palinode, the former a humble Protestant, the latter a complacent, worldly Catholic. Piers laments the suppression of the good Algrind, a straightforward allegory of the arrest of Edmund Grindal, the reforming archbishop of Canterbury, who was eventually replaced by the more conservative John Whitgift.[164] The allusion to Grindal's harsh treatment is made more forcefully in the 'July' eclogue, in which the unfortunate shepherd has a shellfish dropped on his head by the soaring female eagle, leaving him lying in 'lingring payne' (line 228). The narrator, Thomalin, expresses his sympathy for Algrind, and the fable can be read as one of excessive regal power punishing the innocent, good citizen, who simply wishes to tend his flock properly. Spenser's recycling of one of Erasmus's *Adages*, in which the eagle is represented as a cruel and bullying tyrant, helps provide *The Shepheardes Calender* with an antimonarchical *frisson*.

Spenser's sceptical assessment of the virtue of Elizabethan government increased as Elizabeth's reign continued into the 1590s, and he came to place more emphasis on the role of the queen's servants as virtuous protectors of her rule.[165] In Book V of *The Faerie Queene*, published in 1596, he shows a series of ineffective, incompetent and malicious female figures and rulers – Florimell, Munera, Radigund, Mercilla – either failing to cope with the task of government or deliberately opposing and subverting the attempts of Artegall, the Knight of Justice, to reform the state. Only Britomart, the warrior woman who will marry Artegall, and so found a dynasty, possesses any significant virtue. Yet she stands as a cruel antitype of Elizabeth, who had failed as a warrior queen by not supporting military intervention in the Netherlands and not sending over enough troops to reconquer Ireland, as well as failing to continue her dynasty beyond her lifetime by not having children. The Book ends with Gloriana, a figure of 'the most excellent and glorious person of our soveraigne the Queene' ('Letter to Ralegh', p. 716), prematurely recalling Artegall from the 'salvage island' before he has had the chance to establish true justice (5.12.27). The queen is shown working to prevent proper government, not establish it. But as readers we can hardly be surprised. In his allegorical representation of the trial of Mary Queen of Scots in canto 9, Mercilla had to be forced by her male counsellors to pursue the right course of action and have Mary/Duessa executed (5.9.36–50).[166] The longer he lived, it would appear, the less Spenser placed his faith in the queen, and the more in her counsellors.

In *A View of the Present State of Ireland* (*c.*1596), Spenser had made extensive reference to George Buchanan, and had evidently read his works by the mid-1590s, probably earlier. Buchanan is cited to prove the common ancestry of the Irish and the Scots, part of his fear that the English in Ireland could be caught in a pincer movement between the two peoples, especially if James VI became king of England when Elizabeth died (a likely prospect by the mid-1590s).[167] But it is improbable that Buchanan's influence was solely limited to this area of Spenser's writings, especially given the impact that *The Faerie Queene* had at the Scottish court. James expressed outrage at the representation of the trial and execution of his mother, Mary Stuart, and refused to allow the second edition of *The Faerie Queene* to be sold in Scotland because of 'som dishonourable effects (as the King deems thereof) against himself and his mother deceased', later demanding ' that Edward [*sic*] Spenser for his fault be duly tried and punished'.[168] James clearly felt that Spenser's poetic narration of the trial of Duessa was likely to hinder his chances of achieving his lifetime ambition of uniting the crowns of England and Scotland, by slandering Mary as guilty of 'vyld treasons, and outrageous shame' (stanza 40) in her attempts to overthrow Mercilla (Elizabeth). The accusations made by the courtier, Zele, make Duessa's crimes public through a series of personifications:

> Then brought he forth, with griesly and grim aspect,
> Abhorred *Murder*, who with bloudie knyfe
> Yet dropping fresh in hand did her detect,
> And there with guiltie bloudshed charged ryfe:
> Then brought he forth *Sedition*, breeding stryfe
> In troublous wits, he forth *Incontinence* of lyfe,
> Even foule *Adulterie* her face before,
> And lewd *Impietie*, that her accused sore. (V.ix.48)

It is hardly surprising that James took umbrage at these lines. He may have had no personal affection for his mother, whom he had not seen since childhood, but they obviously reflected badly on the house of Stuart, already a tainted bloodline in many English eyes because of its association with the worst elements of Catholicism.[169] Furthermore, Spenser's comments echo the savage criticisms of Mary's behaviour made by her Scottish detractors, the most important being Buchanan. Spenser describes Mary as guilty of murder, presumably of Lord Darnley, a crime linked to sedition, as she has caused the deaths of the subjects who have died in the wars she has caused; unable to control her natural female vices by reason (the word 'incontinence' links her to Malecasta in Book III, canto I, who falls for the disguised Britomart, perhaps making her a type of Mary); faithless in marriage and in politics; and sacrilegious, overturning the Reformation in favour of reactionary French Catholicism. In short, exactly how Buchanan represented her in *Ane detectioun of the duinges of Marie Quene of Scottes* and his *History of Scotland*.[170] The Faerie *Queene* shows that it is the men who advise the female monarch – undoubtedly including Spenser himself – who should really run the country. The representation of the trial of Mary looks suspiciously like a demonstration of Buchanan's theory of kingship, whereby the monarch serves the people and is answerable to them.

It was probably through his growing connection to the earl of Essex immediately before his death that Spenser came to contribute a commendatory poem to Lewis Lewkenor's translation of Contarim's *The Commonwealth and Government of Venice* (1599).[171] The Lewkenor family were clients of Essex.[172] Contarini's work was an enthusiastic endorsement of the merits of Venice as the best constitution in the world. The sonnet is not one of Spenser's most remarkable. It contrasts the evils of the second Babylon, Rome, with the goodness of Venice, which Spenser praises for its beautiful buildings, 'flower of the worlds delight', but more significantly for its 'policie of right' (*Shorter Poems*, p. 502), both commonplace judgements of the worth of the city-state.[173] Placed alongside his use of Buchanan's theories, Spenser's willingness to be associated in print with Lewkenor's translation indicates the direction in which he appears to have been travelling in the 1590s.

The fact that the two most prominent English poets writing in the 1580s and 1590s, who helped determine the future course of English literature and an English literary career, should be keen to display their interest in republican ideas was not lost on other writers.[174] Sidney and Spenser certainly paved the way for others to explore republican political issues, even if they did not adhere to republican ideals themselves. A case in point is Sidney's friend and editor, Fulke Greville (1554–1628), who came from an old Warwickshire family and was certainly known to Shakespeare, possibly acting as his first patron.[175] Much of Greville's work remained in manuscript until after his death – the publication of *Mustapha* (1609) was without his consent – and he destroyed his play *Antony and Cleopatra* because it reflected rather too carefully on the rebellion of the earl of Essex, with whom Greville had been closely associated in the 1590s.[176] It is evident that his two surviving plays, *Mustapha* (c.1594–96) and *Alaham* (c.1598–1600), neither of which were performed publicly, provide extensive discussions of resistance theory based on his reading of *Vindiciae, Contra Tyrannos,* one of Sidney's favourite political works.[177] Greville, certainly when he revised his plays in the early 1600s, had little sympathy for armed rebellion, but this may be indicative of a change in political attitudes after the accession of James as well as a personal conviction.[178] He was, nevertheless, a keen student of Machiavelli, and, like Francis Bacon, had great faith in the value of parliaments.[179]

The plays are concerted attacks on the vices of overbearing rulers, but they argue the case that anarchy is worse than tyranny. People need security and order, ideally under the law, and the worst ruler is a weak one, such as Alaham, who is more interested in his comforts and assisting his friends and allies than enforcing the law properly. Both plays stress the need for kings to heed wise counsel so that they realize when something untoward happens, an argument for the constitutional importance of parliament. Greville also places emphasis on the need for true religion to play its part in good government, and favours the security of a hereditary rather than an elective kingship.[180] There are many assumptions here in common with the political arguments made in the 1590s: the need for counsel, for monarchs to obey the law, reason to be the key principle of government, the fear that tyranny will erode the people's liberty and the concomitant fear of rebellion if a monarch treats subjects too harshly, the hope that religious differences can be either solved or placed to one side, and so on, all affirming a belief in the principle of the 'mixed' constitution.[181] Nevertheless, the central political fear has changed from the need for subjects to force the hands of their rulers in order to ensure proper justice and liberty, to the need for rulers to behave well and be attentive to their kingdoms.[182]

Greville's political opinions are meticulously laid out in his poetry, most obviously in 'A Treatise of Monarchy'. This long poem of 664 stanzas in a form that resembles rhyme royal (ababcc, not ababbcc), argues that hereditary monarchy is the best form of government.[183] It was probably completed in the early 1600s, but was started in the 1590s.[184] Nevertheless, Greville's political anatomy and history is evidently touched by republican thought, a word he uses to describe states in stanzas 1, 14, 276, 325, and elsewhere. Greville charts the political progress of monarchy from its inception to its frequent degeneration into tyranny, warning his readers that 'thrones are not indefinite', that 'pow're bounded is with wrong and right' (stanza 40) and it is the duty of the good counsellor to 'lymitt the excesses of a Crowne' (stanza 45). The story of the end of the republic is told, yet again, with only a slight twist:

> *Caesar* was slaine by those that objects were
> Of grace, and engines of his tiranny.
> *Brutus* and *Cassius* worke shall wittnes beare,
> Even to the comfort of posterity,
> That prowd aspirers never had good end,
> Nor yet excess of might a constant frend. (stanza 70)

Caesar is, as usual in work written in the 1590s, cast as a tyrant. But Brutus
and Cassius are seen as equally ambitious and self-serving, tyrants who
never got to rule, unlike Caligula and Nero (stanza 74). It is tempting to
speculate how this verse read in the first version of the poem, assuming
that Greville revised it. Whatever the genesis of the poem, it is clear that
Greville needed to make use of the history of the Roman republic as a
central reference point for his readers. This would seem to indicate that it
was difficult for any political writer in the 1590s and 1600s to ignore or
summarily dismiss arguments for a republic. A contrary case could not be
assumed but had to be argued. By a deft sleight of hand in the verse cited
above, Greville transforms the story of the end of the republic into one of
the end of constitutional monarchy, Caesar, Brutus and Cassius all being
cast as enemies of the middle way. It is a neat manoeuvre, which testifies
to the dominant role of the history of the republic in English political life.

In contemporary Europe Greville is positively encouraging to republics, principally because they oppose the might of Spain:

> The pride of such inferiors did constraine
> The *Swise* against the *Austrians* cantonise;
> Soe were the *Belgians* likewise forc't againe
> A new *Republique* finely to devise;
> In which that Monarch [i.e., the King of Spain's representative,
> the Duke of Alva] was compeld to treat
> As with states equall free, not equall great. (stanza 102)

The republics established here enable their citizens to stop tyrants whose
desire is to 'Abridge our freedome, to lord over us' (stanza 100), and, in
section 6 of the poem (stanzas 192–238), Catholicism and tyranny are
shown to have an identical agenda. The reference to Spain suggests that
this verse was written in the 1590s when Spain's power was at its height
and most Protestant European states devoted their foreign policy to
halting Iberian imperial ambitions, and indicates that the poem may have
been less obviously celebratory of monarchy in earlier forms.[185]

However, in the later stages of the poem Greville weighs in against
republicanism, as he compares monarchy favourably with alternative
systems of government (aristocracy, stanzas 580–609; democracy, stanzas

610–40). The republic is seen as an unstable political form, veering from tyranny to popular rule, and the history of Athens is no less chaotic. Caesar was not without his faults, but 'he that brought back Monarchie / Err'd less, then he who sett the people free' (stanza 591). The banishment of the Tarquins was an unqualified good, but Rome soon degenerated from its unified state and 'fell shee into manie-headed powre', until the people eventually realized that they were better off with a 'brave Monarchall state' (stanza 592), a stable political form that could offset the dangerous swings that other states experienced. Greville's aim is to outplay the republicans at their own game and show that constitutional monarchy is the best form of government that ensures stability and grants the people maximum liberty.[186] Whereas admirers of the Roman or Venetian republics argued that these were the most stable constitutional forms, mixing together all the desirable elements of government, Greville, following James, claims that monarchy provides all these goods.[187] It is a compelling case, but it also reveals how clearly republicanism had set the political agenda in Shakespeare's England.

PART II

Shakespeare and Republicanism

Introduction II: Shakespeare's early republican career

It is hard for us to know for certain in which order Shakespeare wrote his early works, what he wrote before his works were published, or just how many of his plays were the product of collaborative authorship. He first appeared as a published author in 1593–94, when four works were printed: the 'bad' quarto of *2 Henry VI, The first part of the contention betwixt the two famous houses of Yorke and Lancaster; The most lamentable Romaine tragedie of Titus Andronicus*; and the two poems, *The Rape of Lucrece* and *Venus and Adonis*.[1] It is likely that the two plays were published for commercial reasons, as Peter Blaney has recently claimed, designed to make money for the Lord Chamberlain's Men when the theatres were closed because of the spread of the plague from 1592 to 1594.[2] It is also likely that Shakespeare published the two narrative poems for the same reason to make up for the sharp drop in income he must have experienced.[3]

The publication of four works in a single year assumes further importance if we suspect that Shakespeare had already been working in the theatre for a number of years. In 1594 Shakespeare was already thirty, and if we make the assumption that his earliest plays were staged in 1592, from when the first extant records of them date, he must have started a theatrical career relatively late in life.[4] Christopher Marlowe had his first plays staged when he was twenty-three and George Peele in his late teens, while he was a student at Oxford.[5] It is most plausible to assume that Shakespeare spent these years 'with some theatrical company or other, as apprentice writer and actor, learning his trades'.[6] It is probable, especially given the number of plays that have been lost and the number of performances that have gone unrecorded, that Shakespeare had plays performed before this date.[7] We cannot know for certain when the career of the prolific Henry Chettle began, for example, as so few of his plays have survived.[8] The same is true of the equally productive Thomas Heywood.[9] Plays were published with any regularity only from the late 1580s onwards, so those performed on the public stage before this time

were unlikely to be preserved.[10] As many scholars have argued, Thomas
Nashe's reference to the reappearance of the heroic Talbot on the stage in
Henry VI, Part One, Henry Chettle's slighting reference to Shakespeare as
an 'upstart crow' in *Greene's Groatsworth of Wit*, and Francis Mere's high
estimation of Shakespeare's writing in *Palladis Tamia* (1598) suggest either
that Shakespeare became well established as a poet of note very rapidly, or
that his career began earlier than many have suggested.[11] If this longer
career is assumed, then Shakespeare's decision to fashion himself as a
republican author takes on a greater importance.[12] Shakespeare belonged
to an expanding generation of writers who had received a classical education but had no obvious place in the social hierarchy.[13] It is hardly
surprising that many turned to republican political ideas and values,
especially grammar school boys such as Shakespeare, who had to make a
career in London by producing what a wider public wanted.[14]

These four texts could be seen to announce the start of Shakespeare's
career in print, in the same way that Edmund Spenser had proclaimed the
start of his literary career by asserting that he was going to revolutionize
English literature in *The Shepheardes Calender*.[15] This small collection of
works would have singled Shakespeare out as a writer interested in
republican questions and issues. In itself, this might tell us as much about
what people wanted to read as it does about Shakespeare's actual beliefs.
The point is made even more forcefully if we follow Jonathan Bate's
argument that *Titus Andronicus* was written for the reopening of the
theatres in 1594, conceived as a work that would lure audiences back to
public performances.[16] *Titus* is not simply a play about the decline of the
Roman republic, but deals explicitly with the political issues and choices
raised by the history of Rome, as the opening scene makes clear.[17] The
Contention is a play inspired by Lucan's *Pharsalia*, showing the terrible
effects of the civil war of powerful factions on the innocent populace, with
the implication that a better way of governing must surely be possible.
Behind the work lie Lodge's *The Wounds of Civil War* and – possibly –
Samuel Daniel's adaptation of Lucan's Roman history to England, *The
Civil Wars*, also published in 1594.[18] *The Rape of Lucrece* is the story of the
foundation of the Roman republic. The fact that Shakespeare's poem is
here simply advertised on the title page in huge letters as 'Lucrece' might
well suggest that the poem was published with the intention of its making
a significant political impact, perhaps attracting readers keen to see how
such a controversial story would be retold.[19] *Venus and Adonis* is the least
straightforwardly political of the three, although it does signal an Ovidian
subject matter, providing a link to the recently murdered Marlowe, and it

can be read as a critical account of the social and political mechanisms operating at Elizabeth's court.[20]

Shakespeare was following a trail blazed by Marlowe and Lodge, both of whom had a major influence on the first half of his writing career.[21] It is evident that Shakespeare – or his publishers – felt that these particular works might sell well and they provide us with further evidence of the ways in which Elizabethan authors represented themselves. It is surely no accident that the two poems were published by Richard Field, another native of Stratford. Field was the publisher of two of the most prestigious literary works of the sixteenth century, George Puttenham's *The Arte of English Poesie* (1589) and Sir John Harington's translation of Ariosto's *Orlando Furioso* (1591), which may well have attracted an ambitious young author to his stable of writers. In addition, Field published devotional works, but he was also one of the main English publishers of material dealing with the French wars of religion. Equally significantly, he published a number of translations of key political works of the sixteenth century, including Lipsius's *Six Bookes of Politiques or Civil Doctrine* (1594), and later, Geoffrey Fenton's translation of Guicciardini's *History of Italy* (1599) and William Fulbecke's *An Historicall Collection of the continuall factions, tumults, and Massacres of the Romans and Italians* (1601).[22] Katherine Duncan-Jones speculates that 'Shakespeare regularly used Field's printing house in Blackfriars . . . as a working library, and even did his writing there', as Field's books would have given him 'unlimited access to the historical sources he needed'.[23] Certainly having his poetry published by Field placed the works for sale among political texts at Field's print shop.

The dedication of the poetry to the earl of Southampton is a further detail that points to Shakespeare presenting himself to the public as a republican author. Southampton was closely connected to the earl of Essex, by now the key patron for authors of challenging and problematic political works, a position that brought him unwanted dedications.[24] Essex sent his secretary, Henry Cuffe, to Paris in the early 1590s to expound Aristotle to Southampton and the earl of Rutland, a move which many have read as a sign of Essex's interest in republican politics.[25] As Martin Dzelzainis has pointed out, 'In choosing the foundational event of the Roman republic as his topic, Shakespeare in fact showed a remarkably shrewd sense of what was likely to appeal to his patron's political tastes.'[26] The relationship presumably worked both ways, announcing Shakespeare as a radical author all the more likely to produce exciting theatrical works that challenged received conventions and analysed topical subjects.[27]

Such evidence indicates that Shakespeare was keen to be seen as a writer interested in political questions, and, specifically, republican issues. What is also notable is his desire to engage with a wide variety of republican texts and examples, from ancient Rome to contemporary Venice, from a native English tradition to the writings of the Italian *politiques*, from questions of political representation to an imaginative rethinking of English history in terms of republican counterepic. Perhaps his first engagement with republican thought – assuming that Shakespeare did not write the *Ur-Hamlet* – was with Lucan's *Pharsalia*, which he was not alone in applying to the bloody course of English history.

CHAPTER 3

Shakespeare's Pharsalia *: the first tetralogy*

In the opening scene of *Henry VI, Part One* the Duke of Bedford attempts to sum up the feelings of the realm and his hopes for the future as his elder brother's coffin proceeds on its last journey:

> Henry the Fifth, thy ghost I invocate:
> Prosper this realm, keep it from civil broils,
> Combat with adverse planets in the heavens.
> A far more glorious star thy soul will make
> Than Julius Caesar or bright –
> *Enter a Messenger*[1]

The speech is, of course, a moment of heavy dramatic irony, as even the least historically literate of playgoers would have been aware that the events of Henry VI's reign were a catalogue of 'civil broils', suggesting that 'adverse planets' had a more than usual interest in the lives of the inhabitants of the British Isles.[2] Indeed, the Messenger informs the assembled nobles that the crown's lands in France, obtained during Henry's reign, are under threat. As they divide up to perform different roles vital to the organization of the realm – proclaiming the new boy king, preparing military reinforcements – it becomes clear that Henry's death has exposed the unstable nature of their temporary union. With a power vacuum at the centre, unscrupulous and ambitious aristocrats will seize their chance to dominate public affairs. There has already been an argument between the Lord Protector, the Duke of Gloucester, and the Bishop of Winchester about the relationship between church and state (lines 33–45). The scene ends with an ominous self-address from the Bishop, in which he signals his selfish ambition:

> Each hath his place and function to attend;
> I am left out; for me nothing remains;
> But long I will not be Jack-out-of-office.
> The King from Eltham I intend to steal,
> And sit at chiefest stern of public weal. (173–77).[3]

We do not know exactly what Bedford would have said about Julius Caesar looking down from the heavens on England, but the comparison between the man who forced the Roman Senate to establish him as dictator for life, making him, in effect, the first Roman emperor, and Henry V, is both suggestive and, in terms of the hereditary succession of the monarchy, intensely problematic. Gloucester's praise of the dead Henry, 'England ne'er had a king until his time. / Virtue he had, deserving to command' (lines 8–9), implies not only that Henry was a fortunate aberration, but also that loyalty to the monarch is conditional on the king 'deserving to command'. Henry V achieves this in France, his military virtue binding together an otherwise disparate army assembled from the four nations of the British Isles.[4] But if we are invited to regard Henry as Julius Caesar in the – chronologically – earlier play, the comparison implies that the English king was a military ruler whose death would inevitably leave the country with more problems than opportunities. Faction, conquest and violence, as any account of his life available to an English Renaissance reader emphasized, defined Caesar's career.[5] He rose to prominence through his successes in the Mithridatic Wars, in Spain, in Gaul and in England; came to power through his victory in the civil war with Pompey; subsequently defeated the remains of the senatorial party led by Cato in Africa, and, in his last campaign, the sons of Pompey in Spain; and was then assassinated a year later.[6] The result was a further civil war and the establishment of imperial Rome. No monarch could have felt proud of his legacy if all he had achieved were the triumphs of Caesar.

Bedford's words appear to be an echo of the opening lines of Lucan's *Pharsalia* – an approximate but nevertheless distinct reference.[7] Having castigated Rome for the disasters it has heaped upon itself through the late republic's indulgence in extensive civil wars, Lucan appears to change tack and he praises Nero for military achievements that match those of Caesar. Marlowe's translation renders them as:

> Yet Rome is much bound to these civil arms,
> Which made thee emperor, thee (seeing thou, being old,
> Must shine a star) shall heaven (who thou lovest)
> Receive with shouts, where thou wilt reign as king,
> Or mount the sun's flame-bearing chariot,
> And with bright restless fire compass the earth[.][8]

Lucan's lines, whether he intended it or not, opened themselves up to be read ironically, when Nero became universally known as a deranged tyrant, and Lucan was forced to commit suicide after taking part in Piso's failed conspiracy. If Henry V is then linked to Nero via their mutual comparison to Julius Caesar, all three being cast as stars looking down on the earth, then the extent of the disaster which is about to befall England is clear. The degeneration of the Roman republic from a thriving and egalitarian body politic of citizens into a fractious and unstable world in which the strongest and most ambitious fight for control serves as a model for England during the bloody civil wars known as the Wars of the Roses. The three *Henry VI* plays – as well as *Richard III* – are Shakespeare's *Pharsalia*.

It is unlikely that we will ever know exactly how much Shakespeare wrote of the three *Henry VI* plays, nor when they were first performed onstage. Part One first appeared in print in the folio, and may well have been written – or revised – after Parts Two and Three.[9] Nevertheless, it is usually assumed that it was first performed at the Rose in 1592 and was the play seen by Thomas Nashe when he asked, rhetorically, 'How would it have joyed brave Talbot . . . to think that after he had lain two hundred years in his tomb, he should triumph again on the stage', and asserted that ten thousand spectators had seen the play.[10] It is possible that Nashe was one of Shakespeare's co-authors, so that his comments are a sly promotion of his labours, perhaps even written for those who already knew this (and if Nashe was the author of Act 1, as Burns and Taylor argue, then our appreciation of the ironies surrounding the reference that links Caesar, Nero and Henry V, is more pronounced).[11] Nashe, who co-wrote *Dido, Queen of Carthage* (as the 1594 edition advertised on the title page), provides us with a further link between Shakespeare and Marlowe, whose historical play *Edward II*, written in the early 1590s, is a further republican context for Shakespeare's early histories (see above, p. 65).

It is quite likely that Parts Two and Three were written somewhat earlier – probably in the late 1580s or early 1590s – perhaps designed as a pair to cash in on the success of the two parts of Marlowe's *Tamburlaine*.[12] Again, they are probably collaborative works, perhaps with Robert Greene (Part Two), perhaps with Marlowe, Greene and Peele (Part Three), but it is virtually impossible to tell without any external evidence.[13] Both appeared, without authorial identification on the title page, in 1594 and 1595 respectively, as octavos that differ in significant ways from the later versions published in the folio, probably because they were records of versions of the plays that were actually staged, the folio text deriving from the working papers in the possession of the theatre company.[14] The extensive titles make clear to any prospective reader that they will encounter a detailed narrative of the English civil wars of the fifteenth century. Part Two was published as *The first part of the contention betwixt the two famous houses of Yorke and Lancaster with the death of the good Duke Humphrey: and the banishment and death of the Duke of Suffolke, and the tragical end of the proud Cardinall of Winchester, with the notable rebellion of Jacke Cade: and the Duke of Yorkes first clayme to the crowne* (1594) (hereafter *Contention*), and Part Three as *The true tragedie of Richarde Duke of Yorke and the death of good King Henrie the sixt: with the whole contention betweene the two houses, Lancaster and Yorke; as it was sundry times acted by the Right Honourable the Earle of Pembrooke his servantes* (1595) (hereafter *True Tragedie*).

The textual problems of *Henry VI* are arguably even more daunting than those of *Hamlet*.[15] We do not know how much of the three plays Shakespeare actually wrote; we do not know whether they were conceived as a trilogy, which would make them unique in this period of theatre history (although, given the experimental nature of the Elizabethan theatre, this is not a reason to dismiss the possibility out of hand), or as a pair, with *Henry VI, Part One* appearing as a 'prequel' to cash in on the success of the *Contention* and *True Tragedy*; we do not know the precise textual relationship between the different versions of Parts Two and Three; and we cannot be sure of the dates of any of them.[16] What we can be sure of is that Shakespeare, near the start of his career, was heavily involved in a dramatic project that sought to bring the history of the English civil war to public attention, realizing either its commercial potential, or that it was a venture designed to mould public opinion, and, quite probably, both.

It is often asked why Shakespeare chose to begin his career with plays on the life of Henry VI, especially when he later wrote plays narrating the histories of the three kings who preceded him, and what he hoped to achieve in writing works that are so at odds with subsequent dramatic taste.[17] The answer may well be that they were conspicuously designed to represent Henry's troubled reign as the English civil war, a means of adapting Lucan onstage to suit the republican climate of Elizabeth's 'second reign', as well as establishing English literature as a Latinate European culture alongside that of France and Italy.[18] If Spenser was the English Virgil, and Marlowe the English Ovid, then perhaps we should see the early Shakespeare as the English Lucan, a republican poet who could write about troubled times that had a bearing on current political issues and which also represented one nightmarish vision of the future.[19] The subsequent appearance of the spectacularly violent *Titus Andronicus* can only have strengthened the impression that Shakespeare had Lucan in mind when trying to forge a literary identity. Nashe's comments about the popularity of Talbot on the stage – even if they are self-promoting – and the fact that three plays could be produced on the same subject, suggest that Shakespeare and his collaborators knew exactly what they were doing. Given the uncertainty of the succession in the 1590s, the anxiety induced by the range of candidates, the growing interest in alternative forms of government, classical and contemporary, the protracted war with Spain, and the fear of the French civil wars of religion being imported across the Channel, it is easy to see why these plays were so popular and why they had such an impact on the development of the English theatre.[20] Lucan's narrative of the disastrous effects of the struggle between Caesar and Pompey on the people of Rome and its environs was an obvious vehicle for the expression of this combination of issues.

Lucan was very much in vogue in the early 1590s.[21] Marlowe's translation of Book One circulated in manuscript and Arthur Gorges was at work on his translation of the *Pharsalia*.[22] This eventually appeared in 1614, with the title *Lucans Pharsalia: Containing The Civill Warres betweene Caesar and Pompey*, a balanced description of the contents that resembles the style of the titles of the octavos of the *Henry VI* plays.[23] Samuel Daniel adapted the *Pharsalia* to English history in his long chronicle poem, *The first fowre bookes of the civile wars between the two houses of Lancaster and Yorke*, published in 1595.[24] Like Lucan's epic, this work was never finished but was gradually expanded, the last instalment reaching the marriage of Edward IV in 1609.[25] Much has been made of the relationship between Daniel's poem and Shakespeare's *Richard II*, the two works shadowing each other throughout their early publishing histories. Shakespeare read *The Civil Wars* when writing his play, and then Daniel revised his poem in 1609 to take account of Shakespeare's work, also making use of the two *Henry IV* plays for good measure.[26] An assumption generally made is that Shakespeare was not a close reader of Lucan and read the Roman poet through the work of his more scholarly contemporary.[27] This may, of course, be true, but it leaves out of the account the impact of the *Henry VI* plays.[28] If these were inspired by Lucan, as seems likely, and they date from the late 1580s or early 1590s, then it may be more plausible to argue that it was the design of the *Henry VI* plays that had the crucial influence on the vogue for Lucanizing English history.[29]

There are many similarities between Lucan's unfinished epic poem and the various versions of the *Henry VI* plays. Both show the dreadful effects of ruthless ambition on the principal historical actors, and, more to the point, those who have to serve them or get caught up in forces beyond their control. Both show the conflict of sides that are not quite evenly balanced and the triumph of the stronger and more brutal faction over the more sympathetic group: the mighty Caesar over the fading, ineffectual Pompey, and the Yorkist faction led by Richard, Duke of Gloucester, and then his son, Richard III, whose fate might seem to mirror that of Julius Caesar (military triumph leading to rule, but without respite, before being betrayed – by Buckingham – and then murdered), over the hapless Henry VI. The destructive civil war in each work leads to the establishment of a dictatorship: Caesar, through a combination of strategy and good fortune, is able to eliminate all traces of Pompey's faction, as well as to sweep aside the objections of the citizens of Rome and their republican institutions. Caesar triumphs through merit, what the republic was supposed to value and promote, but ends the republic in doing so, hurtling Rome into a brave new political world. The same can be said of the Yorkist faction, who feel that they have a better right to the throne than Henry, a disparity that he acknowledges at the start of the *True Tragedie*, but, more importantly, that they are more regal in style and substance than he is. The plays endorse this reading of history, but show that it only leads to the triumph of Richard III, who has no idea how to rule, only how to seize the throne, a failure that results in the triumph of the Tudors, a dynasty that was just about to end when the plays were first performed.[30] It is inconceivable that many of the audience, given the plotting that was taking place to decide on the succession, would not have made a connection between the chaos that led to the advent of the Tudors and the chaos that could very well ensue after their rule ended.[31] The decline and fall of the Roman republic into a cycle of civil war punctuated by the dictatorship of the powerful and unscrupulous, whose families then destroy the body politic as well as themselves, is shown to be uncomfortably close to the tragic history of England, past, present and future.

There are other links that can be made. The witchcraft professed by Joan La Pucelle in *Henry VI, Part One* and Eleanor Cobham in *Henry VI, Part Two* perhaps recalls that of the *Pharsalia*, Book VI, when Pompey's army consult witches to conjure up the spirits of the dead before the crucial battle of the war, Pharsalia (the news is predictably bad). The sequence of bloody battles in the *True Tragedie* – Wakefield, Towton,

Barnet and Tewkesbury – give that particular play a sense of prolonged conflict, with huge forces moved over significant distances, a fraught series of tactical encounters that see the balance swing one way then another, before the inevitable victor triumphs, mirroring one key aspect of the appeal of Lucan's poem to many seventeenth-century readers, absorbed by military issues.[32] Neither work has a clear hero: the reader/audience is simply asked to think how he or she would behave when presented with a series of stark choices between undesirable outcomes, there being no immediate possibility of establishing a viable body politic. The slaughter and waste of human life that characterizes the English civil war plays is probably the most obvious link between the two works. Each represents all levels of society drawn into the conflict, and shows the dreadful effect that war has on ordinary citizens, Lucan through the fate of individual soldiers, Shakespeare through the scene in which King Henry has to witness the tableau of parricide in *Henry VI, Part Three*, as well as the rebellion of Jack Cade in *Henry VI, Part Two*.[33]

Of course, there was nothing new in representing grisly forms of death in literary works.[34] Placing emphasis on the destruction of ordinary people caused by the actions of their supposedly heroic superiors is, however, a radical departure in both Latin literature and English drama. The heroic duel to the death between Aeneas and Turnus in the final book of the *Aeneid* is a conspicuous attempt to transfer the glory of the epic conflicts of the *Iliad* to the newly founded imperial Rome, a key literary example of *translatio imperii*.[35] Lucan's poem, written after the cruel and destructive reigns of Tiberius, Caligula and Claudius, is designed to expose the hollow foundations on which imperial Rome was built. In David Quint's words, Lucan 'traces the foundation of the imperial ascendancy of Augustus and the Julio-Claudians back not to a hoary, Homeric past but merely to one generation earlier, to the civil strife between Julius Caesar and Pompey that had destroyed the republic'.[36] Quint suggests further that the 'republican ideal' that Lucan promotes is oligarchic in character and he points to the 'element of class conflict' in the poem, one that pits 'a warrior nobility at odds with a central monarchy determined to limit their power'.[37]

Of course, this is correct, but one might further suggest that the class conflict could be seen to range rather more widely, something that later readers recognized. After the English Civil War, responses to the *Pharsalia* concentrated on the images of slaughter and destruction of ordinary people, as Nigel Smith has noted.[38] The graphic description of the horrible death of Lycidas, a sailor on one of Caesar's ships which is surrounded by Greek vessels during the sea campaigns in Book III, is a case in point. The sheer length of the description of Lycidas's death and the macabre fascination with anatomical detail indicates that Lucan is conspicuously parodying Virgil's epic similes of military might:

As a grappling-iron was fastening its grasping hooks on to a ship, it pierced Lycidas. He would have been submerged in the deep but for his comrades, who held on to his legs as he swung. He was torn and split apart and blood did not spurt out as from a wound; slowly from his broken veins it falls everywhere, and as the stream of life passed into his separated limbs it was intercepted by the waters. From none in death has life departed by so wide a path. The lowest part of his torso handed over to death limbs empty of vitals; but where the swelling lung lies, where the organs are warm, the fates stuck for a long time and, after a long struggle with this portion of the man, took all his parts with difficulty.[39]

The image has a number of resonances. The demands it places on our attention force us to confront the squalid and tragic nature of an ordinary man's death. The wealth of detail – the grappling iron piercing Lycidas, his comrades trying to save him and only succeeding in prolonging his agony, the blood seeping from his body into the sea rather than spurting out (a pointed contrast to the heroic wounds inflicted by the warriors in the *Aeneid*), and the slow process of necrotization passing upwards through the body – provides Lycidas with an importance and individuality that he did not possess in life. We are made aware of his significance even though he does not matter to the military leaders who are prepared to sacrifice him in their pursuit of glory. The death of Lycidas stands as a pointed – undoubtedly deliberate – contrast to the death of Turnus at the end of the *Aeneid*. The one leads to the establishment of a great empire, a heroic sacrifice in keeping with the ideal of imperial might; the other is part of the death of an ideal, that of the republic, Lycidas's broken body representing the destruction of a Rome run for and by its citizens. The mighty epic similes that describe Caesar as a thunderbolt (Book I, lines 151–57), and Pompey as an ancient oak (Book I, lines 136–43), are here reduced to the agony of a single dying man of no real consequence, a democratic gesture reminding the reader what poetry can do and the political resonances that it has. Lucan reinforces this point in the following lines, which describe the spectacular fate of an unnamed young man who experiences 'a unique form / of hideous death' when he is 'by chance . . . transfixed by the beaks of converging vessels':

The middle of his chest was split apart by such tremendous blows, the bones were ground away, his limbs could not prevent the bronze of the beaks resounding; from his crushed belly the blood mixed with entrails spouted gore through his mouth. (lines 652–58)

When Turnus has received his deathblow from Aeneas, he implores the victor to 'Make use of what Fortune has given' him.[40] However, in the world of the *Pharsalia* we are constantly made aware that it is the human titans, the mighty oak, and to a much greater extent, the thunderbolt, who determine the course of men's fates. Caesar is described as 'greedy for the fight' (Book VI, line 28) before the battle of Pharsalia, and later, 'satiated with the slaughter of Emathia' (Book IX, line 950), in direct contrast to the detached figure of Cato who, when drawn into the conflict, 'waged a civil war without desiring power / or fearing slavery' (Book IX, lines 27–28). After his victory, Caesar sees 'the fields drenched sufficiently with Hesperian / blood', and sees fit to grant life 'to worthless souls, to columns / whose death would have had no point' (Book VII, lines 728–31), acts of mercy which serve only to remind us of the power that Caesar has over the lives of those he leads as well as those he fights, and the carelessness with which he exercises it.[41] Lucan shows how the horror visits everyone present at the field of slaughter:

> The ghost of a murdered citizen
> stands there; each man is tormented by a terrifying
> [vision all his own:
> *he* sees faces of old men, *he* the forms of younger men,
> *he* in all his dreams is harried by his brother's corpse,
> in *this* breast is his father – all these shades are in Caesar.
> (lines 772–76)

Everyone may be touched by the horror and their part in it, but the guilt is clearly Caesar's. Lucan then addresses Caesar directly, further reminding him of his responsibility for the carnage, and making sure that no reader of the *Pharsalia* can have been in any doubt who caused all the death and destruction: 'Drink these waters, Caesar, breathe this air, if you can, / But the rotting hordes rob you of Pharsalian / fields, they rout the conqueror and possess the plains' (lines 822–24).

The obvious precursors of the English civil war plays – Marlowe's *Tamburlaine, The Massacre at Paris* and *Edward II*, as well as Lodge's *The Wounds of Civil War* – do, of course, show conflict and destruction. They do not, however, focus so clearly and explicitly on the relationship between the sins of the leaders and the suffering of the people, which is one reason why the *Henry VI* plays appear to be more consciously influenced by the representation of civil war in the *Pharsalia*. There is little to compare with the scene at the battle of Towton (1461), by far the bloodiest battle of the war (some 28,000 men perished).[42] The lone figure of Henry, isolated from the fighting, muses on the pains of high office. He states a desire to be 'no better than a homely swain, / To sit upon a hill as I do now, / To carve out dials quaintly, point by point, / Thereby to see the minutes how they run' (2.5.22–25).[43] His reverie is rudely awakened by the entry of 'A Sonne that hath kill'd his Father, at one doore; and a Father that hath kill'd his Sonne at another doore.'[44] When the son, evidently a 'homely swain', searches for the body of the man he has killed in a hand-to-hand combat to see if his victim has a store of coins that will at least yield some profit from the day's slaughter, he discovers that he has killed his father. This shock is balanced by the discovery of the other combatant, who also plans to search his victim for gold, that he has killed his son.

Although he is an ineffective king, Henry is an astute enough commentator to realize the correct moral to the story: 'Whiles lions war and battle for their dens, / Poor harmless lambs abide their enmity' (2.5.74–75). The failure of those who are supposed to govern is the key issue of the play, just as it was in the *Pharsalia*. In fifteenth-century England the lion does not lie down with the lamb but transforms the lamb into a petty lion. Civil war infects the whole realm, as the squabbles over the body of Henry V suggest.[45] Henry may well envy the lives of those who are not born great, but he is then shown what the effects of aristocratic conflict usually are, a blindness already thrown into relief by the previous scene which shows Clifford and Richard, Duke of Gloucester, pursuing their murderous feud, one that does not end when they are both dead. When Henry is finally defeated by the Yorkist forces led by Edward IV, Queen Margaret comments that England has become a 'slaughterhouse' (5.4.78), an appropriate conclusion for a play which owes so much to the *Pharsalia*.

Indeed, throughout the three plays we are constantly aware of the example of Julius Caesar, a malign ghostly presence who haunts the major historical figures, constantly reminding the audience that civil war is likely to produce a dictator.[46] In *Henry VI, Part One*, following on from the initial reference to Caesar in the opening scene, Joan La Pucelle refers to herself as the 'English scourge' (1.2.129), a reference likely to remind readers of Tamburlaine's self-appointed role as the 'scourge of God'.[47] She concludes her speech to the Dauphin with a striking and unfamiliar image: 'Now am I like that proud insulting ship / Which Caesar and his fortune bore at once' (lines 138–39). The reference is not directly to the

Pharsalia, but to Plutarch's 'Life of Julius Caesar'.[48] Nevertheless, the incident referred to did take place during the civil war with Pompey. According to Plutarch, Caesar, separated from his army, disguised himself and undertook a dangerous voyage to Brundisium in an unsuitably small boat so that he could rejoin his troops. When a sudden storm threatened the safety of the sailors, Caesar revealed his identity to the captain and assured him that nothing could happen to them because it was his destiny to rule Rome. The crew, fortified by Caesar's confidence, rowed onwards. However,

perceiving they laboured in vain, and that the pinnace took in abundance of water, and was ready to sink, Caesar then to his great grief was driven to return back again. Who when he was returned unto his camp, his soldiers came in great companies unto him, and were very sorry, that he mistrusted he was not able with them alone to overcome his enemies, but would put his person in danger, to go fetch them that were absent, putting no trust in them that were present.[49]

This is a vitally important allusion for two principal reasons. First, it makes an explicit historical link between the events of the fourteenth century and the end of the Roman republic, sustaining the connection made in the opening scene of the play. Second, Joan is evidently unaware of the outcome of the story, its problematic nature, and the thick layers of irony that surround it. The attempt fails and the moral is that Caesar is supremely and recklessly confident, arrogantly putting no trust in his army. In the short term he is vulnerable. In the medium term he is vindicated with his triumph over Pompey and assumption of power in Rome. In the long term he is more seriously exposed, trusting his advisers and close friends, who conspire and succeed in killing him, an ironic reversal of Caesar's behaviour here – although his later blind trust is again a result of his myopic arrogance, as Shakespeare later dramatized. And, of course, the subsequent history of Rome further complicates our understanding of the behaviour and legacy of Caesar. It is worth noting that Caesar's famous boast, 'Veni, vidi, vici', is mocked in both *Love's Labour's Lost* (1594–98), through Armado's preposterous usage (4.1.70), and *As You Like It* (1599), when Rosalind refers disparagingly to 'Caesar's thrasonical brag' (5.2.30).[50]

Joan, like Caesar, has a complicated and diverse historical significance. She initially succeeds in defeating the English; she is then captured and burnt; but, eventually the French manage to drive the English out of France, culminating in the recapture of Calais during the reign of Mary (1558). The moral would seem to be that confidence in being able to predict the future from any historical point is invariably a sign of hubris.

The English civil wars lead to the advent of the Tudors, so in one sense Joan helps pave the way for the triumph of Elizabeth, weakening the Lancastrian faction, who are defeated by the Yorkists, before losing out to the future Henry VII. But in the early 1590s, England stood at a dangerous crossroads, which was why the link between the Roman and English civil wars was such a potent – and common – one to make.

Furthermore, Joan is represented in this scene in language that uncomfortably recalls the ways in which Elizabeth was represented as a queen specially chosen by God, going beyond other women and assuming masculine virtues. Joan also stands alone in front of the French knights, calling their bluff: 'My courage try, if thou dar'st, / And thou shalt find that I exceed my sex' (lines 89–90). When she defeats the Dauphin in single combat, he has to beg for mercy: 'Stay, stay thy hands. Thou art an Amazon, / And fightest with the sword of Deborah' (lines 104–5). Elizabeth was defended as queen because she had gone beyond her sex, most famously in Bishop John Aylmer's response to John Knox, and was endless portrayed as Deborah and an Amazon, very recently in the well-known Tilbury speech of 1588.[51] The play forms a neat and potent link between Caesar, Joan and Elizabeth, suggesting that the Roman civil war, the Anglo-French war of the fourteenth century / Wars of the Roses, and any future conflict that might result from the succession crisis in the 1590s, were catastrophic events that needed to be linked in the minds of the reader/audience. Elizabeth, impressive Amazonian queen that she was, might well leave a historical legacy that resembled that of Joan La Pucelle – as well as Julius Caesar. When Charles later celebrates Joan as 'Divinest creature, Astrea's daughter' (1.7.4), the connection would seem to be hard to miss, given the ubiquitous comparison of Elizabeth to the goddess of justice.[52] The Duke of Alençon, the namesake of Elizabeth's prospective husband, is also present, making his only real appearance onstage in this scene, one wonders whether Shakespeare was seeing just how far he could push the historical links.[53]

Furthermore, the lines raise the related questions of date of composition and performance. Do they provide evidence that *Henry VI, Part One* was written after the other two plays to build on their success? If so, are these carefully crafted references to Lucan and the civil war between Caesar and Pompey a means of exploiting and developing what was more implicit in the first two plays? This order of composition would suggest that Shakespeare and his co-authors realized the commercial potential of representing English history in a republican way and sought to continue this in subsequent works, as Shakespeare later did when he wrote *Julius*

Caesar as the first play to be performed at the Globe. The careful and resonant intellectual significance of the allusion might also suggest that the lines were designed to be read as much as performed, a further indication of the play's serious nature as a form of English history writing, which seeks to contextualize English history in terms of a foreign past and potential future.

Henry VI, Part One contains further references which suggest that the play was written with Lucan's epic in mind. Talbot, the doomed military hero noted by Marlowe, treats France as Nero treated Rome, boasting to Salisbury that he will 'like thee, Nero, / Play on the lute, beholding the towns burn' (1.5.73–74).[54] The source of the allusion is most probably Suetonius, who represents Nero as obsessed with music, especially his own favourite instrument, the lyre. When he deliberately set Rome on fire, 'Pretending to be disgusted by the drab old buildings and narrow, winding streets', he put on his 'tragedian's costume and sang *The Fall of Illium* from beginning to end'.[55]

The allusive nature of the reference is again complex. Nero does not seem an obvious point of comparison for the stalwart English hero and hammer of the French, Talbot. However, the image does appear at a crux in the play, as a few lines later Salisbury is killed by a stray shot from the battlements of Orléans, inspiring Talbot to vow endless revenge on the French led by Joan and the Dauphin:

> Frenchmen, I'll be a Salisbury to you,
> Puzzel or pucelle, dolphin or dogfish,
> Your hearts I'll stamp out with my horses heels
> And make a quagmire of your mangled brains. (lines 1.5.84–87)

Talbot may be a great military hero but he can do little other than threaten and kill, so that the play establishes a balance of forces: Salisbury and Talbot against Joan and the Dauphin. With Salisbury dead so early in the play – he actually died in 1428 before the siege of Orléans – the odds are stacked in favour of the French. All the efforts of Talbot may be as ineffective – certainly as far as the French are concerned – as those of Nero and it is another sign of hubris that the death of his chief ally occurs after his ignorant boast, demonstrating that he is as poor a reader of history as Joan. We do indeed witness endless violent acts, but they generally take place in England rather than France. The resemblance that Talbot bears to Tamburlaine is also unlikely to be purely accidental.

The other significant aspect of the image, of course, is that Nero was emperor when Lucan wrote *Pharsalia*, the opening lines drawing the

legendary tyrant into the course of the action. The French and the English
are shown not to realize the implications of their conflict as they simply
concentrate, like Lucan's antiheroes, on victory at all costs (and it may
well be relevant that sixteenth-century France, like fifteenth-century
England, was blighted by a vicious civil war).[56] The people who have to
fight the wars have been written out of the struggle. Given the catastrophic violence that develops in the subsequent plays – ones that had
probably already been written – Talbot's myopia assumes a further
importance, sealed with his Lucanesque image of violent slaughter.

When Henry VI tries to unite the first warring factions, Gloucester and
Warwick, he employs another arresting image, warning them that 'Civil
dissension is a viperous worm / That gnaws the bowels of the commonwealth' (3.1.72–73). The image has numerous precedents, but it may be
designed to recall a key passage in Lucan that came to have a major
significance in the seventeenth century, 'the extinction and literal evapor-
ation of Cato's army in the Libyan desert'.[57] Some of Cato's army are
killed by the numerous venomous snakes that originate and flourish in the
North African deserts, such as the unlucky Aules, 'standard-bearer of
Etruscan blood', who steps on a 'Dipsas', which fatally wounds him.
Lucan's description makes it clear that there is more at stake here than the
poisoning of a soldier:

> Hardly was there pain or a sensation of a bite, and even death's
> appearance is not malignant and the injury does not look
>   [threatening.
> Look – the silent venom creeps along, and devouring fire
> eats away the marrows and with hot decay it sets the guts ablaze.
> The poison drinks up moisture spread around
> the vital parts and starts to parch the tongue
> on his dry palate; there was no sweat to pass across
> the tired frame, the stream of tears reconciled from the eyes.
> Not the glory of the state, not the authority of saddened Cato
> could stop the burning warrior from boldly scattering
> the standards and in his frenzy seeking far and wide
> the waters which the thirsty poison in his heart demanded.[58]

All that remains of Aules is his name and the manner of his death.
Lucan demonstrates at great length – the description of the deaths of
the soldiers from snakebite continues for more than a hundred lines –
how the army is consumed until nothing remains, a striking emblem of
the effects of civil war, which destroys a society from within, no one being
able to pinpoint exactly when the process of decay and destruction begins.

This is, of course, true of the first Henriad, as it is of the history of republican Rome. As the last lines of this passage indicate, the slide cannot be halted by a return to politics. No such intervention has a chance of saving the infected body politic, as Cato discovers. The future triumph of Caesar already has too much momentum to be prevented.

In the same way, we know that the squabbles over the body of Henry V will lead to the brief glory of Richard III, who, like Caesar, knows more about reaching the throne than how to occupy it. Neither can Aules's frantic, violent activity prevent his death, a fate that might be compared to the mighty Marlovian feats of Talbot, which fail to revive the factitious English body politic. That Henry can identify what is happening to the kingdom he nominally rules does not give him the power to cure the deadly wound. The loyal choric figure, the Duke of Exeter, recognizes this inevitability at the end of the scene. He notes, sardonically, that 'we may march in England or in France / Not seeing what is likely to ensue' (lines 190–91), which not only shows that the Anglo-French and the English civil war are inextricably linked, but also reinforces our sense that neither Joan nor Talbot knows where their military prowess will lead them or the nations they serve. Talbot's death, as Sir William Lucy recognizes, occurs through 'The fraud of England, not the force of France' (4.5.36); Joan denies her true lineage before she is burnt (5.5.23–33), a further indication that she is a displaced character, not quite what she seems to be. Exeter provides another Lucanesque image as a means of commenting on the fate of the English body politic:

> This late dissension grown betwixt the peers
> Burns under feignèd ashes of forged love,
> And will at last break out into a flame.
> As festered members rot but by degree
> Till bones and flesh and sinews fall away. (lines 192–96)

The disturbing image of flesh falling off bones so that the body disappears is one of the key motifs of Lucan's description of the fate of Cato's army. Poor 'miserable Sabellus', bitten by 'a tiny Seps', ceases to possess corporeal form:

> The membrane which binds the belly burst apart, and out melt
> the entrails; and not as much as there should be from an
> > [entire body
> melts into the ground, but the savage poison boils
> the limbs down; death shrinks the whole into a tiny pool of venom.
> All that makes a human being is uncovered by the unholy nature
> > of the killer.[59]

The social whole and the individuals who form it simply disappear. They can only be reconstructed and remembered through literature, a realization central to the work of both Lucan and Shakespeare.

If *Henry VI, Part One* is a 'prequel', then it seems to have been written to develop what is latent in the first two plays. This suspicion is strengthened by possible revisions to *Henry VI, Part Two*. When Suffolk is about to be murdered by the fictional character Walter Whitmore, he compares himself to the great men of the ancient Roman world who suffered similar fates:

> Great men often die by vile Bezonians [beggars];
> A Roman soldier and banditto slave
> Murdered sweet Tully; Brutus' bastard hand
> Stabbed Caesar; savage islanders
> Pompey the Great; and Suffolk dies by pirates. (4.1.136–40)

The *Contention* includes the reference to Cicero and Caesar and Brutus, but does not have the reference to Pompey.[60] Any mention of Pompey was likely to have had the effect of triggering a memory of the *Pharsalia*, especially when juxtaposed with the name of Caesar, indicating that whoever revised the text wanted to stress this particular subtext. Even so, Suffolk's words do him little credit. The example of Cicero, murdered by the agents of Antony when Octavian/Augustus reluctantly agrees that the champion of the republic must be disposed of, is at odds with his attack on Brutus, whose assassination of Caesar Cicero had – guardedly – supported. Suffolk shows that he understands history and politics no better than Talbot or Joan La Pucelle. Suffolk has simply sought glory for himself and paid little attention to the needs of the state. His death, in a sequence of plays in which many innocent people die, is one of those that is richly deserved. Yet again, the references to the history of Rome help determine our responses to the history of England.

Another reference to Caesar towards the end of the *True Tragedie* – not present in the folio – performs a similar role in that play. When Warwick, the powerful king-maker now fighting for the Yorkist faction, is fatally wounded by Clarence, Edward addresses him in words that also recall the most celebrated assassination of all time: '*Et tu* Brute, wilt thou stab *Cesar* too?' (Sig. G3r). The two texts are markedly different at this point.[61] In *Henry VI, Part Three*, Warwick has decided to rejoin the Lancastrian forces and calls Clarence over. In the *True Tragedie*, no such plan is conceived. The line, an adaptation of Suetonius's record of Caesar's rebuke to Brutus when he is about to deliver the fatal blow, 'You, too, my son?', predates the better-known repetition of the words in *Julius Caesar*.[62] It is significant, of course, that Shakespeare – or his co-authors – should make the link between English and Roman history before the famous words are dramatized in their natural historical setting.

The historical precedent is, yet again, a major clue as to how we should read the *True Tragedie*. Edward's identification with Caesar does him no more credit than Suffolk's use of classical historical precedent did, and exposes him as yet another unscrupulous, overambitious figure within the sequence. The jibe that Warwick is really Brutus is designed to represent him as an unscrupulous traitor. However, it also has the effect of emphasizing both his power to make and unmake kings, and the fact that kings do have to be installed by their subjects because they cannot assume control simply by right, the obvious, albeit dangerous, conclusion to draw from reading a history of the Wars of the Roses.[63] Again, the speaker shows that the historical example he cites does not mean what he wants it to mean and makes the position they are trying to articulate more, rather than less, problematic. In comparing English kingship to Roman dictatorship, Edward effectively demystifies and denaturalizes the myth of a hereditary succession, one of the chief political languages used in the play by all claimants to the throne.[64] Warwick is elevated to Edward's equal, an aristocrat who could be king. He may well be a traitor as Edward alleges, but the king's words dignify his actions as those of a republican traitor.

For all the emphasis made by the characters on their legitimate claims to the throne, the *Contention* and the *True Tragedie* show that kingship is a pragmatic office, earned most frequently by successful military victories not natural right.[65] York tries to persuade Warwick and the other assembled nobles that he should be the legitimate ruler of England: 'Let me reveale unto your honors here, / The right and title of the house of Yorke, / To Englands Crowne by lineall descent.' Warwick positions himself as a neutral ready to be persuaded if York can mount a decent defence: 'Then Yorke begin, and if they claime be good, / The Nevills are thy subjects to commaund' (*Contention*, Sig. C4v). Warwick's words are more a scarcely veiled threat than a protestation of loyalty. Warwick can be commanded as a subject if his sovereign can make a good-enough case. In this fractious world unconditional loyalty is a sign of fatal weakness. York's success is based on the fact that he is able to persuade others that he looks and acts like a king, until he overreaches himself and is defeated. Indeed, he is not the only king-like figure in the play. Queen Margaret points out to her husband that the nominal king, Humphrey, Duke of Gloucester, whom she wants dispatched, has a regal bearing and pretension: 'See you not the

Commons follow him / In troupes, crying, God save the good Duke Humphrey, / And with long life Jesus preserve his grace, / Honoring him as if he were a King' (Sig. D4r). The irony is that the murder of the Duke of Gloucester helps pave the way for the rise of York as a pretender, achieved partly through his alliance with the commoner, Jack Cade. Furthermore, it is his son who is then able to become Duke of Gloucester, on the way to his brief rule as Richard III.

York's unholy strategic alliance with Cade in *Henry VI, Part Two*, a link that has no connection in the chronicles available to Shakespeare, further illustrates both the power vacuum in England, and the levelling effect that the questioning of hierarchy inevitably has.[66] Nevertheless, the ground for this dangerous alliance has been carefully prepared for us. In the central scene of the play, Henry swoons when he learns of Gloucester's death, making those around him assume that he is dead.[67] After a long, self-pitying speech by Queen Margaret, Warwick enters with 'many Commons'.[68] He announces that 'the Commons like an angry hive of bees / That want their leader, scatter up and down / And care not who they sting in his revenge' (3.2.125–27). The familiar image of the commonwealth as an ordered hive of bees, central to a whole variety of literary and political works such as John Lyly's *Euphues and his England* (1580) and Charles Butler's *The Feminine Monarchie or a treatise concerning bees* (London, 1609), is transformed from a comforting to a threatening political image.[69] It is hardly surprising that the commons fall under the sway of Cade, promoted by the Duke of York, given the failings of the nation's rulers. The death of the good duke and the actions of the feeble king and self-pitying queen are all drawn to our attention in this scene, verbally and visually, a clear contrast being made between the manic energy of the commons and the inept, insular-looking behaviour of the royal family.

Cade's rebellion is explicitly represented in class terms. One of the rebels, George, claims that 'Jack Cade the clothier means to dress the commonwealth, and turn it, and set a new nap upon it' (4.2.4–5), a complex image that represents England as naked and in need of new (political) clothes, something we have seen to be true, given the failings of the central monarchy and the warring aristocracy. How these words might have been applied to the situation in the early 1590s is a matter for considerable speculation. George further comments that 'the King's Council are no good workmen' (lines 12–13), a double-edged comment that mixes class envy with an astute assessment of how the realm is being governed. Nick's response might seem like faulty syllogistic logic, and therefore easy enough to dismiss out of hand, but it simply follows from what George has already noted: 'and yet is said, "Labour in thy vocation"; which is as much to say as, "Let the magistrates be labouring men"; and therefore we be magistrates' (14–16).[70]

Cade himself does at least pay lip service to the pretence that he has aristocratic blood, when Sir Humphrey Stafford attempts to persuade his followers to return to proper order:

> STAF: Why country-men, what meane you thus in troups,
>   To follow this rebellious traitor Cade?
>   Why his father was but a Brick-laier.
> CADE: Well, Adam was a Gardner, what then?
>   But I come of the Mortimers. (Sig. F4v)

Cade's words draw our attention to the theatrical nature of the moment. He undercuts his claim to be of noble blood with his opening rhetorical question, showing that he knows, as the audience does, that the claim is fictitious: first, because it is false, and, second, because it simply does not matter. Cade's brief period of glory is carnival time, as his vulgar command that 'The pissing conduit run nothing but red wine' (Sig. G1r) indicates, an inversion of the hierarchy that Stafford in vain tries to reestablish.[71] The lower orders have found a voice and can challenge their supposed betters because nothing fits into its place anymore. Cade's question alludes to John Ball's famous rhyme, 'When Adam delved and Eve span, / Who was then the Gentleman?', a rallying cry in the Peasants' Revolt of 1381, which later assumed importance in the civil war of the seventeenth century.[72] His insouciance triggers a metatheatrical moment: Cade's refusal to take the difference between a bricklayer and an earl seriously draws our attention to the fact that we are watching actors performing, men dressed up as kings and aristocrats who are changing places for the duration of the play.[73] When we learn that Cade 'hath sworne / To crowne himselfe King in Westminster' (Sig. G1v), we know that he will succeed if only he has the power, a reminder of what the actors on stage could be if they also had the means that Cade seems to have at that moment.[74]

The only figure in the plays who does seriously believe in natural law and rights is Henry VI, a creed that, paradoxically, makes him incapable of ruling effectively.[75] In the opening scene of the *True Tragedie*, Henry is forced to admit that his title is weaker than that of York, a confession that leads to chaos as different solutions to the problem, all of them unsatisfactory, are proposed. Warwick urges Richard to claim the English crown

(Sig. A2r), but then he is seen changing sides when Edward IV falls for Lady Elizabeth Grey and humiliates Warwick who has been arranging a match with the sister-in-law of the French king. Warwick, yet again, shows that he sees himself as a free agent able to serve which monarch he chooses: 'No more my King, for he dishonours me, / And most himselfe, if he could see his shame.' Queen Margaret, recognizing Warwick's power and success, welcomes him back into the fold: 'Yes *Warwicke* I do quite forget thy former faults. / If now thou wilt become king *Henries* friend' (Sig. F1r). Warwick can see no problem with his behaviour, admitting to the Lancastrians that he left Edward as his ambassador to France, but returned 'his sworne and mortall foe' (Sig. F1v). When Hastings declares, in the following scene, 'Let England be true within it selfe, / We need not Fraunce nor any alliance with them' (Sig. F2r), he speaks truer than he knows. England is being true to its current self in fighting a bloody civil war, needing no help from France to achieve this.

The heart of the trouble has been caused by the abdication of Richard II, as becomes clear in the opening scene when Henry and Richard rehearse their claims to the throne. Henry makes a bold defence of his right to rule, which leaves him more exposed than secure:

> Suppose by right and equitie thou be King,
> Thinkst thou that I will leave my Kingly seate
> Wherein my father and my grandfather sate?
> No, first shall warre unpeople this my realme,
> I, and our colours often borne in *Fraunce*,
> And now in *England* to our heartes great sorrow
> Shall be my winding sheete: why faint you Lords?
> My title's better then his. (Sig. A3v)

The bathos of the last line – one of the few potentially comic moments in an otherwise unrelentingly grim play – points up how hollow Henry's boasts are. As he well knows, his title to the throne rests on Bolingbroke's overthrow of Richard II, a crucial passage in English history that was transformed into a Lucanesque poem by Samuel Daniel soon after Shakespeare co-wrote the *Henry VI* plays.[76] Henry is forced into arguing two weak defences of his kingship. First, that he should possess the throne because of his grandfather's successful rebellion, a manoeuvre that plays into the hands of York: '*King*: Why, *Henrie* the fourth by conquest got the crowne / *Yor*: Twas by rebellion gainst his Soveraigne.' York's rebellion cannot be condemned if the king is going to defend his own right to rule on such flimsy grounds. In an aside, Henry admits that he is at a serious disadvantage: 'I know not what to say, my title's weak' (Sig. A3v). As a result, he changes tack, arguing that a king might adopt an heir:

> Then am I lawfull King, for *Richard*
> The second, in the view of many Lords,
> Resignde the Crowne to *Henrie* the fourth,
> Whose heire my father was, and I am his. (Sig. A4r)

York returns to his insistence that Henry is only king through the rebellion of his ancestors, but Henry has already given himself nowhere to turn. If the crown can be transferred from one monarch to another, then there can be no *necessary* reason why any one line of kings should be preserved in power rather than another. As the audience would have been only too well aware, the Wars of the Roses ended with the triumph of Henry VII, Elizabeth's great-grandfather, who had no more right to rule than the king he deposed.[77] Mary Stuart had a better claim than Elizabeth in the eyes of many, so York's defence of his rebellion could not but have had a topical resonance, especially given Elizabeth's refusal to declare who would be her heir.[78] When York demands that Henry 'Confirme the Crowne to me and to mine heires, / And thou shalt raigne in quiet whilst thou liv'st' (Sig. A4r), the political situation in the play mirrors almost exactly the state of England after the execution of Mary. James, keen to inherit the English throne, pledged loyalty to Elizabeth, on the understanding that he would become the next king of England.[79]

The compromise does not work and fails to prevent the continuation of the civil war, simply serving to divide the nation into ever more dangerously powerful factions. Clifford's protestation of loyalty to Henry shows how far removed England has become from a world in which natural rights rule: 'King *Henrie* be thy title right or wrong, / Lord *Clifford* vowes to fight in they defence' (Sig. A4r). Clifford's personal loyalty to his lord is admirable, especially in a world of poisonous ambition and sly treachery, but it also indicates that there are no commonly agreed rules and laws for people to obey. The constitution does not work, as there is no general consensus about the succession of the crown, which has not remained within one family, nor is there a formal means for passing it on from one monarch to the next.

Three parallels might be cited, providing an insight into the place of the *True Tragedie* within a larger political culture. First, the bloody history of Scotland, which was widely known in England through Holinshed's *Chronicles*, the role played by Mary and later, James, and plays such as *Hamlet*. In Scotland the succession was always contested:

Kenneth III's constitutional changes made little difference to this stubborn fact of Scottish life (see Chapter 6). Second, the contemporary situation in England, with discussion of the succession forbidden even though it was the one political event that was most likely to have an impact on peoples' lives. Third, the anarchy that developed after the decline of the Roman republic, leading to civil war, and the triumph of the dictator Caesar, who ruled by right of conquest.

York emerges as a type of Lucan's Caesar in the *True Tragedie*, resolving to 'win the crowne or die' (Sig. B1v), not caring what horrors he foists on his native land in the process. One of the constant narrative motifs of the *Pharsalia* is a series of constant reminders of the cost of Caesar's ambition:

> added to these horrors [the battles fought], Caesar, be the
> [famine of Perusia,
> and the struggles of Mutina, the fleets overwhelmed
> near rugged Leucas, and the slave wars under burning Etna;
> yet Rome owes much to citizens' weapons, because it was
> [for you that all was done.[80]

Caesar becomes dictator because his abilities enable him to triumph over his enemies. York's success is built on the same principles. In the folio version of *Henry VI, Part Two*, he boasts in an aside when confronting the Duke of Buckingham that he is 'better born than is the King, / More like a king, more kingly in my thoughts' (5.1.28–29), and is frustrated that he has to wait to seize the crown.[81] York fails when his forces are defeated at the Battle of Wakefield. He is taunted when he is crowned with a paper crown by the triumphant Queen Margaret, the words echoing the earlier aside: '*Yorke* cannot speake, unlesse he weare a Crowne. / A Crowne for *Yorke*? and Lords bow low to him? / So: hold you his hands while I do set it on, / I, now lookes he like a King' (*Contention*, Sig. B3v).[82]

Margaret's baiting of York, such a powerful stage image, serves as an emblem of the civil war, one that is developed as a structuring device in the play. It assumes an even greater importance in *Richard III*, reminding the audience that just because events happened some time ago does not mean that they do not have a contemporary significance – the deposition of Richard II being the obvious example.[83] When Margaret confronts Richard, the two trade insults. Eventually, the long list of victims on either side that each can cite assumes the character of a game of rhetorical substitution, so that the civil war becomes a black comedy of name-calling, its horror now deadened:

MARG: Thou slander of thy heavy mother's womb,
Thou loathed issue of thy father's loins,
Thou rag of honour, thou detested –
RICH: Margaret!
MARG: Richard!
RICH: Ha?
MARG: I call thee not.
RICH: I cry thee mercy then, for I did think
That thou hadst call'd me all these bitter names.[84]

   The two powerful and murderous figures appear as disgruntled infants, clever, energetic and quick to react, but far too irresponsible to rule a country. When Richard does ascend to the throne, he has no idea how to govern because he has been trained to plot and fight not pass laws, arbitrate in disputes and plan for the future.[85] Of course, he is not entirely to blame: no one has really governed England for more than a century, unless the triumphs of Henry V in France are counted.[86] It is little wonder that, without proper examples and institutional support, the governing class seem so petty, vindictive and self-interested. The repetitive use of a repetitive rhetorical figure, anaphora, expresses the mindset of those who rule in England:

MARG: I had an Edward, till a Richard kill'd him;
I had a husband, till a Richard kill'd him:
Thou hadst an Edward, till a Richard kill'd him.
Thou hadst a Richard, till a Richard Kill'd him.
DUCH: I had a Richard too, and thou didst kill him;
I had a Rutland too: thou holp'st to kill him.
MARG: Thou hadst a Clarence too, and Richard kill'd him.
                                    (4.4.40–46)[87]

The fact that the two women both blame Richard shows the war playing itself out and finally moving towards a conclusion. The use of rhetorical skills for such a personal goal – revenge – indicates that, like Rome in the age of Caesar, England has lost sight of the noble art of speech and government, rulers no longer seeing themselves as answerable to a wider public.[88] Richmond's closing speech is a conscious attempt to move beyond this stultifying sense of political and linguistic impasse. He plans to 'unite the white rose and the red', and end the tit-for-tat slaughter that has become the norm: 'England hath long been mad, and scarr'd herself: / The brother blindly shed the brother's blood; / The father rashly slaugh-ter'd his own son; / The son, compell'd, been butcher to the site' (5.5.23–26). Richmond's lines are clearly a riposte to the violent killings that have

torn families apart, specifically those that Henry VI witnesses at the battle
of Towton in the *Contention*, as well as the arid insular culture of revenge
that has paralysed the governing class in *Richard III*. Richmond plans to
put an end to the 'civil wounds' (line 40) and create an England worthy of
the peace. In contrast, Richard's world has shrunk ever smaller until he
has lost sight of why a king exists at all. His last, famous line, 'A horse! A
horse! My kingdom for a horse' (5.5.12), confirms our understanding that
he sees the land as the king's possession to use and trade as he pleases, one
of the key definitions of a tyrant.[89] It also shows how much has been lost
in the process.

Richmond makes no specific recommendations as to what this new
England will look like nor how it will be governed. We are given a
framework with which to imagine it, however, one that depends on our
following through key historical comparisons made throughout the sequence of plays. The culmination of the references to Julius Caesar occurs
when Richard is cast as the dictator in a key scene, the last one in which
the two young princes, sons of Edward IV, appear before they are
murdered in what was already understood to be the gravest crime committed by an English king.[90] When Richard urges the two young princes
to stay in the Tower of London for their safety, Prince Edward asks
whether Julius Caesar was responsible for building it. Buckingham tells
him that he was, and the prince presses him about the records, 'say, my
lord, it were not reigister'd, / Methinks the truth should live from age to
age, / As 'twere retail'd to all posterity, / Even to the general all-ending
day' (lines 75–78), introducing an eschatological context. When the prince
overhears Richard's aside, 'So wise so young, they say, do never live long'
(line 79), Richard is forced to equivocate, claiming that he was making a
general historical point, 'without characters [i.e., written records] fame
lives long' (line 81), boasting in a second aside that 'like the formal Vice,
Iniquity', he moralizes 'two meanings on one word' (lines 82–83).[91]
Richard's reference to the stage figure of the Vice alerts us to the significance of this exchange as a metatheatrical moment.[92] The prince
concludes his comments on Julius Caesar using another popular rhetorical
figure, antimetabole ('where two or more words are repeated in inverse
order'): 'With what his valour did enrich his wit, / His wit set down to
make his valour live.'[93] Caesar, according to Prince Edward, has conquered death because he now 'lives in fame, though not in life' (line 88).
He completes the scene with a dramatic irony full of pathos: 'if I live until
I be a man, / I'll win our ancient right in France again, / Or die a soldier,
as I liv'd a king' (lines 91–93), which draws another pointed ironic

comment from Richard, designed for the audience: 'Short summers lightly have a forward spring' (line 94), a reference to the famous second line of the play.

This is a complex and immensely important exchange which draws together most of the significant issues raised not just in *Richard III*, but also the *Henry VI* plays. It has no source, and has tended either to baffle commentators, or has been read as a comment on the vicissitudes of fame.[94] However, the scene assumes a whole new range of meanings when read in the light of the republican analysis of civil war. Prince Edward does not appreciate the historical role(s) of Julius Caesar, seeing him simply as a military conqueror and a builder of empire, symbolized by his construction of the Tower of London. He has clearly based his understanding of Caesar on his reading of Caesar's *Commentaries* on his conquests of Britain and Gaul, a popular work which was translated into English in 1565 (reprinted in 1590), following a partial translation printed in 1530.[95] Caesar's commentaries were a central feature in humanist education systems practised in England in the sixteenth century.[96] Lucan's *Pharsalia* was also an integral part of a humanist education, although this work was studied rather later in the child's schooling. One aspect of the pathos of Edward's words is that he will never have the chance to read this work. He will not live to complete his education and so produce the more rounded judgements that his comments on the nature of history indicate he has the capacity to make, a fate that also befell a more recent prince who received a humanist education, Edward VI.[97]

Caesar was indeed famous and does live in fame as Edward recognizes. However, he was famous not simply for his imperial conquests, but also for destroying the republic and causing a bloody civil war. It is probably this historical narrative that has the greater validity for him as the ruler who will govern after the Wars of the Roses, hence the importance of the discussion of historical record. Humanist reading practices demanded that a reader consider a variety of relevant passages and then choose the most appropriate one for the situation in question.[98] Prince Edward's desire to conquer France for the glory of his country follows directly from his praise of Caesar, indicating that the warrior king serves as his model for his own projected reign. He has the good of his nation at heart – unlike Richard – but not the means, as yet, to implement this empathy. History, however, as the discussion of records and reports demonstrates, delivers a more complex and less secure sense of truth than Edward realizes. Reading the account of Caesar in the *Pharsalia* would change Edward's conviction. Edward's fear of the Tower is a clear sign that his childish consciousness has already registered that all is not well, and his admiration for Caesar – for which there is no historical record – will be tempered when he learns more about him. Edward – like his Tudor namesake – reveals all the signs that he would be a good king if he were given the chance.

This reversibility, in which a particular form of words can be redescribed, recontextualized, and so assigned a different meaning, is one of the chief rhetorical figures employed in arguments throughout the early modern period in England, namely, paradiastole.[99] As John Roe has pointed out, 'Paradiastole registers the ease with which virtue may be depicted as vice, and, contrarily, how vice may be made to look like virtue.'[100] It is this element of reversibility which is so evident in Richard's sly use of proverbs and his asides, especially the calculating line that ends the exchange, which will be read by the characters onstage to mean that the boy is precocious and will have much of value to say before long, but the bond between Richard and the audience means that we know that Edward has little time left to live. Richard revels in his self-appointed role as the 'formal vice', but we also know that his sense of the triumph of the 'glorious summer' ending the 'winter of our discontent' (1.1.1–2) is a false dawn and, like Edward, he and the house of York are also doomed.

This wordplay further reveals the extent of the degeneration of England's body politic, and the disappearance of a forum – a Senate, a parliament – for proper argument on equal terms. Political language has become either the shrill lament uttered by the women characters, or the deceitful banter of the men. Richard's quick wit and humour help disguise and dilute the full impact of his tyrannical behaviour. One of the key effects of the development of tyranny was the decline of proper political debate, based largely on the model of Cicero's extant writings. Arguments could be made for two opposing viewpoints before the audience would decide which was the most persuasive, carefully weighing up the merits of each case. Under tyranny, such reasonable forms of decision-making degenerated into flattery, debased and specious argument, and dictatorial command.[101]

Here we witness the talented young humanist prince, in the middle of an education that will equip him to rule benevolently and wisely, become the butt for the clever but pointless humour of those who will rule as badly as is conceivably possible. Edward is learning how to argue as a humanist prince should. He listens to counsel from his elders and is keen to weigh up the pros and cons of any argument, a laudable trait that Richard uses for his own amusement and as a means of flattering and seducing the audience into imagining that his crimes are roguish rather than wicked. Richard's jokes are, after all, a prelude to murder. Moreover, Richard's manic use of paradiastole, reducing anything virtuous to fodder for his own rise to power, is a criminal abuse of rhetoric, which marks him out as a vicious tyrant, like Milton's Satan, in another republican text.[102] It is no accident that it is Richard who seems like a naughty child in this scene, gleefully subverting the words of the young man he is about to have murdered, and showing that his own words are there simply to serve his purposes. There is no common language of politics under his tyrannous rule.[103] In doing so he shows that he is like Tiberius, Caligula and Nero, the tyrants for whom Julius Caesar paved the way – especially Nero, who had Lucan killed. As the histories of Suetonius and Tacitus revealed, silence rather than eloquence was the best policy under such regimes, even though the disappearance of the body politic led to the decline of Rome as resources were needlessly wasted and fear prevented innovation and proper management.[104]

The murder of Edward is the last slaughter of the English body politic, the good prince killed off by the evil usurper; the humanist republican king falling prey to the tyrant. After this, Richard has no one to teach him how to rule, an art he has neglected to learn, and the way is paved for a return to proper government only, after yet another military campaign, with the advent of the Tudors, who, at least, espoused the humanist ideal of the 'mixed' constitution, even if they did not always live up to it. Perhaps the leading testament of Tudor political theory, one that came to seem increasingly under threat in the 1590s, was Sir Thomas Smith's *De Republican Anglorum*, readily available in Holinshed's *Chronicles*, the main source for the first four history plays.[105] Smith's treatise, written during the first decade of Elizabeth's reign, was the product of his experience of government during the reign of Edward VI, the lost humanist Tudor king, who bears more than a passing resemblance to the precocious Prince Edward in *Richard III*, and so serves as a warning of what might happen if the ruling class lose sight of why they are where they are.[106]

CHAPTER 4

The beginning of the republic: Venus *and* Lucrece

The closure of the London public theatres in the summer of 1592 probably served to increase Shakespeare's involvement with republican literary forms and ideas. The theatres were shut down first because of a riot in Southwark, which broke out after those involved had 'assembled themselves by occasion & pretence of their meeting at a play'.[1] Although the theatres reopened in December, they were closed again in January 1593 because of an outbreak of plague and did not reopen again until after Christmas.[2] Theatre companies and the people they employed had to find alternative means of supporting themselves. Companies offset their loss of income by publishing plays, a means of acquiring a small income from the print run and also with the hope of encouraging audiences back to the theatres when they did reopen.[3] This must have been the reason behind the publication of the *Contention* in 1594, and then the *True Tragedy* a year later, part of a developing vogue for English history in the last years of Elizabeth's reign, with play texts forming lively, animated and brief contributions to debates (the most famous example being *Richard II*).[4] Neither text contains any preliminary material nor any attribution of authorship – although the *True Tragedy*'s title advertises the fact that 'it was sundry times acted by the Right Honourable the Earle of Pembroke his servantes' – possibly a sign of hasty publication.[5]

Shakespeare published three other works in this period which provide substantial clues to his inclinations, whether political or commercial or both, especially when taken together as a group. First he produced the erotic narrative epyllion *Venus and Adonis* (1593), a work on an Ovidian theme; then *The Rape of Lucrece* (1594), a longer poem narrating the events leading up to the foundation of the Roman republic; and a tragedy, *Titus Andronicus* (1594), a fictional Roman play without a source. The two poems were dedicated to the earl of Southampton, who had already become part of the circle of young, disaffected aristocrats, and the writers they brought in their wake, attached to Essex. Essex and his cohorts, most

130

notably Henry Cuffe, 'openly discussed . . . anti-absolutist ideas and oppositional views of history' when they gathered at Essex House.[6] Cuffe, sometime Regius Professor of Greek at Oxford, instructed his master in the ways of reading Lucan, and performed a similar service for Southampton, along with the earl of Rutland, using Aristotle's *Politics* to interpret the texts in so radical a way that he was credited with being the evil genius behind Essex's rebellion and so executed for his scholarship.[7]

Venus and Adonis describes a domineering, but ultimately unsuccessful, goddess in pursuit of an indifferent younger man, who eventually flees her attentions and escapes only through his untimely death at the tusks of a boar.[8] The poem was not always treated as a work of great profundity and many of the earliest readers were more attracted to the erotic nature of the descriptions than to the passages on the passing of youth and the inevitability of death.[9] Shakespeare had probably written *Venus and Adonis* with his potential patron in mind, given that Southampton was about to be forced into making a lucrative match about which he was less than enthusiastic, to the granddaughter of his guardian Lord Burghley, Lady Elizabeth Vere.[10] Equally significantly, the ridiculous figure of Venus, who is spared few indignities in the representation of her aggressive wooing of Adonis, culminating in her throwing him to the ground in a desperate attempt to arouse him, stands as a figure of the ageing queen, as one early – albeit eccentric – reader, William Reynolds, noted in his copy of the poem.[11] This undignified and unqueenly action is motivated by Venus's fear of Adonis resolving to hunt the boar, which it had been prophesied – correctly – would lead to his death.[12] When Adonis announces his decision to depart, Venus is given a long speech on the transitory nature of the world which contains numerous reflections that could apply to other contexts rather closer to home, as her concluding lines demonstrate:

> 'What is thy body but a swallowing grave,
> Seeming to bury that posterity,
> Which by the rights of time thou needs must have,
> If thou destroy them not in dark obscurity?
> If so, the world will hold thee in disdain,
> Sith in thy pride so fair a hope is slain.

> 'So in thyself art made away;
> A mischief worse than civil home-bred strife,
> Or theirs whose desperate hands themselves do slay,
> Or butcher sire that reaves his son of life.
> Foul cank'ring rust the hidden treasure frets,
> But gold that's put to use more gold begets.' (lines 757–68)[13]

Venus's speech has a significance that ranges far beyond her own situation in the poem, the words carefully chosen so that they can be applied to the more public, political situation of England ruled by Elizabeth in the 1590s. The notion of the body as a 'swallowing grave' which buries its own posterity is an eloquent image of human decay, but also functions as a comment on the impending death of the queen who was about to expire without leaving behind any posterity. Elizabeth, Shakespeare allegorically suggests, has neglected the rights of stable succession that her subjects expect, destroying them in a 'dark obscurity', perhaps a reference to her refusal to allow the question of the next monarch to be discussed.[14] The last couplet of this stanza, suggesting that the queen will be reviled because her pride has caused her to fail in her duty, is as aggressive a piece of anti-Elizabethan rhetoric as Spenser's attack on the aged Elizabeth in 'Two Cantos of Mutabilitie'.[15]

The final stanza expresses the common fear of the consequences of Elizabeth's failure, namely civil war. Venus claims that Adonis's frigid chastity is worse than 'civil home-bred strife', a forceful comment, especially given Shakespeare's leading role in the composition of the *Henry VI* plays, two parts of which were about to be published. Elizabeth stands condemned by the goddess of love for failing to see that the consequences of her virginity are more serious than she can possibly have imagined.[16] The disputed succession in the fifteenth century led to carnage that demanded to be interpreted in terms of the great republican antiepic of the ancient world, Lucan's *Pharsalia*. Elizabeth's failure to continue the Tudor dynasty that ended the conflict threatens to repeat this cycle of violence and reduce Tudor rule to the status of an interlude. The father killing his son is perhaps a reference to the scene Henry witnesses when trying to escape the painful rigours of high office and retreat into his own personal world: certainly, the recollection would be fitting here.[17] Adonis's crime is also seen as worse than suicide, the most deadly of all sins because God's creation was destroyed without the possibility of repentance and salvation.[18] By implication, Elizabeth's virginity is also a form of self-murder, a concentration on her personal body at the expense of her public body as monarch.[19]

The forceful political comment contained within *Venus and Adonis* has a number of pertinent resonances designed to appeal to the earl of Southampton. The reversible erotic/political language of the poem continues in the vein of Sidney's *Astrophil and Stella* (c.1582), the sonnet sequence that established the possibilities of the love poem in late

Elizabethan culture.[20] Here the understanding that politics is just as important as love, and that erotic poetry is never quite what it seems to be, is turned with especial venom against the conventions of court poetry, exposing them as a means of masking the true issue, the baneful influence of the monarch. The witty games played out in sonnet culture, whereby conspicuous and clever flattery of the mistress shows the author to be an able and pliant courtier who deserves patronage, are used by Shakespeare to appeal to an earl forced into a match by the queen's chief minister.[21] Southampton's reputation as a disaffected aristocrat interested in political argument provides a further context.[22] The dedication to him of a pornographic work with scandalous political significance simultaneously acknowledged his place within court culture and served to enhance and cement this reputation.[23] The text bore Shakespeare's name and a short dedication to the earl, confirming in conventional terms the unworthy nature of the verses offered. Shakespeare was putting his signature to a work with scandalous overtones, containing the sort of imagery and analysis that attracted the hostile attentions of the authorities in 1599 and led to a number of works by major poets – Everard Guilpin, Joseph Hall, John Marston and Thomas Middleton – being called in.[24]

Shakespeare's instinct for commercial success was vindicated and the poem was, as Sasha Roberts has noted, 'an astute entrance into the realm of print'.[25] *Venus and Adonis* went though eleven editions in Shakespeare's lifetime and some seventeen editions by 1636, making it one of the bestselling poems in England before the Civil War, outstripping everything else that Shakespeare wrote.[26] When considered alongside the conspicuous success of the *Henry VI* plays, Shakespeare's instinct for public taste seems all the more remarkable and it is little wonder that, in a precarious profession, rival dramatists such as Chettle expressed their jealousy in print. Therefore, the fact that Shakespeare published two republicanesque works during the hiatus in theatrical productions suggests that he had calculated that this was exactly what the public wanted to read in the mid-1590s.

It is remarkable how resistant critics have been to reading *The Rape of Lucrece* as a republican work, preferring to concentrate on the poem as a representation of patriarchal violence against women.[27] However, if *The Rape of Lucrece* is read alongside *Venus and Adonis,* then the republican significance of the poem becomes more immediate and apparent.[28] In *Venus and Adonis,* we witness the failure of sexual consummation and the impossibility of new life. Shakespeare's casting of Venus as a frustrated matron is counterbalanced by Adonis's homoerotic, phallic death:

> thus was Adonis slain:
> He ran upon the boar with his sharp spear,
> Who did not whet his teeth at him again,
> But by a kiss thought to persuade him there;
> And nuzzling in his flank, the loving swine
> Sheath'd unaware the tusk in his soft groin. (lines 1111–16)

Nothing can spring from this union. Even the anemone, a token of fragile, ephemeral beauty in Ovid's *Metamorphoses*, becomes a sign of what is lost rather than a brief earthly pleasure.[29] Venus ends the poem retreating into herself, 'weary of the world' (line 1189), like Elizabeth in 1593, and waiting for death, a striking contrast to her earlier vigorous attempt to force the unwilling Adonis into having sex with her:

> Now quick desire hath caught the yielding prey,
> And glutton-like she feeds, yet never filleth.
> Her lips are conquerors, his lips obey,
> Paying what ransom the insulter willeth;
> Whose vulture thought doth pitch the price so high
> That she will draw his lips' rich treasure dry.
>
> And having felt the sweetness of the spoil,
> With blindfold fury she begins to forage;
> Her face doth reek and smoke, her blood doth boil,
> And careless lust stirs up a desperate courage,
> Planting oblivion, beating reason back,
> Forgetting shame's pure blush and honour's wrack. (lines 547–58)

As Coppélia Kahn has noted, the imagery used here bears a striking resemblance 'to that describing Tarquin when he is about to rape Lucrece'.[30] Tarquin and Venus are here related as sexually predatory tyrants.[31] Tarquin leaning over the innocent sleeping body of Lucrece is described in suitably bestial terms:

> As the grim lion fawneth o'er his prey,
> Sharp hunger by the conquest satisfied;
> So o'er this sleeping soul doth Tarquin stay,
> His rage of lust gazing qualified –
> Slak'd not suppress'd, for standing by her side,
> His eye which late this mutiny restrains,
> Unto a greater uproar tempts his veins. (lines 421–27)
>
> Yet, foul night-waking cat, he doth but dally,
> While in his hold-fast foot his weak mouse panteth.
> Her sad behaviour feeds his vulture folly,
> A swallowing gulf that even in plenty wanteth.

His ear her prayer admits, but his heart granteth
No penetrable entrance to her plaining:
Tears harden lust, though marble wear with raining. (lines 554–60)

The similarities between the two descriptions are remarkable. Both represent the act of sex in an analogous fashion, suggesting that Shakespeare has transformed Venus – albeit briefly – into a rapist. Each poem represents the predatory sexual tyrant as a carnivore stalking a prey, Venus as a vulture, Tarquin as a lion, then a vulture, and finally a cat stalking a mouse; the sexual act is seen in terms of appetite (Venus is 'glutton-like', Tarquin is driven on by 'sharp hunger'); both have their sexual urges inflamed by the prospect of success and the lack of resistance of the sex object; Venus feels 'careless lust', Tarquin, 'a rage of lust'; both experience a rush of blood to the head (Venus's 'face doth reek and smoke, her blood doth boil', Tarquin experiences a 'greater uproar' that 'tempts his veins'); both lose control of reason and are quite indifferent to the consequences of their actions; and, most significantly of all, the emphasis on the political nature of the language of rape in *Venus and Adonis* (Venus's lips are 'conquerors', forcing Adonis to pay 'what ransom the insulter willeth') forges a connection to the other most political of all rapes.

The representation of Venus and Tarquin as similar creatures forces the reader of the poems to make connections between the two regal figures, especially if we remember that they were dedicated to the same reader. The failure of the attempted sexual act in *Venus and Adonis* results in stasis, death and a lack of regeneration; the success of Tarquin's rape leads to spectacular political change, the end of the Roman monarchy and the establishment of the republic. Indeed, the event was so traumatic that the Romans were never able to return to a monarchy:

After Tarquinius was banished and his stocke, the name of kinges was banished, and that forme of regiment chaunged, not that, that estate of governement was ill, but bycause theyr Princes placed in that sole and excellente estate, after theyr will and lustie relinge, of reason and all moderation neglected, tyrannical and outragious factes were committed by them . . . that estate of governement was dissolved, and chaunged through the evill maners of Princes[.][32]

If Venus is seen as a type of Elizabeth, then Shakespeare's poem reads as a stinging attack on the sterile courtly culture of the second half of her reign once the queen had passed the age when there would be any point in her marrying. Elizabeth's attempts to control the marriages of her courtiers, and her fury when matches of which she had not approved took place, had become notorious, the most recent example being Sir Walter

Ralegh's marriage to Elizabeth Throckmorton (1592).[33] Southampton already saw himself as a victim of the queen's overzealous interest in others' personal lives. *Venus and Adonis* implies that the queen's own matrimonial failure has made her a ridiculous figure, showing an unhealthy interest in younger men, one that does not simply cast her in a bad light, but has the potential to damage the lives of the subjects she is supposed to protect. She may be less culpable than the tyrannical Tarquins, but her actions cast doubt on the ability of the monarchy to survive, a reading of Roman history that was readily available to those who sought out the most obvious texts.[34]

Elizabeth's failure to complete the sex act places the realm in danger. Shakespeare, I would suggest, is drawing a pointed contrast between Venus/Elizabeth and the virtuous Lucrece, a truly noble woman whose actions benefit her fellow citizens. Elizabeth/Venus's repellent virginity – intact despite her vigorous efforts to lose it – is emphasized by the virtuous chastity of Lucrece.[35] Shakespeare's poem shows us the development of Lucrece from pliant subject to potential king-killer in her long speeches that make up the bulk of the poem's narrative once Tarquin has entered her chamber. The issues raised – suicide weighed against murder – are the same as those debated in *Hamlet*. Katharine Eisman Maus reads *The Rape of Lucrece* as a poem which shows 'two people making important decisions'. Tarquin surrenders to his personal lust and neglects to act as a king. Lucrece chooses to kill herself, but the poem forces us to ask: 'What if Lucrece had resolved to kill Tarquin rather than herself?'[36]

The Rape of Lucrece differs from earlier versions of the story in placing such emphasis on the character of Lucrece.[37] Livy's narrative highlights the tyranny of Tarquin who, enflamed by lust, 'determined . . . to debauch her'. Lucretia is represented as a passive victim:

[Tarquin] made his way into Lucretia's room determined to rape her. She was asleep. Laying his hand on her breast, 'Lucretia,' he whispered, 'not a sound! I am Sextus Tarquinius. I am armed – if you utter a word, I will kill you.' Lucretia opened her eyes in terror; death was imminent, no help at hand. Sextus urged his love, begged her to submit, pleaded, threatened, used every weapon that might conquer a woman's heart. But all in vain: not even the fear of death could bend her will. 'If death will not move you,' Sextus cried, 'dishonour shall. I will kill you first, then cut the throat of a slave and lay his naked body by your side. Will they not believe that you had been caught in adultery with a servant – and paid the price?' Even the most resolute chastity could not have stood against this dreadful threat.[38]

Lucretia is seen purely in terms of her chastity, a judgement she accepts herself. She defines herself in relation to her sexual purity/impurity, and, once she has extracted a promise from her father and husband to take revenge on Tarquin, she stabs herself, her final words being, 'Never shall Lucretia provide a precedent for unchaste women to escape what they deserve.' The 'unhappy girl' has produced an epitaph of studied ambiguity: is she committing suicide because she realizes how the patriarchal world will see her dishonour and so kills herself to give women a means of escaping this stain? Or is she, whatever her menfolk might protest to the contrary, convinced that the crime inevitably sullies the victim? However we read Livy's narrative, it is clear that an absolute division of the sexes is established, one that defines women in relation to their sexuality. Women inhabit the private sphere: political action is the prerogative of men.[39] Tarquin abuses his power, and the result is that the republic is established over the body of a dead woman, once she has been moved out from the private into the public sphere ready for other men to act on her behalf:

Lucretia's body was carried from the house into the public square. Crowds gathered, as crowds will, to gape and wonder – and the sight was unexpected enough, and horrible enough, to attract them. Anger at the criminal brutality of the king's son and sympathy with the father's grief stirred every heart: and when Brutus cried out that it was time for deeds not tears, and urged them, like true Romans, to take up arms against the tyrants who had dared to treat them as a vanquished enemy, not a man amongst them could resist the call.[40]

The exclusion of women from the establishment of the republic is complete. The dead Lucretia stands as a symbol of Tarquin's tyranny; the crowd sympathizes with her father (no mother is mentioned); Brutus urges them on to act as true Romans, and the men banish the Tarquins. From its inception, the story repeated the misogyny of the rape.

Ovid, who tells the story in the *Fasti*, emphasizes Lucretia's silence, and portrays her as too traumatized by her ordeal to speak with any coherence or eloquence:

> She is silent a long time, and veils her face, in shame;
> Her tears in a perennial stream.
> Both father and husband console her tears; they beg
> For a sign, and weep and quake with blind fear.
> Three times she tried to speak, three times she stopped; she dared
> A fourth time but did not lift her eyes.
> 'Shall we owe Tarquinius this too? Am I to speak,'
> She asks, 'To speak my wretched dishonour?'
> She narrates what she can. The final part was left.

She sobbed, and her matronly cheeks flushed.
Father and husband pardon what she was forced to do.
'The pardon you give,' she said, 'I reject.'
No delay: she pierced her breast with hidden steel[.][41]

As in Livy, Lucretia feels her own dishonour keenly and has to be avenged by men. In a melodramatic denouement, Brutus rips the knife out of her breast and swears to exact a proper vengeance on the Tarquins, arguing that he has 'cloaked [his] manhood long enough' (line 844). Ovid's retelling of the story, a source that Shakespeare probably used, repeats the division of the sexes established in Livy.[42]

It is hardly surprising that St Augustine, analysing the relationship between earthly and heavenly achievements, should attack Lucretia as an example of false pride because of her suicide. Augustine separates Lucretia into the 'highly extolled' pagan matron and the 'innocent chaste, outraged Lucretia' whom she murders, arguing that either Lucretia experienced some form of guilt because of her participation in the sexual act, or that she abrogated the authority of God to herself. Either way, she cannot stand as a proper example for Christian women to imitate.[43] Augustine, like Ovid, was merely developing an antifeminism already inherent in Livy's narrative.

Versions of the story available to Shakespeare emphasized either the victimization of Lucretia and the issues of guilt and shame, as in Chaucer's *Legend of Good Women*, available in various sixteenth-century editions, or the political implications of the transformation of Rome from monarchy to republic.[44] Casual references to the rape are common. In Antonio de Guevara's *The Diall of Princes*, translated into English by Sir Thomas North in 1557 (and popular enough to be reprinted in 1568, 1582 and 1619), Guevara discusses the flaws of kings and the problems they cause: 'By the faith of a good man I sweare unto you . . . that if the miserable *Tarquyne* hadde bene beloved in Rome, he had never bene depryved of the Realme, for committinge adulterye, wyth Lucretia.'[45] The rape is downgraded to adultery, and the crime referred to as a 'lyghte offence' which a prince needs to avoid if he wants to stay in power (Guevara is following Cicero's dictum that princes need to be loved by the people).[46]

More significant is the version in William Painter's collection of prose tales, *The Palace of Pleasure*. Painter's version, which is about the same length as Livy's, places emphasis on the actions of Brutus and the helplessness of Lucretia. Painter describes the coup that removes the Tarquins as a genuinely popular revolt against tyranny, expanding the brief description of Livy ('the populace took fire, and were brought to demand the abrogation of the king's authority and the exile of himself and his family'[47]):

[T]he people out of all places of the citie, ranne into the market place. Where Brutus complained of the abhominable Rape of Lucrece, committed by Sextus Tarquinius. And therefore he added the pride and insolent behaviour of the king, the miserie and drudgerie of the people, and howe they, which in time paste were victours and Conquerors, were made of men of warre, Artificers and Labourers. He remembered also the infamous murder of Servius Tullius their late kinge. These and such like he called to the peoples remembraunce, whereby they abrogated and deposed Tarquinius, banishing him, his wife, and children.[48]

Painter tells the story as one of a degraded people, who have been reduced from citizens to humble workers, being shocked out of their servility and reasserting their political rights. The king's tyrannical behaviour ensures that not only is he banished and his dynasty ended, but that the very institution of monarchy disappears, a reading in line with George Buchanan's use of Livy in *De Jure Regni apud Scotos Dialogus*, in which he develops the radically republican argument that evil kings can be overthrown with impunity.[49] The passage also informs readers that the Tarquin dynasty came to power because of the murder of the legitimate king, Servius Tullius, a detail that might well then have reminded them of the deaths of certain English kings: Richard II, and, possibly, Richard III.[50] This popular, republican – and thoroughly male – version of the rape occupied a central place within the English political imagination in late Elizabethan times. William Fulbecke, in his *Historical Collection* of Roman history leading up to the reign of Augustus, begins with some comments on the banishment of 'vainglorious Tarquin' for the 'shameful rape of Lucrece'. Fulbecke laments the Roman rejection of monarchy and points out the irony of their 'loathing one king' only to suffer 'manie tyrants'.[51] Nevertheless, he understands how the advent of the republic happened: 'for what could be more unjust, or more contrarie to the free estate of a citie, then to subject the whole common weale to the rule of manie potentates, and to exclude the people from all right and interest in publique affaires?'[52] Tarquin has, in fact, helped establish liberty (p. 8).

Shakespeare's *Lucrece* is written with both versions of the story in mind. The poem stands as part of the well-established English tradition of complaint poetry, where a female voice eloquently laments her fate.[53] Lucrece's journey from servile subject of the king to an outspoken critic of the excesses of monarchy, prepared to use violence, absorbs the political transformation which she had traditionally been seen to cause. There is little need for Brutus in Shakespeare's version because Lucrece has already done all the work for the reader. Hence it is a sign of the poem's sophisticated political character, rather than the interference of a heavy-handed editor, that it has a prose description of the establishment of the republic as a preface the poem as 'The Argument'.[54] Shakespeare, making use of the accounts in Ovid's *Fasti*, as well as Livy's *History of Rome*, ends with the standard political moral as read by Buchanan, Painter and Fulbecke. Brutus, speaking next to Lucrece's body, makes 'a bitter invective against the tyranny of the King. Wherewith the people were so moved, that with one consent and a general acclamation the Tarquins were all exiled, and the state government changed from kings to consuls' (*Poems*, p. 66). However, the poem itself simply ends with the memorable, but potentially bathetic, two feminine couplets:

> And so to publish Tarquin's foul offence;
> Which being done with speedy diligence,
> The Romans plausibly did give consent
> To Tarquin's everlasting banishment. (lines 1852–55)

The use of these feminine rhymes is perhaps a means of reminding us that the republican case is based on the actions of a woman.[55] Brutus's speech (lines 1818–41) does not have the dramatic character it has in Ovid, Livy or Painter because Lucrece has already reached the conclusion that Rome needs to reestablish its 'country rights' (line 1838).[56] In transferring the political significance of her violation to the victim herself, Shakespeare refashions and combines two distinct poetic traditions. Furthermore, in doing so, he establishes the virtuous, beautiful, politically agile and literate Lucrece as a pointed contrast to the self-absorbed and unattractive Venus/ Elizabeth. The countering of one form of antifeminism is cleverly used to establish another.

At the start of the poem, Lucrece's proud husband, Collatine, boasts of her 'sov'reignty' (line 36), a virtue that places her apart from other women and shows his confidence in his wife's ability to conquer her passions. He is proved right when Lucrece is discovered spinning while the other wives are out 'dancing and revelling' (p. 65). But his boast proves to be his undoing as it 'Suggested [tempted] this proud issue of a king' (line 37). As John Kerrigan has pointed out, 'By vaunting his wife's virtue . . . Collatine puts it on a level with Tarquin's regal pride.'[57] The comparison suggests further that Lucrece is herself a proud monarch

– like Elizabeth – and will have her views profoundly changed in a work that describes the advent of republicanism.

When Tarquin does confront Lucrece, we do not witness the conflict of two mutually exclusive political languages, that of absolutism and that of contractual theory, as we might expect.[58] Rather, both protagonists accept that a constitutionally limited monarchy is a desirable political form. The problem is that Tarquin cannot confine his appetites within the boundaries established, and Lucrece is consequently forced to consider more revolutionary action. Tarquin is represented as a tyrant, admitting to himself that his 'will is strong past reason's weak removing' (line 244). The narrator elaborates on this clash between reason and appetite, referring to Tarquin as a traitor, whose 'greedy eyeballs' commit 'high treason' in misleading his heart (lines 369–70). Given that the expanded treason statutes that were passed by the Tudors all sought to strengthen the power of the monarchy and define more forms of verbal opposition to the regime as treachery than had been prohibited in the late Middle Ages, the extent of Tarquin's arrogant abrogation of constitutional powers is clear enough.[59] While still attempting to persuade Lucrece to commit adultery, he proposes a means of circumventing the law that will satisfy his desires, confirm his real power and leave the constitution intact:

> 'But if thou yield, I rest thy secret friend;
> The fault unknown is as a thought unacted.
> A little harm done to a great good end
> For lawful policy remains enacted.' (lines 526–29)

Tarquin's argument is that Lucrece should submit to him as a means of preserving Roman liberty; the barely suppressed threat is that if she does not yield to him he will undermine the state when he becomes king.[60] Tarquin's reason informs him that he is acting in a manner ill-befitting the heir to the throne; his will is too strong for him to control. Any monarch who cannot limit his appetites is a tyrant who must be overthrown in the interests of the people. In a discussion about kings who seize kingdoms 'by violence and without the consent of the people', Buchanan argues that tyrants often disguise their true natures because they are aware of the consequences of their actions, 'For the hatred aroused by a single misdeed loses them all gratitude for their ostentatious generosity.' Their aim is to act 'for the sake of their own absolute power rather than the advantage of the people' and to 'enjoy their own pleasures' rather than governing in the interests of the people they are supposed to serve.[61] This dishonest and closed form of government encourages the further vice of bad rule, flattery, the 'nurse of tyranny and the most grievous plague of lawful kingship'.[62]

Lucrece refuses to remain silent and dares to challenge Tarquin. His desire to separate his private act from his public person produces a corresponding division in Lucrece's understanding of him: 'In Tarquin's likeness I did entertain thee: / Hast thou put on his shape to do him shame?' (lines 596–97). Lucrece tries to separate the private from the public body of the future king. She then explores the consequences of Tarquin's as yet uncommitted crime in lines that show her political ideas changing as we read:

> 'Thou seem'st not what thou art, a god, a king:
> For kings like gods should govern everything.
>
> 'How will thy shame be seeded in thine age,
> When thus thy vices bud before thy spring?
> If in thy hope thou dar'st do such outrage,
> What dar'st thou not when once thou art a king?
> O be remember'd, no outrageous thing
> From vassal actors can be wip'd away:
> Then kings' misdeeds cannot be hid in clay.
>
> 'This deed will make thee only lov'd for fear;
> But happy monarchs still are fear'd for love.' (lines 601–11)

Lucrece stands as the ideal subject in these lines, transforming herself arguably into a citizen when threatened by the illegal actions of the monarch, a role that prefigures her representation as the body politic itself when Tarquin rapes her. In the first lines cited here, she sees kings as god's representatives on earth, able to govern everything, the familiar statement of divine right theory in Europe, and an interpretation of the role of the monarch within the English constitution which the Tudors intermittently asserted as theirs.[63] In the second stanza, she develops her ideas, speculating on what Tarquin might do when he has become king if he is prepared to act so badly before he has assumed power. The implications of this train of thought undermine the premiss with which she started. If kings need to be suitable for their office, then they have no absolute right to rule. If they rule to serve the people, then the people have a right to expect proper regal behaviour. The last line of this stanza might have been written with Buchanan's recently published *History of Scotland* in mind. Buchanan's long work was designed in part to show that history exists to record the misdeeds of kings so that their subjects can learn how to choose their monarchs wisely and to depose those who show signs of being unsuitable to rule.[64] Lucrece's actions lead to the deposition of the Tarquins before Sextus Tarquinius has had a chance to govern, the implication being that prevention may be better than cure.

Lucrece uses the language of feudal subjection to persuade Tarquin not to commit the crime he has announced he will carry out. She argues that 'no outrageous thing' can be 'wip'd away' from 'vassal actors'. This startling choice of words has no precedent in any of Shakespeare's sources – along with the rest of this speech. The two lines have a series of complex effects on the reader. The use of the word 'vassal' establishes a relationship of servitude between a subject and a lord or sovereign which was conspicuously archaic in Elizabethan England, a social practice which the common law tradition had eventually made obsolete.[65] If, under the feudal system, lowly subjects could not hide their crimes, then how much worse was it for kings who were more squarely in the public gaze and had a duty correspondingly greater because of their status? And, as a reader alert to the contemporary significance of these lines would have realized, in Elizabeth's reign when all were equal under the law, the misdeeds of the monarch were even more vulnerable to public scrutiny.[66] Lucrece's political meditation is dramatic and she is in the process of rejecting the very concepts she uses to articulate her argument.

The last lines cited here juxtapose two famous political maxims, the one formulated as a reaction to the other. 'This deed will make thee only lov'd for fear' is a citation of Machiavelli's famous, iconoclastic statement that it is much better for monarchs 'to be feared than loved'.[67] Machiavelli was rewriting Cicero's dictum that it was better for a prince to inspire loyalty through love than fear.[68] Lucrece's words could be read as a Ciceronian commonplace. More plausibly, I would suggest, they might be seen as a rather more active intervention in contemporary political debate, changing Machiavelli's reversal of the terms back to their original relationship. In doing so she is placing her faith in one of the central pillars of republican theory as a form of resistance to Tarquin's tyranny. Lucrece has travelled a vast journey in these eleven lines, from accepting that the king is like a god, to seeing the monarch as having a duty to rule justly in the interests of his subjects. This political awakening is then applied – by implication – to the poem itself: 'For princes are the glass, the school, the book, / Where subjects' eyes do learn, do read, do look' (lines 615–16). Anyone who learns from the behaviour of Tarquin, as Lucrece suggests, will almost certainly come to the conclusion the Romans came to: that they would be better off without kings ever again.

Lucrece's rhetoric, as Colin Burrow points out, 'is a textbook example of political oratory in this [i.e., Elizabethan] period', designed to counsel the monarch against a destructive course of action.[69] Lucrece explains that she sues for 'exil'd majesty's repeal' (line 640), but her pleas are unsuccessful. Nevertheless, the lines point to a very different future. Lucrece means here, in line with her earlier separation of the office and person of the king, that Tarquin is exiled from himself in his duty as king. But we all know that Tarquin and his line really are banished from Rome at the end of the poem, and that even a protracted war with the newly established republican armies fails to restore the dynasty.[70] The eventual effect of Tarquin's base desires is to make Romans value their freedom even more: 'The hard-won liberty of Rome was rendered the more welcome, and the more fruitful.'[71] Lucrece's failure at this stage does not imply that resistance to Machiavellian tyrants is futile; rather, it suggests that the rhetoric of counsel may have to be abandoned in favour of more drastic – i.e., republican – measures.[72]

Even though Tarquin interrupts her flow to warn her that her resistance only inflames him more (lines 645–46) – an argument that prefigures the Romans' enjoyment of their newfound liberty in Livy's *History of Rome* – Lucrece's speech continues, raising many of the key political questions debated in the 1590s. In doing so Lucrece shows that she can turn the metaphors that Tarquin uses against him, demonstrating that her increasingly republican rhetoric is the master of his self-regarding defence of his power. The overtly sexual nature of Tarquin's imagery – 'my uncontrolled tide / Turns not, but swells the higher by this let [hindrance]' – is cleverly turned against him, in itself a refiguring of his boast that his lust for her 'Turns not'. Lucrece reminds Tarquin what his duties will be as a hereditary king:

> 'Thou art', quoth she, 'a sea, a sovereign king,
> And lo there falls into thy boundless flood
> Black lust, dishonour, shame, misgoverning,
> Who seek to stain the ocean of thy blood.' (lines 652–55)

The references to the dishonour, shame and misgovernment that Tarquin's intentions will cause are familiar enough attacks on regal and aristocratic abuses of power.[73] More startling is the argument that Tarquin will corrupt the bloodline of the Roman kings if he carries out the tyrannous act of rape. A bloodline attainted by treason risked losing its nobility unless the monarch intervened, arguments that were used to disbar Mary Stuart from the English throne for plotting against Elizabeth, while preserving the claim of her son.[74] Once again, the monarch's treachery points the reader to recent Scottish history. Republican arguments against hereditary kingship, most notably those advocated by George Buchanan, argued that there was no advantage to be gained from this political system which was only ever introduced to benefit the ruling family.[75] Speaking as himself in *De Jure Regni*, Buchanan pointedly asks Thomas Maitland to imagine 'someone from the ranks of an assembly of a free people freely asking our king: "What if some king has a stupid son? What if he is mad? Will you establish as our rulers *those who cannot rule themselves*?"' (my emphasis).[76] Tarquin clearly cannot rule himself and control his gargantuan sexual appetite, and, as Lucrece points out, such behaviour will 'stain the also ocean of [his] blood', tainting his children and making them also unfit to rule.[77] This is an explicitly republican argument, one that, as Buchanan's writings demonstrate time and again, places power in the hands of the people not their rulers.[78]

Furthermore, the argument that a tainted bloodline had no right to rule had a particular contemporary resonance for readers in the 1590s. Arguments in favour of Elizabeth as the legitimate monarch of England had always had to counter the equally strong claims of Mary Stuart. Mary was sometimes excluded because of her Catholicism.[79] However, this was obviously a problematic argument for any supporter of a dynasty because it opened up the possibility that other objections to the form of religion that a monarch professed could be used as a means of excluding them, or, indeed, other objections *per se*. For many, the argument that the monarch could be excluded because he or she came from a corrupted bloodline not fit to rule seemed a more promising line to take. As Anne McLaren has argued, Buchanan represented Mary as 'a woman overmastered by lust, drawing on the powerful homology of the person of the monarch and the state of his or her realm to justify her removal from office'.[80] Establishing the need for a Protestant succession involved the radical step of 'undermining the salience of blood *qua* blood as a determinant of monarchical identity'.[81] James's claim could be made through his religion rather than his mother.[82]

This point is central to the narrative of the poem as Lucrece repeats the allegation in her long speech reflecting on the consequences of her rape, representing nature as foul and degenerate:

> 'Why should the worm intrude the maiden bud,
> Or hateful cuckoos hatch in sparrows nests?
> Or toads infect fair founts with venom mud,

> Or tyrant folly lurk in gentle breasts?
> Or kings be breakers of their own behests?
> *But no perfection is so absolute*
> *That some impurity doth not pollute.*' (my emphasis; lines 848–54)

The list of vile animals reminds readers that nature is not perfect and cannot be relied upon as an infallible guide to personal and political behaviour. As John Danby pointed out long ago, two notions of nature, the benign and the malign, were commonly available for Elizabethans.[83] Lucrece's lines implicitly make the case that nature will not serve as a way of establishing political models, as many theorists of kingship claim.[84] The republic was almost invariably seen as an artificial human construct, the best form of government built at the furthest remove from the 'bad' state of nature. The republic of Venice, for example, which Shakespeare was to study and praise in *Othello* – another work which reminds us that nature is often 'bad' and that evil is invariably disguised – was frequently described as an 'artificial angel', because its inhabitants had managed to create an almost ideal form of society which had lasted for a millennium.[85] If there is no perfection in nature without impurities that pollute the sacred bloodline of kings, then society must always work to achieve perfection and can take nothing for granted, one of the basic premises of republican thought.[86] Tarquin's excessive desire and abuse of his power invalidate his right to rule: some lines later, Lucrece refers to Tarquin's deeds making him 'degenerate' (line 1003).[87]

The two poems addressed to Southampton both contain rulers whose behaviour is defined by their lust, surely reminding readers of the behaviour of the recently executed queen who had sought to rule them. If she could be removed from the succession, then so might any monarch. Elizabeth's argument that if Mary were executed, the conduct of other monarchs might be subject to hostile scrutiny would appear to be fulfilled in Shakespeare's two poems.[88] *Venus and Adonis* and *The Rape of Lucrece* work most powerfully as political statements if read together. The lust of the monarchs stands in pointed contrast to the virtue of Lucrece. Tarquin's tyrannical self-regard helps her develop an articulate critique of hereditary monarchy, leading eventually to the establishment of the republic. The next stanza continues with an analysis of the dreadful effects of Tarquin's flaws, as 'shall these slaves be king, and thou their slave: / Thou nobly base, they basely dignified' (lines 659–60). Tarquin has overridden the Roman rule of law and introduced the condition of slavery, reducing his subjects to this lowest of all human conditions, just as he has transformed himself into a slave to his base passions.[89] The republican political vision of free citizens making free choices – as expressed, for example, by Buchanan – stands as a laudable ideal in contrast.[90] Liberty and slavery are incompatible states.[91] Lucrece is adeptly pointing out that Tarquin is moving Romans backwards rather than forwards. Tarquin has no means of answering her charges and eventually simply stops her by interrupting her eloquent flow of speech: 'So let thy thoughts, low vassals to thy state' – / 'No more', quoth he, 'by heaven I will not hear thee' (lines 666–67). We do not need to hear any more at this point because Lucrece has worked out her political ideas in front of us.

In a sense, the establishment of the republic as an ideal is already taking place, which is why we need so little detail of the first Brutus's role in the poem. Lucrece is the real architect of the republic, a fact that has been hidden from view, just as the rape in the dark is unseen and needs to be brought into the light of day. Shakespeare equates darkness and tyranny: 'When most unseen, then most doth tyrannize' (line 676). Tyranny thrives in conditions of secrecy when it is easy for rulers to hide what they are doing; the republic functions when all is revealed and society is open, exactly as republican theorists such as Buchanan had argued.[92] Shakespeare's version of the myth of the founding of the republic shows that the contract between people and ruler has been broken by the king. If Tarquin had listened to Lucrece's counsel, the monarchy would have been preserved, but he chooses to let his appetites rule him and so establish a state of slavery for himself and his subjects. In consequence, the republic, the child of a rape, is born – paradoxically, a welcome development resulting from a heinous act.[93]

Lucrece concludes that her suffering cannot be redressed by legal means and that her attempt to argue with Tarquin has been a waste of time: 'For me, I force not argument a straw, / Since that my case is past the help of law' (lines 1021–22). This statement – once again, without precedence in any possible source – shows that Lucrece feels that the means of feasible redress are closed to her. Given that we have seen how her attempts at advising Tarquin through the adoption of the rhetoric of counsel have been brushed aside, we surely conclude that she is right to dismiss the legal route. Her situation recalls that of Hieronimo in Thomas Kyd's *The Spanish Tragedy*, which had enjoyed a success on the commercial stage rivalled only by Marlowe's *Tamburlaine*. Moreover, Kyd and Shakespeare may have collaborated in the late 1580s.[94] Hieronimo found that he could not attract the attention of the Spanish king and so obtain justice for his murdered son Horatio. As Hieronimo cries out, 'Justice, O justice, gentle king', the king ignores his pleas because he is more interested in securing the diplomatic match with Portugal that will conclude the peace treaty which is in both countries' interests.[95] In the following scene, Hieronimo makes his most famous speech, 'Vindicta mihi!', one that evidently helped shape English revenge tragedy in the 1590s, being frequently cited. Hieronimo rejects the possibilities of earthly and divine justice and appropriates the function of just avenger for himself:

> Strike, and strike home, where wrong is offer'd thee,
> For evils unto ills conductors be,
> And death's the worst of resolution:
> For he that thinks with patience to contend
> To quiet life, his life shall easily end. (3.13.7–11)

Hieronimo stages a version of the tragic story of Soliman and Perseda which enables him to dispose of the chief agents of his woe.

As has routinely been noted, the style of *The Spanish Tragedy* owes much to the violent and moralistic drama of Seneca.[96] Its arguments, as with other revenge tragedies such as *Hamlet*, are also indebted to the language of monarchomach theory as found in works such as *Vindiciae, Contra Tyrannos* and Gentillet's *Anti-Machiavel*. Hieronimo's actions may stand condemned at the end of the play, equating Catholicism with a barren pagan universe in which pagan classical gods such as the figure of Revenge hold sway. But the fact that they have been afforded extensive dramatic representation guaranteed that the debates they generated reached a wide audience in London. It is hard not to believe that Lucrece's statement does not owe something to Hieronimo's decision and actions in *The Spanish Tragedy*.

Moreover, a case can be made that Kyd was consciously hinting that his play had republican overtones and could be linked to such foundational narratives as the rape of Lucrece. *The Spanish Tragedy* appears to have no obvious sources.[97] Horatio is murdered by the son of the Portuguese viceroy (king), Balthazar, and Lorenzo, the king of Spain's nephew, their actions perhaps recalling the role and actions of Tarquin. More tellingly, Hieronimo's line 'Heaven covereth him that hath no burial' (3.13.19) is a direct echo of a key line in the *Pharsalia*, 'the man who has no funeral urn is covered by the sky'.[98] Lucan's words are a memorial for the dead slain at the battle of Pharsalia, a reminder that even the unknown soldier should have a place in an epic poem. They are also an indictment of the slaughter caused – in the main – by Julius Caesar, who is challenged to look at the results of his ambition. The poet asks him a rhetorical question as he leaves the battlefield: 'You – exacting punishment from the nations in corpses without burial – / Why do you flee this carnage? Why do you desert these stinking fields?' (lines 820–21). The dead are buried in the open air so that they can be honoured by those who salute them, like the poet himself. They also stand as an indictment of the cruel conqueror who turns away and on to more pleasant and selfish things.

Kyd's choice of allusion gives his play a republican edge. Hieronimo is forced to challenge the basis of the monarchy in which he serves because the king cannot administer the law impartially – just as Lucrece is forced to mount a violent challenge to Tarquin. Horatio is a victim of dynastic ambition which loses sight of the fact that the monarch is there to serve the people rather than use the populace as his vassals or slaves – the same error that Tarquin makes. The fate of Hieronimo's son, as the quotation his father uses demonstrates, resembles that of the dead armies left on the fields of Pharsalia.

Both Kyd and Shakespeare show that they realize that the issues involved in republican thought in the 1590s cannot easily be separated from theories of resistance to tyrants, a link repeated time and again in the available literature. Lucrece argues that the sins of the king should not remain secret and so be visited on the people:

> 'Why should the private pleasure of some one
> Become the public plague of many moe?
> Let sin alone committed, light alone
> Upon his head that hath transgressed so;
> Let guiltless souls be freed from guilty woe:
> For one's offence why should so many fall,
> To plague a private sin in general?' (lines 1478–84)

The logic is, once again, akin to that found routinely in both Catholic and Protestant resistance theory.[99] Tarquin has neglected his realm and so deserves to lose it. The imagery of light and darkness suggests that if the deeds of the monarch are made clear to the people, they will decide to depose him. Lucrece's speech shows that there is little need for the acts of Brutus to be recorded because her words have already made the case for the republic. The next stanza argues that the Trojan War was caused by 'one man's lust' and that had 'doting Priam checked his son's desire, / Troy had been bright with fame and not with fire' (lines 1489–91).[100] The argument shows that Lucrece can easily use historical examples in the same way that Renaissance readers were encouraged to do.[101] Her long discussion of the war (lines 1366–1561), inspired by the wallhangings she sees, would probably have reminded Elizabethan readers of the connections they made between the English civil wars and those of Rome which led to the end of the republic, especially given the possibility felt so keenly in the 1590s that England might undergo a political change as catastrophic as that experienced by the Roman monarchy.[102]

Lucan is referred to on the opening pages of the two most widely read Tudor works of English history, Edward Hall's *Chronicle containing the History of England during the reign of Henry the Fourth and the succeeding monarchs to the End of the Reign of Henry the Eighth* (1548), and Raphael Holinshed's *Chronicles of England, Scotland and Ireland* (1587 ed.). Hall refers to the fame of emperors spread by history which has judged Augustus to be noble, Trajan merciful, Nero cruel, and Caligula ungracious, and he argues that history serves to expose the evil ways of bad kings and so help others correct the vices they display in future years. He compares the civil discord in the reign of Henry IV to the conflict between Caesar and Pompey, 'by whose discorde the bright glory of the triumphant Rome was shadowed and eclipsed'.[103] Holinshed also makes reference to the same line of Roman emperors – Augustus, Tiberius, Claudius and Nero – at the start of his history of the British Isles, showing how constant a reference point this period of Roman history was for English readers. He then cites Lucan to show that the world was divided during the reigns of Augustus, Claudius and Nero, demonstrating that civil conflict has been the norm throughout world history.[104] A further subtext, of course, was the reign of Henry VI.

Lucrece's suicide, I would suggest, can be read as a displaced assassination of the king, in the same way that Hamlet's most famous soliloquy can be read as a meditation on the same subject. In fact, she does ask Collatine to kill the king before she kills herself:

> 'And for my sake, when I might charm thee so,
> For she that was thy Lucrece, now attend me:
> Be suddenly revenged on my foe, –
> Thine, mine, his own. Suppose that thou dost defend me
> From what is past: the help that thou shalt lend me
> Comes all too late, yet let the traitor die,
> For sparing justice feeds iniquity.' (lines 1681–87)

It is hard to imagine a more direct request for political assassination. The phrase 'suddenly revenged' can only mean one thing, especially when supplemented by the elaboration that Tarquin is the enemy of everyone, including himself (a reference back to her description of the relationship between the king and slavery). The connection made in the last two lines between the death of the treacherous son of the king and the need to implement justice therefore has to be read as a defence of tyrannicide when the law cannot be applied. Lucrece's earnest request markedly resembles the opening pages of Buchanan's *De Jure Regni* where he tries to establish a distinction between lawful and just monarchs who should be obeyed and tyrants who have no right to life. As Buchanan points out to Thomas Maitland, 'The common people . . . approve of the murder of tyrants but are concerned at the misfortunes of kings.'[105] Later on, the need to kill tyrants becomes a categorical imperative demanded by God. When Maitland tries to use the Bible to defend a milder course of action, he is given a stern lesson in historical interpretation by Buchanan: '[W]hen you take refuge in the argument that all tyrants must be obeyed because God through His prophet ordered His people to obey one particular tyrant, you will receive the immediate response that *all tyrants must be killed* by their subjects since it was God's bidding that Ahab was killed by the commander of his own troops' (my emphasis).[106] Proper justice requires vigorous enforcement, and, if all are equal under the law, then the monarch must suffer the consequences of his – or her – sins as any lowly subject would, precisely the point that Lucrece makes.[107]

The Tarquins are not killed but banished after the Romans give their 'consent' in the final lines of the poem. This may indicate that Lucrece is seen to go too far in her demands, or it might suggest that they do not go far enough. Shakespeare leaves both possibilities open. When Collatine is listening to Lucrece's last speech, the emotions he experiences, and the metaphors with which they are described, make him resemble Tarquin:

> As through an arch the violent roaring tide
> Outruns the eye that doth behold his haste,
> Yet in the eddy boundeth in his pride
> Back to the strait that forc'd him on so fast,
> In rage sent out, recall'd in rage being past:
> Even so his sighs, his sorrows make a saw,
> To push grief on and back the same grief draw. (lines 1667–73)

Collatine's grief is described as a surging passion that threatens to overwhelm his reason and his senses, just as Tarquin's lust overrode his. An identical violent torrent is unleashed by the rape. The parallel description also leaves the question of the ending open. Is Collatine actually like Tarquin, an oppressor of women within whom tyranny is waiting to break out? Or does he stand as a corrective to Tarquin, the emotion he experiences serving to blot out the memory of Tarquin's transgression and so help heal the wound that Lucrece – and Rome – have experienced? If the poem points us in any particular direction, it is that the rape of the virtuous Lucrece should be avenged by the death of the tyrant.[108] Lucrece's death serves to restore the traditional privileges and freedoms that Roman citizens have enjoyed, as Brutus, who seizes the knife from Lucrece's side, seizes control. He swears that

> By all our country rights in Rome maintained,
> And by chaste Lucrece' soul that late complained
> Her wrongs to us, and by this bloody knife,
> We will revenge the death of this true wife. (lines 1838–41)

Brutus understands the need to avenge the rape, even if the people tone down the punishment accorded to Tarquin.

The Rape of Lucrece contains a series of ironies, or displacements, that require us to read its status as myth and history with due care and attention. Lucrece speaks for more than half of the poem and develops a sophisticated understanding of political issues in the course of her argument with Tarquin and subsequent meditations on her unhappy fate, yet she concludes that argument is futile and that she is too polluted to carry on living (lines 1021–22, 1700–22). Her death, not that of the king, paves the way for the establishment of the republic, with men acting to expunge the faults of men over the dead body of a woman.[109] Yet the real establishment of the republic occurs through the words of Lucrece and the intellectual journey she undertakes.

. How should we read the political significance of Shakespeare's poem and figure its range of meanings in terms of the culture out of which it emerged in the 1590s?[110] I would suggest that the republican virtue of Lucrece stands as a pointed contrast to the lustful and selfish tyranny of the rulers represented in the two poems dedicated to Southampton, Venus and Tarquin. Together they form a composite picture of the perils of monarchy, each showing that inside every ruler lurks a tyrant waiting to escape. Furthermore, neither manages to produce an heir, despite their attention to the sexual act, a failure that highlights the dangers of their rule. The monarchs Shakespeare undoubtedly has in mind are Elizabeth and Mary, the two queens living within the British Isles each of whom claimed that they had the sole right to rule England.[111] Lucrece stands as the body politic, abused as a possession by the monarch, who fails to see that the people who make up the state have voices and rights as well as corporeal existence, as her increasingly articulate speech proves.[112] In fact, her demand that the king be killed is hard to refute, given her portrayal in the poem. The seemingly bathetic note on which the poem ends opens up the possibility that more radical action would have been appropriate, although how this reading might have been translated to England in the last years of Elizabeth's reign will remain an open question. Rather clearer is the contrast drawn between the virtuous female subject and the bad monarch, a dichotomy that Shakespeare was to develop in what was probably his next work, *Titus Andronicus.* The animus against women that has often been detected in *Lucrece* may well, ironically enough, depend on the impressive virtue of the protagonist, a factor that becomes clearer if we read the two poems together. Lucrece is represented as a male fantasy, a self-sacrificing figure, prepared to die for a political ideal, and thus a pointed contrast to the queen in the guise of Venus in *Venus and Adonis.*[113] Given its foundational narrative, republicanism rarely managed to escape from the discourses of misogyny that enveloped it, especially the forms that emerged in England in the 1590s.[114]

CHAPTER 5

The end of the republic: Titus Andronicus and Julius Caesar

When the theatres reopened on 27 December 1593, only one new play seems to have been performed by the Lord Chamberlain's Men at Henslowe's Rose Theatre, Shakespeare's *Titus Andronicus*. The play was staged some four weeks into the season, on 24 January 1594, presumably because it took a month to rehearse and to make sure that it was ready for professional performance. Like *Henry VI, Part One, Titus* appears to have been a notable success, achieving the best takings of the season, and would undoubtedly have enjoyed a long run had not a restraining order, due to yet another outbreak of the plague, forced the theatres to close yet again.[1] And, as with the *Henry VI* plays, *Titus* is almost certainly the product of co-authorship, a strong case having been made by Brian Vickers for the conspicuously classical George Peele as the author of the first and last scenes.[2] Opinions differ as to whether *Titus* was specially written for the reopening of the theatres in late 1593, making it 'the pivotal play in Shakespeare's early career', as Jonathan Bate suggests, or whether it was a revival of a work first performed in the late 1580s or early 1590s, and then probably rewritten for the grand reopening.[3] Either way, it is clear that *Titus* was considered to be a potentially popular work that was likely to entice audiences back to the theatre in the mid-1590s.

Titus is one of the few Shakespeare plays that probably has no direct source, although it has been argued that the chapbook *The History of Titus Andronicus, The Reanowned Roman General* and the ballad *Titus Andronicus' Complaint*, printed in the eighteenth century, were discoveries of old texts that may have predated Shakespeare's play.[4] Even if these were works used by Shakespeare (or his collaborator/s), they lack the explicitly political framing that he gives to the play in the first act, and the controversial – and frequently misinterpreted – closing scene. Even if Shakespeare did not write these scenes, but was employed to flesh out the poetic carnage of Acts II–IV, his involvement in such a project indicates the direction his work was taking, alone and in collaboration. *Titus* is undoubtedly a strange, hybrid play, which builds on the successes of spectacular historical drama, such as the *Henry VI* plays; Roman plays, such as Lodge's *Wounds of Civil War*; exotic drama such as Peele's *The Battle of Alcazar* and Marlowe's *Tamburlaine*; the Machiavellianism of plays, such as *The Jew of Malta*; and revenge tragedy, such as Kyd's *The Spanish Tragedy*.[5] All the great successes of the theatre in the late 1580s and early 1590s are signalled by various aspects of *Titus*: hideously choreographed violence; strange and wonderful settings; revenge and Senecan excess; memorable, emblematic speeches and images; moral judgements that allow the play to appear to be an ethical work, while allowing the possibility of more subversive readings; a great investment in wonderful costumes, and carefully planned use of the resources the stage can offer.[6]

Arguably, however, the most significant aspect of *Titus*'s experimental, commercially driven nature, is its republicanism. This, after all, is a play set at an unspecified point soon before the collapse of the Roman empire, and the triumph of the 'barbarian' forces who ushered in the Dark Ages, related in works such as Pedro Mexia's *Historia Imperial y Cesarea*, which was not translated into English until 1604.[7] If any of the authors of *Titus* used one work to establish the imaginative universe of their play, it was probably the *History* of the Greek author Herodian (AD c.165–c.250). Herodian's *History* traces the fates of the emperors from the death of the virtuous Marcus Aurelius to AD 238, charting the spectacular rises and falls of a series of lesser-known emperors – Commodus, Severus, Julian – who usually occupy the imperial seat after a plot and die prematurely, often poisoned (rather like most Scottish monarchs).[8]

Herodian reinforces a reader's impression of the nature of Roman history derived from the stories of the advent of the republic and its decline into tyranny. He announces at the start that the history takes place 'when the Romane superioritie was commyted to the arbitrement of one man'.[9] Virtuous emperors, such as Marcus Aurelius, are rare, and even ones who start out with the potential to rule well, such as Commodus, are misled by their peer group, become corrupted, and end up as vicious tyrants, like Tiberius in Tacitus's *Annals*.[10] Life is an endless cycle of violence, often breaking out in the form of spectacularly bloody crimes. Furthermore, the *History* contains a wealth of detail of the Roman conflict with the barbarians in Britain and Germany, as well as two characters named Saturninus (a supporter of Plautian, a challenger of the emperor,

Severus, who appears in Book III) and Bassianus (who appears soon after the empire has been divided in Book IV). These bear little relation to their namesakes in *Titus*, but suggest that Shakespeare may have consulted the *History* when writing his play.[11] Emperors are elected, as they are in *Titus*, but often under straightened conditions and with severe military encouragement, a striking resemblance to the changes of dynasty represented in the opening and closing scenes in *Titus*.

The opening scene of *Titus* also conjures up an image of Rome at a much earlier juncture in its history, the transformation from the republic to the empire. It is this startling, fictional historical setting, one produced in line with Sir Philip Sidney's well-known dictum that the best history is really poetry because it is able to tell moral truths which are not constrained by the world of fact, that constitutes the innovative heart of the play.[12] Furthermore, the refiguring of the rape that established the Roman republic, through Chiron and Demetrius's rape and dismemberment of Lavinia, reinforces our understanding that we are witnessing a dark parody of a crime that led to popular outrage and the establishment of political liberty. In the world of *Titus*, the body politic has degenerated so much that Lavinia cannot be granted the dignified exit of Lucrece, and her abuse only fuels revenge and a further cycle of violence.[13]

In the first two speeches of the opening scene, we witness the clash of two distinct perceptions of the ordering of political life. The unnamed emperor has died and his sons now compete for power. The eldest, Saturninus, argues the case for primogeniture as an overriding principle of political selection and right to rule:

> Noble patricians, patrons of my right,
> Defend the justice of my cause with arms.
> And countrymen, my loving followers,
> Plead my successive title with your swords.
> I am his first-born son that was the last
> That wore the imperial diadem of Rome:
> Then let my father's honours live in me,
> Nor wrong mine age with this indignity. (1.1.1–8)

Saturninus's words are designed to close off debate and establish him as the legitimate ruler of Rome.[14] He appeals only to the assembled patricians and has no time for the wider political classes gathered to greet the triumphant returning forces after their victories over the Goths. He also shows that his idea of honour is one based on an aristocratic ideal of military prowess, that he expects absolute obedience from his subjects, and that he values military might over rational argument and debate. It is hard to imagine a political manifesto further away from the republican ideals, in itself a sign of how far Rome has degenerated away from its ideal Polybian state.[15] If Saturninus's words remind readers of Roman rulers, it will be either Tarquin – especially if we bear in mind that his rule witnesses the rape of Lavinia – or the worst of the Julio-Claudians.

Bassianus's speech is rooted in an ideal of consent, the ruler having to rely on the support of the people to obtain power, a political model that resembles the civic republicanism of numerous European thinkers, perhaps most notably that of George Buchanan.[16] Bassianus appeals to

> Romans, friends, followers, favourers of my right,
> If ever Bassianus, Caesar's son,
> Were gracious in the eyes of royal Rome,
> Keep then this passage to the Capitol,
> And suffer not dishonour to approach
> The imperial seat, to virtue consecrate,
> To justice, continence and nobility;
> But let desert in pure election shine,
> And, Romans, fight for freedom in your choice. (lines 9–17)

Bassianus's words stand directly opposed to those of Saturninus. While the latter appeals to a limited upper tier of the populace, the former legitimizes his bid for the highest office through an appeal to the citizens at large, his opening line anticipating the words that Mark Anthony would use to overthrow the oligarchic republic that Brutus wished to reestablish in *Julius Caesar* (3.2.74). Bassianus addresses the gathered crowd as 'friends', imagining them as his equals. His vocabulary signals his political position as he uses a series of key words to establish his principles: 'virtue', 'justice', 'continence', 'nobility', 'desert', 'election', and 'choice', terms that mark him out as a candidate steeped in republican ideology. His desire to be continent is undoubtedly derived from Aristotle's writings on the cardinal virtues and marks his opposition to Saturninus's patrician scorn for confining his appetites, demonstrated in his speech and later in his actions throughout the play.[17] It also shows that Bassianus wants to be a virtuous ruler, like Marcus Aurelius, and not a tyrant like Tarquin, or the wild young emperors represented in Herodian.[18] It is harder to attach any specific register to the ubiquitous words 'virtue' and 'justice', but they too point to Bassianus's desire to win an election on his merit and future performance as a ruler rather than his birthright.[19] 'Desert' can be glossed as 'merit', the sense of the line being that Bassianus wants to persuade the assembled citizens to elect him as leader because he is a suitable candidate not because of his birth, the cardinal principle of republican government.[20] Whereas Saturninus wants the patricians to fight to defend his honour if his right to rule is threatened, a claim that is implicitly tyrannical, Bassianus demands that Romans fight for their liberty, their ancient privileges under threat at the end of empire.

Bassianus's last line continues the links between forms of government, virtue and military prowess that Saturninus's speech had inaugurated. The claims made on behalf of the third candidate for the imperial see further explore these connections. Marcus, a tribune, proposes that his brother, the successful warrior Titus, has a legitimate chance of being elected as emperor. Marcus cites his brother's successes against the Goths, and his military virtue, as reasons for the people to elect him:

> A nobler man, a braver warrior,
> Lives not this day within the city walls.
> He by the senate is accited home
> From weary wars against the barbarous Goths,
> That with his sons, a terror to our foes,
> Hath yoked a nation strong, trained up in arms. (lines 25–30)

The ways in which the three candidates present themselves before the assembled Romans raise the familiar question of the relationship between military virtue and republican liberty, a central dilemma in Machiavelli's writings.[21] Was the ideal form of the republic actually a military one? Virtue functioned best when it was endlessly tested, allowing no room for complacency to flourish, making war the ideal condition for the growth of republican liberty. However, this was an unstable phase, because it was most likely that a society dominated by military values would eventually be transformed into 'a tyranny, which may well be exercised by a Pompey or Caesar, once a citizen but now so far perverted as to use the sword as an instrument of political power'.[22]

Titus does indeed represent a society that finds it impossible to end conflict and transform itself from a culture of war to one of peace. Titus has proved a terror to the enemies of Rome, but after this scene he becomes a threat to its internal stability. The long opening scene becomes more and more redolent with prophetic ironies, suggesting that even if Shakespeare did not write this section of the play, whoever did clearly cooperated closely with him to produce a play that is carefully integrated into a functioning whole. Titus is praised by his daughter, Lavinia, as a warrior 'Whose fortunes Rome's best citizens applaud' (line 167), and then further urged by Marcus to stand for election as emperor:

> Titus Andronicus, the people of Rome,
> Whose friend in justice thou hast ever been,
> Send thee by me, their tribune and their trust,
> This palliament of white and spotless hue,
> And name thee in election for the empire
> With these our late-deceased emperor's sons.
> Be *candidatus* then and put it on,
> And help to set a head on headless Rome. (lines 182–89)

Titus, of course, helps keep the body politic of Rome headless. He refuses to stand himself and puts his support behind Saturninus, praising his 'virtues' (line 229), when the opening two speeches have made it quite clear which of the two sons is seriously interested in fostering virtue in Rome. Titus's choice shows that he has not made the transition from war to peace and still thinks in terms of strong, aggressive leadership – appropriate in the army, but not necessarily a desirable form of ordinary government, especially in a state that enjoyed its best years when it had a republican constitution. The fact that he has just agreed to the sacrifice of Tamora's son to appease the gods, a decision which fuels the cycle of revenge that dominates the main action of the play, shows how far Titus is from the civilized reputation of Rome's legacy.[23] It is not clear from these opening exchanges whether Titus really has any substantial popular support, a political problem revisited in the last scene of the play. He is supported by his brother, who acts as a tribune, and is praised by his daughter. A director of the play can choose to represent this scene as one in which a tyrant in embryo thwarts the legitimate republican/democratic aspirations of the citizens of Rome; or one in which the outcome has already been carefully stage-managed, with the principal candidates cut off from the electorate.[24]

We see Rome as a self-parody in this opening scene. The ideals of the republic are present in Bassianus's speech, but the forces that dominate the victors reveal that the Romans are really driven by much darker forces, ones that highlight the similarities there are between supposedly civilized Roman society and the barbarian Goths, symbolized at the end of the play by Aaron's baby.[25] In Herodian's *History*, Rome is continually threatened by the barbarians and protected only by the banks of the Isther.[26] But the political discussion and election are designed to remind the reader/ audience of the last days of the decaying republic, specifically, I would suggest, the famous passages at the start of Sallust's account of Catiline's conspiracy and the Jugurthine War, each a pivotal point in the history of Rome, the first illustrating the accelerating decline of the Roman republic, the second the advanced state of moral degeneracy that afflicted the empire from its inception.[27]

Sallust discusses his own unsuitability for public life in the first chapter of his account of Catiline's conspiracy, a failure he attributes to his adherence to the noble ideals of the republic:

Now being a young man amongst others, was taken from my Booke, and thrust into the worlde, wherein I found many things were opposite to my disposition. For, instead of modesty, abstinence, and frugall Liberality, I found all places accustomed to Impudence, Bribery, and Avarice. Which although my very soule did loath, as a Virgin undefiled with these contagious abuses, yet by reason of my tender yeares (as it could not otherwise fall out) in the very centre of so many fretting and inciting failties, I could not escape the humour of Ambition. For beeing spotlesse in all other Vanities, the same desire of preferment which had atached others with boldnes and ambition, seized also upon me[.][28]

The historian charts his own corruption and failure to live up to his principles as a sign of how severely Rome was rapidly degenerating as the ideals of the republic were fading. Only by retreating into the world of his books can Sallust regain his virtue, the republic of letters replacing the political reality of the republic: 'retyring my selfe to my Booke, from whence ydle ambition had once almost withdrawn me, I have resolutely set me downe, briefly to relate the glorious actions of the Roman people, and with the greater courage, because my pen is free from hope, from feare, or any other partialities of the commonwealth' (p. 58). Under a corrupt state, only the detached are free to make informed and responsible judgements, a message that assumed an equal, if not a greater significance in the writings of Tacitus and the phenomenon of 'Tacitism'.[29]

The prefatory remarks to Sallust's history of the Jugurthine War are, if anything, even more suggestive than those which preface the history of Catiline's conspiracy and equally relevant to *Titus* because they describe the epic conflict between Rome and the powerful Numidians, militaristic North African barbarians.[30] Sallust's history shows how the unscrupulous Jugurtha was able to mount a serious challenge to Rome through the extensive use of bribery and corruption because so many high-ranking Roman officials were easy to purchase. Sallust explains that he has chosen to write his history because of the invaluable political lessons it offers. The Jugurthine War is an important event in the history of Rome

First, because it was weighty, cruell, and doubtfull: Secondly, for that about this time, the people avowed their first discontents against the surquedrie [pride] of the *Roman* Nobility: a contention whereby al Divine and humaine lawes were wrapped in confusion; & afterward proceeded into such raging fits of succeeding madnesse, that *Italy* was almost wasted, before their civill warres ended. (p. 125)

Sallust's comment is studiously ambiguous and deliberately avoids the question of causation so vital in charting the reasons for the decline of the republic. He simply informs the reader that the overarching pride of the Romans and the war against Jugurtha happened at the same time as part of the same process, but does not say which came first. What is clear is that the civil wars are a disaster for Rome and its allies, and that the rise of ambitious men – such as Julius Caesar – is a sign that the republican constitution can no longer contain the disruptive elements within the body politic. Chaos is the inevitable result.

An identical situation has arisen in *Titus*. The trappings of the republican ideal are still extant in the arguments of Bassianus; the importance of the tribunes, the elected mediators between the people and the Senate, and the praise rightly given to figures such as Titus who serve Rome well and are rewarded for this, rather than expecting honour to be granted simply through an accident of birth. However, not only are such features too weak to protect the state against the unholy alliance of a self-declared tyrant and his barbarian allies, they are also already corrupted and complicit with the patrician and autocratic drift of Roman society. The only tribune we see in action is Titus's brother, and, via his advocacy of Titus, he manages to transfer goodwill, if not active support, to Saturninus. The words of Bassianus, which sound very like the ideal of the 'mixed constitution' current in Sir Thomas Smith's writings and elsewhere in Elizabethan political thought, are unworkable without a political will to enforce them.[31] The play shows that the republic is reverting to the bad model of the tyrannical monarchy enforced by the Tarquins, foolishly surrendering the liberty it has gained of its own volition. This was, indeed, a commonly expressed fear in Roman political writing. Cicero, for example, in his famous speech defending Gaius Rabirus from the absurd charge of treason, argued that the aims of Julius Caesar's 'democratic party' could be seen in their use of slogans:

For those phrases of yours . . . are foreign not only to Roman liberty and clemency but even to Romulus or Numa Pompilius: Tarquin, haughtiest and most cruel of tyrants, provides your torture-chamber with those mottoes which . . . you delight to record, such as 'Veil his head, hang him to the tree of shame.'

Such phrases, I say, have long since disappeared from our state, overwhelmed not only by the shadows of antiquity but by the light of Liberty.[32]

Cicero's point is that if the language of monarchy is accepted as valid currency, then the arguments will start to shift in that direction and away from the freedoms that the republic worked so hard to introduce. Cicero's speech casts his opponents' language as the return of the properly repressed, an atavistic moment in which the negation of the Roman state returns to threaten the people. The extensive savagery that is unleashed by the actions of the opening scene emphasizes this process. The images of cannibalism suggest that the Romans are complicit in their dreadful fate, as they have consumed themselves.[33] The parallel to the political language employed in the first scene of *Titus*, and the subsequent events that take place in the play, are easy to map out. Once the Romans have accepted that mottoes such as 'Plead my successive titles with your swords' and 'let my father's honours live in me' should be established as the rock on which they will build their government, then the political game will be run from above, as Cicero feared, and as history proved to be the case.

Titus shows the triumph of older values of honour, symbolized at the start of the play in the tombs that stand as a background to the political arguments of the first scene.[34] Images of hunting start to dominate the play, as an aristocratic culture sweeps aside republican political values, a neat reversal of the social changes that many commentators felt were taking place in Elizabethan England.[35] The principal victim of this newly dominant masculine culture is Lavinia. When Saturninus decrees that a hunt shall be held to celebrate his new power, Demetrius reminds his brother that there may be other possibilities: 'Chiron, we hunt not, we, with horse nor hound, / But hope to pluck a dainty doe to ground' (2.1.25–26). They are spurred on by a piece of cunning advice given by the villainous Moor, Aaron, when they express their desire to him:

> 'Tis policy and strategem must do
> That you affect, and so must you resolve
> That what you cannot as you would achieve,
> You must perforce accomplish as you may.
> Take this of me: Lucrece was not more chaste
> Than this Lavinia, Bassianus's love.
> A speedier course than the lingering languishment
> Must we pursue, and I have found the path. (1.1.604–11)

This speech and the subsequent action it generates are replete with political symbolism. Chiron and Demetrius murder Bassianus and then rape and mutilate Lavinia in a passage of horrific violence that still shocks audiences today.[36] The Ovidian and Senecan contexts of these scenes have long been recognized.[37] But the main significance of the action is that the transformation of the Roman monarchy to the republic is shown to be reversing itself through the repetition of the rape. At the start of the play, Lavinia is engaged to Bassianus, the would-be republican ruler, a projected union that points towards a hopeful future for Rome. The triumph of Saturninus, and his union with Tamora, results in the death of Bassianus, and the dismemberment of Lavinia. Whereas the dignified suicide of Lucrece led to the establishment of the republic, the survival of the mutilated Lavinia serves as a visual reminder of the liberties Rome has lost.[38] The violation of Lucrece inspired a popular movement that sought to correct abuses and move Rome forwards into a more enlightened political state; that of Lavinia serves only to inaugurate a bloody cycle of revenge that drags Rome back to the realms of savagery. In Shakespeare's poem, Lucrece herself charts the change in Roman consciousness resulting from Tarquin's actions; in *Titus,* Lavinia is left mute and in the power of her father, whose political naivety has helped cause her downfall.

The parallels do not end here. Aaron leads Tamora's sons on with his description of Lavinia's chastity, exactly as Tarquin's lust had been increased through Collatine's boasting and Lucrece's chastity. Aaron uses the word 'policy', the key term that denotes the language of reason of state, outlined in Machiavelli's writings, but also in such figures as Botero, Justus Lipsius, and Guicciardini, and, most crucially here perhaps, Tacitus.[39] He also refers to 'stratagem' and 'plots' and then later manages to disguise the crime by having Titus's sons, Quintus and Martius, blamed for the murder of Bassianus. Such language and actions mark Aaron out as the stage Machiavellian villain pioneered in a figure such as Barabas in Marlowe's *The Jew of Malta.* Barabas, in a play that casts him as a disciple of Machiavelli, also uses the word 'policy' as a means of casting aside conventional moral restraints.[40] The phrases and language of reason of state now define Rome's political character, having the precise effect that Cicero feared. Given that Machiavelli consciously sought to undermine and reverse Cicero's political pronouncements, most famously in the assertion that it is better for princes to be feared than loved, it is hard to dispute that *Titus* is making a deliberate political statement.

Perhaps Shakespeare's boldest move is to revise and transform Marlowe's deliberate association between villainy, policy and the alien. It was a commonplace of Roman history that as Rome expanded and

became more powerful, absorbing new peoples, it lost its ancient, republican traditions, partly through the sheer scope of the territories that had
to be controlled, which necessitated greater centralization and the concentration of power in one man; partly through the triumph of military men
who exercised a greater influence in Roman society; and partly through
the absorption into the body politic of barbarians who, hardly surprisingly, had no interest in Roman political traditions.[41] *Titus* shows that
the decline of the republic leads directly to the triumph of the savage
barbarism of the Goths and the Moors, an unholy alliance that engulfs
and overwhelms the civilization of republican Rome, dragging the city
back into the Dark Ages. When Bassianus is murdered and Lavinia raped,
both Aaron and Tamora are labelled as barbarians within a few lines
(2.2.78, 118). The wheel has come full circle and Rome is now governed by
a dictator who is an even worse tyrant than the Tarquins.

The just avenger, Lucius, Titus's sole surviving son, makes precisely
this comparison as he swears to avenge the ills that have afflicted his
family, his soliloquy coming immediately after Titus has been sent back
his severed hand along with the heads of his other sons:

> If Lucius live, he will requite your wrongs
> And make proud Saturnine and his empress
> Beg at the gates, like Tarquin and his queen.
> Now will I to the Goths and raise a power,
> To be revenged on Rome and Saturninus (3.1.297–301)

Lucius rightly recognizes what Saturninus has become.[42] But his projected
solution is part of the problem, showing how far Rome has degenerated
from the days of the inception of the republic. Lucius simply equates
Saturninus with Rome, showing that he has accepted Saturninus's political logic. His desire is for revenge, not justice, and he determines to leave
the city and act alone in raising a Goth army, a pointed contrast to the
actions of Brutus against the Tarquins. Gothic savagery, a reminder of
Rome's own hybrid, savage origins – the city was founded by men who
had been raised by wolves, one killing the other in their struggle for
mastery – is both the poison and the cure.[43]

The ending of the play shows only an ominous and uncertain future
for Rome. Two images of unstable hybridity haunt the pacified city.[44]
First, Aaron and Tamora's baby is displayed and its origins noted by
Marcus: 'Behold the child: / Of this was Tamora delivered, / The issue of
an irreligious Moor' (5.3.119–21). However, attention is immediately
transferred to the father who is buried up to his chest in the earth and

left to starve. Aaron is defiant to the end: 'I am no baby, I, that with base prayers / I should repent the evils I have done / . . . If one good deed in all my life I did / I do repent it from my very soul' (lines 184–85, 188–89), adding a note of comedy to an otherwise unrelentingly brutal theatrical experience. The baby, as John Gillies argues, stands as a sign of the degeneration of Rome: 'Just as Lucrece's body is "adulterated" by rape, so is the Roman body-politic adulterated by the "blackamoor child"', a striking contrast to the pure Roman left to govern, Lucius, Titus's last remaining son, 'who represents himself as the unadulterated issue of Rome, "That have preserved her welfare in my blood" (5.3.109)'.[45]

The point is well taken, but the second image at the end of the play probably suggests that Lucius is either mistaken or disingenuous in asserting his purity. He has, after all, defeated Saturninus with the army of the Goths. Lucius is proclaimed emperor, but who actually supports him? Editors routinely reassign 5.3.145, Marcus's cry, 'Lucius, all hail, Rome's gracious emperor', giving it to 'All Romans', indicating that Lucius is a popular choice of emperor and that a proper order has been restored to Rome.[46] However, it is equally possible that Lucius is staging an Andronici coup, having his brother proclaim support for him. This would suggest that the ending shows a corrupted Rome that has failed to learn from its history and the same political errors will be repeated by the Andronici, who will inevitably degenerate into tyrants, propped up by the Goth army.[47] Just as Saturninus turned into Tarquin, Lucius has become Saturninus. Rome no longer has the institutions that can preserve the virtue of its citizens. Its body politic has become a bloody mess like Lavinia, rather than a healthy and robust torso. Exactly how this structural failure occurs – whether the institutions fail the people or the people the institutions – Shakespeare, like Sallust, does not say.[48] But it is clear that the political language that Bassianus speaks at the start of the play has no relevance at the end. There is no collective body politic left and individuals act out of self-interest, whether to advance themselves, or to avenge wrongs. Rome itself is adulterated.

What relevance might *Titus* have had in 1594? Read one way, it is a simple republican morality tale, warning of the dangers of tyranny and the problem of the inevitable decline of republics.[49] *Titus* shows that a more constitutional form of government, which relies on greater participation from a wider political class than is currently involved in making decisions, would be of benefit to any regime (that the exact details of this political form are not worked out in the play does not invalidate the point).[50] The parody of this form of government which emerges at the end of the play serves only to emphasize its importance. Nevertheless, *Titus*, in common with many of Shakespeare's early works, appears to argue a case for a limited monarchy, a mixed constitution and a fairer form of government. Concentration on the dramatic pyrotechnics of *Titus* have blinded many readers to its explicitly political messages. Structurally the play begins and ends with scenes centred around constitutional issues, and at its heart is a striking dramatic emblem that carefully refigures some dominant motifs of Roman literature and history: most importantly, the rape of Lucrece. As T. J. B. Spencer remarked nearly fifty years ago: 'It is not so much that any particular set of political institutions is assumed in *Titus*, but rather that it includes *all* the political institutions that Rome ever had. The author seems anxious, not to get it all right, but to get it all in.'[51]

The conflict of the Goths and Romans may well be intended to signal the complicated relationship between England and Rome, explored in such Jacobean history plays as John Fletcher's *Bonduca* (1609–14?) and Shakespeare's later work, *Cymbeline* (c.1610).[52] Neil Rhodes has made the compelling case that *Titus* draws attention to itself as an experimental play, the union of Goths and Romans suggesting the conflict between civilized and barbarian in classical tragedy, as well as the cultural relationship between a developing English literary culture and its classical antecedents. What the play promises is 'a drama which could be described equally as neo-classical and neo-Gothic, an educated barbarism'.[53] If so, *Titus* also makes clear that this new hybrid drama will explore the relationship between Roman political forms and historical events, and English politics and history, a task Shakespeare had already carried out in the English civil war plays, as well as the narrative poems. *Titus* itself presents a political culture helplessly out of control and hurtling headlong into the worst excesses of tyranny.[54] There are various possibilities open to the Romans at the start of the play to lead their state towards peace and plenty, as they have just defeated their enemies. Unfortunately, they choose the worst option, that of hereditary succession, in itself a subversive and aggressive action to represent on stage. The fact that this form of government leads directly to tyranny, and that the other options would have been better for Rome, would appear to be a comment on the forms of government existing in late Elizabethan England. That the crown was likely to pass to a Scottish king who was largely unknown in England at this point, but who ruled a kingdom notable for its tyrants – especially his mother – would seem to make the parallel even more obvious.[55] The publication of Robert Parsons's *A Conference about the Next Succession to the Crowne of Ingland* in the same year that *Titus* was probably first performed (1594), further indicates the topical nature of the play, especially its opening scene.[56]

Five years later, the Chamberlain's Men, having established themselves as a major company able to attract large audiences, made their new home at the Globe Theatre near Southwark Cathedral.[57] The first play they performed was Shakespeare's *Julius Caesar*. Yet again, a work on a conspicuously republican theme marks a key moment in Shakespeare's career, indicating that such subjects clearly caught the public imagination and that he wished to be known as the playwright who explored republican history.[58] The performance was watched by the Swiss traveller Thomas Platter and his party, perhaps an indication of the significance of the event. Platter notes that he 'witnessed an excellent performance of the tragedy of the first Emperor Julius Caesar', suggesting that he realized the significance of the play as a work about the death of the republic and the rise of imperial Rome.[59] Platter makes only two other references to the theatre in his account of London, observing that a playhouse can be seen on the south bank of the Thames west of the Tower, next to 'two rings for bull and bear baiting', and that prostitutes, a huge problem in the city, 'haunt the town in the taverns and playhouses'.[60] Platter's comments suggest that he was not a habitual theatregoer – one reason why his comments on *Julius Caesar* are so limited in comparison to his comments on other aspects of London life (inns, palaces, executions) – which further emphasizes the importance of the staging of the play.

Julius Caesar has often been read as though it could be accommodated into one of the prevailing modes of tragedy, its formal classification, principally because the main characters appear more 'rounded' and have greater psychological depth than those in Shakespeare's earlier plays.[61] It has also been read as a play of studied balance, exposing the limitations of creeping tyranny and the republican argument for selective political assassination.[62] However, the play appears in a different light if we read it as a work designed to intervene in the political debates of a culture that has a keen interest in republican history, issues and questions, an ambition that its first staging clearly signals. One of the great clichés of Shakespeare criticism is that the real hero of the Roman plays is Rome itself.[63] *Julius Caesar*, like *Titus Andronicus*, depicts a dying and perverted republican Rome that has lost the ability to inspire its citizens to behave virtuously.[64] Without this basic requirement the republic cannot function as a political force and will be superseded by a more suitable form of government, one that matches the needs and desires of the people. Rome has returned to a state that resembles the last days of the monarchy under the Tarquins – not quite the bloody anarchy that characterized the dying city under threat from the barbarians – rather than the apotheosis of the republican ideal.

However, as Shakespeare was undoubtedly aware, the republic was always an ideal that was in the process of becoming or receding. Its most celebrated writings describe either the hope that came with its foundation or the need to preserve a constitution about to disappear for ever. The main republican figure from the last days of the republic was not Brutus, whose actions are a parody of those of his famous ancestor, but Cicero, one of the most influential intellectual influences on the development of sixteenth-century European thought.[65] Cicero appears in Shakespeare's play as a minor character. The fact that he does not join the conspirators shows how their actions, however they are presented, are at odds with the proper goals of the republic.

Cicero is indeed a shadowy figure in *Julius Caesar*. The conspirators are aware of his presence and importance, but they never discover what he thinks even though he is always close to the main sites of the action. As Caesar enters after the games, Brutus describes Cicero in terms that indicate his importance, as well as the anxiousness he inspires in the conspirators. He says that Cicero 'Looks with such ferret and such fiery eyes / As we have seen him in the Capitol / Being crossed in conference by some senators'.[66] The conspirators do not know which way Cicero's sympathies will turn, a significant problem for them because of his status as one of the central figures in the republic, whose goal was a culture of deliberative oratory, designed to facilitate a public forum in which citizens could debate central issues on equal terms.[67] Given his central importance in late sixteenth-century England, the audience would have registered this failure as an exposure of the limitations of the conspiracy to assassinate Caesar. Cassius decides to send Caska to sound out Cicero. That this is done in secret, while Antony and Caesar discuss the loyalties of the Senate elsewhere on stage, reveals how fragmented Roman political culture has become, and how far from the stated aims of republicans such as Cicero.[68]

It is also significant that it is Caska who is sent to discover Cicero's loyalty. Caska is one of the most edgy of the conspirators, as Cassius tells him (1.3.57–78), keen to scoff at Caesar's pretensions, and later he is the first to stab him in the Capitol with the words, 'Speak hands for me!' (3.1.76), a sign that the oratory of the republic has run its course and the new form of political argument is violence. The scene which contains Caska's encounter with Cicero further reveals Caska's nervousness, a marked contrast to the Cicero's detachment. Caska, who enters with a drawn sword, lists all the strange phenomena happening in the city: tempests, unusual tides, a slave whose hand 'did flame and burn / Like twenty torches joined' (1.3.16–17) yet who remained unscathed, a lion wandering at large, a large group of women who swear that they have seen men engulfed in fire in the streets, and an owl screeching in the market-place at noon. Yet Cicero remains a model of calm: 'Indeed it is a strange-disposed time. / But men may construe things after their fashion / Clean from the purpose of the things themselves' (lines 33–35). Given Caska's state of mind, it is not certain that everything he claims to have seen really exists. The scene serves as a counterpart to the portents observed by the equally sensitive Calpurnia (2.2.13–31). Nevertheless, it is Cicero's point that is the most telling. There are signs available to be interpreted, but the private meanings they yield shows that political culture in Rome is rapidly disintegrating. The search for shared meanings available to everyone is an implicit goal of Cicero's major works, notably his attempts to establish a workable Roman constitution in his dialogues on the commonwealth and the laws; and his vast array of speeches defending individuals accused of crimes by the state.[69]

Two other works are of even greater relevance to *Julius Caesar*. Cicero's last philosophical treatise, *De Officis (Of Duties)*, was one of the most influential books published in England in the sixteenth century, occupying a central place in the school curriculum, going through numerous editions and translations, and being cited whenever there were discussions of virtue, government and citizenship.[70] *De Officis* was an attempt to articulate the political and ethical values of the Roman republic, outlining the duties Roman citizens owed to the collective state that was their country. The work, however, was composed after the assassination of Julius Caesar, when it seemed to Cicero that the ideals to which he had dedicated his life were in danger of disappearing for ever. It was dedicated to his son, Marcus, in itself a sign of the loss of values held in common and of a public sphere. Cicero is sharply critical of the militarized culture that has taken over Roman society and is openly nostalgic for the community and friendship that the republic fostered.

Cicero's social vision might usefully be linked to the opening scene of *Julius Caesar* in which the tribunes, Flavius and Murellus, try to persuade the plebeians to remove scarves tied on statues to celebrate Caesar's victory over Pompey (for which they are later said to have been 'put to silence' (1.2.285)).[71] Cicero pays due respect to citizens who behave well and help the republic through amassing wealth. The highest plaudits, however, are reserved for those who promote the public culture of the republic: 'Our judgement should be that the achievements which are greatest and show the greatest spirit are those of the men who rule the republic. For their government reaches extremely widely and affects the greatest number.'[72] As public culture declined in importance, resulting in the loss of oratory as a mode of public argument, greater emphasis was placed on the significance of conversation as a means of preserving the values of the republic.[73] As a result, there was also greater stress on the republican celebration of friendship.

Cicero's dialogue on friendship, *De Amicitia*, is the other work that is of most relevance to Shakespeare's play. Like *De Officis*, it was a key plank in the intellectual culture of sixteenth-century Europe.[74] Cicero's protagonists argue that friendship helped distinguish men from beasts, and was to be valued above virtually all worldly things.[75] Friendship cannot exist unless the two men involved are virtuous – a condition the treatise reiterates several times – making it a republican goal, one that can preserve the spirit of the republic even if the constitution is absent (fos.10, 29). Friendship 'is geeven by Nature to bee an ayde to Vertue' (fo.36). Tarquin, significantly enough, helped friends to unite against him and found friendship when he was expelled from office (fos.14, 24), indicating that friendship was not a virtue easy for monarchs to practise. Friendship can withstand many disputes and disagreements, but not 'dissemblinge' (fos.13, 29, 39), another point that is repeated at regular intervals. Moreover, friendship is not at odds with a Stoic philosophy of indifference to the world, as friends make each other's lives better through their relationships, establishing examples for others to copy (fo.14). Friends must not break the law, as this invalidates their friendship and shows that they are too attached to the world to treat it with the correct amount of Stoic detachment (fos.18–19). Friends need to 'delighte in Justice and equitie' (fo.35).

Julius Caesar portrays a state that bears only a passing resemblance to the republican ideals established by Cicero, who, knew that he was preserving for posterity an ideal that was dying. All the main conspirators, as well as the principal characters, in the play meet their untimely deaths in the aftermath of the assassination of Julius Caesar. Brutus and Cassius perish in the civil war with the combined forces of Antony and Octavius, each committing suicide during the Battle of Philippi. Before the battle, they receive letters informing them that seventy senators have been put to death as a result of their actions, 'Cicero being one' (4.3.176). Plutarch's 'Life of Cicero' informs us that Cicero was 'not only fearful in wars, but timorous in pleading' (p. 597). Nevertheless, he uses his impressive bearing, derived from his formidable oratorial skills, to confront the murderers Antony has sent, and meets his end with dignity:

Cicero . . . commanded his men to set down his litter, and taking his beard in his left hand, as his manner was, he stoutly looked the murderers in the faces, his head and beard being all white, and his face lean and wrinkled, for the extreme sorrows he had taken: divers of them that were by, held their hands before their eyes, whilst Herennius did cruelly murder him. So Cicero being three score and four years of age, thrust his neck out of the litter, and had his head cut off by Antonius' commandment, and his hands also, which wrote the orations . . . against him. (p. 610)

Shakespeare would have known this account.[76] The absence of Cicero's voice within the play serves only to draw attention to his writings, and the lack of importance they have at this crucial historical juncture. Cicero's thought has no role in the militarized society that was developing under Caesar, something the opening scene demonstrates, as Caesar returns to celebrate a victory over his fellow Romans. His minor part in the action of *Julius Caesar* shows that he has become a private rather than a public citizen, anxious to keep his thoughts to himself (not surprisingly, perhaps, as according to Plutarch his death results as much from his attacks on Antony in his speeches as his association with the conspirators). But neither is he able to play any role in the conspiracy, a misguided attempt to restore the values of the republic to Rome. In between the two violent extremes the republic has retreated with Cicero, although its goal of individual liberty can, of course, be revived later.[77]

Shakespeare represents Roman society as a toxic mixture of decayed republicanism and emergent tyranny. There is no shared public culture, a fact emphasized by the stage arrangements which carefully divide up the characters into small groups whispering secrets to each other (few plays make such extensive use of the aside and clandestine meeting). Trials were one of the main features of the republic – as exemplified in Cicero's wide range of speeches, words that lead to his murder – but Flavius and

Murellus can be silenced, Caesar assassinated, and seventy senators put to death without any due legal process at all. Superstition rather than reason, one of the defining attributes of republican society, dominates everyday life as portents are witnessed and interpreted in different ways.[78] Far from existing as a successful 'mixed' constitution, classes are at odds with each other, the tribunes opposing the actions of the Senate and the senators eager to displace the military commander who plays an uncertain role but whom they fear will emerge as a tyrant and end the liberties they have enjoyed as citizens of the republic.[79]

The word 'liberty' is not mentioned in the first two acts. However, after the assassination of Caesar it becomes the watchword of the conspirators as a means of justifying their actions. As soon as Caesar is dead, Cinna cries, 'Liberty! Freedom! Tyranny is dead! / Run hence, proclaim, cry it about the streets' (3.1.78–79), as though producing the words themselves ensured that the reality would immediately follow. This was, of course, the case when Tarquin was deposed – although, even then, a protracted war had to be fought with the forces loyal to the Roman monarchy. Yet, when Brutus directs that they all bathe their hands 'Up to the elbows' and cover their swords in Caesar's blood, 'Then . . . walk forth even to the market-place', waving their weapons and crying ' "Peace, Freedom, and Liberty" ' (lines 108–10), the naivety of the conspirators' assumptions is painfully, almost comically, evident.[80]

This scene, one that Shakespeare invented, shows that the actions of the second Brutus are a parody of those of the first. We know that the attempt to restore the republic was always doomed to fail. The institutions of the republic are too feeble to be revitalized. Those who supposedly guard their spirit have either retreated into private life, like Cicero, or replaced collective action with violent conspiracy. Whereas there was strong popular support for the birth of the republic, as all historical accounts make clear, in *Julius Caesar* the conspirators have to persuade the people to follow their lead. Their isolation from the population they supposedly represent makes them acutely vulnerable to more astute populist politicians such as Antony. Liberty appears as a concept that suddenly erupts in the aftermath of a bloody act, something that almost has to be imposed on a reluctant, uncomprehending people who, like the conspirators, have lost sight of what functions their institutions – the Senate and other political offices, the law courts, the forum, and so on – actually serve. Caesar's rise to potential tyranny is not simply a result of his own efforts. Rome exists as a militarized culture weary from years of civil war, very similar to the society that Shakespeare had already represented in *Richard III* in which post-civil war England bore a striking resemblance to imperial Rome. Rome has gone too far to be saved from itself. In Plutarch's 'Life of Marcus Brutus', Faonius, a follower of Marcus Cato the Stoic, makes the telling point 'that civil war was worse than tyrannical government usurped against the law' (p. 822).

The actions and behaviour of the characters further demonstrate how much the ideals of the republic have decayed and not yet been replaced by the more austere philosophy of imperial Rome, designed as a means of living under tyranny. Brutus and Portia are shown to be an affectionate and well-matched couple in their only scene together. Yet, for all her loyalty, virtue and republican credentials, Brutus will not tell Portia the substance of his secret plans, however hard she pleads with him. Their marriage exists as a parallel to that of Caesar and Calpurnia – Caesar ignores his wife's advice not to venture out on the Ides of March (2.2) – when political logic suggests that they should be strikingly different. Portia reminds Brutus that there should be no secrets within a marriage (2.1.279–81), but he maintains his silence even though he praises her as his 'true and honourable wife' (lines 287), a description that is both gender-neutral and could also be read as casting her as a loyal republican, honour being the reward of true virtue.[81] Portia's protestations show that she realizes that it is her sex that has served to exclude her from the conspiracy. Commenting on his praise of her virtue, Portia argues:

> If this were true, then I should know this secret.
> I grant that I am a woman: but withal
> A woman that Lord Brutus took to wife.
> I grant I am a woman: but withal
> A woman well reputed, Cato's daughter.
> Think you I am no stronger than my sex
> Being so fathered and so husbanded?
> Tell me your counsels. I will not disclose 'em.
> I have made strong proof of my constancy,
> Giving myself a voluntary wound,
> Here in the thigh. Can I bear that with patience
> And not my husband's secrets? (lines 291–301)

Portia asks to be treated as an equal and to be allowed to share Brutus's life in an exchange which is Shakespeare's invention and therefore a gloss on the private lives of eminent Romans in the dying republic. The culture of secrecy and spying, a situation that would have reminded many playgoers of their own times, dictates otherwise, but if Brutus were acting to save his wife pain and suffering, he evidently fails.[82] Roman philosophy was characterized by Stoicism, but we witness the rash and rather over-passionate suicide of Portia, a parody of the Stoic ideal as represented via the death of Cato, her father, one of the heroes of the *Pharsalia*, and later Lucan and Seneca the Younger.[83] Portia appeals to one of the central Stoic principles, 'constancy' (line 298), struggling with her weak, female nature. Her self-inflicted wound is an act that protests too much, which, in Cynthia Marshall's words, 'directs attention inward, toward the vulnerable interior of her bodily self'.[84] Furthermore, it apes the violent plot of her husband, as well as showing how debased the ideals of the republic have become, so that self-mutilation stands as a sign of honour (given what represents virtue in his marriage, it is perhaps hardly surprising that Brutus imagines that an excess of blood will symbolize liberty).[85]

Republicanism was invariably cast as a masculine phenomenon, and was established over the dead body of a woman, as the myth of the birth of the republic demonstrates. Portia's heroic struggle with herself, which reads like a parody of Elizabeth's professions of her androgynous nature, shows that the strength of the republic is ebbing away and it is returning to the effeminacy/hypermasculinity of tyranny.[86] When left alone in her last scene (2.4), Portia again appeals to 'constancy', demonstrating that women's role in late republican Rome is to suffer in isolation: 'Set a huge mountain 'tween my heart and tongue. / I have a man's mind, but a woman's might. / How hard it is for women to keep counsel' (lines 6–8). Portia is overwhelmed by fear after her discussion with the soothsayer, another sign that reason has been usurped by superstition in Rome. The broken syntax of her last words before her suicide further indicates the crisis of values in Rome:

> Ay me, how weak a thing
> The heart of woman is. O Brutus,
> The heavens speed thee in thy enterprise.
> Sure the boy heard me. Brutus hath a suit
> That Caesar will not grant. O, I grow faint:
> Run, Lucius, and commend me to my lord.
> Say I am merry. Come to me again
> And bring me word what he doth say to thee. (lines 40–47)

The lines are hardly the most memorable in the play. However, they reveal a number of points that confirm our understanding of the action. Portia is struggling to maintain an equilibrium that proves impossible, as is the rest of Rome. Her chaotic syntax and distracted thought patterns express the confusion that is endemic in Rome. She is perturbed by Brutus's enterprise yet dependent on him for direction, again, just like the rest of Rome. And she has no real sense of his plans, imagining that he has a suit to take to Caesar, a notion undoubtedly gleaned from overhearing the conversations of the conspirators. Her death, unlike that of Lucrece, which it repeats and so parodies, leads nowhere. The exhausted Brutus, on the verge of death and defeat, simply notes the causes: she was 'Impatient of my absence' and was afraid of the growing power of Octavius and Antony's army (4.3.150–52).

Marriage is not the only relationship between supposed equals which does not function properly in the play. Friendship is also shown not to work as the republican ideal of Cicero demanded it should, Cicero's own isolation within Roman society dramatically pointing up the gap between theory and practice. Friendship has become a private and furtive affair, whereas *De Amicitia* stated that it should be a relaxed and public manifestation of a healthy society. Brutus and Cassius clearly have a mutual bond of comradeship expressed in their final words to each other before the fateful Battle of Philippi (5.1.120–26). But their relationship is increasingly characterized by argument and division, most fatefully in Brutus's famous insistence that Antony be allowed to deliver Caesar's funeral oration (3.1.232–42), and then later with their dispute over tactics in the next act, which sees Brutus sweeping aside Cassius's objections to his plan that they seek an immediate confrontation with the enemy. On each occasion Cassius's commonsense is overruled by Brutus's disastrous principles: each time with the polite use of the term 'pardon' (2.2.235; 4.3.211). Cicero explicitly warns friends against this sort of behaviour. Friendship needs to preserve truth and virtue and will not work properly if the two friends involved do not allow themselves to correct each other when the occasion demands. Cicero states that 'freendes must often times bee both admonished and chidden . . . And this is to bee friendly taken, when it is done freendlye and of good will' (fo.38). Brutus is at fault for refusing to take advice, and Cassius is to blame for not correcting his friend.

There are other flaws in their friendship. When they first meet and start to plot the overthrow of Caesar, we might imagine that Brutus and Cassius act as equals planning an enterprise together. But when Brutus departs, Cassius reveals that he is manipulating his partner, leading him towards a predetermined course of action, using what he sees as Brutus's good nature, universal popularity and high principles:

Well, Brutus, thou art noble: yet I see
Thy honourable mettle may be wrought
From that it is disposed. Therefore it is meet
That noble minds keep ever with their likes.
For who so firm that cannot be seduced?
Caesar doth bear me hard, but he loves Brutus.
If I were Brutus now, and he were Cassius,
He should not humour me. I will this night
In several hands in at this window throw,
As if they came from several citizens,
Writings all tending to the good opinion
That Rome holds of his name – wherein obscurely
Caesar's ambition shall be glanced at.
And after this, let Caesar seat him sure,
For we will shake him, or worse days endure. (1.2.306–21)

Although the last lines show that Cassius does have honourable motives
for wanting to assassinate Caesar, we also learn that he has personal
reasons for wishing to do so, having been slighted by the dictator. In
Huguenot treatises that argued that tyrants could be assassinated, such
as *Vindiciae, Contra Tyrannos,* magistrates who undertook such drastic
actions were supposed to be pure in spirit as befitted their role as servants
of God and the people.[87] Cassius is evidently not such a creature.
Shakespeare is following Plutarch's hostile description of Cassius's motives: 'Cassius being a choleric man, and hating Caesar privately, *more
than he did the tyranny openly,* he incensed Brutus against him' (my
emphasis) ('Life of Marcus Brutus', p. 819). Cassius plans to use Brutus
because he is trusted, and admits that he would not be persuaded by his
own arguments, an observation that establishes an inherent imbalance in
their alliance. The attempt to fake popular support by throwing stones at
the window once again stresses the fragmented nature of Roman society
and the isolation of the conspirators.

Cassius's behaviour further violates the rules of proper friendship as
determined by Cicero. Cicero argues that dissimulation invalidates friendship: 'Dissimulation in all thinges is euill (for it taketh away the righte
judgement of truthe and corrupteth it) yet namely to Friendshippe it is
most repugnant. For it raseth out the truth, without which, the name of
Frendshippe cannot endure' (fo.39). (Republican) friendship depends on
virtue and any violation of this fundamental principle renders proper
friendship invalid: 'For sithens the opinion of Vertue is the breeder of
frendshippe, it is harde for Frendshippe to remayn, if a man swerve from

Vertue' (fo.18). Cicero also argues that friendship is invalidated if a friend tries to persuade another to commit an unlawful act. The assassination of Caesar may or may not fall under this heading, but Cassius's impure motives reveal the dangers involved in such an enterprise.[88]

Casssius grows more passionate towards Brutus near the end of the play, petulantly demanding that Brutus kill him because Brutus loved Caesar more than him: 'Strike as thou didst at Caesar: for I know, / When thou didst hate him worst, thou lov'dst him better / Than ever thou lov'dst Cassius' (4.3.104–6). In contrast, Brutus tries to be as little affected by the mutable nature of the world as is possible. Throughout *Julius Caesar*, Brutus attempts to treat everyone with equal concern, rationally assessing how he should behave towards them. Following Stoic principles, he does not react with excessive grief to the death of his wife; he persuades himself that it is best if Caesar is killed, even though he is Caesar's friend; he allows Antony to speak to the people in the name of fairness and friendship, even though it is obvious to all concerned that this is a recipe for disaster; and he maintains his friendship with Cassius on general, egalitarian, republican principles. When they part for the last time, Cassius utters words of affection for his friend, 'For ever and for ever farewell, Brutus: / If we do meet again, we'll smile indeed; / If not, 'tis true parting was well made' (5.1.120–22). Brutus sticks to more general, quasi-philosophical terms and practical matters:

> Why then, lead on. O that a man might know
> The end of this day's business ere it come:
> But it sufficeth that the day will end,
> And then the end is known. Come ho, away. (lines 123–26)

The similarity to his reaction to the death of Portia is striking. Cicero, arguing for the central importance of friendship in men's lives, claims that 'A man void of al affections is like a logg or a stone' (fo.22), a perpetual danger that Stoicism courted.[89] Brutus certainly runs the risk of appearing too detached from the world to be properly human.

The friendship of Cassius and Brutus has to be weighed against that of Antony with his now-dead friend, Caesar. Antony's passionate loyalty to Caesar is more obviously appealing than Brutus's detached indifference to people and loyalty to an ideal. Brutus's willingness to use friendship for his own ends, revenge on the conspirators, balances Cassius's manipulation of Brutus to persuade him to help carry out the killing of Caesar. Once again, the society of Rome appears as a perversion of republican principles. Antony's funeral oration for Caesar is Shakespeare's expansion of the bare details provided by Plutarch who notes that he mingles 'his oration with lamentable words', and so moves them 'unto pity and compassion' for the dead Caesar. When he shows the people the 'bloody garments of the dead, thrust through in many places with their swords', Antony puts 'the people into such a fury' that they burn Caesar's body in the market-place and then run 'to the murderers' houses to set them afire, and to make them come out and to fight' ('Life of Marcus Antonius', p. 689). Antony's statement when he is left alone on stage in Shakespeare's play, 'Now let it work. Mischief, thou art afoot: / Take thou what course thou wilt' (3.2.251–52), shows that he is prepared to use friendship to further his personal revenge, just as Cassius was.

The central feature of the republic at its height was rhetoric, the public art of persuasion, enabling listeners to weigh up the evidence on either side of any argument and choose the right way forward.[90] The rights and wrongs of Brutus's assassination of Caesar was, in fact, a historical case that was often cited as an example of a problem that should be debated by aspiring orators eager to persuade an audience.[91] In his dialogue *Brutus*, written in *c.*55 BCE, before the assassination (44 BCE), Cicero represents Marcus Junius Brutus as an urbane and keen student of oratory, keenly aware of its passage from Greece to Rome and its central place within the social fabric of the republic.[92] Titus Pomponius Atticus constructs a familial and intellectual genealogy linking Brutus and his namesake and ancestor:

Who, for example, can suppose that Lucius Brutus, the founder of your noble family, was lacking in ready wit, who interpreted so acutely and shrewdly the oracle of Apollo about kissing his mother; who concealed under the guise of stupidity great wisdom; who drove from the state a powerful king, son of a famous king, and freeing it from the domination of an absolute ruler fixed its constitution by establishing annual magistrates, laws, and courts; who abrogated the authority of his colleague so that the very memory of the regal name might be obliterated? All this certainly could not have been accomplished without the persuasion of oratory.[93]

Atticus's use of a series of rhetorical questions – a form of anaphora (repetito), 'where the same word is repeated at the beginning of a sequence of clauses or sentences' – serves to link the political and social purpose of oratory to the generations of the Brutus family.[94] Lucius Junius Brutus's oratorial skills, even though they are not immediately apparent, are instrumental in driving out the hated monarchy of the Tarquins. The keen interest shown in oratory by Marcus Junius Brutus is part of the same process. In using his own powers of persuasion, Atticus establishes the continuity of the republic.

Cassius persuades Brutus to join the conspiracy by using exactly the same parallel:

> O, you and I have heard our fathers say
> There was a Brutus once that would have brooked
> Th'eternal devil to keep his state in Rome
> As easily as a king. (1.2.157–60)[95]

However, what we witness in *Julius Caesar* is the paucity of republican oratory, a confirmation of the republic's drastic decline. Brutus, for all his obvious qualities as the 'noblest Roman of them all', the only one of the conspirators whom Antony acknowledges acted out of pure motives rather than 'envy of great Caesar' (5.5.68–69), is an ineffective orator. His virtue is at odds with the body politic, as his troubled personal relationships with Portia and Cassius demonstrate. Whereas Cicero's Brutus is a key figure who holds the Roman republic together, Shakespeare's is easily outmanoeuvred and defeated by Antony, a better friend and orator, whose angry passion serves him well. The Stoic ideal of the rule of reason and the control of the emotions has been superseded by fierce tribal loyalties as dictatorship and tyranny replace the republic.[96]

Brutus's soliloquy in his orchard betrays a circular reasoning that does not follow the accepted rules of forensic oratory, established principally by Cicero:

> It must be by his death: and for my part
> I know no personal cause to spurn at him
> But for the general. He would be crowned;
> How that might change his nature, there's the question.
> It is the bright day that brings forth the adder,
> And that craves wary walking . . .
> . . . and to speak truth of Caesar
> I have not known when his, affections swayed
> More than his reason. But 'tis common proof
> That lowliness is young ambition's ladder
> Whereto the climber upward turns his face;
> But when he once attains the upmost round
> He then unto the ladder turns his back,
> Looks in the clouds, scorning the base degrees
> By which he did ascend. So Caesar may.
> Then, lest he may, prevent. (2.1.10–15, 19–27)[97]

Given that what is to be carried out is effectively a legal judgement, that Caesar deserves to die, Brutus should adhere to the guidelines for judicial oratory in making the case against Caesar. Instead, he decides what has to be done before his fellow conspirators arrive, an indication of the perverse relationship that exists between the public and the private spheres in Rome. What should be an art of persuasion has become a personal meditation in which the answer is already known and the reasoning follows the conclusion. The imperative ('must') is followed by a series of conditionals ('would', 'might', 'may'), indicating that the cart has been placed before the horse. There is, in fact, no evidence in Brutus's speech – nor in the play – that Caesar will definitely become the tyrant that Brutus claims he will. What is certain is that his assassination leads to tyranny – although whether Brutus's actions are a sufficient or necessary condition of the triumph of Augustus and the reigns of Tiberius, Caligula, Claudius and Nero is impossible to prove.

Thomas Wilson, the author of _Arte of Rhetorique_ (1560), one of the most influential English treatises on rhetoric in the sixteenth century, follows Cicero in dividing oratory into three distinct forms: demonstrative, deliberative and judicial.[98] Demonstrative oratory was used 'when a man is commended or dispraised, for any acte committed in his life'; deliberative oratory is designed to 'perswade, or disswade, entreate, or rebuke, exhorte, or dehorte, commende, or comforte any man'; and judicial oratory 'is an earnest debatyng in open assemblie in some weightie matter before a judge, where the complainaunt commenseth his action, and the defendaunt thereupon aunswereth at his peril to al suche thynges as are laied to his charge'.[99] Brutus's soliloquy could be read as a combination of all three types of oration: the speech does 'dispraise' Caesar for acts he may well commit as dictator; it is designed to persuade the speaker that he is acting in the right way; and it condemns Caesar to death. Of course, Brutus is not entirely to blame for the impure and eccentric nature of his argument. There is no public forum for him to practise his oratory, a problem Cicero experienced in his own career and which resulted in his placing greater emphasis on the virtues of friendship than the arts of public persuasion. Wilson, again following Cicero, argued that any speech should conform to a pattern, having seven parts: the entrance or beginning; the narration; the proposition; the division; the confirmation; the confutation; and the conclusion.[100] Yet Brutus's speech demonstrates no principle of organization: the argument does not develop logically; the examples are not persuasive because they are not based on any observation or evidence; there is no consideration of the contrary case, specifically in the use of proverbial wisdom (Caesar climbing the ladder of ambition), which is not balanced by an argument with an opposite case leading to a considered conclusion.

Brutus's speech is not, of course, an oration as such. However, given what is at stake, it appears to be a shadow of the proper sort of argument that ought to be made. Certainly the extensive arguments made in monarchomach literature were clear that resistance to tyrants who were oppressing the people was the only available option for would-be liberators. The questions posed centred around the issue of who could carry out the deed, not whether tyranny could be predicted and killed before it hatched, as Brutus's concluding metaphor claims (lines 31–34).[101]

The speech Brutus gives in the market-place after Caesar's death confirms our understanding of his lack of rhetorical skills, a failing that exposes the absence of republican sophistication rather than simply demonstrating his plain honesty or commitment to the ideals of Stoicism.[102] Brutus speaks in prose and makes the unconvincing case that, although he loved Caesar in many ways, he killed him because 'he was ambitious' (3.2.26), an argument that does not even reach the rhetorical level of his soliloquy. He is demonstrating his lack of interest in, even contempt for, the public institutions and spaces that used to characterize republican Rome and which his ancestor helped establish, persuading the people to take action against the Tarquins after the rape of Lucrece. Antony is able to subvert Brutus's use of the term 'honour' with ease, partly because he has only to dispute the one negative trait that Brutus has attributed to Caesar, 'ambition'. Brutus makes no mention of the disastrous effects of the civil wars, of the silencing of the tribunes, of the decline of the republic, or of the fears he and the other conspirators have for the future, allowing Antony to represent the dead Caesar, not without reason, as a populist in tune with the immediate needs of the ordinary citizens, as he reads out Caesar's will promising each citizen seventy-five drachmas and leaving his orchards and private arbours beside the Tiber for their 'common pleasures' (line 241).[103] Antony uses one of the most important cultural and political legacies of the republic, public oratory, to help destroy the republic, continuing the civil wars that signalled its decline into dictatorship. He also uses his friendship with Caesar – another chief republican virtue – to the same end as he demonstrates in his soliloquy over the dead body of Caesar:

O pardon me, thou bleeding piece of earth,
That I am meek and gentle with these butchers.
Thou art the ruins of the noblest man
That ever lived in the tide of times.
Woe to the hand that shed this costly blood. . .
A curse shall light upon the limbs of men:
Domestic fury and fierce civil strife
Shall cumber all the parts of Italy:
Blood and destruction shall be so in use,
And dreadful objects so familiar,
That mothers shall but smile when they behold
Their infants quartered with the hands of war. (3.1.254–58, 262–68)

Shakespeare's dramatic representation of Antony's speech is a significant elaboration of the brief description of his words in Plutarch's 'Life of Marcus Brutus'.[104] Antony is a war monger who does not have the good of the state at heart – unlike Brutus – and his reputation for a fatal combination of reckless cruelty and sensual indulgence is a more culpable version of Brutus's paralysing division of his life into the public and private spheres.[105]

The political charge of a staging of the story of *Julius Caesar* in 1599 is obvious enough, even if it is only in relatively recent times that the relationship has been recognized.[106] As Ian Donaldson has pointed out, 'it is reasonable to say that any play concerned with conspiracy, political ambition, and the assassination of a ruler was bound to be of absorbing interest to audiences in England in the late 1590s, who would no doubt have seen some broad resemblances to their own times in the political uncertainties and jockeyings for power of late Republican Rome'.[107] The connections the play makes between the two historical situations are perhaps rather more wide-ranging than even this perceptive comment suggests. *Julius Caesar* does not just chart the power struggles of an elite which clearly resembled those taking place in the last years of Elizabethan England and expose the uncertainty of the succession. Such connections were routinely made in the drama of the 1590s and would have done little on their own to distinguish the play from numerous other works competing for the attention of the theatregoing public.[108] More significantly, Shakespeare's play represents a necrotic body politic that has abandoned its healthy republican institutions and values, allowing its citizens to lapse into vice. Brutus's attempt to reestablish republican values is itself tainted by these vices – secrecy, contempt for the citizenry, the decline of the art of persuasion, and so on – and so doomed to failure, represented most eloquently in his naive faith that bathing oneself in the victim's blood will ensure the support of the populace. Republican values have become reduced to the public badge of murder. As in the early English history plays, the public sphere shrinks from the general control of the many to the concern of a few who, to adapt the words of Thersites in *Troilus and Cressida*, a play written in the wake of *Julius Caesar*, 'yoke [them] like draught-oxen and make [them] plough up the war'.[109] Shakespeare may not, of course, be alluding to a specific war, although everyone in London knew that war in Ireland was imminent in 1599, and his next play, *Henry V*, is written as an 'at war' play.[110] But the disenfranchised citizens of Rome had no stake in their collective destiny and it may have been this aspect of their lives that struck the English audience at the Globe. Certainly their political and intellectual life bore little resemblance to that outlined in the extensive writings of Cicero, which were supposedly one of the chief sources of Elizabethan culture.

CHAPTER 6

The radical Hamlet

Perhaps more than any other Shakespeare play, *Hamlet* has a problematic history, one that is intimately connected with its political charge. We know that a play called *Hamlet* was performed in – or before – 1589. Thomas Nashe wrote in his preface to Robert Greene's prose romance *Menaphon* (1589) that 'English *Seneca* read by candle-light yeelds many good sentences, as *Blood is a begger*, and so forth; and if you intreate him faire in a frostie morning, hee will affoord you whole Hamlets, I should say handfuls of Tragicall speeches.'[1] Nashe makes what many have taken to be a pun on the name of the author of this lost play, the *Ur-Hamlet*:

let blood line by line and page by page, at length must needes die to our Stage; which makes his famished followers to imitate the Kid in *Aesop*, who, enamoured with the Foxes newfangles, forsooke all hopes of life to leape into a newe occupation; and these men, renouncing all possibilities of credite or estimation, to intermeddle with Italian Translations[.][2]

From this, it is assumed, quite reasonably, that the author of this lost play must have been Thomas Kyd.[3] Writing in 1596, Thomas Lodge refers to a 'ghost which cried so miserably at the Theatre, like an oyster-wife, *Hamlet, revenge*', which indicates that the play was well known by then, and Philip Henslowe writes of a production of *Hamlet* in June 1594 at Newington Butts Theatre.[4] No trace remains of this play, which is perhaps not surprising, given that few plays performed in the 1580s survive in written form, and it was only in the 1590s that the commercial possibilities of drama in print seem to have been realized.[5]

Shakespeare's *Hamlet*, undoubtedly an adaptation of this lost play, assuming that Shakespeare had no part in writing the earlier version, was written and produced between mid-1599 and July 1602.[6] It exists in a quarto published in 1603 (Q1), a version which used to be dismissed as a 'bad' quarto based on the memorial reconstruction of an actor, or as a version for a reduced, touring company. A longer version of the play appeared in a second quarto (Q2) (1604–5), before a revised further version appeared in the folio of 1623 (F), apparently based on Q2, but containing some cuts and additions.[7]

Hamlet exists in radically different forms, a textual problem that can be explained in various ways. Q1 differs in a number of ways from Q2 and F, notably containing a version of the 'To be or not to be' speech which bears only a passing resemblance to the famous counterpart. A short scene, 14, contains a dialogue between Gertrude and Horatio that summarizes the details of Hamlet's voyage to England contained in Act IV, scene 7, and Act V, scene 2 in Q2 (other material is also missing here: there is no mention of pirates, for example).[8] Both passages are carefully written, suggesting either detailed revision, or an alternative version rather than a mangled source.[9] Polonius is called Corambis, Reynaldo is called Montano, and there are numerous verbal changes, some deliberate, some undoubtedly mistranscriptions.[10]

The plot differs significantly. Some of the major distinctions are as follows: the unnamed king who is the Claudius figure has no opening speech showing that he is a competent leader and skilful courtier; he does not acknowledge that he has a guilty conscience before the 'To be or not to be' speech (3.1.48–53); his speech in the prayer scene is half its normal length (3.3.36–72); there is no acknowledgement of Hamlet as an especially popular ruler (1.5.2–11 and 4.7.16–24); and he plays a more aggressive role in the plans for dispatching Hamlet in the final scene. Corambis is made even more irritating and foolish than he is in Q2, repeating himself when instructing Montano in scene 6 and making Ophelia accompany him when he informs the king of her description of Hamlet's odd behaviour, which also makes Ophelia seem more pliable and naive than in Q2. She does not answer Gertrude when told to observe Hamlet's madness (scene 7; 3.1.37–41). Gertrude's role is similarly played down. The king provides no explanation of his reasons for marrying her (scene 2), and she says little when the disaffected Hamlet enters the banquet hall. She later has to witness her son being humiliated by Rosencrantz and Guildenstern in silence (scene 7), and then sees her husband and son trading insults without intervening (scene 11). However, she is shown to be allied more to Hamlet than to the king through some lines which are not in Q2, the most significant of which has her exclaim, 'I never knew of this most horrid murder' (scene 11, line 84), when Hamlet confronts her with the ghost's revelations. She can be read as a more sympathetic character than she is in Q2. Hamlet is characterized as a somewhat less complex character than he is in Q2, more committed to the revenge of his father, and less in control of his plans. This is mainly due to his having only 60 per cent of the lines he has in Q2, but also because he is probably represented as a younger man: the gravedigger makes no mention of him as aged thirty (5.1.142–47, 161–62).[11] The plot moves at a much more rapid pace, most noticeably in the acceleration of Hamlet's plan to expose the king's crime. The gap between the arrival of the actors and the perform-ance of *The Murder of Gonzago* is considerably shorter. The exchange between Hamlet and Ophelia is moved forward so that it takes place just after Corambis's plan to spy on the lovers, which may be, as Katherine Irace suggests, 'a deliberate theatrical alteration designed to speed the action'.[12] Many of the insults aimed at Rosencrantz and Guildenstern in Act 4 are missing.

Structurally, *Hamlet* is a messy and often chaotic play – hardly surpris-ing, given its complicated textual history – especially if produced in a virtually complete longer version, and so it stands out as unusual among Shakespeare's works.[13] It was clearly revised and rewritten in parts, and provides suggestive evidence that certain texts were written to be read rather than performed (which would also emphasize the importance of the topical and political nature of the texts).[14] Dr Johnson noted that the 'action is indeed for the most part in continual progression, but there are some scenes which neither forward nor retard it' and Harley Granville-Barker argued that the play 'illustrates no consistent dramatic purpose on Shakespeare's part'.[15] Played certain ways, Hamlet can seem to be a tortured and tragic figure, and this is indeed how he has usually appeared on stage from the eighteenth century onwards.[16] Yet the comments of Thomas Nashe would indicate that observers of the early version that Shakespeare adapted probably saw a more robust play firmly in the mould of Senecan revenge tragedy, a tradition that Shakespeare's play is often thought to modify, even parody.[17]

What might this first version of *Hamlet* have looked like? It is hard to tell, of course, given the multilayered nature of its composition, especially if we make the reasonable assumption that Q1 is not necessarily an early version of the play. It is likely, I think, that it would have been the more straightforward revenge tragedy that people have generally assumed the *Ur-Hamlet* to be. Harold Jenkins is representative in suggesting that the play had a plot of 'murder, madness, and revenge [with] its style evidently remarkable for its Senecan sententiousness, [so that it] must therefore have had a strong likeness to Kyd's . . . *Spanish Tragedy*'.[18] This seems to be a plausible reconstruction of key elements of the play. Equally import-ant, I would suggest, is that this first *Hamlet* would have contained many of the details of the murder of the old Hamlet, as well as the 'mousetrap' plot, and, indeed, Nashe's comments suggest that this was the case. The surviving texts of *Hamlet* show that it is a play with key republican elements, as well as being a work that displays a considerable interest in Scottish history, entirely appropriate for a topical play written soon after the execution of Mary Queen of Scots, and an explanation of why it was revived in the last years of Elizabeth's reign. Much is often made of the defeat of the Spanish Armada, but it is more likely that the key event that defined the anxious and fractious character of the 1590s was the execution of Mary.[19] Anti-Marian propaganda continued well after Mary's death (8 February 1587), as a means of blackening the character of Elizabeth's likely successor, her son, James VI, as Spenser's *The Faerie Queene* demonstrates.[20] The complex history of *Hamlet* in the last years of Elizabeth's reign is a sign of these political concerns.

In writing *Hamlet*, Shakespeare turned to what might have seemed a relatively obscure source, but it was a tale with immense and obvious political charge in the late 1580s, in the immediate aftermath of the execution of Mary Queen of Scots, and in the late 1590s, with the death of Elizabeth ever more imminent, and the threat of the Essex faction culminating in the abortive rebellion of 1601. The story of Amleth is that of a legendary prince of Denmark first narrated in Saxo Grammaticus's *Historiae Danicae* (written at the end of the twelfth century and first published in 1514), and then retold in François Belleforest's *Histoires Tragique* (1570). This French collection, used by many English writers in the late sixteenth century, was undoubtedly Shakespeare's principal source. Thomas Nashe probably recognized this in his comment about meddling with Italian translations, as the earliest stories Belleforest included all derived from the Italian novella writer Matteo Bandello.[21] The story of Hamlet already had an overlaid textual history before it was transformed into a play, changing from a story of blood revenge in a Norse saga, to an Italianate novella of treachery and deceit with a grim conclusion, to a sensational story masquerading as a morality tale.

It is also clear that Belleforest's version has a pronounced republican theme, something that Shakespeare exploits and expands. Any tale of the assassination of a malicious king would remind readers of the story of the banishment of Tarquin, because any such change was likely to lead to a transformation of the form, as well as the occupant, of the ruling office. The story appears time and again throughout Shakespeare's career, more frequently than in that of any other Renaissance English dramatist. In *Hamlet*, the link between the founding of the Roman republic and the story of the murderous infighting at the Danish royal court is made explicit. Hamlet feigns madness to buy himself time before he acts, a tactic employed by Lucius Junius Brutus, and one that makes his name especially appropriate ('Brutus' means 'fool' or 'madman'). Brutus is the nephew of the king – like Hamlet – and he decides to adopt a role when he learns of the actions of the king, Tarquin Superbus. The fullest source is Livy's *History of Rome*:

Now Brutus had deliberately assumed a mask to hide his true character. When he learned of the murder by Tarquin of the Roman aristocrats, one of the victims being his own brother, he had come to the conclusion that the only way of saving himself was to appear in the king's eyes as a person of no account. If there were nothing in his character for Tarquin to fear, and nothing in his fortune to covet, then the sheer contempt in which he was held would be a better protection than his own rights could ever be. Accordingly he pretended to be a half-wit . . . He even submitted to being known publicly as the 'Dullard' (which is what his name signifies), that under cover of that opprobrious title the great spirit which gave Rome her freedom might be able to bide its time.[22]

Brutus is taken by two sons of Tarquin, Arruns and Titus, to consult the Delphic oracle. They learn that the next king of Rome will be the first of them to kiss his mother. Brutus becomes the chosen one when he pretends to fall and so kisses the ground, his mother earth.[23]

Hamlet and Lucius Junius Brutus are similar – although hardly identical – figures. Each pretends to be insane in order to escape the evil machinations taking place at court; each is singled out by supernatural forces as the hope for the future of their countries; and each becomes the next ruler, Brutus establishing the Roman republic, Hamlet becoming king briefly while dying. In Q2, Claudius admits that Hamlet is a popular figure and that dealing with him might be very dangerous:

> The other motive
> Why to a public court I might not go
> Is the great love the general gender bear him,
> Who, dipping all his faults in their affection,
> Work like the spring that turneth wood to stone,
> Convert his gyves to graces; so that my arrows,
> Too slightly timber'd for so loud a wind,
> Would have reverted to my bow again,
> But not where I had aim'd them. (4.7.16–24)

The power of the king is strictly limited by his ability to control the masses, and there are bounds he dare not overstep, exactly the problem that led to the downfall of Tarquinus Superbus. The popular avenger in the surviving play is actually Laertes rather than Hamlet, as he gains the public vote when he returns to Elsinore, informed of his father's death. The messenger informs Claudius that

> The rabble call him lord,
> And, as the world where now but to begin,
> Antiquity forgot, custom not known –
> The ratifiers and props of every word –
> They cry, 'Choose we! Laertes shall be king.'
> Caps, hands, and tongues applaud it to the clouds,
> 'Laertes shall be king, Laretes king'. (4.5.102–8)

In an elective monarchy, such opposition is especially dangerous for the incumbent monarch. It might also be seen to recall the popular rebellion of Brutus, who succeeded in overthrowing the Tarquins because of widespread support, as much against the king as for him. Brutus throws off his disguise in the forum and tells the assembled crowd of the king's 'arrogant and tyrannical' behaviour in appropriating his subjects' property and allowing his son to rape Lucrece, along with Tarquin Superbus's numerous other evil acts: 'The effect of his words was immediate: the populace took fire, and were brought to demand the abrogation of the king's authority and the exile of himself and his family.'[24]

Given that Laertes and Ophelia are additions Shakespeare has made to Belleforest's story (only the Polonius figure features there), it is tempting to speculate that the early *Hamlet* contained one revenge figure only. The later versions enable Shakespeare to draw up a pointed contrast between the simple revenge hero in Laertes, and the brooding, philosophical and ineffective Hamlet, something that has absorbed much modern critical conjecture.[25] Certainly the sense of the play that we gain from Nashe's comments would indicate that this is a distinct possibility. If so, then the later versions indicate that Shakespeare complicated and diluted the rather raw and aggressive form of the first play.

Nevertheless, *Hamlet* stands as a distinctly republican play. The anonymous translation of Belleforest's story, *The Hystorie of Hamblet* (1608), has clearly been influenced by Shakespeare's play.[26] The Argument that prefaces this text, translated faithfully from Belleforest, situates the story of the Danish court within the wider context of a general moral failing, 'envy raigning in the worlde hath in such sort blinded men', and, more specifically, the early history of Rome.[27] Belleforest's reading of Roman history, taken from Livy, sees both cycles and decay, the good transformation of the tyrannical rule of the Tarquins leading to the desirable constitution of the republic, and the bad transition from republic back to tyranny. Human nature might not change and the vices of humanity remain the same whatever the form of government, but it is nevertheless evident that not all these forms are equal:

And not to leave the hystories of Rome, what, I pray you incited Ancius Martinus to massacre Tarquin the Elder, but the desire of raigning as a king, who before had bin the onely man to move and solicite the saide Tarquinius to bereave the right heires and inheriters thereof? What caused Tarquinius the Proud traiterously to imbrue his hands in the blood of Servius Tullius, his father in law, but onely that fumish and unbridled desire to be commander over the cittie of Rome? which practise never ceased nor discontinued in the said principall cittie of the empire, as long as it was governed by the greatest and wisest personages chosen and elected by the people; for therein have been seen infinite numbers of seditions, troubles, pledges, ransommings, confiscations and massacres, onely proceeding from this ground and principle, which entereth into mens hearts, and maketh them covet and desirous to be heads and rulers of a whole common wealth. And after the people were deprived of that libertie of election, and that the empire became subject to the pleasure and fantasie of one man, commanding al the rest, I pray you peruse their bookes . . . and you shall see how poysons, massacres, and secret murthers, were the means to push them forwards that durst not openly attempt it[.][28]

Under the guise of declaring that nothing ever changes, this potted history shows how different the (Roman) republic was from the empire, a message that pervades every extant telling of the story of Hamlet. The republic may not be able to transform mankind as its most vociferous supporters would wish it to, a theme that had dominated discussions of republicanism in Italy in the fifteenth and sixteenth centuries, and assumed increasing importance in seventeenth century political thought in England and America when republican government became a reality.[29] Nevertheless, these prefatory comments show what is at stake when constitutions that provide liberty for the majority of citizens are pitted against ones that take it away.

Hamlet is a neatly circular work, with its end in its beginning. We see the soldiers on the battlements of Elsinore at the start of the play, awaiting the invasion forces of Fortinbras, prince of Norway, who is keen to avenge his father's death at the hands of Hamlet senior (thus adding a further dimension to the cycle of revenge and showing how uncomfortably close Hamlet and Fortinbras are, even though they have to be enemies). The action of the play shows the royal family destroying itself from within, another characteristic of histories of republican and imperial Rome, most notably the Julio-Claudians, whose history was narrated in Tacitus's

History and *Annals*, material that was as familiar to English readers as Livy's *History of Rome*, and was very much in vogue in the 1590s. When the Danish royal family have destroyed themselves in the very last scene, Fortinbras is able to take over the crown, elected by the dying Hamlet who has only been king for a matter of minutes (5.2.360–61). The cyclical nature of the play makes the history of Denmark seem very like that of Rome, raising the same issues of continuity, change and political form, and, without necessarily resolving any of them, shows how relevant those issues are for English audiences in those 1590s.

Hamlet's resemblance to Lucius Junius Brutus is only one of the complex republican contexts and themes that this messiest of plays signals and develops. *Hamlet* also makes use of recent Scottish history, as has often been noted.[30] Why might Shakespeare have been interested in Scotland, and what connected Scotland to republicanism in English minds? No one who paid any attention to Elizabethan current affairs could fail to take careful note of events north of the border. Elizabethan England was in fact neatly framed by its relationship with Scotland: most specifically through the Stuart claim to the English throne, but also because Scotland was acknowledged as the site of the most advanced and controversial political ideas in post-Reformation Europe. For many Protestants, Scottish political thought was a source of inspiration and a means of their fighting back against corrupt and tyrannical rulers; for many monarchs and their advisers, keen to preserve the status quo, the same ideas threatened to undermine stability and their legitimacy. These issues were most immediately relevant in England, which would probably be ruled by a Scottish monarch when Elizabeth died, whether that occurred in the 1560s or the 1600s, unless a concerted effort was made to prevent this outcome.[31]

Scotland was also a divided and fractious land. It appeared to some observers as an example of the worst form of state, where bitter religious conflict defined the body politic, as was the case in late sixteenth-century France, especially after the Massacre of St Bartholomew's Day (23 August 1572).[32] In Scotland aggressive and implacably divided factions of Protestant and Catholic nobles fought for control over the monarch. It is no accident that while Mary Stuart was a Catholic, her son, James VI, was brought up as a Protestant. Mary was the product of a French Catholic education, overseen by her mother-in-law, Catherine de Medici – making the link between Scotland and France explicit for English observers. James had to endure as tutor the overbearing Protestant humanist George Buchanan, who was determined to impress on his young charge the need to serve his people well and so helpfully bombarded him with examples of the fates of evil tyrants who had disobeyed God's word.[33] As if this were not enough, James was later kidnapped (August 1582) by a group of Protestant noblemen, the Ruthven lords, who were determined to have him recognize the supremacy of the Scottish Kirk and banish his Catholic favourite, Esmé Stuart, first duke of Lennox.[34]

It is little wonder that Shakespeare's one Scottish play, *Macbeth*, although the action takes place in the eleventh century, makes a direct allusion to contemporary religious divisions. Immediately after the murder of Duncan, the Porter compares Scotland to hell and imagines the damned knocking at the gates. One of these is 'an equivocator, that could swear in both the scales against either scale; who committed treason enough for God's sake, yet could not equivocate to heaven' (*Macbeth*, 2.3.8–11).[35] Clearly the primary allusion is to the trial speeches of Father Garnett, one of the condemned Gunpowder Plot conspirators, in which he sought to extract himself from charges of treason through the use of deliberately specious reasoning and dishonest wordplay.[36] But the Porter's words also indicate that Scotland was known to have been a disunited kingdom with powerful and hostile figures gaining access to the monarch through force and guile – as in the Ruthven Raid. Given that James's aim from the very start of his reign as king of England was to achieve a formal unity between the two kingdoms, such reminders of the problems he had left behind in Scotland were indeed potent warnings of a troubled future.[37]

The impact of Scotland on English politics and political thought was profound.[38] When Elizabeth became queen on 17 November 1558, Catholic monarchs throughout Europe declared their allegiance to Mary Stuart as the true hereditary monarch, establishing a problem that would shadow Elizabeth's reign even after the execution of Mary in 1587.[39] Equally, a piece of spectacularly unfortunate timing saw the publication of John Knox's polemic against women rulers, *The First Blast of the Trumpet Against the Monstrous Regiment of Women*, in the same year. Knox, as is well known, had Mary Tudor in mind but his work caused considerable difficulty for the Scottish Kirk in subsequent years as they sought substantial aid from Elizabeth to combat the Catholic threat in Scotland.[40] Nevertheless, Knox's intervention neatly encapsulates the problematic relationship between the English authorities and Scottish religious and political affairs. Knox later backtracked on his claims that women should never be allowed to rule, arguing rather disingenuously in his encounter with Mary Stuart that he had made no effort to challenge her right to rule and had written his book 'most especially against that wicked Jezebel of England [i.e., Mary Tudor'] and that he had never intended to 'hurt you or your authority'.[41]

As any reader of *The First Blast* would have known, this was simply not true. For Knox asserted there, in stridently misogynist terms, signalled by the marginal note, 'Causes why women should not have pre-eminence over men':

For who can deny it but repugneth to nature that the blind shall be apppointed to lead and conduct such as do see; that the weak, the sick and impotent persons shall nourish and keep the whole and strong; and finally, that the foolish, mad and frenetic shall govern the discreet and give counsel to such as be sober of mind? And such be all women compared unto man in bearing of authority. For their sight in civil regiment is but blindness, their strength weakness, their counsel foolishness, and judgement frenzy, if it be rightly considered.[42]

Furthermore, later in the same work Knox articulated a theory of kingship which indicated that sovereignty was the prerogative of the godly such as himself and not the monarch (and he repeated his injunction that God 'hath sanctified and appointed for man only . . . to occupy and possess as His minister and lieutenant, secluding from the same all woman'). Using his understanding of Old Testament history Knox argued:

If any think that the forewritten law did bind the Jews only, let the same man consider that the election of a king and appointing of judges did neither appertain to the ceremonial law neither yet was it mere judicial, but that it did flow from the moral law as an ordinance, having respect to the conservation of both the Tables.[43]

Here the marginal note informs the reader that 'The election of a king floweth from the moral law.' Knox's political ideas were by no means consistent and coherent and do not really amount to a resistance theory to tyrannical government.[44] The one central idea is the supremacy of biblical injunctions and the need for the monarch to conform to these rather than exercising his or her own means of government. Nevertheless, they closely resemble arguments produced in monarchomach Huguenot treatises such as *Vindiciae, Contra Tyrannos*, which made explicit links between theories of resistance developed in France and Scotland. *Vindiciae, Contra Tyrannos* gives arguments of hereditary monarchy short shrift because authority resides in the (godly) people whose monarch is there to serve them:

All kings were wholly elected from the beginning. Those who today seem to come to the kingdom by succession must first be constituted by the people. Finally, although it has been the custom in some regions for the people to choose its kings for itself from a certain lineage on account of some outstanding merits, it chooses the stem and not the offshoot. Its choice is not such that if degeneration occur, it may not elect another. The offspring of that stem are not so much born, as made, kings; they are held to be not so much kings, as candidates for kingship.[45]

The argument is an ingenious one, suggesting that any dynasty rules only because the people choose it and that no line of kings and queens has any right to rule, whatever might appear to be the case and whatever claims they might make themselves. Knox and the authors of *Vindiciae, Contra Tyrannos* show how inextricably intertwined were the questions of sovereignty and legitimacy, the problem of religion and loyalty, the issue of female government, and the complicated relationship between the Tudors and the Stuarts.

Such arguments were developed even more radically by George Buchanan.[46] Buchanan argued throughout his published works that any godly person could dispose of a tyrant, not just magistrates [i.e., government officials], reserving especial ire for Mary Stuart. Her later behaviour and refusal to bow to the wishes of her Protestant subjects after she returned to Scotland when her first husband, Francis II of France, died in 1560, ensured that Buchanan represented her as a worse Jezebel than Knox had Mary Tudor. Buchanan saw her as a tyrant justly excluded by her people after she had her second husband, Lord Darnley (father of his pupil, James VI), murdered in 1567. Mary was guilty of numerous crimes: imposing her false religious beliefs on the Scots against their wishes; arrogantly refusing to listen to the sensible advice of her courtiers; promoting her favourites at the expense of others; making little effort to control her natural female deficiencies (unlike Elizabeth); plotting treason against God, lawfully elected monarchs and the godly, and so on.[47]

However, Mary was not an exception but the culmination of a long line of dreadful Scottish monarchs who met deservedly grisly ends. A key reign in Buchanan's *History of Scotland* was that of Kenneth III, who ended the long tradition of elective monarchy in Scotland. Buchanan's sense of the significance of Kenneth's reign is encapsulated in the version narrated in Holinshed's *Chronicle of Scotland* (1587), a source Shakespeare made extensive use of when writing *Macbeth*.[48] Kenneth is elected by an assembly of 'nobles and great peers'. He starts as a good monarch, a vast improvement on the previous king, Culene, who was so notorious for his 'filthie sensualitie' that he was murdered by Calard, whose daughter he 'had ravished before time among divers others', while on his way to a parliament assembled at Scone where he was about to be deposed (and where Kenneth was then chosen as king).[49] Kenneth is notable for his public show of moral restraint, which he carefully cultivates to win over the people:

For the nature of the *Scotishmen* is, that first the nobles, and then all the residue of the people transform themselves to the usage of their prince: therefore did *Kenneth* in his owne trade of living shew an example of chastitie, sobrietie, liberalitie, and modestie, misusing himself in no kind of vice, but refraining himself from the same. He banished all such kind of persons as might provoke either him or other unto anie lewd or wanton pleasures . . . He tooke busie care in causing the people to avoid sloth, and to applie themselves in honest exercises, judging (as the truth is) that to be the waie to advance the common-wealth from decaie to a flourishing state. (p. 301)

The passage is notable for its careful praise of Kenneth's virtues as a monarch, justly regarding him as a successful ruler who leads his people well, but also implying that he is repressing a less virtuous side of his nature, one that may surface later. Kenneth copes well with recalcitrant nobles and establishes a series of successful laws that help purge the realm of evildoers. He defeats the Danes, the Viking raiders who terrified northern Europe throughout the tenth and eleventh centuries. As a result, he 'was greatlie praised, loved, and dread of all of his subjects: so that great quietnesse followed in the state of the common-wealth, greatlie to the advancement thereof' (p. 309).

But Kenneth was not famous for any of these achievements, as Buchanan and Thynne were clearly aware. The really significant event of his reign was his transformation of the Scottish constitution when he ended the principle of elective monarchy and established the system of primogeniture.[50] Kenneth makes this crucial change for wholly discreditable motives, through the 'blind love he bare to his own issue'. He poisons the heir apparent, his cousin, Malcolm Duff, prince of Cumberland, escaping detection only through the goodwill of the people: 'But though the physicians understanding by such evident signes as appeared in his bodie, that he was poisoned, yet such was the opinion which men had of the kings honour and integritie, that no suspicion at all was conceived that it should be his deed' (p. 309).

Kenneth is highly successful at going through the motions so that he can cover his tracks, the narrative suggesting that the skills that made him a good ruler now help him become a master criminal. The narrative highlights 'the cloked love . . . which he had shewed him [Malcolm] at all times'; the extensive mourning arrangements, 'that his funeral should be celebrated in everie church and chapel for his soule'; and the tears Kenneth sheds whenever his name is mentioned, convince virtually everyone of the king's genuine grief, until well after the event, when a few nobles begin to suspect that all is not as it should be, 'but yet because no certeintie appeared, they kept their thoughts to themselves' (pp. 309–10).

At a council at Scone, Kenneth makes a powerful speech to persuade his people to agree to accept the principle of primogeniture. He argues that elected monarchy causes division and sedition in the realm, hindering the peace, stability and prosperity of the commonwealth, often leading to 'sundrie murthers, occasions of civill discord, and other wicked practices', and that it would be better if 'the son should without anie contradiction succeed the father in the heritage of the crowne and kinglie estate' (p. 310). Kenneth's son Malcolm is duly declared heir apparent by being made the new prince of Cumberland, and a new act declares that the eldest male heir of the deceased king should succeed him as king of Scotland, a brother's son preceding a sister's son, with a clause enabling the peers of the realm to appoint a regent in the case of a minority (p. 311).

Kenneth now has everything he wants and tries to win over the hearts of the people. However, he is troubled by a guilty conscience and one night a ghostly voice warns him that God knows his actions and that his issue will be punished for his crimes. Kenneth confesses his act to the bishop of Movean who assures him that God forgives those who sincerely repent. Nevertheless, not all of Kenneth's subjects are so magnanimous. On a hunting trip in the Highlands, Kenneth lodges at the castle of Fenella, who hates him – not surprisingly, as he has had her son put to death. Moreover, she is a relation of Malcolm Duff. She has a beautiful tower built, 'covered over with copper finelie ingraven with diverse flowers and images'. Inside she places a statue of the king, holding a golden apple 'set full of precious stones', which will trigger off a series of crossbows hidden behind the 'rich cloths of arras wrought with gold and silk, verie faire and costlie', when handled. Kenneth duly removes the apple to get a closer look and is killed.[51]

The relevance of these events, issues and questions to *Hamlet* is simultaneously obvious and obscure. Why Shakespeare would not have been able to write a play that dealt directly with the Scottish succession is rather easier to comprehend: Elizabeth had forbidden any discussion of the succession and by the last years of the sixteenth century the most likely successor to Elizabeth was James VI of Scotland.[52] James VI married Anne of Denmark in 1589, which might have provided a topical contextual trigger for the play; the character of Gertrude, however she was represented, would surely have reminded the audience of the recently executed Mary Stuart, an adulterous queen whose third marriage was made possible by a murder to which she may or may not have been an accessory.[53] The topical relevance of *Hamlet* in 1589 would have been clear enough, however well disguised, making it a 'functionally ambiguous' work.[54] Later on, if the play was rewritten and revived as early as 1599, as Harold Jenkins suspects, the unfortunate case of Sir John Hayward's *The Life and Raigne of King Henrie IIII*, and the ban on history plays, would have served to make *Hamlet* an ideal vehicle for allusive political comment once again.[55] Given Shakespeare's interest in the question of succession, as both an imminent event and a political problem, throughout the 1590s, it would be odd if he had not turned his attention to either Holinshed's *Chronicle of Scotland* or the political debates that were taking place north of the border.[56]

However, using material available in Holinshed to write a play about a problematic Scottish king who murders his cousin to keep his dynasty in power, or about one who is legitimately deposed, or about one who tyrannizes his subjects, was not a serious option in the years 1589–1603 with the authorities already alerted to the dangerous and subversive use to which history could be put. Holinshed's *Chronicles* attracted the unwelcome attention of the censors who took exception to a number of passages, Thynne's 'Continuation' of 'The History of Scotland' being a case in point. The Privy Council called in the 1587 edition of the *Chronicles* and ordered the removal of 'such mention of matter touching the King of Scottes as may give him cause for offense'. Passages which then had to be excised included criticism of James's favourite, Esmé Stewart, and many details of Anglo-Scottish relations 1584–86, which might have showed James's actions in a bad light.[57] Given this level of censorship and sensitivity, it is clear that any direct analysis of Scottish events would have had to be rather more obliquely and allegorically represented. Indeed, the only three plays on obviously Scottish themes produced between 1590 and 1603 are Robert Greene's comedy, *The Scottish History of James IV* (1590), and two lost plays, the tragedy of *Robert II of Scotland* (for which in 1599 Philip Henslowe advanced 40 shillings to a series of writers, including Ben Jonson, Henry Chettle and Thomas Dekker) and Charles Massey's *Malcolm, King of Scots* (1602).[58]

Nevertheless, the plot of *Hamlet* seems saturated with suppressed and disguised references to Scottish history, all designed to express the anxiety felt by English subjects at the prospect of a Scotsman inheriting their throne. The murder of Old Hamlet takes place in an orchard, as did the murder of Mary Stuart's second husband.[59] His body broke out in boils, 'Most lazar-like, with vile and loathsome crust / All my smooth body', as did the dead body of Darnley, according to Buchanan (1.5.72–73). It was commonly argued in anti-Marian propaganda that Mary's partner in crime and next husband, James, earl of Bothwell, committed adultery with her before Darnley's death, as Old Hamlet alleges was the case with Gertrude and Claudius; that the period of mourning for Darnley was far too short, as Hamlet claims was the case with his father; and that Bothwell was markedly inferior in appearance to Darnley, a judgement that Hamlet says anyone who saw Claudius beside his father would also have made.[60] Furthermore, as Howard Erskine-Hill points out, 'There is as much difference and resemblance between the murder of Hamlet the King and the Darnley tragedy, as between the murder of Gonzago and the murder of Hamlet the King', and he argues that the play 'dramatized the position of King James VI . . . the tragically incapacitated inheritor of the unnatural scene into which he had been born'.[61]

Shakespeare uses the impending change of dynasty to speculate more widely and philosophically on the nature of government and the forms of political action that can be countenanced. It is noticeable that key sections of the language of the play's most famous speech, Hamlet's soliloquy on suicide (3.1) could easily have come from the arguments of such mon-archomach treatises advocating the right of citizens to assassinate their ungodly rulers as *Vindiciae, Contra Tyrannos*.[62]

> To be, or not to be, that is the question:
> Whether 'tis nobler in the mind to suffer
> The slings and arrows of outrageous fortune,
> Or to take arm against a sea of troubles
> And by opposing end them . . .
> For who would bear the whips and scorns of time,
> Th'oppressor's wrong, the proud man's contumely,
> The pangs of dispriz'd love, the law's delay,
> The insolence of office, and the spurns
> That patient merit of th'unworthy takes
> When he himself might his quietus make
> With a bare bodkin? (3.1.56–60; 70–76)

The speech is nicely balanced in its hesitant embrace of violence as a solution to problems. When Hamlet meditates on the nature of suffering and action, we cannot be sure whether he is planning 'to take arm against a sea of troubles' by ending his own life or by ending that of the person who has caused his misery. Equally, the desire to achieve 'quietus' (settling a debt) through the use of a 'bare bodkin' (dagger), does not indicate whether the intended target is his own breast or another's, and the mention of 'oppressor' and 'office' in the immediately previous build-up of phrases suggests that Hamlet's mind is at least partly on the sins of Claudius. Furthermore, political assassination invariably led to the death of the perpetrator, as is the spectacular case at the end of the play. Assuming the mantle of God's avenger against tyranny was a dubious honour, as, successful or not, death awaited the chosen one. The soliloquy may well be a meditation on Hamlet's death, through his own choice and brought about by his own actions, but not quite as has been assumed.

Indeed, many of the significant political questions that *Hamlet* poses derive from those asked in a text such as *Vindiciae, Contra Tyrannos.* Is Claudius a good ruler and are the effects of his rule just and beneficial for his subjects? Would it have been better on balance if Fortinbras had taken Denmark and ruled it instead (after all, this is what does happen at the end of the play, and England was about to surrender its crown to a foreign monarch for the second time in half a century)? Should obedient subjects accept their lot and obey their ruler however he or she obtained power? Or is their duty to oppose him or her and try to restore the legitimate ruler (assuming one has a claim)? Such comparisons are invited by the play when Polonius tells Hamlet that he 'did enact Julius Caesar. I was killed i'th'Capitol. Brutus killed me' (3.2.102–3), prefiguring not only his own death, but also that of Claudius, as well as demonstrating how potent political narratives shadow the stories of other events, waiting for percep-tive readers to make the connections between them.[63] Polonius is clearly not such a reader and his need to explain the fate of the character he played shows that he has no idea that others might already know and understand the story of Caesar and attribute significance to his life and death. The murder of Caesar was a key moment in republican history, but one that came too late to save the republic as its institutions had already decayed too far to be saved. Hence the act of the second Brutus was a parody of the act of the first, especially in Shakespeare's version of the story. The implication here is either that Hamlet has waited too long or that he is right to procrastinate. Political assassination simply will not provide any desirable result in Claudius's Denmark, even though figures

such as Polonius may well deserve nasty ends. Perhaps we should conclude that Fortinbras's eventual triumph is inevitable, rather like that of
James VI.

Nevertheless, Hamlet's last action before he dies is to kill Claudius,
showing that his soliloquy has a prophetic purpose in the plot. He justifies
his actions through his exclamation, 'The King – the King's to blame'
(5.1.326). Hamlet undoubtedly means Claudius, although the audience
might see an irony if it is thought that the real villain is the ghost of
the Old Hamlet.[64] Claudius has murdered his brother, the legitimate
king, and subsequently married his wife. It is not clear whether he has
destroyed a workable political process in doing so: Hamlet claims only
that Claudius has stolen his rightful kingdom after the King has been
exposed as 'A murderer and a villain, / . . . That from a shelf the precious
diadem stole / And put it in his pocket' (3.4.97–101) (Claudius publicly
declares Hamlet his successor in his first scene [1.2.8–9]). After the
mousetrap play, he is represented as cut off from God. He admits that
his 'offence is rank, it smells to heaven; / It hath the primal eldest curse
upon't – / A brother's murder' (3.3.36–38), aligning him with the cursed
race of Cain. His attempts to pray are futile: 'My words fly up, my
thoughts remain below. / Words without thoughts never to heaven go'
(97–98). Claudius has violated God's law, a capital crime according to
Vindiciae, Contra Tyrannos: 'The king . . . if he neglects God, if he goes
over to his enemies, if he commits felonies against God, forfeits the
kingdom by this very right and often loses it in practice.'[65] His court
becomes a labyrinth of deceit in which all human relationships are
poisoned: fathers spy on sons and daughters; friends betray friends;
private utterances become public, invariably distorted in the process with
disastrous consequences. When he knows that his crime has been exposed,
Claudius plans to murder the heir to the throne to save his secret.

Yet it would be a crude reading of the play that saw Claudius's rule as
entirely negative. There is a pointed contrast between the bloody and
violent military world represented in the opening scene and the revelry
at court shown in the second, with only Hamlet standing aside from
the guests as a self-marginalized malcontent. The Old Hamlet's pride in
the warrior culture he inhabits, gambling his country on the outcome of
single combat, is replaced by the sensible diplomacy of Claudius, who in
dispatching Voltemand and Cornelius to Norway seems to have preserved
peace for Denmark. Modern kingship has started to impose order on a
lawless and anarchic kingdom. The tragedy is in fact precipitated by
exposing the king's crime rather than keeping it concealed.

Claudius's reign bears striking similarities to that of Kenneth III. Both are relatively efficient kings who preserve the territorial integrity of their countries, Kenneth achieving this by defeating the Danes. Both act swiftly and efficiently to establish law and order, and are prepared to be utterly ruthless to impose their will. One of Kenneth's first acts as king is to have five hundred 'idle loiterers as used to live by spoil and pillage . . . hanged upon gibbets . . . and commandment given . . . that their bodies should not be taken downe, but there to hang still to give example to other, what the end was of all such as by wrongfull means sought to live idelie by other mens labours' (Holinshed, *Chronicle of Scotland,* p. 304). Both achieve power as elected monarchs, Claudius assuming the throne as brother of the dead king, Kenneth as son of the murdered Malcolm I, whose reign was followed by those of Indulph and Culene. Both are murderers, committing desperate acts, in Kenneth's case to ensure that his progeny remain on the throne, in Claudius's to marry the queen. Both preside over courts that contain hostile and suspicious opponents. And both are assassinated by people closely related to those they have killed: Kenneth by an unspecified relation, Claudius by the son of his victim, his bereaved nephew. Each death is associated with a dramatic event: Kenneth's with the golden apple and the crossbows behind the arras, Claudius's with the tournament in the last scene, as well as the mousetrap play.

Such links are suggestive, rather than conclusive proof that Shakespeare had these key events in Scottish history in mind when he wrote *Hamlet.* But any relationship between the historical narrative and the dramatic plot seems more plausible if they are read alongside the connections already noted between the murder of Old Hamlet and its counterpart, the murder of Gonzago, and the murder of Lord Darnley. One of the noted features of anti-Marian propaganda was its virulent misogyny.[66] Buchanan's *Ane detectioun of the duinges of Marie Quene of Scottes,* published in English in 1572, the substance of which was frequently repeated in the next thirty years, represented Mary as a selfish, lecherous whore who would not hesitate to satisfy her whims before those of her subjects and who had no scruples about murder. Buchanan describes her elopement with Bothwell as fuelled by a dangerous lust which endangers her and the people she is supposed to rule:

Though she learned there on good authority that his life was safe, her affection could brook no delay, and she betrayed her *infamous lust* by setting out at a bad time of year, heedless of the difficulties of the journey . . . When he [Bothwell] had been brought there [Jedburgh], their staying together and familiarity were hardly consistent with the honour of either. Then, either because of their daily and nightly exertions, which were dishonourable to themselves and infamous in the eyes of the people, or by some secret dispensation of providence, the Queen fell into so severe a sickness that there remained little hope of recovery (my emphasis).[67]

As James Phillips has noted, the Protestant case against Mary was 'directed not against her religion *per se*, but rather against what was portrayed as the weakness and immorality of her character', the advantage of such an argument being that the deposition of the queen could be justified 'on personal rather than religious grounds'.[68] Hamlet's aggressive misogyny when he confronts his mother with her complicity in Claudius's deeds (3.4) is a standard feature of criticism of *Hamlet*, singling the play out as the Shakespearean work that contains the most striking examples of antifeminist rhetoric.[69] Hamlet impugns his mother's virtue and represents Gertrude's relationship with Claudius as one based on a desire that is wholly inappropriate for a woman. He refers to 'an act / That blurs the grace and blush of modesty, / Calls virtue hypocrite, takes off the rose / From the fair forehead of an innocent love' (40–43). Here the audience cannot be sure whether Hamlet is most enraged about her complicity in the murder of her husband (and the surviving texts never allow the reader/audience to be certain that she knew about Claudius's guilt), or her choice of sexual partners, an ambivalence mirrored in anti-Marian propaganda.[70] His subsequent speech, comparing the merits of the two brothers, can only strengthen a suspicion that it is Gertrude's sex that irks Hamlet most. He concludes the encounter by instructing his mother on what she should avoid, and in doing so, dwells on her intimate relations with Claudius:

> Not this, by no means, that I bid you do?
> Let the bloat King tempt you again to bed,
> Pinch wanton on your cheek, call you his mouse,
> And let him, for a pair of reechy kisses,
> Or paddling in your neck with his damn'd fingers. (183–87)

The only queen known to a late Elizabethan audience who would have behaved with similarly indiscrete and destructive passion was Mary Queen of Scots, the mother of the man most likely to become the next king of England. *Hamlet* seems to contain numerous clues that ask a literate audience to make connections with Scottish history and politics. In fact, if I am right in my readings, one of the wittiest jokes the play contains is the imagined marriage of Kenneth III as Claudius and Mary Queen of Scots as Gertrude, a union which represented the most frightening aspects of Scotland for an Elizabethan audience, and posed the question of what a union between England and Scotland might entail when James became king.

Given the multilayered nature of the texts of *Hamlet*, uncovering a political archaeology is especially problematic. However, unless we wish the play to be cast adrift of any political significance – and *Hamlet* is a work that constantly asks its audience to make topical and political connections – then such a task must be undertaken.[71] My contention is that *Hamlet* is a play that confronts its audience with the dilemma of how they would act when faced with an unjust and unpalatable succession, leaving them governed by a ruler who has obtained power by nefarious means. One crucial context for the play is the banishment of the Tarquins, effected by Lucius Junius Brutus, a model for the actions that Hamlet considers undertaking. Of course, there are other complicating factors – apart from Hamlet's own procrastination – that prevent him from behaving like Brutus. Claudius is shown to be a relatively efficient king, probably rather better than Hamlet's father, certainly in Q2 and F. Political debate in the second half of the sixteenth century made clear distinctions between taking actions against tyrants who oppressed people and those who had gained the throne through usurpation, a theme Shakespeare developed in his history plays.[72] Furthermore, Polonius's reference to himself as Caesar serves to remind Hamlet that not all political assassinations provide beneficial results. Certainly this proves to be the case when Polonius is killed. It is hard to see that a prompt assassination of Claudius would lead to better government, let alone the establishment of a republic.

The second context is Scottish history, ancient and recent. The execution of Mary Queen of Scots meant that the next ruler of England was most likely to be James VI, who in 1589 had just married and so was likely to be able to found a dynasty, and by 1600 had actually done so with the birth of his two sons, Henry (b.1594) and Charles (b.1600).[73] The rights and wrongs of the possible succession were endlessly debated, in tracts and pamphlets (a dangerous undertaking), and, obliquely, on the stage, despite the fact that such dialogue was forbidden.[74] *Hamlet*, a play written about a usurpation in which an apparently complicit queen turns a blind eye to the murder of the king, reminded its audience of events in Scotland which had already had a bearing on English history and were probably going to have a more significant influence in the next few years. Perhaps the *Hamlet* that did the rounds in the late 1580s and early 1590s suggested that political assassination was a viable solution to the problem of an unwanted and dangerous monarch. More likely, it implied, as the later versions of the play do, that the union of England and Scotland might bring such political ideologies in its wake.

Such a reading may seem rather forced, and it would be absurd to reduce the play to an allegory of Scottish involvement in the English succession. Nevertheless, by the time *Hamlet* was revived Shakespeare was probably aware that Mary Queen of Scots had been represented allegorically in a literary work – in the second edition of Spenser's *The Faerie Queene* (1596) – and that (as discussed earlier) James had demanded that the author be punished because any slanderous attack on his dead mother might affect his chances of claiming the English throne (the exclusion of Mary was based on her unsuitability and her lack of virtue so the same case could be made against the son). The result was a major scandal.[75] It was highly unlikely that a dramatist would have been keen to reflect openly on the problems James might bring with him from Scotland to England – political uncertainty and instability, religious conflict, corruption at court, sexual scandal, lack of personal morality and unscrupulous behaviour. But a coded warning to whoever might want to listen, adding spice to an already heady mixture of plots and narratives, perhaps seems a more plausible reason for producing a play, especially one first performed at the very end of Elizabeth's reign. *Hamlet* makes no attempt to offer any solution to the problems it highlights, so it cannot be read as a propagandist play designed to persuade its audience to follow a particular course of action, as earlier court dramas were.[76] Rather, the bleak atmosphere of despair that characterizes the play can be attributed in part to the fear that the sort of intrigues and political disasters represented were about to engulf England when James eventually travelled south to claim his contested birthright. It would not be a surprise if many did turn to their histories of Rome to see if there could be a better option.

CHAPTER 7

After the republican moment

Shakespeare remained interested in republican issues throughout his writing career. His later plays all show an absorbing interest in the question of the prerogative of the monarch and the problem of creeping tyranny, an issue central to republican thought.[1] Plays such as *Coriolanus* (1607–8) and *Pericles* (1609) demonstrate a concern for the republican need to 'define civic virtue and create a sustainable balanced state'.[2] *Macbeth* (1605–6) is a trenchant study of tyranny, as, to a lesser extent, are *King Lear* (1605–6), *The Winter's Tale* (1610–11) and, arguably, *The Tempest* (1611–12).[3] *Timon of Athens* (1607–8) is an analysis of greed and government that is surely designed to reflect badly on the notorious court culture and promotion of favourites that many witnesses saw as the defining characteristic of James's reign.[4]

However, the republican moment had passed with the death of Elizabeth.[5] The accession of James was achieved with an ease and a confidence that few could have predicted in the 1590s. The dreaded apocalyptic consequences of the contested succession never happened. James turned out to be a safe, ecumenical Protestant, eager to inherit his English kingdom without antagonizing his subjects unduly.[6] He proved not to be the destructive Catholic offspring of Mary that many had feared; nor was he the sectarian low-church Protestant that the English also associated with Scotland.[7] In fact, one of the chief threats to James, the Gunpowder Plot, was hatched because, in the wake of the Somerset House Conference of 1604, Catholics expected more tolerance and power than they were actually given.[8] James, as is well known, was widely condemned as a monarch for his absolutist tendencies, corruption, profligacy, ill manners, promotion of favourites, intemperance, lack of dignity, and so on, but it is at least arguable that his role as a peacemaker and mediator between religious extremes prevented the outbreak of dangerous civil strife and contained the opposition to his government to a carping, albeit large, minority.[9]

More importantly, many of his subjects appear to have recognized the stability that James brought, Shakespeare among them.[10] One of the first Shakespeare plays that the newly established King's Men performed at court was *Measure for Measure*, acted in the Banqueting Hall on St Stephen's Night (26 December) 1604. It was probably written earlier that year and then performed at the Globe after 9 April when the theatres reopened after closure caused by another outbreak of the plague.[11] The play is replete with comments on James's reign, exploring the relationship between corruption, vice and government, posing the fundamental question of whether such problems can be eliminated or whether they are an ineradicable constituent of human nature.[12] The opening exchange between the Duke and his adviser, Escalus, leads the audience to expect a play that explores political issues:

> Of government the properties to unfold
> Would seem in me t'affect speech and discourse,
> Since I am put to know that your own science
> Exceeds, in that, the lists of all advice
> My strength can give you . . .
> The nature of our people,
> Our city's institutions, and the terms
> For common justice, y'are as pregnant in
> As art and practice hath enriched any
> That we remember. (1.1.3–7, 9–13)[13]

As it turns out, the metaphorical use of 'pregnant' proves to be unusually appropriate to the development of the play.

This link is, of course, quite deliberate. *Measure for Measure* shows that government is inextricably mired in the problems caused by the vices of its officers, a fundamental issue that the Duke's speech suggests he has overlooked. In the following scene, we learn that Claudio has been sentenced to death for making Juliet pregnant. When the condemned man's sister, Isabella, pleads for his life, Angelo, the substitute governor, promises to pardon him only if she submits to his lust for her, a desire that warps his political judgement and precipitates the main action of the play. The subplot concerns the struggle of the brothel run by Mistress Overdone, a microcosm of the spiritual state of Vienna, to resist Angelo's attempts to rid the city of the vice it provides for the inhabitants.

The Duke is implicated in the plot in a significant way. Disguised as a friar, he is slandered by Lucio for his supposed lechery.[14] When the Friar/

Duke responds that he has 'never heard the absent Duke much detected for women; he was not inclined that way' (3.2.118–19), we know that the ostensible meaning is that the Duke is not promiscuous. However, the play leaves open the possibility that the Duke is not keen on women for other reasons – by implication, his preference for men. Given that James's enthusiastic relationship with young men from the time of his ardour for his cousin, Esmé Stuart, onwards, appears to have been common knowledge in England as well as Scotland, it is hard not to believe that this is a reference that makes a clear connection between Vienna and London.[15]

Measure for Measure, as has often been noted, is a play of endless substitutions.[16] In essence, there are two processes taking place; the substitution of the woman as sexual partner, culminating in the 'bedtrick' whereby Mariana is substituted for Isabella; and the substitution of the heads of the executed criminal, culminating in the death of Ragozine, 'a most notorious pirate' (4.3.70), who only appears – if at all – as a disembodied head.[17] The two plotlines are linked in numerous ways, not least because Mistress Overdone's servant, Pompey, has to serve as assistant to the executioner, Abhorson, in order to obtain a pardon for his sexual crimes. Politics and vice are neatly linked and reversed – substituted – through the use of these two figures: Abhorson, whose name is a version of the common curse, the son of a whore, a frequent insult in Shakespeare's plays; and Pompey, the flawed and failed republican hero.[18]

Measure for Measure, in so far as Vienna stands for London, does not represent the capital city of James's early reign in a positive way, revealing the city to be corrupt, hypocritical and riddled with open and hidden vice.[19] Nevertheless, the play can be seen as an endorsement of the status quo, however qualified this might be. The Duke is indeed a flawed and unattractive leader in many ways, but no alternative form of government is either deemed desirable or, indeed, proposed.[20] But what is most significant for my argument here is that Shakespeare appears to provide a series of hints through the use of numerous plot motifs that republicanism is no longer a viable, current political philosophy. The use of the name Pompey, the losing republican leader in the civil war with Julius Caesar, for a brothel employee, in a play that reveals that all men are fundamentally the same weak and feeble creatures, slaves to their basest desires, strongly suggests that the republican ideal of a society that can promote virtue and eliminate vice is not likely to feature prominently in this particular play. Pompey first appears in the second scene of the play, which introduces us to the Viennese underworld. He informs his employer that the 'houses in the suburbs' (1.2.88) are to be closed down, a means of halting the burgeoning sex trade.[21] Mistress Overdone exclaims, 'Why, here's a change indeed in the common-wealth!' (lines 96–97). However, this feared transformation does not take place as the series of substitutions which are enacted throughout the play leave the moral, social and political order untouched. The line serves to highlight our sense that *Measure for Measure* parodies republicanism as a means of signalling its contemporary irrelevance.

The inauguration of the Roman republic was precipitated by the rape of a virtuous citizen by a corrupt and secretive king who forced her to expose his tyrannical behaviour as a means of cleansing the body politic. Shakespeare's representation of this foundational story had placed heavy emphasis on the transformation of Lucrece from a subservient subject into an articulate citizen ready to die for the ideals of her country. An identical situation is revisited in *Measure for Measure*. Angelo, the substitute governor, is corrupted by power when he fails to control his repressed, secret desires, and tries to force himself on Isabella, abusing his authority and neglecting his duties as upholder of the law in order to carry out his plan. The resemblance of the encounter between Angelo and Isabella to that of Tarquin and Lucrece is evident throughout their first meeting in Act 2. When Isabella threatens to expose Angelo he responds:

> Who will believe thee, Isabel?
> My unsoil'd name, th'austereness of my life,
> My vouch against you, and my place i'th'state
> Will so your accusation overweigh,
> That you shall stifle in your own report,
> And smell of calumny. I have begun,
> And now I give my sensual race the reign:
> Fit thy consent to my sharp appetite;
> Lay by all nicety and prolixious blushes
> That banish what they sue for. Redeem thy brother
> By yielding up thy body to my will;
> Or else he must not only die the death,
> But thy unkindness shall his death draw out
> To ling'ring sufferance. Answer me tomorrow,
> Or, by the affection that now guides me most,
> I'll prove a tyrant to him. As for you,
> Say what you can; my false o'erweighs your true. (2.4.153–69)

Angelo's words recall the logic, style and argument of Tarquin's to Lucrece in Shakespeare's poem. Both men reveal themselves as tyrants, allowing their reason to be overthrown by their will (appetites).[22] Angelo declares that he has given his 'sensual race the reign', a graphic image of kingship being overthrown; Tarquin confesses that his 'will is strong past reason's weak removing' (line 243). Angelo argues that his supposed virtue will enable him to keep his reputation because no one will believe Isabella's accusations. Tarquin makes an analogous case: Lucrece should keep his crime hidden in order to hide the stain to her reputation. An undetected crime is not really a crime at all:

> 'But if thou yield, I rest thy secret friend;
> The fault unknown is as a thought unacted.
> A little harm done to a great good end
> For lawfull policy remains enacted.' (lines 526–29)

The law can be upheld if the tyrant's behaviour remains secret so that life can continue as normal. Angelo's plan is to use the law to fulfil his own desires and then hide behind its mystique. What the law cannot bring into the light the tyrant claims, does not, really exist. However, through this abuse of public authority the docile subject is made active and the secrets that those in power seek to keep hidden are exposed. The darkness that is necessary for Tarquin's crime to take place succumbs to light as the republic, an open form of government, is established. And the obsessively secret machinations of the Viennese rulers – not just Angelo, but also the 'old fantastical duke of dark corners' (4.3.157) – are placed under public scrutiny through Isabella's claims.

Nevertheless, *Measure for Measure* resists and deflects the potential for social, moral and political change. For all the initiatives designed to control and regulate the city's sexual underworld, the play ends with an acknowledgement that vice cannot be easily removed because everyone is subject to it.[23] The crucial events which threaten to inaugurate change simply do not happen. Claudio is not executed and neither is the dissolute Barnadine. Lucio only faces humiliation and Angelo is forced to marry Mariana. The Duke is able to resume power in Vienna as though he had never surrendered it to a deputy. He may not be an ideal ruler, but he does bring stability of sorts to the city he rules, returning at the end of the play to tie up all the strands of the plot.

Most importantly, the rape does not take place: the revolutionary event that conceived the republic is missing. Isabella, unlike Lucrece, does not feel so polluted by her violation that she needs to kill herself, even though her encounters with Angelo and then Claudio (2.4; 3.1) imply that she might follow Lucrece's example.[24] Rather, it is her brother who is threatened with death for the sin of fornication, a lesser crime than rape, one that did not dispute that both parties had performed consensual

sexual intercourse and which was dealt with in England by the ecclesiastical, not the conciliar and ancient courts.[25] His story ends happily with
his impending marriage to Juliet, whose pregnancy also stands in marked
contrast to the nonissuing union of Lucrece and Tarquin. In addition,
Angelo does not suffer for his neglect of Mariana and the couple are
united after the performance of the 'bed trick', an illusory rape that
actually preserves the status quo. The comic universe of *Measure for
Measure* results in the establishment of a series of unions – albeit ones
that may not be ideal – rather than a traumatic violation that has wider
implications.

The 'republican moment' of Elizabeth's last years had been inaugurated
by the execution of Mary Queen of Scots, who was her obvious successor.
The treason committed by the monarch, the crime that sealed her fate, is
recalled in Tarquin's actions in Shakespeare's poem.[26] Near the end of the
last act of *Measure for Measure*, Shakespeare includes an incident, one that
seems to threaten the happy conclusion of the comedy, that would also
have reminded the audience of Mary's death. It is assumed that Claudio
has been executed, whereas he is disguised among the assembled company. In what seems to be a superfluous exchange and a heavy-handed
plot device, the Duke introduces doubts about the legality of the
supposed execution of Claudio as he quizzes the Provost:

> DUKE: I have bethought me of another fault.
>   Provost, how came it Claudio was beheaded
>   At an unusual hour?
> PROV:　　　　　　　　It was commanded so.
> DUKE: Had you a special warrant for the deed?
> PROV: No, my good lord: it was by private message.
> DUKE: For which I do discharge you of your office.
>   Give up your keys.
> PROV:　　　　　　　Pardon me, noble lord;
>   I thought it was a fault, but knew it not;
>   Yet did repent me after more advice. (5.1.454–62)

The exchange concludes, rather pointlessly and undramatically, with the
Provost claiming that, because of his doubts about the legality of the
process he has followed, he has spared the life of Barnadine. Barnadine
now appears and the 'muffl'd fellow' (line 484) next to him proves to be
Claudio. The episode seems to be a clumsy parody of yet another
substitution motif.

However, the incident does make sense if it is read as a clear recollection of the disputes and uncertainty which accompanied the execution of

Mary. Elizabeth was understandably reluctant to have another monarch beheaded after due legal process, an event that would place any English monarch as subject to the rule of law and put them on the same footing as the subjects they ruled. By doing so she was handing over substantial authority to the 'Bond of Association', who had declared that they would use force to protect the queen from her enemies, enabling them to judge the actions of kings and queens.[27] This was a dangerous concession that had republican implications, indicating that the merit of kings and queens could be as important as their bloodlines.[28]

As a result, Elizabeth sought to distance herself as much as possible from the signing of Mary's death warrant. Only the rumour of an invasion force of Spanish troops landing in Wales enabled the Privy Council to get Elizabeth to sign the document on 1 February 1587. Elizabeth signed the warrant when it was brought to her by William Davison, her second secretary. He had it sealed at once and presented to the Privy Council so that the execution could proceed. However, Elizabeth subsequently ordered Davison to wait until she gave a further command before he sealed and sent on the document, enabling her to claim that he had disobeyed her. Davison became the scapegoat whose actions enabled Elizabeth to argue that she had not wanted to let the execution go ahead but that her hand had been unfairly forced by her privy councillors. Davison was threatened with execution by royal pre-rogative, was fined 10,000 marks – later remitted – and imprisoned in the Tower for eighteen months instead.[29]

The conversation in *Measure for Measure* seems to recall many of the details of Mary's death. The supposed execution of Claudio is at 'an unusual hour', apparently preventing any attempt to have the process halted. Mary was executed a week after the warrant was signed by Elizabeth in Fotheringay Castle, a gloomy, obscure and secure prison, where she had spent her final days, the timing and location also prevent-ing any last-minute intervention.[30] The mention of a 'special warrant', which, it transpires, does not exist, and the command by 'private message' further suggest that confusion surrounding Mary's execution. The final detail, the Duke punishing the officer who carried out the act, also serves to remind the audience of Mary's fate. However, the purpose of this carefully crafted comparison is actually to signal its irrelevance to con-temporary English political life. The execution has not been carried out, so the consequences that were precipitated by Elizabeth's actions have no place in the world of *Measure for Measure*, just as they have, by implication, no place in Jacobean England. Time has moved on.

Equally significantly, *Measure for Measure* almost goes out of its way not to point any moral to its story, one reason why it has been classified as a 'problem comedy' (along with its problematic conclusion).[31] There is no obvious moral order that can be detected in the matches made at the end of the play, notably that between Angelo and Mariana, and the Duke and Isabella, which has enabled directors to interpret the ending in radically different ways.[32] The problems that beset Vienna are likely to continue: certainly there is no positive action taken by government to eliminate them successfully. The city's institutions – its government, the law, and personal and social relations – do not appear to have the power to change its citizens for the better, and vice versa.[33]

Yet this is the central claim made by republicans: that they know how to make society and human nature more virtuous, that if only society were to be transformed as they suggest, government will serve the people better, everyone's behaviour will improve, and the citizens will be more content. *Measure for Measure* appears to challenge all such plans to change human nature. Despite the apparently overheard discussion of government that opens the play, the Duke is restored to his rightful place and political and personal life continue as they always have done. Lucio's punishment is meted out according to the authority of the Duke, who first threatens him with whipping and hanging for the crime of slandering the head of state – after he has been forced to marry the woman he has impregnated and abandoned. It is only when Lucio pleads with a neat chiasmus – 'Your Highness said even now, I made you a duke; good my lord, do not recompense me in making me a cuckold' (5.1.513–15) – that the Duke commutes the punishment to what Lucio then establishes as the realm of metaphor:

> DUKE: Upon mine honour, thou shalt marry her.
>   Thy slander I forgive, and therewithal
>   Remit thy other forfeits. – Take him to prison,
>   And see our pleasure herein executed.
> LUCIO: Marrying a punk, my lord, is pressing to death,
>   Whipping, and hanging. (lines 516–21)

These are complicated and densely allusive lines that have generally been ignored by commentators. In what sense does Lucio think he has made the Duke? Literally, he makes the Duke by pulling off his mask. But presumably the answer is also that in attributing heroic feats of debauchery to him, he transforms him from a remote figure into one in touch with the needs and desires of his people. The Duke's administration of justice is not designed to set the audience at their ease and dissipate the tension of the final scene. Only one speech separates the implementation of a rigorous and brutal punishment from a lenient sentence, a rare transformation in a play where things stubbornly refuse to change. This rapid *volte face* surely makes Lucio's representation of his fate as a metaphorical death rather too close to an external reality, especially when the Duke's riposte is 'Slandering a prince deserves it' (line 522). We are reminded throughout this exchange that the Duke either can do, or thinks he can do, exactly as he pleases, a position that seemed to many of James's subjects to represent that of their king.[34] Whether he punishes Lucio severely, or demonstrates clemency, the Duke reinforces his own power.[35]

The reference to 'pressing to death' further suggests silenced, helpless subjects crushed by the weight of authority. There is undoubtedly a bawdy reference to Lucio being smothered beneath his domineering new wife, with the familiar pun on death as orgasm. The other reference is to the legal process of *peine forte et dure*, whereby the guilty party would be slowly pressed to death if they refused to incriminate themselves by entering a plea. The prisoner would be killed by a combination of 'heavy irons and scanty food and water'.[36] The advantage of refusing to plead was that the prisoner's family was able to inherit their property, which would otherwise be forfeit to the crown in cases of, as here, slandering of the king.[37] Lucio's slander of the Duke and his description of his fate reminds the audience of what the penalty could be for criticizing the actions and words of the monarch. What Lucio says is not true, and it is plausible to argue that his eventual fate is just and even-handed, in line with the biblical injunction announced in the play's title.[38] Nevertheless, *Measure for Measure* portrays a state in which there is no authority outside that of the governor's personal rule – a situation that resembled what many thought were the desires of England's new monarch.[39] If Lucio told the truth, he still might experience the same fate, as there are no institutions which could provide legal redress. Authority is dark and mysterious and sometimes silence is the best strategy of resistance; or, put another way, the constitution is less 'mixed' than dysfunctional. There is no forum for public discussion and debate, a harsh reality that the Viennese simply have to accept, just as Isabella has to accept the Duke's marriage proposal.

The episode also provokes one last question. Has the Duke imple- mented justice as he thinks he has? Lucio's crime repeats that of the pardoned Claudio, who was, however, initially punished and had to face the possibility of the death penalty. It also stands as a mirror image of that of Angelo who suffers no punishment other than public shame for his transgression. The play leaves us with two conclusions. First that, whatever the designs of governors, under this political system there will always be one law for the powerful and one for the powerless. Second, that this situation will continue indefinitely, human nature being as weak and fallible as it is.

It would be wrong, however, to think that *Measure for Measure* was Shakespeare's last word on republicanism. The republican moment had indeed passed, but a republican interest in the functioning of institutions, a concern that is clearly present in *Measure for Measure*, would still continue. *Othello* was written at about the same time – it is not certain whether it was one of the last plays performed during Elizabeth's reign or one of the first in James's.[40] While Vienna is represented as a problematic autocracy, Venice receives a much more positive portrayal, in line with that of other English travellers who were invariably attracted to the life and government of Europe's oldest surviving republic.[41]

Venice was seen by many English authors as the most desirable city-state in Europe, an 'artificial angel' notable for its wealth, relative tolerance of strangers (in marked contrast to much of the rest of Italy), and a sophisticated, complex but clear constitution that brought out the best in its citizens. As Vittorio Conti has pointed out, 'the word "republic" was all but a synonym for Venice. When "republic" was mentioned, Venice was automatically evoked.'[42] The most important features, as noted by English observers such as William Thomas and made widely available through Lewis Lewkenor's translation of Gaspar Contarini's *The Commonwealth and Government of Venice*, were the preservation of liberties through the rotation of political offices and the practice of universal adult male suffrage.[43] While the rest of Europe suffered periodic bouts of chaos and change – England's version of this Continental malaise is recorded in Shakespeare's histories, for example – Venice had remained constant for a thousand years. As if this were not enough to attract the admiration of Englishmen, it was also a natural ally of such moderate Protestant countries as England, being in dispute with Rome.[44]

Shakespeare used Lewkenor's translation of Contarini extensively when he wrote *Othello*.[45] It is notable that the Venetian republic makes every effort to use Othello's services and treat him with proper respect in the first act, after Brabantio has intervened in the council meeting to discuss the imminent threat from the Turks. Racism does exist in Venice, as the actions and thoughts of Brabantio, Iago and Roderigo demonstrate (although it is also notable that Iago and Roderigo are Spanish names, suggesting that they may, like Othello, be strangers within the realm), and it is possible that the Venetian authorities employ Othello (who is, after all, their second choice after Marcus Luccios) as an expediency.[46] Nevertheless, they make every effort to deal with racial prejudice – in marked contrast to Shakespeare's earlier representation of Venice in *The Merchant of Venice*.[47] It is quite possible to argue that Iago is able to cause the tragedy only because the subsequent action takes place in Cyprus, a Venetian colony, rather than the metropolitan centre itself.[48]

What we see in the first act of *Othello* is the city's institutions struggling – with considerable success – to make its citizens behave virtuously, a key republican concept and one that evidently absorbed Shakespeare's imagination. Citizens in Venice are not necessarily more naturally virtuous than they are elsewhere. Moreover, Shakespeare's plays contain numerous examples of characters who exhibit similar vices to those on display in the first act of *Othello*, and it is worth noting that one of the critical commonplaces made by commentators from Thomas Rymer onwards is that it is the tragedy that most closely resembles a comedy.[49] However, unlike Vienna in *Measure for Measure*, in which the city authorities are shown to be encouraging vice rather than preventing it, those in Venice appear have the power to rein in the bestial instincts and behaviour of its citizens. A great deal is made of the inclinations of individuals. When he learns that his daughter has eloped with Othello, Brabantio remarks that 'This accident is not unlike my dream' (1.1.140), an illustration of the racist fantasies of miscegenation that torment him.[50] In contrast, Desdemona tells the court in the trial scene that she 'saw Othello's visage in his mind' (1.3.253), a problematic line in terms of its conceptualization of the contrast between skin colour and goodness, but one that shows her drawn to what she sees as virtue. Iago, hardly surprisingly, expresses sentiments more in line with those of Brabantio, beginning with his soliloquy at the end of the same scene. This sees the process of what Coleridge famously called 'the motive-hunting of motiveless malignity', as Iago searches for a substantial form on which to anchor his feelings of overwhelming hostility towards Othello.[51] Iago claims that his chief strategy will be to turn the good qualities of his victims against them:

> The Moor is of a free and open nature
> That thinks men honest that but seem to be so,
> And will as tenderly be led by th'nose
> As asses are.
> I have't, it is engendered! Hell and night
> Must bring this monstrous birth to the world's light. (lines 398–403)

Such a plan makes him, of course, a dangerous enemy. However, it depends on his actions remaining undetected, of the state being too weak to defend its citizens and there being no due process at the end of the plot to investigate the different stories of events. This is indeed what happens in the play, as Othello takes the law into his own hands, first publicly shaming his wife, and then killing her in a parody of a judicial process.[52] The murder of Desdemona in 4.2. stands as a pointed and deliberate contrast to the trial scene in 1.3, illustrating the vast gulf between life in Venice and life in the outpost of Cyprus. It is evident that Emilia's sensible and clear-headed testimony would have prevented the final denouement had it been given in a Venetian court, one of the many aspects that makes *Othello* such a hard play to watch as audiences often imagine that the tragedy will be prevented at any moment.[53]

Othello shows that individual virtue is often too weak to survive on its own in the face of a concerted attempt to undermine it by a determined enemy, that it can only flourish if nurtured and protected by powerful state institutions, an argument central to republican theory as it developed in Europe.[54] Republics had a need to promote two mutually complementary forms of virtue: the positive duty of the citizen to live an active life (*vita activa*) supporting and furthering the ideals of the republic; and a negative duty to prevent the development of abuses which could lead to the establishment of tyranny. Both of these ideals are seen as central features of the Venetian republic by Contarini. He describes the founding of the republic:

With this then exceeding vertue of mind did our ancestors plant and settle this such a commonwealth, that since the memory of men, whosoever shal go about to make compare between the fame & the noblest of the ancients, shal scarcely find any such: but rather I dare affirme, that in the discourses of those great Philosophers, which fashioned & forged commonwealths according to the desires of the mind, there is not any to be founde so well fayned and framed[.][55]

Everything about Venice is marked by perfection and virtue. It is the concept of the 'exceeding vertue of mind' of the founders of the republic and is not only the best constitution ever devised by mankind, but also the best that could possibly have been designed. Whereas other states simply have as their goal the improvement of nature, Venice actually manages this feat. Following Aristotle, Contarini opens his third book by arguing that the young should obey the old, as a principle of government is to perfect what has been given to mankind by nature:

Every institution and government of man, the neerer it aspireth to the praise of perfection and goodnesse, the nearer shold it imitate nature, the best mother of all thinges: for so hath she disposed the order of the whole world, that those thinges which are devoide of sence and understanding, shoulde bee ruled and governed by those that have sense and knowledge: and therefore in this assemblie of men, (which of us is called Citie) olde men ought to bee preferred before the younger sort[.] (p. 64)

The Commonwealth and Government of Venice shares a common political discourse with numerous other sixteenth-century European political – and nonpolitical – texts.[56] Yet, even when it uses the most familiar of clichés, they are given a republican significance.

The mixed constitution of the republic is also seen as the best means of preventing the unwelcome development of tyranny through its ability to control and regulate dangerous elements – such as Brabantio's racism or Iago's destructiveness – and always return to the balanced status quo. Contarini employs the familiar image of the body politic to show how the Venetian council – the very body represented in session in the third scene in *Othello* – steers the city-state away from the unhappy fate that befalls most other political systems:

Our elders did with a marvellous & in manner divine providence forsee, that as in mans bodie, through the corruption and putrefaction of one humor, many & most daungerous diseases doe commonly happen, which growe in time to bee the causes of death: so also in a commonwealth there are sometimes wicked and disloyall citizens, that are causes thereunto of great troubles and calamities, whiles they aspire rather to the pride of a wicked and unjust commandement, then to the praise of an honest and quiet obedience carried away in those damnable endevors eyther with ambition, and desire of rule, or oppressed with intollerable debt, or otherwise having committed some haynous wickedness or crime, for which they stand in doubt or punishment: such as we reade was in *Rome, Catiline, Silla, Marius* and finally, *Julius Caesar* . . . The like we reade of sundry commonwealthes of the Greekes . . . But in these times of ours *Italy* it selfe hath yeelded us sufficient examples . . . For which cause our prudent elders laboured to establish this commonwealth of ours in all perfection and beauty, and to strengthen the same with such & so holesome lawes, that it might as much as in mans wisedome lyeth, prevent the inconvenience of so monstrous and miserable a fall . . . they thoughte it not amisse . . . to create in this our citie some magistrate of authority and power, whose office above all other things should be, to have especial care to see that among the citizens should not arise any strife or dissention . . . and to prevent factions, or the attemptes of any wicked citizen that shoulde conspire against the liberty of the commonwealth[.] (pp. 77–78)

Venice's stability stands in marked contrast to all other political systems. The emphasis placed on Julius Caesar is significant. Contarini is pointing out, probably following Polybius, that, for all the sophistication of its carefully crafted constitution, the Roman republic was eventually undone by an ambitious, ruthless and self-interested individual.[57] Venice stands alone as the republic that has lasted and will endure for the foreseeable future, preserved through scrupulous attention to the mechanics of government. It is this process, the attempt to preserve internal cohesion and harmony, that we see at work in the first act of *Othello*, as the assembled council and Duke simultaneously prepare to meet the threat of the Turks and smooth over troubles within the city itself.

Iago represents his actions as an assault on the virtue of the protagonists. He acknowledges their essential goodness and plans to use their admirable qualities as the means of destroying them. He frequently uses the word 'virtue', always in an attempt to undermine a belief in it. At the end of 1.3, Iago is left onstage with Roderigo who recognizes that their plot to separate the newlyweds has failed miserably. Roderigo laments his inability to influence his destiny: 'I confess it is my shame to be so fond, but it is not in my virtue to amend it' (1.3.318–19). Iago seizes on Roderigo's usage to argue that, on the contrary, one's own will is paramount and can overrule everything else:

Virtue? a fig! 'tis in ourselves that we are thus, or thus. Our bodies are gardens, to the which our wills are gardeners. So that if we will plant nettles or sow lettuce, set hyssop and weed up thyme, supply it with one gender of herbs or distract it with many, either to have it sterile with idleness or manured with industry – why, our power and corrigible balance of this lies in our wills. (lines 320–27)

Iago's logic and perception of nature can be seen to invert the language of republicanism as reproduced in Contarini's text. There, nature and the good society are in harmony, whereas Iago sets the one against the other. For Contarini, virtue is the highest ideal of nature; for Iago, it is a delusive ideology imposed on citizens to make them conform. For Contarini, the state is the object of comparison, the good state being a natural form; for Iago, the self is the individual's own garden to cultivate as he or she wishes. Elsewhere, they conceive man and the natural world in similar ways, but from opposite perspectives. Contarini sees human nature inclining towards virtue and only perverse wills trying to undermine or sever this link; Iago tries to persuade Roderigo that he can make of himself what he wills. As with the better-known case of Menenius's fable of the belly in *Coriolanus*, we are shown how analogical language is never stable and can be used to very different ends.[58]

This exchange plays a crucial role in the play, establishing Iago as an antirepublican villain, committed to the destruction of all forms of virtue, including the political virtue that was so important in Venice. Iago's lines can also be read as a response to the praise the Duke bestows on Othello as a means of reconciling his father-in-law to the marriage and reintegrating Brabantio into the mainstream of Venetian life: 'If virtue no delighted beauty lack / Your son-in-law is far more fair than black' (lines 290–91). The Duke's lines are an attempt to establish nature and virtue as complementary, although Brabantio refuses to be mollified and leaves warning Othello to watch out for his duplicitous daughter. Iago's subsequent meditation on virtue pursues this theme of separation and isolation, casting himself in the role of the outsider who threatens the stability of the republic. When Iago articulates his plot in his soliloquy after the brawl scene, he does so in terms that refer back to this earlier speech, as well as the murder of Gonzago in the 'mousetrap' play in *Hamlet*, which also has a republican significance:[59]

> For whiles this honest fool [Cassio]
> Plies Desdemona to repair his fortune,
> And she for him pleads strongly to the Moor,
> I'll pour this pestilence into his ear:
> That she repeals him for her body's lust.
> And by how much she strives to do him good
> She shall undo her credit with the Moor –
> So wil I turn her virtue into pitch
> And out of her own goodness make the net
> That shall enmesh them all. (2.3.348–57)

Iago's plot, freed from the control of the institutions of Venice, works in the military environment of the Cyprus garrison. Othello, as has often been noted, regards his own virtue in terms of military success.[60] He sees the success and failure of his marriage in terms of his prowess on the battlefield, his virtue connecting the two crucial areas of his life:

> I had been happy if the general camp,
> Pioneers and all, had tasted her sweet body,
> So I had nothing known. O now for ever
> Farewell the tranquil mind, farewell content!
> Farewell the plumed troops and the big wars
> That makes ambition virtue! (3.3.348–53)

In Venice Othello is regarded as a worthy citizen of the state and his good qualities can flourish. When he strikes Desdemona in front of the newly arrived Venetian dignitaries, Lodovico comments that his action 'would not be believed in Venice' (4.1.241) and then registers his shock that the man they all had such faith in had let them down so badly:

> Is this the noble Moor whom our senate
> Call all in all sufficient? This the nature
> Whom passion could not shake? whose solid virtue
> The shot of accident nor dart of chance
> Could neither graze nor pierce? (lines 264–68)

Othello is a virtuous man in many ways, but his qualities are found to be wanting when he faces a concerted and brilliant attack from where he least expects it, within the ranks of his own army. He is transformed into a bloodthirsty savage, an example of the bestial state of nature that Venice strives so hard to negate.[61] Iago's plot can be seen as analogous to the internal threats to states described by Contarini. These were launched by evil and perverse citizens – Catiline, Scylla, Marius and Julius Caesar – who managed to undermine even the best of states such as republican Rome. Venice itself can fight off such attacks through the strength of its magnificent constitution, its institutions and elaborate series of laws, checks and balances. However, none of these work in Cyprus and the ruthless individual can accomplish the triumph of the will.

As well as maintaining his interest in institutions, Shakespeare also dramatized the final destruction of the Roman republic when he wrote *Antony and Cleopatra*, completed at some point between 1604 and 1608.[62] The play shows the break-up of the triumvirate established between Octavius, Antony and Lepidus to fight the republican army of Cassius and Brutus in the last two acts of *Julius Caesar*.[63] Antony has become enraptured by the queen of Egypt, Cleopatra, but briefly returns to fight alongside his allies to defeat the rebellion of Pompey's son, the last gasp of republican resistance to the newly established empire, marrying Octavia, Octavius Caesar's sister, as a sign of his renewed commitment to their cause. However, on the advice of his soothsayer, he returns to Egypt, leaving Octavius and Lepidus finally to defeat Pompey when a truce breaks down. Octavius turns on Lepidus and has him executed, then moves to destroy Antony and Cleopatra, who have now declared themselves rulers of the Eastern empire. The last two acts depict the heroic deaths of the lovers and the triumph of Octavius, whose words celebrating his victims close the play:

> No grave on earth shall clip in it
> A pair so famous. High events as these
> Strike those that make them, and their story is
> No less in pity than his glory which
> Brought them to be lamented. Our army shall
> In solemn show attend this funeral,
> And then to Rome. Come, Dolabella, see
> High order, in this great solemnity. (5.2.358–65)

The tribute appears generous but is, at heart, self-serving. The glory of Antony and Cleopatra is emphasized, but only so that it reflects well on 'his glory [i.e., Octavius's] which / Brought them to be lamented'. Octavius has won, and Shakespeare's lines show that he intends the monument to serve his purpose more than theirs. The play reminds us, however, that there are other ways of representing and reading the surviving evidence.[64]

Shakespeare was not the only English writer to produce a stage version of this eminently dramatic story, and he was following in a tradition established by Mary Sidney, who translated Robert Garnier's *Marc Antonie* (1578) as *Antonius* (1592) for private performance, and Samuel Daniel, who wrote a *Tragedie of Cleopatra* (1594), for a similar type of audience.[65] It is likely that he knew both plays and made use of them as part of his research for his own work.[66] Nevertheless, Shakespeare was the only English dramatist who staged the complete story of the end of the Roman republic from the triumph of Julius Caesar to the victory of Augustus, the first proper Roman emperor.[67]

The significance of the story as that of two royal lovers who sacrifice the world for their passion was already well established before Shakespeare wrote *Antony and Cleopatra*. Daniel's portrait of Cleopatra was clearly hostile and he represents her as a queen who cannot control her desire and lust, who will throw away all she has gained for her people as an imperial conqueror for her own selfish ends. The Chorus are the ordinary Egyptians who must suffer her whims:

> And *Cleopatra* now,
> Well sees the dangerous way
> She tooke, and car'd not how,
> Which led her to decay.
> And likewise makes us pay
> For her disordered lust,
> The int'rest of our blood:
> Or live a servile pray,
> Under a hand unjust,

As others shall thinke good.
Thus hath her riot wonne:
And thus she hath her state, herselfe and us undone. (lines 222–33)

If we also consider that the actions of Cleopatra and Antony lead to a contested succession, then the play can be read along with many other works as the sort of topical dramatic allegory that flourished in the 1590s.[68] Given Daniel's later problems with *Philotas*, the case would seem hard to ignore.[69] Cleopatra's lust can easily be translated into Elizabeth's virginity as an excessive concern for the private self rather than the body politic.

Antony and Cleopatra presents Cleopatra in a far more nuanced way. Her decision to pursue her private desires is not such an obviously wrong choice as it is in Daniel's version of her story, even if it does have disastrous consequences.[70] Nevertheless, Shakespeare's representation of the final chapter of the protracted civil wars that destroyed the Roman republic does have obvious topical resonances. Margot Heinemann has argued that the 'chaotic world of Antony and Cleopatra could . . . be seen as moving towards the reign of corrupt emperors described by Tacitus', the historian who had been promoted by many as the preeminent critic of corrupt imperial rule, and, moreover, a writer increasingly mistrusted by James I.[71] Such a reading would suggest that more attention ought to be paid to the relatively shadowy figure of Octavius, the future emperor, Augustus.

In the most sustained reading of the play in terms of contemporary politics, H. Neville Davies has argued that a contemporary audience must have seen Octavius as a figure of James: 'it is inconceivable that a dramatist late in 1606 . . . could have failed to associate Caesar Augustus and the ruler whose propaganda was making just that connection'.[72] James cast himself as the heir of the first Roman emperor, a man who inherited an empire and who was able to bring peace and plenty to his people, spreading around the benefits accumulated in more straitened times.[73] His famous motto, *Beati Pacifici* (blessed are the peacemakers), had its origin in the Sermon on the Mount (Matthew 5.9), but also owed much to James's perception of the beneficial legacy of Augustus. Many authors, such as Henry Petowe and Samuel Rowlands, sought to represent the king in terms that he would appreciate, as a mighty Caesar.[74] However, other subjects who were rather less impressed by James compared him to later emperors, such as Tiberius, exposing the problematic nature of the historical analogy, which, with a minimal effort of historical scholarship, could be turned against the king.[75]

James's conception of himself and his role as monarch was undoubtedly part of his reaction against the republican inclinations of his tutor, George Buchanan.[76] In itself, this deliberate reversal indicates how central republican ideas, images and iconography were to the politics of the British Isles in the late sixteenth and early seventeenth centuries. Augustus is the most ambivalent figure represented in Tacitus's *Annals*, the work of Roman history that had probably had the greatest influence on English political life in the 1590s. It is notable that Tacitus actually provides two views of Augustus and encourages his readers to think carefully which one they find the most persuasive in the light of the evidence of his life that he assembles. The history opens with the funeral of Augustus. Tacitus suggests that debates over the character of the dead emperor inspired as much argument among the citizens of Rome as those over the assassination of the dictator, Julius Caesar:

On the day of the funeral the troops were out, apparently for protective purposes. This caused much jeering from people who had witnessed, or heard from their parents, about that day (when the nation's enslavement was still rudimentary) of the ill-starred attempt to recover Republican freedom by murdering the dictator Caesar – a fearful crime? or a conspicuously glorious achievement?[77]

For some, Augustus had been a pragmatic hero who had guided the state from crisis to crisis until some semblance of order could be restored. He may have been cruel at times and responsible for harsh and arbitrary government, but he had never lost sight of the rights and needs of the citizens of Rome:

Filial duty and a national emergency, in which there was no place for law-abiding conduct, had driven him to civil war – and this can be neither initiated nor maintained by decent methods . . . However, Augustus had put the State in order not by making himself king or dictator but by creating the Principate. The empire's frontiers were on the ocean, or distant rivers. Armies, provinces, fleets, the whole system was interrelated. Roman citizens were protected by the law. Provincials were decently treated. Rome itself had been lavishly beautified. Force had been sparingly used – merely to preserve peace for the majority. (p. 35)

This reading of Augustus makes him a republican at heart, determined to preserve the liberties Romans have enjoyed, even if short-term problems mean that his methods seem to be pursuing the opposite path. He cannot be held responsible for the actions of subsequent emperors.

For others, Augustus was the first in a long line of oppressive tyrants. He removed the checks and balances of the constitution, paving the way for his bloody successors:

Filial duty and national crisis had been merely pretexts. In actual fact, the motive of Octavian, the future Augustus, was lust for power. Inspired by that, he had mobilized ex-army settlers by gifts of money, raised an army – while he was only a half-grown boy without any official status – won over a consul's brigade by bribery, pretended to support Aextus Pompeius (I), and by senatorial decree usurped the status and rank of a praetor. Soon both consuls had met their deaths . . . Then he had forced the reluctant senate to make him consul . . . His judicial murders and land distributions were distasteful even to those who carried them out. (p. 36)

Tacitus does not adjudicate this argument, but he does give more space to criticisms of Augustus than to praise of him, concluding with a discussion of how people thought that he 'seemed to have superseded the worship of the gods when he wanted to have himself venerated in temples' (p. 36). It is easy to see why James became suspicious of Tacitus when he wanted to represent himself as Augustus, especially when more positive assessments of his character were provided in Suetonius, who claims that Augustus twice 'seriously thought of restoring the Republican Constitution'.[78]

Shakespeare was undoubtedly alluding to the political issues raised by the story of the last days of the Roman republic in *Antony and Cleopatra*: but how, exactly? A clue is provided in 2.7., the galley scene, which may have been inspired by James's meeting with his brother-in-law, Christian of Denmark, aboard a ship in 1606.[79] Pompey's younger son and the triumvirs share a banquet as a celebration of their truce aboard Pompey's galley. Menas, one of Pompey's chief supporters, makes strenuous efforts throughout the meal to propose a plan to his master, despite the constant stream of rebuffs that he experiences. Although he judges that Menas must be mad, Pompey eventually agrees to walk with him and to hear his proposition. Menas asks Pompey if he would like to be 'lord of the whole world', a question he has to repeat (lines 62, 64), as Pompey assumes his loyal servant must be drunk like everybody else – apart from one – on the ship. Menas explains that he has abstained from drink and that a decision awaits Pompey, one that the audience would have recognized was every bit as momentous as Caesar crossing the Rubicon.[80] Menas states that Pompey could be, if he is daring enough, 'the earthly Jove' (line 69).

Pompey is sufficiently tempted to ask how this glory might be achieved, but he eventually declines the offer:

> POMPEY: Show me the way.
> MENAS: These world-sharers, these competitors,
> Are in thy vessel. Let me cut the cable,
> And when we are put off, fall to their throats.
> All then is thine.
> POMPEY: Ah, this thou shouldst have done
> And not have spoken on't. In me 'tis villainy;
> In thee't had been good service. Thou must know
> 'Tis not my profit that does lead mine honour;
> Mine honour, it. Repent that e'er thy tongue
> Hath so betrayed thine act. Being done unknown,
> I should have found it afterwards well done,
> But must condemn it now. Desist and drink.
> [*Returns to the others.*]
> MENAS (ASIDE:) For this,
> I'll never follow thy palled fortunes more.
> Who seeks and will not take, when once 'tis offered,
> Shall never find it more. (lines 70–84)

This is a vitally important exchange that resonates with central issues, not just those explored within the confines of *Antony and Cleopatra*, but throughout Shakespeare's career. Pompey does not appear in the play again. Within an act his defeat has become old news, so much so that when Eros mentions the fact to Enobarbus, his sad fate is eclipsed by that of Lepidus, who has been used by Octavius and, no longer serving any purpose, has been imprisoned and condemned to death (3.5). Pompey's failure to seize the day spells his doom, as Menas realizes. Pompey himself may have a sense of his future. His last lines are a reconciliation with Antony that seeks to ignore their long-standing enmity: 'O, Antony, you have my father's house. / But what? We are friends! Come down into the boat' (lines 129–30). Rather than banishing the long, bitter legacy of the civil wars that have destroyed the republic, Pompey's words serve only to remind those present of their enduring relevance, that it is personal feuds that dictate the course of world politics. Antony, the loyal friend of Julius Caesar, enjoys the confiscated property of the old warrior hero of the republic, Pompey, whom Caesar defeated in one stage of the civil wars, recalled in the first scene of *Julius Caesar*. Only in the carnival of drunken revelry can reality be suspended and the past be – temporarily – put to sleep.[81]

Pompey becomes yesterday's man as soon as he has made his speech. The issue raised – yet again – is the familiar dilemma of the assassination of the tyrant central to resistance theory as well as republicanism, already analysed in *Hamlet* and *Julius Caesar*. In fact, *Antony and Cleopatra* provides a neat, balanced counter-weight to the earlier Roman play. Whereas the actions of Brutus and Cassius eventually serve only to hasten the demise of the republican ideal they espouse, here it is Pompey's nonaction that seals his fate. The later play qualifies and recontextualizes the earlier one. We could conclude that chance dictates fate so that sometimes such action serves a purpose and sometimes it is doomed to failure, the central problem being that it is hard to determine when the time is ripe, as the examples of the three defenders of the republic demonstrate. Or, that events have conspired so much against the republic that it is in terminal decline and cannot be saved whatever action is taken. Either way militates against Menas's proposed course of action.

The exchange, which has no obvious source, has a further dimension relevant to the eclipse of the republic and its ideals.[82] Pompey does not agonize over the legitimacy of the action, as Hamlet and Brutus do. Rather, he is worried about his own association, as a Roman aristocrat, with the proposed assassination. Menas can carry out the action in secret, but Pompey cannot be seen to have had a hand in it. He explains this as a code of 'honour', one that is rooted in a comprehension of public appearance not ethical behaviour. This code would have reminded the audience of the dying cult of honour of their own aristocracy rather than the culture of the republic, making Pompey more akin to Achilles and his macho posturing in *Troilus and Cressida* than Cicero or the first Brutus.[83] Pompey's words indicate that the ideals of the republic have sunk even lower and become more perverted than they had in *Julius Caesar*, when there was at least some form of commitment to the restoration of liberty and public culture. In *Julius Caesar*, Cicero had given way to Brutus, who may have been more embroiled in subterfuge and violent action than in the service of republican institutions. In *Antony and Cleopatra*, the representative of the republic is the son of its great warrior hero, Pompey, the defeated opponent of Julius Caesar in the *Pharsalia*. He has his chance to influence the future of the world, but fails to take it and instantly disappears to the dust heap of history. His stated ideals show that had he done so, he would undoubtedly have been no better than those he sought to replace. At this point in history, there is no plausible distinction to be made between the guardians of the republic and their opponents.[84]

Antony and Cleopatra witnesses the destruction of an age of heroes. The revelry in the galley scene is emblematic of the excess inherent in the story of Antony and Cleopatra who sacrifice the world for their love.[85] However, we need to remember who they are and what they represent. Antony's passion for Cleopatra mirrors his friendship for Caesar in *Julius Caesar*, a virtue out of control that shows that he has lost sight of all reason and responsibility and does not care about the consequences of his actions for others (precisely the sort of calculations that even a misguided character such as Brutus makes endlessly). Antony remains 'drunk' throughout the play. Cleopatra, as many commentators have noted, bears more than a passing resemblance to Elizabeth, partly through her androgyny, partly through her love of regal display, a connection that earlier writers seem to have already made.[86] The famous description that Enobarus provides of his queen in the barge may well recall the glories of a more recently bygone age, punctuated by royal progresses (a form of display that her successor instinctively avoided):

> The barge she sat in, like a burnished throne,
> Burned on the water; the poop was beaten gold;
> Purple the sails, and so perfumed that
> The winds were love-sick with them; the oars were silver,
> Which to the tune of flutes kept stroke, and made
> The water which they beat to follow faster,
> As amorous of their strokes. For her own person,
> It beggared all description: she did lie
> In her pavilion, cloth-of-gold of tissue,
> O'erpicturing that Venus where we see
> The fancy outwork nature. On each side her
> Stood pretty dimpled boys, like smiling cupids,
> With divers-coloured fans, whose wind did seem
> To glow the delicate cheeks which they did cool,
> And what they undid did. (2.2.200–14)[87]

Agrippa's seemingly admiring comment, 'O, rare for Antony!' (line 215) also serves to remind us that such a display is for the benefit of a few rather than the many, perhaps a further sign of how remote the behaviour of Antony and Cleopatra is from the ideals of the Roman republic. They have made themselves exotic wonders rather than admirable political leaders.[88]

In marked contrast is the behaviour of the coming man of the new era, Octavius. While everyone around him is drunk and unable to see clearly into the future, he remains scornfully sober. While the supposed allies pursue their revels deep into the night, singing a drinking song, 'Cup us till the world go round', Octavius leaves early and warns Antony what the affairs of state require: 'Good brother, / Let me request you off. Our graver business / Frowns at this levity' (2.7.119–20). The future Augustus is a shadowy figure, suggesting that either of Tacitus's assessments of his character might be correct. We cannot be sure, when he objects to Antony's grandiloquent declaration of his power and decides to avenge his sister's dishonour at the hands of her unfaithful husband, whether Antony's betrayals inspire his actions or whether they had been predetermined and his erstwhile ally had simply provided Octavius with good excuses to act.[89] Octavius does indeed use his friends ruthlessly and abandons them without sentimentality when it suits his larger designs, but then they are hardly admirable characters. We may admire the heroic passion of Antony in particular, as some seventeenth-century writers and audiences obviously did.[90] However, Antony is, at best, a problematic character, always prepared to allow his passion to govern his reason, as he demonstrated to such deadly effect after the assassination of his friend, Julius Caesar. Octavius, in contrast, preserves the ascetic code of the Stoic ideal, the principal philosophy of the republic, subordinating his emotions and appetites to his rational capacities. But he uses his abstinence to smooth his way to power, not to preserve a proper detachment from the world. After all, as many of the audience would have been well aware, it was Octavius who had agreed to the murder of Cicero, the guardian of republican values, putting his name down when the triumvirates agreed to sacrifice a man each as a sign of their mutual loyalty.[91]

It is hard, given his portrayal in the play, to read Octavius straightforwardly as James, as some critics have suggested we do. James was regarded by his contemporaries as profligate, incautious, sensual and dedicated to peace at almost any price.[92] Shakespeare, perhaps following Tacitus more than Plutarch, represents Octavius as devious, secretive, intensely private in his thoughts (in two plays depicting remarkably open and frank declarations by most of the principal characters), ambitious and militaristic in his bearing and style.[93] Nevertheless, the topical resonance of *Antony and Cleopatra* seems hard to deny. Perhaps one of Shakespeare's points is that James is foolish to ape Octavius, a ruler with whom he would appear to have little in common. If so, the contrast instead of a comparison is not all to James's disadvantage. James would appear to be a rather more charismatic and sympathetic leader than the first Roman emperor. More significantly, perhaps, Octavius had simply emerged victorious from the civil wars that killed off the Roman republic because he was the most ambitious and efficient military leader, a sign that individuals had become much more important than the institutions they were supposed to serve. Octavius's adherence to Stoic asceticism was less part of an overall philosophy than a means to a self-interested end. On the other hand, James was simply another king. He had succeeded a queen whose sex, behaviour, circumstances and longevity had opened up the possibility of the establishment of a republic, an unrealized political goal that was to become a reality for a brief time later in the century.[94] James had not killed a political ideal as such, but had provided a new-found – albeit somewhat flawed – stability for his subjects. Perhaps this achievement meant that, for Shakespeare, he was actually more like the compromised but attractive heroes of the ancient world – an Antony, a Pompey, or even a Cicero – than the role model he had mistakenly chosen.

Conclusion

Given that Shakespeare's plays and poems were conceived with current issues in mind, it is clear enough that they changed in focus, style and, of course, content, over the two, or two and a half, decades during which they were written. Works such as *The Winter's Tale*, although it represents a king behaving tyrannically, has little in common with the frenetic urgency of the political comment in the three *Henry VI* plays.[1] Moreover, it would be reductive to imagine that a history of republicanism could be written against a constant ideal of republican thought, as though times and circumstances did not change, and the issues, hopes and fears of historical figures did not alter accordingly. Nevertheless, this is what routinely happens. Historians establish definitions of republicanism that are either overarchingly inclusive, or narrowly exclusive, and make the concomitant assumption that republicans are made for life, once they have been persuaded of the truth of their chosen creed.[2]

The reality, as the case of Shakespeare demonstrates, is probably more messy and more interesting. We have no direct insight into Shakespeare's mind, as we have to reconstruct his thought processes from his surviving literary works, all of which are mediated in a variety of complex ways. Not only were his plays hardly a direct expression of Shakespeare's innermost convictions, they were also often written in collaboration with other writers, a fact about early modern dramatic composition with which we are only just starting to come to terms.[3] It is hard to answer with any certainty many of the questions we might like to ask. Was Shakespeare a convinced republican in the same way that Algernon Sidney was?[4] This is a possibility, but it is, I suspect, unlikely, although a case can be made that some of Shakespeare's contemporaries may have had more than a passing inclination towards a constitution without a monarch, the strongest form of republican thought in this period.[5] Or was Shakespeare a self-interested man on the make who had the ability to absorb and recycle ideas without too much difficulty, and had an eye for an opportunity, as well as a keen sense of which way the land lay? He clearly did not let political issues dominate his output and wrote numerous plays – principally comedies – that have, at best, an oblique relationship with such topics. Moreover, other surviving evidence and informed conjecture has enabled biographers to represent Shakespeare's character in this way, as the recent work of Katherine Duncan-Jones demonstrates.[6] Yet, if this was the case, and it was Shakespeare's *Richard II* that was staged before Essex's men on the night of the attempted *coup* in 1601, then he was caught up in events beyond his control that demanded a certain degree of conviction and carried a risk that was unlikely to be purely self-interested. Whichever way we interpret the evidence involves a large degree of speculation.

The answer probably lies somewhere in between, something that has to be explained in terms of the complicated and frustrating nature of evidence from the early modern period, and the discontinuous and fragmentary history of early republicanism in England. Many of Shakespeare's early works are based on explicitly republican stories and highlight and develop republican themes and issues. Other works, most obviously such early comedies as *The Two Gentlemen of Verona* or *The Comedy of Errors*, are likely to prove far less happy hunting grounds for republican spotters. Shakespeare was also involved in projects that might seem to provide evidence against his republicanism, such as the collabora- tive work *Sir Thomas More*, probably written in 1593–94, but never performed. Here, it has been argued, Shakespeare was a politically accept- able figure added to a potentially scandalous team of Henry Chettle, Thomas Dekker and Anthony Munday, to deflect attention from a project that was attracting unwelcome interest from the authorities.[7]

I think it is hard to place great significance on this episode, especially as we do not know whether this conjecture is really plausible, nor whether the play was actually written in the early 1590s. But let us assume that we can date it accurately. We then need to bear in mind that Elizabethan censorship and strictures were more often aimed at religious transgression than political dissent, and Munday and Dekker were already known as among the 'hotter' sort of Protestants writing for the London stage.[8] In the wake of the Marprelate controversy (1588–89), the play's potentially seditious charge against foreigners may have been enough to arouse suspicion, rather than any other reason. Shakespeare was certainly not known for his religious writing, and, given that hand D concentrates on the danger of resident aliens, it is by no means clear that Shakespeare's part in the play was that innocuous. Moreover, it soon became clear that

Munday and Shakespeare were hardly compatible ideologues when Munday helped write the 1599 *Sir John Oldcastle* for the Admiral's Men in response to Shakespeare's denigration of a Protestant hero in *King Henry IV, Part One*.[9]

Shakespeare's control over the writing of *Sir Thomas More* would appear to have been severely limited and its content not necessarily something he endorsed. And the fact that it was not included by Heminge and Condell in the first folio, while hardly conclusive proof, given the plays that were omitted, further suggests that it was not a work which featured prominently in the Shakespeare canon. In short, such examples have been read to fit the common assumption that Shakespeare was a conservative writer. But in fact, Shakespeare appears to have fashioned himself as a writer who dealt with complex and troubling political – specifically, republican – issues, from the start of his career. He was clearly happy to write on other issues, but his concern with republicanism continued throughout the 1590s, and then long after the republican moment of the last years of Elizabeth's reign had passed, as his plays focused on the ways in which individuals and institutions functioned.[10]

Of course, there was no republican party or faction for Shakespeare to join. Politics at court still centred around powerful individuals.[11] But if we concentrate on the machinations of high political intrigue and omit the wealth of ideas that were produced elsewhere, we lose sight of a political history that had a huge impact on the lives of people excluded from this world of politics, many of whom seemed to think they should play a significant part within it. Such histories are invariably unstable, making it hard to chart a history of republicanism in England in a linear way, and they depend on the contingency of particular circumstances. And, as often as not, the evidence for this history does not always appear in the most obvious places. Nevertheless, it is a history that has remained hidden from view for far too long and one which helped determine the career of the world's most celebrated writer.

Notes

INTRODUCTION I: WAS SHAKESPEARE A REPUBLICAN?

1 See Blair Worden, 'English Republicanism', in J. H. Burns and Mark Goldie, eds., *The Cambridge History of Political Thought, 1450–1700* (Cambridge: Cambridge University Press, 1991), pp. 443–75.

2 A pioneering work which is an exception – even though it is not about Shakespeare – is Julie Sanders's *Ben Jonson's Theatrical Republics* (Basingstoke: Macmillan, 1998). For reflections on the methodological problems that beset a study like this, see Douglas Bruster, *Quoting Shakespeare: Form and Culture in Early Modern Drama* (Lincoln: University of Nebraska Press, 2000), ch. 1. For an alternative view, see Robert D. Hume, *Reconstructing Contexts: The Aims and Principles of Archaeo-Historicism* (Oxford: Clarendon Press, 1999).

3 See, for example, Graham Holderness, *Cultural Shakespeare: Essays in the Shakespeare Myth* (Hatfield: University of Hertfordshire Press, 2001).

4 For a witty exploration of this problem, see Richard Burt, *Unspeakable Shaxxxspeares: Queer Theory and American Kiddie Culture* (Basingstoke: Macmillan, 1998).

5 See Gary Taylor, *Reinventing Shakespeare: A Cultural History from the Restoration to the Present* (London: Hogarth, 1989), chs. 1–3; Michael D. Bristol, *Big-Time Shakespeare* (London: Routledge, 1996).

6 Brian Vickers, *Shakespeare, Co-Author: A Historical Study of Five Collaborative Plays* (Oxford: Oxford University Press, 2002), pp. 7–10, *passim*. See also Jonathan Hope, *The Authorship of Shakespeare's Plays* (Cambridge: Cambridge University Press, 1994); MacDonald P. Jackson, *Studies in Attribution: Middleton and Shakespeare* (Salzburg: Salzburg University Press, 1979).

7 *Mr. William Shakespeares Comedies, Histories, & Tragedies: A Facsimile of the First Folio, 1623*, introduction by Doug Moston (London: Routledge, 1998). For comment, see David Scott Kastan, *Shakespeare and the Book* (Cambridge: Cambridge University Press, 2001); Douglas A. Brooks, *From Playhouse to Printing House: Drama and Authorship in Early Modern England* (Cambridge: Cambridge University Press, 2000); Lukas Erne, *Shakespeare*

as Literary Dramatist (Cambridge: Cambridge University Press, 2003); Patrick Cheney, *Shakespeare, National Poet-Playwright* (Cambridge: Cambridge University Press, 2004) (I am extremely grateful to Professor Cheney for allowing me to see this book at the proof stage).

8 See Erne, *Shakespeare as Literary Dramatist*; Eric Sams, *The Real Shakespeare: Retrieving the Early Years, 1564–1594* (New Haven: Yale University Press, 1995).

9 Stephen Orgel, *Imagining Shakespeare: A History of Texts and Visions* (Basingstoke: Palgrave, 2003), pp. 14–15.

10 Andrew Gurr, *The Shakespearian Playing Companies* (Oxford: Clarendon Press, 1996), p. 43, *passim*.

11 Orgel, *Imagining Shakespeare*, pp. 126–27; Peter Thomson, *Shakespeare's Professional Career* (Cambridge: Cambridge University Press, 1992), pp. 156, 177.

12 For analysis, see Martin Butler, *Theatre and Crisis, 1632–42* (Cambridge: Cambridge University Press, 1984).

13 David Scott Kastan, 'Performances and Playbooks: The Closing of the Theatres and the Politics of Drama', in Kevin Sharpe and Steven Zwicker, eds., *Reading, Society and Politics in Early Modern England* (Cambridge: Cambridge University Press, 2003), pp. 167–84.

14 Gurr, *Shakespearian Playing Companies*, p. 4. See also Andrew Gurr, *The Shakespearean Stage, 1574–1642* (3rd ed., Cambridge: Cambridge University Press, 1999); Roslyn Lander Knutson, *Playing Companies and Commerce in Shakespeare's Time* (Cambridge: Cambridge University Press, 2001); Grace Ioppolo, ed., *Shakespeare Performed: Essays in Honour of R. A. Foakes* (Newark: University of Delaware Press, 2000), pt. 1.

15 See Rebecca Solnit, *A Book of Migrations: Some Passages in Ireland* (London: Verso, 1997), p. 4.

16 See Pauline Kiernan, *Staging Shakespeare at the New Globe* (Basingstoke: Macmillan, 1999). A sceptical assessment of the motives behind the project is provided in Holderness, *Cultural Shakespeare*, ch. 5.

17 See Gurr, *Shakespearean Stage*, ch. 6.

18 For a recent analysis, see Robert Matz, *Defending Literature in Early Modern England: Renaissance Literary Theory in Social Context* (Cambridge: Cambridge University Press, 2000). See also Richard Helgerson, *Self-Crowned Laureates: Spenser, Jonson, Milton and the Literary System* (Berkeley: University of California Press, 1983); Andrew Hadfield, *Literature, Politics and National Identity: Reformation to Renaissance* (Cambridge: Cambridge University Press, 1994), ch. 4.

19 See Richard Helgerson, *The Elizabethan Prodigals* (Berkeley: University of California Press, 1976); Michael G. Brennan, *Literary Patronage in the Renaissance: The Pembroke Family* (London: Routledge, 1988); Eleanor Rosenberg, *Leicester, Patron of Letters* (New York: Columbia University Press, 1955); Richard Rambuss, *Spenser's Secret Career* (Cambridge: Cambridge University Press, 1993); Alan Stewart, *Close Readers: Humanism and Sodomy in Early Modern England* (Princeton: Princeton University Press, 1997).

20 It is now thought that the famous attack was written by Henry Chettle and not Robert Greene, the purported author of *Greene's Groatsworth of Wit: Bought with a Million of Repentance* (1592); see the edition by D. Allen Carroll (Binghampton, N.Y.: MRTS, 1994), pp. 131–45.

21 Katherine Duncan-Jones, *Ungentle Shakespeare: Scenes From His Life* (London: Thomson, 2001), pp. 149–51, *passim*; Park Honan, *Shakespeare, A Life* (Oxford: Oxford University Press, 1998), ch. 12, *passim*.

22 See Harold Jenkins, *The Life and Work of Henry Chettle* (London: Sidgwick and Jackson, 1934); Charles W. Crupi, *Robert Greene* (Boston: Twayne, 1986).

23 See David Bevington, *Tudor Drama and Politics: A Critical Approach to Topical Meaning* (Cambridge, Mass.: Harvard University Press, 1968). See also Andrew Hadfield, *Shakespeare and Renaissance Politics* (London: Thomson, 2003).

24 See Greg Walker, *Plays of Persuasion: Drama and Politics at the Court of Henry VIII* (Cambridge: Cambridge University Press, 1991); David Lindley, ed., *The Court Masque* (Manchester: Manchester University Press, 1984); Stephen Orgel, *The Illusion of Power: Political Theatre in the English Renaissance* (Berkeley: University of California Press, 1975).

25 Gurr, *Shakespearian Playing Companies*, p. 241. On *Gorboduc*, see Bevington, *Tudor Drama and Politics*, ch. 11; Greg Walker, *The Politics of Performance in Early Renaissance Drama* (Cambridge: Cambridge University Press, 1998), ch. 6.

26 See Ian W. Archer, 'Popular Politics in the Sixteenth and Seventeenth Centuries', in Paul Griffiths and Mark S. R. Jenner, eds., *Londinopolis: Essays in the Cultural and Social History of Early Modern London* (Manchester: Manchester University Press, 2000), pp. 26–46.

27 The debate is staged in Anthony B. Dawson and Paul Yachnin, *The Culture of Playgoing in Shakespeare's England: A Collaborative Debate* (Cambridge: Cambridge University Press, 2001).

28 Barbara Freedman, 'Elizabethan Protest, Plague and Plays: Rereading the "Documents of Control"', *ELR* 26 (1996), 17–45.

29 On the Privy Council, see David Loades, *Power in Tudor England* (Basingstoke: Macmillan, 1997), ch. 3; J. G. A. Guy, 'The Privy Council: Revolution or Evolution?', in Christopher Coleman and David Starkey, eds., *Revolution Reassessed: Revisions in the History of Tudor Government and Administration* (Oxford: Oxford University Press, 1986), pp. 59–85.

30 F. S. Siebert, *Freedom of the Press in England, 1476–1776: The Rise and Decline of Government Controls* (Urbana: University of Illinois Press, 1952); Janet Clare, *'Art Made Tongue-Tied by Authority': Elizabethan and Jacobean Dramatic Censorship* (2nd ed., Manchester: Manchester University Press, 1990).

31 Richard Dutton, *Mastering the Revels: The Regulation and Censorship of English Renaissance Drama* (Basingstoke: Macmillan, 1991); Dutton, *Licensing, Censorship and Authorship in Early Modern England: Buggeswords* (Basingstoke: Palgrave/Macmillan, 2000).

32 See John Stubbs, *John Stubb's **Gaping Gulf** with Letters and Other Relevant Documents*, ed. Lloyd E. Berry (Charlottesville, Va.: University of Virginia Press, 1968); Cyndia Clegg, *Press Censorship in Elizabethan England* (Cambridge: Cambridge University Press, 1997); Clegg, *Press Censorship in Jacobean England* (Cambridge: Cambridge University Press, 2001).

33 See Kevin Sharpe, *Remapping Early Modern England: The Culture of Seventeenth-Century Politics* (Cambridge: Cambridge University Press, 2000), pp. 46–7. For a recent overview, see Andrew Hadfield, ed., *Literature and Censorship in Renaissance England* (Basingstoke: Palgrave/Macmillan, 2001).

34 John Hayward, *The First and Second Parts of John Hayward's **The Life and Raigne of King Henrie IIII***, ed. John J. Manning (London: Royal Historical Society, 1991; Camden Society, 4th series, Vol. 42). For one possible example of the impact of Stubbs's fate, see Andrew Hadfield, 'Sidney's "poor painter" and John Stubbs's *Gaping Gulf*', *Sidney Newsletter and Journal* 15.2 (Fall 1997), 45–48.

35 For differing views, see Annabel Patterson, *Censorship and Interpretation: The Conditions of Writing in Early Modern England* (Madison: University of Wisconsin Press, 1984); Janet Clare, 'Censorship and Negotiation', in Hadfield, ed., *Literature and Censorship*, pp. 17–30.

36 For discussion, see Clare, *'Art Made Tongue-Tied by Authority'*, pp. 68–72. For more general reflections on this problem, see Richard Burt, '(Un)Censoring in Detail: The Fetish of Censorship in the Early Modern Past and the Postmodern Present', in Robert C. Post, ed., *Censorship and Silencing: Practices of Cultural Regulation* (Los Angeles: Getty Research Institute, 1998), pp. 17–41.

37 For analysis, see Andrew Hadfield, *Spenser's Irish Experience: Wilde Fruyt and Salvage Soyl* (Oxford: Clarendon Press, 1997), pp. 78–84; Jean Brink, 'Constructing *A View of the Present State of Ireland*', *Sp. Stud.* 11 (1990, published 1994), 203–28.

38 Stubbs, *Gaping Gulf*, ed. Berry, introduction; Brian P. Levack, *The Civil Lawyers in England, 1603–1641: A Political Study* (Oxford: Clarendon Press, 1973), pp. 237–38, *passim*; Andrew Hadfield, *Shakespeare, Spenser and the Matter of Britain* (Basingstoke: Palgrave/Macmillan, 2003), ch. 8.

39 Rebecca Lemon, 'The Faculty Verdict in "The Crown v. John Hayward"', *SEL* 41 (2001), 109–32.

40 G. P. V. Akrigg, *Shakespeare and the Earl of Southampton* (London: Hamilton, 1968), pt. 1, ch. 12; Hadfield, *Shakespeare and Renaissance Politics*, p. 183.

41 See Anna Beer, *Sir Walter Raleigh and his Readers in the Seventeenth Century: Speaking to the People* (Basingstoke: Macmillan, 1997), ch. 4.

42 See Joel B. Altman, *The Tudor Play of Mind: Rhetorical Inquiry and the Development of Elizabethan Drama* (Berkeley: University of California Press, 1978); Ronald Knowles, *Shakespeare's Arguments with History* (Basingstoke: Palgrave/Macmillan, 2002); Neil Rhodes, *Shakespeare and the Origins of English* (Oxford: Oxford University Press, 2004), ch. 3.

43 See Andrew Hadfield, '"We see our faults only in the English Glass": John Lyly's *Euphues* and National Identity', *Nationalismus und Subjektivitat* (Johann Wolfgang Goethe-Universität Zentrum zur Erforschung der Frühen Neizeit, 1995), 260–71; Robert White, 'The Cultural Impact of the Massacre of St Bartholomew's Day', in Jennifer Richards, ed., *Early Modern Civil Discourses* (Basingstoke: Palgrave/Macmillan, 2003), pp. 183–99, at pp. 192–94.

44 Although see the cautious reading of Katherine Duncan-Jones: *Sir Philip Sidney: Courtier Poet* (London: Hamish Hamilton, 1991), pp. 148–52. See also Barbara Brumbaugh, 'Temples Defaced and Altars in the Dust: Edwardian and Elizabethan Church Reform and Sidney's "Now Was Our Heav'nly Vault Deprived of the Light"', *Sp. Stud.* 16 (2002), 197–229.

45 Stephen Alford, *The Early Elizabethan Polity: William Cecil and the British Succession Crisis, 1558–1569* (Cambridge: Cambridge University Press, 1998); John Guy, *Tudor England* (Oxford: Oxford University Press, 1988), pp. 268–71, 331–36, *passim*.

46 Robert Parsons [Doleman], *A Conference about the Next Succession to the Crowne of Ingland* (1594), p. 263.

47 Robert Lacey, *Robert, Earl of Essex: An Elizabethan Icarus* (London: Weidenfeld and Nicolson, 1970), pp. 127, 308; *DNB* entry on 'Robert Parsons'.

48 Peter Wentworth, *A Pithie Exhortation to Her Majestie for Establishing her Successor to the Crowne* (1598). On Wentworth, see J. E. Neale, 'Peter Wentworth', in E. B. Fryde and Edward Miller, eds., *Historical Studies of the English Parliament: Volume 2, 1399 to 1603* (Cambridge: Cambridge University Press, 1970), pp. 246–95. See also Jennifer Loach, *Parliament under the Tudors* (Oxford: Oxford University Press, 1991), pp. 52–53; J. E. Neale, *Elizabeth I and her Parliaments: Volume 2, 1584–1601* (London: Cape, 1957), p. 262.

49 See Marie Axton, *The Queen's Two Bodies: Drama and the Elizabethan Succession* (London: Royal Historical Society, 1977).

50 See, for example, Kevin Sharpe, *Remapping Early Modern England*, pt. 1; Blair Worden, *The Sound of Virtue: Philip Sidney's **Arcadia** and Elizabethan Politics* (New Haven: Yale University Press, 1996); Kevin Sharpe and Peter Lake, eds., *Culture and Politics in Early Stuart England* (Basingstoke: Macmillan, 1994).

51 See, for example, Roy Strong, *Art and Power: Renaissance Festivals, 1450–1650* (Woodbridge: Boydell, 1973); David Howarth, *Images of Rule: Art and Politics in the English Renaissance, 1485–1649* (Basingstoke: Macmillan, 1997).

52 The classic study is David Norbrook, *Poetry and Politics in the English Renaissance* (rev. ed., Oxford: Oxford University Press, 2002). See also David Loewenstein, *Representing Revolution in Milton and his Contemporaries: Religion, Politics, and Polemics in Radical Puritanism* (Cambridge: Cambridge University Press, 2001).

53 For further discussion, see my 'Shakespeare and Republicanism: History and Cultural Materialism', *Textual Practice* 17 (2003), 461–83. Some comments here are incorporated from this essay.

54 See, for example, Jonathan Goldberg, 'The Politics of Renaissance Literature: A Review Essay', *ELH* 49 (1982), 514–42; Jean E. Howard, 'The New Historicism in Renaissance Studies', *ELR* 16 (1986), 13–43; Alan Liu, 'The Power of Formalism: The New Historicism', *ELH* 56 (1989), 721–71; Jonathan Dollimore and Alan Sinfield, eds., *Political Shakespeare: New Essays in Cultural Materialism* (Manchester: Manchester University Press, 1985); H. Aram Veeser, ed., *The New Historicism* (London: Routledge, 1989).

55 As hostile accounts such as Brian Vickers's *Appropriating Shakespeare: Contemporary Critical Quarrels* (New Haven: Yale University Press, 1993), acknowledge. See also Jonathan Dollimore, 'Critical Developments: Cultural Materialism, Feminism and Gender Critique, and New Historicism', in Stanley Wells, ed., *Shakespeare: A Bibliographical Guide* (Oxford: Oxford University Press, 1990), pp. 405–28.

56 The history is now familiar enough: see Terry Eagleton, *Literary Theory: An Introduction* (Oxford: Blackwell, 1984); Catherine Belsey, *Critical Practice* (London: Methuen, 1980).

57 E. M. W. Tillyard, *The Elizabethan World Picture* (Harmondsworth: Penguin, 1963, rpt. of 1943).

58 E. M. W. Tillyard, *Shakespeare's History Plays* (London: Chatto and Windus, 1944), cited in Jonathan Dollimore, *Radical Tragedy: Religion, Ideology and Power in the Drama of Shakespeare and his Contemporaries* (Brighton: Harvester, 1984), p. 90.

59 See Graham Holderness, *The Shakespeare Myth* (Manchester: Manchester University Press, 1988); Alan Sinfield, 'Theatres of War: Caesar and the Vandals', in Sinfield, *Faultlines: Cultural Materialism and the Politics of Dissident Reading* (Oxford: Oxford University Press, 1992), ch. 1.

60 Many of the key texts, in addition to those already cited, appeared in *Textual Practice*: see Richard Levin, 'Bashing the Bourgeois Subject', *Textual Practice* 3 (1989), 76–86; Catherine Belsey, 'The Subject in Danger; a Reply to Richard Levin', *Textual Practice* 3 (1989), 77–80; Catherine Belsey, 'Towards Cultural History – in Theory and Practice', *Textual Practice* 3 (1989), 159–72; Jonathan Dollimore and Alan Sinfield, 'Culture and Textuality: Debating Cultural Materialism', *Textual Practice* 4 (1990), 91–100; Richard Levin, 'Son of Bashing the Bourgeois Subject', *Textual Practice* 6 (1992), 264–70.

61 Dollimore and Sinfield, eds., *Political Shakespeare*, p. viii.

62 Sinfield, *Faultlines*, p. 35.

63 Again, a well-known issue, which developed out of American New Historicism rather than British Cultural Materialism: see, for example, Jonathan Goldberg, *James I and the Politics of Literature: Jonson, Shakespeare, Donne, and their Contemporaries* (Baltimore: Johns Hopkins University Press, 1983); Stephen Greenblatt, 'Invisible Bullets: Renaissance Authority and its Subversion, *Henry IV* and *Henry V*', in Dollimore and Sinfield, eds., *Political*

Shakespeare, pp. 18–47; Leonard Tennenhouse, 'Strategies of State and Political Plays: *A Midsummer Night's Dream, Henry IV, Henry V, Henry VIII*', in Dollimore and Sinfield, eds., *Political Shakespeare*, pp. 109–28; Tennenhouse, *Power on Display: The Politics of Shakespeare's Genres* (London: Methuen, 1986).

64 For relevant political discussion, see James Emerson Phillips, *Images of a Queen: Mary Stuart in Sixteenth-Century Literature* (Berkeley: University of California Press, 1964); Susan Doran, *Monarchy and Matriarchy: The Courtships of Elizabeth I* (London: Routledge, 1996); David Loades, *The Reign of Mary Tudor: Politics, Government and Religion in England, 1553–58* (2nd ed., London: Longman, 1991); Anne N. McLaren, *Political Culture in the Reign of Elizabeth I: Queen and Commonwealth, 1558–1585* (Cambridge: Cambridge University Press, 1999); McLaren, 'Gender, Religion, and Early Modern Nationalism: Elizabeth I, Mary Queen of Scots, and the Genesis of English Anti-Catholicism', *AHR* 107 (2002), 739–67.

65 Norbrook, *Poetry and Politics*, p. 271. See also Annabel Patterson, *Shakespeare and the Popular Voice* (Oxford: Blackwell, 1989). For other examples of sophisticated historical analyses of Renaissance literature and politics, see Peter C. Herman, '"O, 'tis a gallant king": Shakespeare's *Henry V* and the Crisis of the 1590s', in Dale Hoak, ed., *Tudor Political Culture* (Cambridge: Cambridge University Press, 1995), pp. 204–25; Martin Dzelzainis, 'Shakespeare and Political Thought', in David Scott Kastan, ed., *A Companion to Shakespeare* (Oxford: Blackwell, 1999), pp. 100–16; Alan Sinfield, '*Macbeth*: History, Ideology, and Intellectuals', in *Faultlines*, pp. 109–42.

66 See, as opposite examples of these tendencies, Terence Hawkes, *Shakespeare in the Present* (London: Routledge, 2002); Sharpe, *Remapping Early Modern England*. That Hawkes is an astute reader of the historical contexts of literature and Sharpe a historian employed in an English Department only serves to emphasize the unfortunate effects of this division.

67 For reflections on this problem, see David Scott Kastan, 'Are We Being Interdisciplinary Yet?', in *Shakespeare after Theory* (London: Routledge, 1999), pp. 43–55. Kastan's attempts to mediate between theory and history have not always been appreciated by those keen to defend their territory; see Hawkes, *Shakespeare in the Present*, pp. 1–2.

68 See, especially, Michel Foucault, *The Order of Things*, trans. anon. (London: Tavistock, 1970); Foucault, *The History of Sexuality, Volume I*, trans. Robert Hurley (New York: Vintage Books, 1980); Judith Butler, *Gender Trouble: Feminism and the Subversion of Identity* (London: Routledge, 1990).

69 See, for example, Jean E. Howard, *The Stage and Social Struggle in Early Modern England* (London: Routledge, 1994), ch. 1, for an overview and a discussion of the significance of this transformation of Renaissance studies.

70 For analysis, see Andrew Hadfield, *The English Renaissance, 1500–1620* (Oxford: Blackwell, 2001), pp. 3–5; David Aers, 'Reflections on Current Histories of the Subject', *Literature & History*, 2nd series, 2, ii (1991), 20–34.

71 Hugh Grady, *Shakespeare, Machiavelli, and Montaigne: Power and Subjectivity From **Richard II** to **Hamlet*** (Oxford: Oxford University Press, 2002), p. 1.

72 Howard, *Stage and Social Struggle*, p. 21.

73 The series description for Cambridge University Press's 'Cambridge Studies in Renaissance Literature and Culture' indicates how dominant 'Cultural Historicism' has become: 'Since the 1970s there has been a broad and vital reinterpretation of the nature of literary texts, a move away from formalism to a sense of literature as an aspect of social, economic, political, and cultural history . . . Recent writing on the nature of representation, the historical construction of gender and of the concept of identity itself, on theatre as a political and economic phenomenon and on the ideologies of art generally, reveal the breadth of the field.'

74 See Kastan, *Shakespeare after Theory*, ch. 1, for an incisive discussion of this problem.

75 *Political Shakespeare* contains essays on both the history of representations, adaptations and criticism of Shakespeare, and the contemporary critical context of his work. It is a great pity that far more capital has been made of the former rather than the latter type of writing in the subsequent two decades.

76 See, for example, Derek Cohen, *The Politics of Shakespeare* (Basingstoke: Macmillan, 1993); Leon Harold Craig, *Of Philosophers and Kings: Political Philosophy in Shakespeare's **Macbeth** and **King Lear*** (Toronto: University of Toronto Press, 2001); Joseph Alulis and Vickie Sullivan, eds., *Shakespeare's Political Pageant: Essays in Literature and Politics* (Lanham: Rowman & Littlefield, 1996); Tim Spiekerman, *Shakespeare's Political Realism: The English History Plays* (Albany: State University of New York Press, 1991); John Alvis and Thomas G. West, eds., *Shakespeare as Political Thinker* (Wilmington, Del.: ISI Books, 2000); Thomas Rist, *Shakespeare's Romances and the Politics of Counter-Reformation* (Lampeter: Edwin Mellen Press, 1999); Molly Smith, *Breaking Boundaries: Politics and Play in the Drama of Shakespeare and his Contemporaries* (Aldershot: Ashgate, 1998); Nina S. Levine, *Women's Matters: Politics, Gender, and Nation in Shakespeare's Early History Plays* (Newark: University of Delaware Press, 1998); Dympna Callaghan et al, eds., *The Weyward Sisters: Shakespeare and Feminist Politics* (Oxford: Blackwell, 1994); Alexander Leggatt, *Shakespeare's Political Drama: The History Plays and the Roman Plays* (London: Routledge, 1988). Two old historicist studies that do consider such issues are W. Gordon Zeeveld, *The Temper of Shakespeare's Thought* (New Haven: Yale University Press, 1974); George W. Keeton, *Shakespeare's Legal and Political Background* (London: Pitman, 1967). See also Howard Erskine-Hill, *Poetry and the Realm of Politics: Shakespeare to Dryden* (Oxford: Clarendon Press, 1996).

77 Annabel Patterson, *Reading Between the Lines* (Madison: University of Wisconsin Press, 1993).

78 My debt to a whole range of historians, political theorists and literary scholars will become evident in the next two chapters.

79 See the trenchant scepticism of Blair Worden's essay, 'Republicanism, Regicide and Republic: The English Experience', in Martin van Gelderen

and Quentin Skinner, eds., *Republicanism: A Shared European Heritage*, 2 vols. (Cambridge: Cambridge University Press, 2002), I, pp. 307–27.

80 J. G. A. Pocock, *The Machiavellian Moment: Florentine Political Thought and the Atlantic Republican Tradition* (Princeton: Princeton University Press, 1975); Quentin Skinner, *The Foundations of Modern Political Thought*, 2 vols. (Cambridge: Cambridge University Press, 1978), I, ch. 6.

81 See Sister Miriam Joseph, *Rhetoric in Shakespeare's Time: Literary Theory of Renaissance Europe* (New York: Harcourt, Brace & World, 1962), p. 26.

82 On the story of Judith, see Margarita Stocker, *Judith, Sexual Warrior: Women and Power in Western Culture* (New Haven: Yale University Press, 1998). Dr Stocker does not develop any potential republican argument, however.

83 See D. R. Woolf, *Reading History in Early Modern England* (Cambridge: Cambridge University Press, 2000), ch. 2.

84 See E. A. J. Honigmann, *Shakespeare: The Lost Years* (Manchester: Manchester University Press, 1985); Richard Wilson, 'Shakespeare and the Jesuits', *TLS*, 19 December 1997; Wilson, *Secret Shakespeare: Studies in Theatre, Religion and Resistance* (Manchester: Manchester University Press, 2004).

FORMS OF REPUBLICAN CULTURE IN LATE SIXTEENTH-CENTURY ENGLAND

1 Patrick Collinson, 'The Monarchical Republic of Queen Elizabeth I', *BJRLM* 69 (1986–87), 394–424; '*De Republica Anglorum*: Or, History with the Politics Put Back', in *Elizabethan Essays* (London: Hambledon Press, 1994), pp. 1–29.

2 Collinson, '*De Republica Anglorum*', p. 18. See also David Cannadine, *Class in Britain* (New Haven: Yale University Press, 1998), pp. 53–54.

3 For discussion, see Anne N. McLaren, *Political Culture in the Reign of Elizabeth I: Queen and Commonwealth, 1558–1585* (Cambridge: Cambridge University Press, 1999); McLaren, 'Gender, Religion, and Early Modern Nationalism: Elizabeth I, Mary Queen of Scots, and the Genesis of English Anti-Catholicism', *AHR* 107 (2002), 739–67; Constance Jordan, 'Woman's Rule in Sixteenth-Century British Political Thought', *RQ* 40 (1987), 421–51; Susan Doran, *England and Europe in the Sixteenth Century* (Basingstoke: Macmillan, 1999), pp. 59–68; Mortimer Levine, *The Early Elizabethan Succession Question, 1558–1568* (Stanford: Stanford University Press, 1966); Levine, *Tudor Dynastic Problems* (London: Allen and Unwin, 1973).

4 Stephen Alford, *The Early Elizabethan Polity: William Cecil and the British Succession Crisis, 1558–1569* (Cambridge: Cambridge University Press, 1998), p. 109; Levine, *Early Elizabethan Succession Question*, ch. 4.

5 Alford, *Early Elizabethan Polity*, p. 115; Collinson, '*De Republica Anglorum*', pp. 18–19.

6 Collinson, 'Monarchical Republic', p. 412.

7 Ibid., p. 416. On the assassination of William of Orange, see J. H. Elliott, *Europe Divided, 1559–1598* (London: Collins, 1968), pp. 283–98.

8 Anthony Fletcher, *Tudor Rebellions* (3rd ed., London: Longman, 1985), ch. 4; R. and M. H. Dodds, *The Pilgrimage of Grace, 1536–7, and the Exeter Conspiracy*, 2 vols. (Cambridge: Cambridge University Press, 1915); Felix Raab, *The English Face of Machiavelli: A Changing Interpretation, 1500–1700* (London: Routledge, 1965), pp. 34–40.

9 Thomas Starkey, *A Dialogue between Pole and Lupset*, ed. T. F. Mayer (London: RHS, 1989).

10 T. F. Mayer, *Thomas Starkey and the Commonweal* (Cambridge: Cambridge University Press, 1989); J. K. McConica, *English Humanists and Reformation Politics* (Oxford: Clarendon Press, 1965), ch. 6.

11 Mayer, *Thomas Starkey*, pp. 218–19.

12 Andrew Hadfield, *Literature, Politics and National Identity: Reformation to Renaissance* (Cambridge University Press, 1994), ch. 2; John N. King, *English Reformation Literature: The Tudor Origins of the Protestant Tradition* (Princeton: Princeton University Press, 1982).

13 See Christina H. Garrett, *The Marian Exiles: A Study in the Origins of Elizabethan Puritanism* (Cambridge: Cambridge University Press, 1938).

14 Quentin Skinner, *The Foundations of Modern Political Thought*, 2 vols. (Cambridge: Cambridge University Press, 1978), II, pt. 3; Robert M. Kingdon, 'Calvinism and Resistance Theory, 1550–1580', in J. H. Burns and Mark Goldie, eds., *The Cambridge History of Political Thought, 1450–1700* (Cambridge: Cambridge University Press, 1991), pp. 193–218.

15 See James Emerson Phillips, *Images of a Queen: Mary Stuart in Sixteenth-Century Literature* (Berkeley: University of California Press, 1964); Roger A. Mason, ed., *Scots and Britons: Scottish Political Thought and the Union of 1603* (Cambridge: Cambridge University Press, 1994), *passim*.

16 Francis Oakley, 'On the Road from Constance to 1688: The Political Thought of John Major and George Buchanan', *JBS* 2 (1962), 1–31; J. H. Burns, 'The Political Ideas of George Buchanan', *SHR* 30 (1951), 61–68; George Buchanan, *The Political Poetry*, ed. and trans. Paul J. McGinnis and Arthur H. Williamson (Edinburgh: SHS, 1995).

17 See George Buchanan, *De Jure Regni Apud Scotos [or a Discourse concerning the due privilege of Government in the Kingdom of Scotland]* (1721); *Ane detectioun of the duinges of Marie Quene of Scottes* (1571); *The History of Scotland written in Latin by George Buchanan; faithfully rendered into English*, J. Fraser (London, 1690). On Buchanan's reception in England, see James E. Phillips, 'George Buchanan and the Sidney Circle', *HLQ* 12 (1948–9), 23–55; I. D. McFarlane, *Buchanan* (London: Duckworth, 1981), ch. 12, *passim*.

18 For comment, see Andrew Hadfield, *Shakespeare and Renaissance Politics* (London: Thomson, 2003), *passim*; Annabel Patterson, *Shakespeare and the Popular Voice* (Oxford: Blackwell, 1989), ch. 4.

19 Mark Goldie, 'The Unacknowledged Republic: Officeholding in Early Modern England', in Tim Harris, ed., *The Politics of the Excluded, c.1500–1850* (Basingstoke: Macmillan, 2001), pp. 153–94, at p. 154. See also David Weil Baker, *Divulging Utopia: Radical Humanism in Sixteenth-Century England* (Amherst: University of Massachusetts Press, 1999), pp. 92–93; Paul Hammond, *Dryden and the Traces of Classical Rome* (Oxford: Oxford University Press, 1999), pp. 75–76.

20 Nicholas Udall, *Respublica: An Interlude for Christmas 1553*, ed. W. W. Greg (Oxford: Oxford University Press, 1952).

21 On Smith, see Mary Dewar, *Sir Thomas Smith: A Tudor Intellectual in Office* (London: Athlone, 1964); Cathy Shrank, *Writing the Nation in Reformation England, 1530–1580* (Oxford: Oxford University Press, 2004), ch. 4; Stephen Alford, *Kingship and Politics in the Reign of Edward VI* (Cambridge: Cambridge University Press, 2002), *passim.*

22 *A Discourse of the Commonweal of This Realm of England, attributed to Sir Thomas Smith*, ed. Mary Dewar (Charlottesville: University of Virginia Press, 1969), introduction; appendix B.

23 *Discourse of the Commonweal*, p. 16; Cicero, *On the Commonwealth and On the Laws*, ed. James E. G. Zetel (Cambridge: Cambridge University Press, 1999), p. 1, 'since our country provides more benefits and is a parent prior to our biological parents, we have a greater obligation to it than to our parents'. More generally, see Cicero, *De Officiis*, trans. Walter Miller (London: Heinemann, 1913), as this was one of the most widely read classical works in Renaissance England; Howard Jones, *Master Tully. Cicero in Tudor England* (Nieuwkoop: Bibliotheca Humanistica & Reformatorica, Vol. LVII, 1981). On the political background and significance of humanism, see Richard Tuck, *Philosophy and Government, 1572–1651* (Cambridge: Cambridge University Press, 1993), ch. 1.

24 An assumption that limits Richard Helgerson's otherwise fascinating survey, *Forms of Nationhood: The Elizabethan Writing of England* (Chicago: University of Chicago Press, 1992).

25 *Discourse of the Commonweal*, p. 29. See also Arthur B. Ferguson, *The Articulate Citizen and the English Renaissance* (Durham: Duke University Press, 1965), chs. 3, 7.

26 Dewar, *Thomas Smith*, pp. 110–14.

27 See Sir Thomas Smith, *De Republica Anglorum: A Discourse on the Commonwealth of England (1583)*, ed. L. Alston (Shannon: Irish University Press, 1972, rpt. of 1906). Subsequent references to this edition in parentheses in the text. On William Harrison, see G. J. R. Parry, *A Protestant Vision: William Harrison and the Reformation of Elizabethan England* (Cambridge: Cambridge University Press, 1987).

28 *The Politics of Aristotle*, ed. and trans. Ernest Baker (Oxford: Oxford University Press, 1946), bk. IV. Louis Le Roy's French translation of

Aristotle with his commentary was later translated into English: *Aristotles Politiques, Or Discourses of Government Translated out of Greeke into French . . . by Loys Le Roy* (London, 1598).

29 Livy, *The Early History of Rome (Books I–V of The History of Rome)*, trans. Aubrey De Sélincourt (Harmondsworth: Penguin, 1960), bk. I. On Livy's sympathies, see P. G. Walsh, *Livy: His Historical Aims and Methods* (Cambridge: Cambridge University Press, 1961); T. J. Luce, *Livy: The Composition of His History* (Princeton: Princeton University Press, 1977).

30 See McLaren, *Political Culture in the Reign of Elizabeth I*, ch. 7.

31 See Glenn Burgess, *The Politics of the Ancient Constitution: An Introduction to English Political Thought, 1603–1642* (Basingstoke: Macmillan, 1992), pp. 123–24, *passim*; J. G. A. Pocock, *The Ancient Constitution and the Feudal Law: A Study of English Historical Thought in the Seventeenth Century* (rev. ed., Cambridge: Cambridge University Press, 1987), pp. 65, 259.

32 See also G. R. Elton, ed., *The Tudor Constitution: Documents and Commentary* (Cambridge: Cambridge University Press, 1972), pp. 234–35.

33 See Martin van Gelderen, 'Aristotelians, Monarchomachs and Republicans: Sovereignty and *respublica mixta* in Dutch and German Political Thought, 1580–1650'; Hans Erich Bödeker, 'Debating the *respublica mixta*: German and Dutch Political Discourses around 1700'; Vittorio Conti, 'The Mechanisation of Virtue: Republican Rituals in Italian Political Thought in the Sixteenth and Seventeenth Centuries', in Martin van Gelderen and Quentin Skinner, eds., *Republicanism: A Shared European Heritage*, 2 vols. (Cambridge: Cambridge University Press, 2002), I, pp. 195–217; I, pp. 219–46; II, pp. 73–83.

34 Blair Worden, 'Republicanism, Regicide and Republic: The English Experience', in van Gelderen and Skinner, eds., *Republicanism*, I, pp. 307–27, at p. 313.

35 Sir John Fortesque, *A learned commendation of the politique lawes of Englande*, trans. Richard Mulcaster (London, 1567). Subsequent references in parentheses in the text. For commentary, see Pocock, *Ancient Constitution and the Feudal Law*, pp. 275–88, *passim*; Burgess, *Politics of the Ancient Constitution*, pp. 6–7, 36–38, *passim*; Constance Jordan, *Shakespeare's Monarchies: Ruler and Subject in the Romances* (Ithaca, N.Y.: Cornell University Press, 1997), pp. 23–25, 88–89, *passim*. My discussion of Fortesque is indebted to these works.

36 Aristotle, *The Politics of Aristotle*, ed. and trans. Ernest Baker (Oxford: Oxford University Press, 1946), p. 241; Janet Coleman, *A History of Political Thought*, 2 vols. (Oxford: Blackwell, 2000), I, pp. 214–16; Rebecca Bushnell, *Tragedies of Tyrants: Political Thought and Theater in the English Renaissance* (Ithaca, N.Y.: Cornell University Press, 1990).

37 On the dominant influence of Aquinas on late medieval political thought, see J. B. Morrall, *Political Thought in Medieval Times* (Toronto: University of Toronto Press, 1997, rpt. of 1980), pp. 70–86; Coleman, *History of Political Thought*, II, ch. 2.

38 On the influence of Polybius on republican thought, see Zera S. Fink, *The Classical Republicans: An Essay in the Recovery of a Pattern of Thought in Seventeenth Century England* (Evanston: Northwestern University Press, 1962), p. 3.

39 Polybius, *The Rise of the Roman Empire*, trans. Ian Scott-Kilvert (Harmondsworth: Penguin, 1979), p. 311. Subsequent references to this edition in parentheses in the text.

40 On Stoicism, see Coleman, *History of Political Thought*, I, ch. 5. For further discussion of the vital political significance of Stoicism in the sixteenth century, see Jessica Wolfe, *Humanism, Machinery and Renaissance Literature* (Cambridge: Cambridge University Press, 2004), *passim*.

41 See Edward Said, *Culture and Imperialism* (London: Chatto and Windus, 1993).

42 Aristotle, *Politics*, pp. 224–34.

43 Ibid., pp. 243–50.

44 See Susan Doran, 'The Politics of Renaissance Europe', in Andrew Hadfield and Paul Hammond, eds., *Shakespeare and Renaissance Europe* (London: Thomson, 2004), pp. 21–52.

45 Documents are collected in Elton, ed., *Tudor Constitution*, ch. 1.

46 See Norman Jones, 'Parliament and the Political Society of Elizabethan England', in Dale Hoak, ed., *Tudor Political Culture* (Cambridge: Cambridge University Press, 1995), pp. 226–42; Jennifer Loach, *Parliament under the Tudors* (Oxford: Oxford University Press, 1991), chs. 6–7; David Dean, *Law-Making and Society in Late Elizabethan England: The Parliament of England, 1584–1601* (Cambridge: Cambridge University Press, 1996); Michael Graves, *Elizabethan Parliaments, 1559–1601* (2nd ed., London: Longman, 1996), chs. 6–7.

47 John Guy, 'Introduction: The 1590s: The Second Reign of Elizabaeth I?', in Guy, ed., *The Reign of Elizabeth I*, pp. 1–19, at pp. 11–12.

48 See, for example, Jonathan Goldberg, *James I and the Politics of Literature: Jonson, Shakespeare, Donne, and their Contemporaries* (Baltimore: Johns Hopkins University Press, 1983); Leonard Tennenhouse, *Power on Display: The Politics of Shakespeare's Genres* (London: Methuen, 1986), ch. 4.

49 See Jenny Wormald, 'James VI and I: Two Kings or One?', *History* 68 (1983), 187–209; Wormald, 'James VI and I, *Basilikon Doron* and *The Trew Law of Free Monarchies*: the Scottish Context and the English Translation'; J. P. Sommerville, 'James I and the Divine Right of Kings: English Politics and Continental Theory', both in Linda Levy Peck, ed., *The Mental World of the Jacobean Court* (Cambridge: Cambridge University Press, 1991), pp. 36–54, and pp. 55–70.

50 See J. P. Kenyon, ed., *The Stuart Constitution: Documents and Commentary* (2nd ed., Cambridge: Cambridge University Press, 1986), ch. 2.

51 Roger Ascham, *The Scholemaster* (1571), ed. John E. B. Mayor (London: Bell, 1934), p. 196; T. W. Baldwin, *William Shakspere's Small Latine and Lesse Greeke*, 2 vols. (Urbana: University of Illinois Press, 1944), I, p. 262.

52 D. R. Woolf, *Reading History in Early Modern England* (Cambridge: Cambridge University Press, 2000), p. 34; Ascham, *Scholemaster*, pp. 225–31.

53 Laurentius Grimaldus, *The Counsellor: exactly portraited in two bookes*, trans. anon. (London, 1599), pp. 8–9; Markku Peltonen, *Classical Humanism and Republicanism in English Political Thought, 1570–1640* (Cambridge: Cambridge University Press, 1995), pp. 107–8.

54 Richard Tuck, *Philosophy and Government, 1572–1651* (Cambridge: Cambridge University Press, 1993), pp. 42, 95–96, 110–2; W. M. Spellman, *European Political Thought, 1600–1700* (Basingstoke: Macmillan, 1998), p. 108.

55 Johnson Kent Wright, 'The Idea of a Republican Constitution in Old Régime France', in van Gelderen and Skinner, eds., *Republicanism*, I, pp. 288–306, at p. 289.

56 Kevin Sharpe, *Reading Revolutions: The Politics of Early Modern England* (New Haven: Yale University Press, 2000), pp. 80, 84, *passim*.

57 More generally, see Woolf, *Reading History*; Kevin Sharpe, *Remapping Early Modern England: The Culture of Seventeenth-Century Politics* (Cambridge: Cambridge University Press, 2000), pp. 87–90.

58 *The Hystories of the most famous and worthy Cronographer Polybius: Discoursing of the warres betwixt the Romanes & Carthaginenses, a riche and godly Worke, conteining holsome counsels & wonderfull deuises against the incombrances of fickle fortune, Englished by C. W. [Christopher Warton] Whereunto is annexed an Abstract, compendiously coarcted out of the life & wothy actes, perpetrate by oure puissant Prince king Henry the fift* (London, 1568). Subsequent references in parentheses in the text. On the practice of making such historical parallels, see Tom McAlindon, *Shakespeare's Tudor History: A Study of **Henry IV, Parts 1 and 2*** (Aldershot: Ashgate, 2001), p. 27.

59 Polybius, *Histories*, bks. 11–15. See also A. C. Spearing, *Medieval Dream Poetry* (Cambridge: Cambridge University Press, 1976), pp. 8–11, *passim*; Marcel Le Glay, Jean-Louis Voison, Yann Le Bohec and David Cherry, *A History of Rome* (2nd ed., Oxford: Blackwell, 2001), pp. 74–80.

60 See Peltonen, *Classical Humanism and Republicanism*, pp. 73–102; Vincent Carey, 'The Irish Face of Machiavelli: Richard Beacon's *Solon his Follie* and Republican Ideology in the Conquest of Ireland', in Hiram Morgan, ed., *Political Ideology in Ireland, 1534–1641* (Dublin: Four Courts, 1999), pp. 83–109. See also Sydney Anglo, 'A Machiavellian Solution to the Irish Problem: Richard Beacon's *Solon His Follie*', in Edward Chaney and Peter Mack, eds., *England and the Continental Renaissance: Essays in Honour of J. B. Trapp* (Woodbridge: Boydell and Brewer, 1990), pp. 153–64.

61 For discussion, see Andrew Hadfield, 'Censoring Ireland in Elizabethan England, 1580–1600', in Hadfield, ed., *Literature and Censorship in Renaissance England* (Basingstoke: Palgrave/Macmillan, 2001), pp. 149–64, at pp. 155–58.

62 See Sharpe, *Remapping Early Modern England*, ch. 2; Burgess, *Politics of the Ancient Constitution*. For an opposing reading of early modern political

conflict, see J. P. Sommerville, *Politics and Ideology in England, 1603–1640* (Harlow: Longman, 1986). On religious borrowings and overlapping, see Alison Shell, *Catholicism, Controversy and the English Literary Imagination, 1558–1660* (Cambridge: Cambridge University Press, 1999).

63 Niccolò Machiavelli, *The Discourses*, trans. Leslie Walker, rev. Brian Richardson, ed. Bernard Crick (Harmondsworth: Penguin, 1970). For commentary, see Gisela Bock, Quentin Skinner and Maurizio Viroli, eds., *Machiavelli and Republicanism* (Cambridge: Cambridge University Press, 1990); Coleman, *History of Political Thought*, II, ch. 6; Quentin Skinner, *The Foundations of Modern Political Thought*, 2 vols. (Cambridge: Cambridge University Press, 1978), I, pp. 180–86; J. G. A. Pocock, *The Machiavellian Moment: Florentine Political Thought and the Atlantic Republican Tradition* (Princeton: Princeton University Press, 1975), ch. 7; Paul A. Rahe, 'Situating Machiavelli', in James Hankins, ed., *Renaissance Civic Humanism* (Cambridge: Cambridge University Press, 2000), pp. 270–308; David Armitage, 'Empire and Liberty: A Republican Dilemma', in van Gelderen and Skinner, eds., *Republicanism*, II, pp. 29–46.

64 Richard Beacon, *Solon his Follie, or A Politique Discourse Touching the Reformation of common-weales conquered, declined or corrupted* (1594), ed. Clare Carroll and Vincent Carey (Binghampton, N.Y.: MRTS, 1996), p. 18. Subsequent references to this edition in parentheses in the text.

65 On the use of Greek history and philosophy, see Eric Nelson, *The Greek Tradition in Republican Thought* (Cambridge: Cambridge University Press, 2004). Nelson argues that there was a separate Greek strain of republicanism in Europe and America, which emphasized the need for property to be redistributed equably. This aspect of republicanism, while important in works such as More's *Utopia*, assumes a greater significance later in the seventeenth century after the works of James Harrington and so has not been considered at length in this study.

66 On the Desmond Rebellion, see Steven G. Ellis, *Tudor Ireland: Crown, Community and the Conflict of Cultures, 1470–1603* (London: Longman, 1985), pp. 221–23.

67 Machiavelli, *Discourses*, pp. 110–11.

68 See Carey, 'Irish Face of Machiavelli', pp. 106–9.

69 Beacon makes considerable reference to Jean Bodin's *Les Six Livres de la République* (Paris, 1986), translated as *The six books of a common-weale*, by Richard Knolles (1606). One of Bodin's principal concerns is to define the central importance of magistrates in defining the monarchy: see Beacon, *Solon his Follie*, introduction, pp. xxxviii–ix; Julian H. Franklin, 'Sovereignty and the Mixed Constitution: Bodin and his Critics', in Burns and Goldie, eds., *Cambridge History of Political Thought*, pp. 298–328.

70 Plutarch, *The lives of the noble Grecians and Romanes compared together by that graue learned philosopher and historiographer, Plutarke of Chaeronea ; translated out of Greeke into French by James Amyot . . . ; and out of French into Englishe, by Thomas North* (London, 1579), pp. 142–66.

71 Beacon, *Solon his Follie*, introduction, pp. xxxix–xli; Patrick Collinson, *The Elizabethan Puritan Movement* (Oxford: Clarendon Press, 1967), pp. 164–65; Hardin Craig, Jr., 'The *Geneva Bible* as a Political Document', *PHR* 7 (1938), 40–49; Katherine R. Firth, *The Apocalyptic Tradition in Reformation Britain, 1530–1645* (Oxford: Oxford University Press, 1979), p. 125.

72 Compare Edmund Spenser's representation of the Souldan (Sultan) (*The Faerie Queene*, ed. A. C. Hamilton (London: Routledge, 2001), V, p. viii. On the links between the Irish and the Spanish, see J. J. Silke, *Ireland and Europe, 1559–1607* (Dundalk: Dundalgan, 1966).

73 Plutarch, *Lives*, pp. 722–63.

74 For discussion of such issues in a Scottish context, see Arthur H. Williamson, *Scottish National Consciousness in the Age of James VI* (Edinburgh: Donald, 1979); David Hume of Godscroft, **The British Union**: *A Critical Edition and Translation of David Hume of Godscroft's* **De Unione Insulae Britannicae**, ed. Paul J. Mc Ginnis and Arthur H. Williamson (Aldershot: Ashgate, 2002).

75 *Vindiciae, Contra Tyrannos, or, concerning the legitimate power of a prince over the people, and of the people over a prince* (1579), ed. George Garnett (Cambridge: Cambridge University Press, 1994), p. 3. Subsequent references to this edition in parentheses in the text. See also John Knox, *On Rebellion,* ed. Roger A. Mason (Cambridge: Cambridge University Press, 1994); Kingdon, 'Calvinism and Resistance Theory', pp. 197–200.

76 On the notion of paratexts, see Gerard Genette, *Paratexts: Thresholds of Interpretation*, trans. Jane E. Lewin (Cambridge: Cambridge University Press, 1997).

77 The significance of the name is not clear, but the Belgian nationality reminds readers of the struggle of the Protestant Low Countries for independence from Spain.

78 On the intellectual contexts of *The Prince*, see Niccolò Machiavelli, *The Prince*, ed. Quentin Skinner and Russell Price (Cambridge: Cambridge University Press, 1988); J. R. Hale, *Machiavelli and Renaissance Italy* (Harmondsworth: Penguin, 1961); Quentin Skinner, *Machiavelli* (Oxford: Oxford University Press, 1981), ch. 2.

79 See Innocent Gentillet, *A Discourse Upon the Meanes of Wel Governing and Maintaining in Good Peace, a Kingdom, or other Principalitie . . . Against Nicholas Machiavell the Florentine*, trans. Simon Patericke (London, 1602); Skinner, *Foundations*, II, pp. 309–10; Kingdon, 'Calvinism and resistance theory', p. 208; Christopher Marlowe, *The Jew of Malta*, ed. N. W. Bawcutt (Manchester: Manchester University Press, 1978), prologue, lines 1–4.

80 Aristotle, *Politics*, pp. 234–54; Mary Ann McGrail, *Tyranny in Shakespeare* (Lanham: Lexington Books, 2001), ch. 1.

81 *Vindiciae, Contra Tyrannos*, introduction, pp. lv–lxxvi; Blair Worden, *The Sound of Virtue: Philip Sidney's* **Arcadia** *and Elizabethan Politics* (New Haven: Yale University Press, 1996), ch. 16, *passim*.

82 Stephanus Junius Brutus, the Celt, *A Short Apologie for Christian Souldiours*, trans. H. P. (London, 1588). Subsequent references in parentheses in the text. For comment, see William C. Carroll, 'Theories of Kingship in Shakespeare's England', in Richard Dutton and Jean E. Howard, eds., *A Companion to Shakespeare's Works, 4 vols., Volume II, The Histories* (Oxford: Blackwell, 2003), pp. 125–45, 136–37.

83 For an overview, see Skinner, *Foundations*, II, pt. 2; J. H. M. Salmon, 'Catholic resistance theory, Ultramontanism, and the royalist response, 1580–1620', in Burns and Goldie, eds., *Cambridge History of Political Thought*, pp. 219–53. See also Richard Wilson, *Secret Shakespeare: Studies in Theatre, Religion and Resistance* (Manchester: Manchester University Press, 2004).

84 On Allen, see *DNB* entry; P. J. Holmes, *Resistance and Compromise: The Political Thought of the Elizabethan Catholics* (Cambridge: Cambridge University Press, 1982), pp. 131–34, *passim*.

85 William Allen, *A Treatise made in Defence of the lawful power and authoritie of Priesthod to remedie sinnes* (1567), B1r. Subsequent references in parentheses in the text.

86 On Elizabeth's assumption of the role and the controversy surrounding her title, see W. P. Haugaard, *Elizabeth and the English Reformation* (Cambridge: Cambridge University Press, 1968).

87 Kingdon, 'Calvinism and resistance theory', pp. 206–14; Skinner, *Foundations*, II, pp. 209–41, *passim*.

88 For discussion, see R. T. Kendall, *Calvin and English Calvinism to 1649* (Oxford: Oxford University Press, 1979), *passim*.

89 Holmes, *Resistance and Compromise*, pp. 35–36; Alison Shell, *Catholicism, Controversy and the English Literary Imagination, 1558–1660* (Cambridge: Cambridge University Press, 1999), pp. 184–85; Evelyn Waugh, *Edmund Campion: Scholar, Priest, Hero, and Martyr* (Oxford: Oxford University Press, 1980, rpt. of 1935).

90 William Allen, *A True, Sincere and Modest Defence, of English Catholiques that suffer for their faith both at home and abrode* (Rouen, 1584), preface. Subsequent references in parentheses in the text.

91 *Leicester's Commonwealth: The Copy of a Letter Written by a Master of Art of Cambridge (1584) and Related Documents*, ed. D. C. Peck (Athens, Ohio: Ohio University Press, 1985).

92 On the crime of 'compassing the king's death', see John Bellamy, *The Tudor Law of Treason: An Introduction* (London: Routledge, 1979), pp. 9–11, 20–23, *passim*. For the operation of the same treason law in a later period, see John Barrell, *Imagining the King's Death: Figurative Treason, Fantasies of Regicide, 1793–1796* (Oxford: Oxford University Press, 2000).

93 On the bull, see John Guy, *Tudor England* (Oxford; Oxford University Press, 1988), chs. 9–10.

94 See Jenny Wormald, *Court, Kirk, and Community: Scotland 1470–16* (London: Arnold, 1981), ch. 9.

95 John Major, *A History of Greater Britain*, ed. A. Constable and A. J. G. MacKay (Edinburgh: Edinburgh University Press, 1892); Hector Boece, *The Chronicles of Scotland*, ed. Raymond Wilson Chambers et al., 2 vols. (Edinburgh: Blackwood, 1938–41).

96 For details, see McFarlane, *Buchanan*; Spellman, *European Political Thought, 1600–1700*, p. 86, *passim*; James M. Aitken, ed., *The Trial of George Buchanan Before the Lisbon Inquisition* (Edinburgh: Oliver and Boyd, 1939).

97 See George Buchanan, *Tragedies*, ed. P. Sharratt and P. G. Walsh (Edinburgh: Scottish Academic Press, 1983); Philip J. Ford, *George Buchanan: Prince of Poets with an Edition of Miscallaneorum Liber* (Aberdeen: Aberdeen University Press, 1982); Buchanan, *Political Poetry*; Buchanan, *De Prosodia Libellius* (Edinburgh, 1590); Buchanan, *De Jure Regni*; Buchanan, *Ane detectioun*; Buchanan, *History of Scotland*.

98 See Buchanan, *Political Poetry*, introduction, p. 12; Hume of Godscroft, **The British Union**, introduction, pp. 1–10.

99 Rebecca W. Bushnell, 'George Buchanan, James VI and Neo-classicism', in Mason, ed., *Scots and Britons*, pp. 91–111, at pp. 96–97.

100 Buchanan, *De Jure Regni*, p. 208. Subsequent references in parentheses in the text.

101 George Buchanan, 'Epithalamium for Francis of Valois and Mary Stewart, of the Kingdom of France and of Scotland', lines 56–59, in Buchanan, *Political Poetry*, p. 128. Subsequent references in parentheses in the text.

102 Buchanan, *Political Poetry*, introduction, p. 3; Roger A. Mason, 'James I, George Buchanan and *The Trew Law of Free Monarchies*', in Roger Mason, *Kingship and the Commonweal: Political Thought in Renaissance and Reformation Scotland* (East Lothian: Tuckwell Press, 1998), pp. 215–41, at pp. 222–23.

103 Buchanan, *History of Scotland*, pp. 193–95. Subsequent references in parentheses in the text. On the significance of Kenneth III, see below, pp. 194–202.

104 On Buchanan's historical method, see Hugh Trevor Roper, 'George Buchanan and the Ancient Scottish Constitution', *EHR* Supplement 3 (1966).

105 On Morton, see *DNB* entry.

106 McFarlane, *Buchanan*, pp. 446–48.

107 Ibid., p. 437; Mason, ed., *Scots and Britons*, pt. 2; Mason, 'James VI, George Buchanan, and *The Trew Law of Free Monarchies*'; Roger A. Mason, '*Rex Stoicus*: George Buchanan, James VI and the Scottish Polity', in John Dwyer, Roger A. Mason and Alexander Murdoch, eds., *New Perspectives on the Politics and Culture of Early Modern Scotland* (Edinburgh: John Donald, 1982), pp. 9–33. On reactions to Mary in a wider context, see Phillips, *Images of a Queen*; Jenny Wormald, *Mary Queen of Scots: A Study in Failure* (London: George Philip, 1988).

108 Guy, *Tudor England*, pp. 334–37.

109 Phillips, 'George Buchanan and the Sidney Circle'; McFarlane, *Buchanan*, pp. 453–55.

110 Christopher Goodman, *How superior powers oght to be obeyd of their subjects* (Geneva, 1558). On Goodman, see Kingdon, 'Calvinism and Resistance Theory', pp. 194–97; Collinson, *Elizabethan Puritan Movement*, p. 46, *passim*.

111 Phillips, 'George Buchanan and the Sidney Circle', p. 45; Worden, *Sound of Virtue*, *passim*; W. D. Briggs, 'Sidney's Political Ideas', *SP* 29 (1932), 534–42. See below, pp. 87–89.

112 Edmund Spenser, *A View of the State of Ireland*, ed. Andrew Hadfield and Willy Maley (Oxford: Blackwell, 1997), pp. 45–46, 51, 60, 63.

113 On the 'Socratic dialogue', see Virginia Cox, *The Renaissance Dialogue: Literary Dialogue in its Social and Political Contexts, Castiglione to Galileo* (Cambridge: Cambridge University Press, 1993), *passim*.

114 Richard A. McCabe, 'The Masks of Duessa: Spenser, Mary Queen of Scot, and James VI', *ELR* 17 (1987), 224–42.

115 Andrew Hadfield, *Shakespeare, Spenser and the Matter of Britain* (Basingstoke: Palgrave/Macmillan, 2003), ch. 10.

116 For arguments that Spenser was influenced by republican thought, see Andrew Hadfield, 'Was Spenser a Republican?', *English* 47 (1998), 169–82; 'Was Spenser a Republican After All? A Response to David Scott Okamura-Wilson', *Sp. Stud.* 17 (2003), 275–90.

117 Stuart Gillespie, *Shakespeare's Books: A Dictionary of Shakespeare Sources* (London: Athlone, 2001), pp. 469–70; William Shakespeare, *Cymbeline*, ed. J. M. Nosworthy (London: Thomson: The Arden Shakespeare, 2000, rpt. of 1955), introduction, pp. xix–xx.

118 McFarlane, *Buchanan*, p. 437; Phillips, 'Buchanan and the Sidney Circle', p. 51.

119 Humphrey Llwyd, *The breviary of Britayne* (London, 1573); Phillips, 'Buchanan and the Sidney Circle', pp. 51–52.

120 On Thynne, see *DNB* entry; Annabel Patterson, *Reading Holinshed's Chronicles* (Chicago: Chicago University Press, 1994), pp. 10, 24, 284.

121 Raphael Holinshed, *Holinshed's Chronicles of England, Scotland and Ireland* (1587), ed. Henry Ellis, 6 vols. (London: Johnson, 1807–8), V, p. 754. Subsequent references to this edition in parentheses in the text. For analysis of Thynne's changes, see Alison Taufer, *Holinshed's Chronicles* (New York: Twayne, 1999), ch. 5; David Norbrook, '*Macbeth* and the Politics of Historiography', in Kevin Sharpe and Steven N. Zwicker, eds., *Politics of Discourse: The Literature and History of Seventeenth-Century England* (Berkeley: University of California Press, 1987), pp. 78–116, at pp. 81–93.

122 Cited in Patterson, *Reading Holinshed's Chronicles*, p. 37.

123 See Burns, 'The Political Ideas of George Buchanan', 60–68; Mason, '*Rex Stoicus*'.

124 McFarlane, *Buchanan*, pp. 224–5, 401, *passim*; Kingdon, 'Calvinism and Resistance Theory', pp. 215–18; Skinner, *Foundations*, II, pp. 342–45.

125 The literature on enthusiasm for Venice's constitutions is enormous: see, for example, Nicolai Rubenstein, 'Italian Political Thought, 1450–1530', in Burns and Goldie, eds., *Cambridge History of Political Thought*, pp. 30–65, at pp. 58–65; Pocock, *Machiavellian Moment*, chs. 7–9; Peltonen, *Classical Humanism and Republicanism*, pp. 102–18; Andrew Hadfield, *Literature, Travel and Colonial Writing in the English Renaissance, 1545–1625* (Oxford: Clarendon Press, 1998), pp. 24–67; Conti, 'Mechanisation of Virtue'.

126 James VI and I, *The Trew Law of Free Monarchies*, in *The Workes* (1616) (Hildesham and New York: Verlag, 1971), pp. 191–210, at p. 203.

127 William Thomas, *Historie of Italie* (1549), fos.73–85. Subsequent references to this edition in parentheses in the text. See also the modern selection, *The History of Italy*, ed. George B. Parks (Ithaca, N.Y.: Cornell University Press, 1963). For comment, see Fink, *Classical Republicans*, ch. 2; Shrank, *Writing the Nation*, ch. 3; Hadfield, *Literature, Travel and Colonial Writing*, pp. 24–32. My comments in the next few paragraphs make use of some of my earlier analysis.

128 See Alford, *Kingship and Politics in the Reign of Edward VI*, ch. 4.

129 For details see David Loades, *Two Tudor Conspiracies* (Cambridge: Cambridge University Press, 1965), chs. 1–5.

130 See Guy, ed., *The Reign of Elizabeth I*; Julia M. Walker, ed., *Dissing Elizabeth: Negative Representations of Gloriana* (Durham, N.C.: Duke University Press, 1998).

131 See below, pp. 214–20.

132 See Cyndia Clegg, *Press Censorship in Elizabethan England* (Cambridge: Cambridge University Press, 1997), pp. 202–5; Richard A. McCabe, '"Right Puisante and Terrible Priests": The Role of the Anglican Church in Elizabethan State Censorship', in Hadfield, ed., *Literature and Censorship*, pp. 75–94.

133 See David McPherson, 'Lewkenor's Venice and its Sources', *RQ* 41 (1988), 459–66.

134 Gaspar Contarini, *The Commonwealth and Government of Venice*, trans. Lewis Lewkenor (London, 1599), 'To the Reader', A1r- A4r. Subsequent references in parentheses in the text. See Pocock, *Machiavellian Moment*, p. 321.

135 See Simon Adams, 'The Patronage of the Crown in Elizabethan Politics: The 1590s in Perspective', in Guy, ed., *The Reign of Elizabeth I*, pp. 20–45; Adams, *Leicester and the Court: Essays on Elizabethan Politics* (Manchester: Manchester University Press, 2002), pt. 1.

136 On the analogy of the 'body politic', see D. G. Hale, *The Body Politic: A Political Metaphor in Renaissance England* (The Hague: Mouton, 1971); Margaret Healy, *Fictions of Disease in Early Modern England: Bodies, Plagues and Politics* (Basingstoke: Palgrave/Macmillan, 2001), pp. 37–40, *passim*; Sharpe, *Remapping Early Modern England*, pp. 111–13, *passim*; Quentin Skinner, *Visions of Politics*, 3 vols. (Cambridge: Cambridge University Press, 2002), ch. 6.

137 Aristotle, *Politiques*, p. 88.

138 See David Norbrook, *Poetry and Politics in the English Renaissance* (2nd ed, Oxford: Oxford University Press, 2002), pp. 87, 115, 118; Blair Worden 'English Republicanism', in Burns and Goldie, eds., *Cambridge History of Political Thought*, pp. 443–75, at p. 446.

139 See David McPherson, *Shakespeare, Jonson, and the Myth of Venice* (Newark: University of Delaware Press, 1990); Gillespie, *Shakespeare's Books*, p. 278; Virginia Mason Vaughan, *Othello: A Contextual History* (Cambridge: Cambridge University Press, 1994), pp. 16–20; Jonathan Bate, 'The Elizabethans in Italy', in Jean-Pierre Maquerlot and Michele Willems, eds., *Travel and Drama in Shakespeare's Time* (Cambridge: Cambridge University Press, 1996), pp. 55–74, at p. 59. For other enthusiastic accounts of Venice by Englishmen, see Fynes Moryson, *An Itinerary Containing His Ten Yeeres Travell* (1617), 4 vols. (Glasgow: MacLehose, 1908) I, pp. 160–96; Thomas Coryat, *Coryat's Crudities* (1611), 2 vols. (Glasgow: MacLehose, 1905), I, pp. 302–427.

140 Peter Burke, 'Tacitism', in T. A. Dorey, ed., *Tacitus* (London: Routledge, 1969), pp. 149–71, at p. 150.

141 Ben Jonson, 'The New Cry', in *Poems*, ed. Ian Donaldson (Oxford: Oxford University Press, 1975), pp. 48–9, line 15. See also Alan T. Bradford, 'Stuart Absolutism and the "Utility" of Tacitus', *HLQ* 46 (1983), 127–55, at p. 137.

142 Modern translations are *On Imperial Rome* (*The Annals*), trans. Michael Grant (Harmondsworth: Penguin, 1956); *The Histories*, trans. W. H. Fyfe (Oxford: Oxford University Press, 1997); *On Britain and Germany*, trans. H. Mattingly (Harmondsworth: Penguin, 1948).

143 Peter Burke, 'Tacitism, Scepticism, and Reason of State', in Burns and Goldie, eds., *Cambridge History of Political Thought*, pp. 479–98, at p. 487. The literature on Tacitus is now substantial. In addition to the works already cited, see J. H. M. Salmon, 'Seneca and Tacitus in Jacobean England', in Peck, ed., *Mental World*, pp. 169–88; Malcolm Smuts, 'Court-Centred Politics and the Use of Roman Historians', in Sharpe and Zwicker, eds., *Culture and Politics*, pp. 21–43; Norbrook, *Poetry and Politics*, pp. 152–3, *passim*; Reid Barbour, *English Epicures and Stoics: Ancient Legacies in Early Stuart Culture* (Amherst: University of Massachusetts Press, 1998), *passim*; Baldwin, *William Shakspere's Small Latine*, *passim*.

144 Sharpe, *Reading Revolutions*, p. 318.

145 Hayward, John, *The First and Second Parts of John Hayward's **The Life and Raigne of King Henrie IIII***, ed. John J. Manning (London: Royal Historical Society, 1991; Camden Society, 4th series, Vol. 42), introduction, p. 2. See also Lisa Jardine and Alan Stewart, *Hostage to Fortune: The Troubled Life of Francis Bacon* (New York: Hill and Wang, 1998), ch. 8; Mervyn James, *Society, Politics and Culture: Studies in Early Modern Culture* (Cambridge: Cambridge University Press, 1988), ch. 9.

146 David Scott Wilson-Okamura, 'Spenser and the Two Queens', *ELR* 32 (2002), 62–84, p. 77.

147 Thomas Hobbes, *Leviathan*, ed. C. B. McPherson (Harmondsworth: Penguin, 1981), p. 369. For comment, see David Norbrook, *Writing the English Republic: Poetry, Rhetoric and Politics, 1627–1660* (Cambridge: Cambridge University Press, 1999), pp. 34–5; Tuck, *Philosophy and Government*, ch. 7; Margot Heinemann, '"Let Rome in Tiber melt": Order and Disorder in *Antony and Cleopatra*', in John Drakakis, ed., *Antony and Cleopatra: Contemporary Critical Essays* (Basingstoke: Macmillan, 1994), pp. 166–81, at p. 176.

148 Quentin Skinner, *Reason and Rhetoric in the Philosophy of Thomas Hobbes* (Cambridge: Cambridge University Press, 1996), pt. 1; *Visions of Politics, Volume III: Hobbes and Civil Science* (Cambridge: Cambridge University Press, 2002), ch. 2.

149 Skinner, *Reason and Rhetoric*, ch. 10.

150 On Saville, see *DNB* entry; David Womersley, 'Sir Henry Saville's Translation of Tacitus and the Political Interpretation of Elizabethan Texts', *RES*, ns, 42 (1991), 313–42.

151 Cornelius Tacitus, *The ende of Nero and beginning of Galba Fower bookes of the Histories of Cornelius Tacitus. The life of Agricola*, trans. Henry Saville (Oxford, 1591), pp. 1–17. Subsequent references to this edition in parentheses. For analysis, see Womersley, 'Saville's Translation of Tacitus'. Richard Greenway translated the other two texts in 1598 as *The Annales of Cornelius Tacitus. The Description of Germanie*. This work was dedicated to Essex, one of the reasons for the panic over Hayward's work, and perhaps also a reason why Bacon made his joke.

152 On the succession, see Susan Doran, *Monarchy and Matriarchy: the Courtships of Elizabeth I* (London: Routledge, 1996). More generally, see Annabel Patterson, *Censorship and Interpretation: The Conditions of Writing in Early Modern England* (Madison: University of Wisconsin Press, 1984)

153 For similar ways of operating at court in an earlier period, see John Guy, 'Tudor Monarchy and its Critiques: From the Wars of the Roses to the Death of Henry VIII', in John Guy, ed., *The Tudor Monarchy* (London: Arnold, 1997), pp. 78–109; Seth Lerer, 'Errata: Print, Politics and Poetry in Early Modern England', in Kevin Sharpe and Steven Zwicker, eds., *Reading, Society and Politics in Early Modern England* (Cambridge: Cambridge University Press, 2003), pp. 41–71.

154 For details, see Tacitus, *The Histories*, bks. 1–2; Le Glay et al., eds., *History of Rome*, pp. 239–42.

155 Justus Lipsius, *Six Bookes of Politickes or Civil Doctrine, written in Latine by Justus Lipsius: which doe especially concerne principalitie. Done into English by William Jones Gentleman* (London, 1594), B1r. On Lipsius, see Burke, 'Tacitism, Scepticism, and Reason of State', pp. 492–3; Jill Kraye, 'Moral Philosophy', in Charles B. Schmitt and Quentin Skinner, eds., *The Cambridge History of Renaissance Philosophy* (Cambridge: Cambridge University Press, 1988), pp. 303–86, at pp. 370–73; Peltonen, *Classical*

Humanism and Republicanism, passim; Skinner, *Foundations,* II, pp. 281–83; Wilson-Okamura, 'Spenser and the Two Queens', pp. 74–77.

156 Justus Lipsius, *Two bookes of constancie. Written in Latine, by Justus Lipsius. Containing, principallie, A comfortable conference, in common calamities. And will serue for a singular consolation to all that are privately distressed, or afflicted, either in body or mind. Englished by John Stradling* (London, 1595).

157 Blair Worden, 'Ben Jonson among the Historians', in Kevin Sharpe and Peter Lake, eds., *Culture and Politics in Early Stuart England* (Basingstoke: Macmillan, 1994), pp. 67–90.

158 The literature on James's political writings is extensive. See, for example, King James VI and I, *Political Writings,* ed. J. P. Sommerville (Cambridge: Cambridge University Press, 1994); Sharpe, *Remapping Early Modern England,* chs. 3–4; Daniel Fischlin and Mark Fortier, eds., *Royal Subjects: Essays on the Writings of James VI and I* (Detroit: Wayne State University Press, 2002); Mark Fortier, 'Equity and Ideas: Coke, Ellesmere, and James I', *RQ* 51 (1998), 1255–82.

159 'An Homily against Disobedience and Wilful Rebellion', in *Certain Sermons* (1574) (Cambridge: Parker Society, 1850), pp. 551–601. The central importance of the homily was asserted, most notoriously, in E. M. W. Tillayrd, *The Elizabethan World Picture* (Harmondsworth: Penguin, 1972, rpt. of 1943). For comment, see Jonathan Dollimore, 'Introduction: Shakespeare, Cultural Materialism and the New Historicism', in Jonathan Dollimore and Alan Sinfield, eds., *Political Shakespeare: New Essays in Cultural Materialism* (Manchester: Manchester University Press, 1985), pp. 2–17, at pp. 5–6; John Drakakis, 'Introduction', in John Drakakis, ed., *Alternative Shakespeares* (London: Methuen, 1985), pp. 1–25, at pp. 14–15.

160 'Homily against Disobedience', p. 599. See also William Tyndale, *The Obedience of a Christian Man* (1528), ed. David Daniell (Harmondsworth: Penguin, 2000).

161 Jonathan Scott, *Algernon Sidney and the English Republic, 1623–77* (Cambridge: Cambridge University Press, 1988), p. 38.

162 Charles Merbury, *A Briefe Discourse of Royall Monarchie, as of the best common weale wherin the subject may beholde the sacred majestie of the princes most royall estate* (London, 1581), p. 8. Subsequent references in parentheses in the text.

163 Thomas Floyd, *The Picture of a perfit Common wealth describing aswell the offices of princes and inferiour magistrates over their subjects, as also the duties of subjects towards their governors. Gathered forth of many authors, aswel humane, as divine* (London, 1600), p. 29. Subsequent references in parentheses in the text. Floyd's political preferences are also expressed in *God and the king. Or a dialogue wherein is treated of allegiance due to our most gracious Lord, King James, within his dominions Which (by removing all controversies, and causes of dissentions and suspitions) bindeth subjects, by an inviolable band of love and duty, to their soveraigne* (Saint-Omer, 1620). For another work using bees as a

political analogy defending the rights of the monarchy, see Charles Butler, *The Feminine Monarchie or a treatise concerning bees, and the due ordering of them* (London, 1609).

164 James VI and I, *Political Writings*, p. 20, 23, 76–78, *passim*.

165 Lucan, *Civil War*, trans. Susan H. Braund (Oxford: Oxford University Press, 1992). For analysis, see David Norbrook, 'Lucan, Thomas May, and the Creation of a Republican Literary Culture', in Sharpe and Lake, eds., *Culture and Politics in Early Stuart England*, pp. 45–66; *Writing the English Republic*, ch. 1.

166 See Lisa Jardine and Anthony Grafton, '"Studied for Action": How Gabriel Harvey read his Livy', *P. & P.* 129 (1990), 30–78; Jardine and Grafton, *From Humanism to the Humanities: Education and the Liberal Arts in Fifteenth- and Sixteenth-Century Europe* (London: Duckworth, 1986).

167 For discussion, see Sommerville, *Politics and Ideology*, p. 4; Burgess, *Politics of the Ancient Constitution*, ch. 1; Sharpe, *Remapping Early Modern England*, pt. 1.

168 See Wormald, 'James VI and I, *Basilikon Doron* and *The Trew Law of Free Monarchies*'; Mason, 'James I, George Buchanan and *The Trew Law of Free Monarchies*'.

169 Aristotle, *Politics*, pp. 168, 182, *passim*; Aristotle, *Politiques*, p. 208.

170 A parallel case is that of Cicero. As has often been pointed out, virtually all writers, whatever political case they are making, refer to Cicero in glowing terms: see Jones, *Master Tully*; Jennifer Richards, *Rhetoric and Courtliness in Early Modern Literature* (Cambridge: Cambridge University Press, 2003), ch. 2. Cicero's most influential work, *De Officis*, was translated into English and reprinted several times throughout the sixteenth century, most importantly by Nicholas Grimald (1556), whose translation was reprinted in 1558 and 1583. See Cicero, *Marcus Tullius Ciceroes three bookes of duties to Marcus his sonne, tourned out of Latine into English, by Nicolas Grimald* (London, 1583).

171 Henry Cross, *The Schoole of Pollicie: or, the araignement of State-abuses. Directing Magistrates, adorning the Court, and beautifying, the whole Common-wealth* (London, 1605), I2r; Edward Forset, *A Comparative Discourse of the bodies natural and politique* (London, 1606), pp. 6–8, 20–21.

172 William Covell, *Polimanteia, or The means lawfull and unlawfull, to judge of the fall of a common-wealth, against the frivolous and foolish conjectures of this age* (London, 1595), Aa2r.

173 Covell's most frequently cited source is Jean Bodin, an absolutist thinker who opposed Huguenot political thought, but who placed great emphasis on the role of magistrates. See Julian H. Franklin, *Jean Bodin and the Rise of Absolutist Theory* (Cambridge: Cambridge University Press, 1973); Franklin, 'Sovereignty and the Mixed Constitution'. Bodin's major political work, *Les Six Livres de la République* (1576), was translated into English in 1606 by Richard Knolles, as *The six bookes of a common-weale*.

174 For details of the Lopez affair, see Jardine and Stewart, *Hostage to Fortune*, pp. 153–9.

175 See Clegg, *Press Censorship in Elizabethan England*, ch. 1, *passim*.

176 Worden, 'Republicanism, Regicide, and Republic', p. 311. See also Worden, 'English Republicanism', in Burns and Goldie, eds., *Cambridge History of Political Thought*, pp. 443–75; Kevin Sharpe, ' "An Image Doting Rabble": The Failure of Republican Culture in Seventeenth-Century England', in Kevin Sharpe and Steven N. Zwicker, eds., *Refiguring Revolutions: Aesthetics and Politics from the English Revolution to the Romantic Revolution* (Berkeley: University of California Press, 1998), pp. 25–56. Quentin Skinner's use of the term 'neo-Roman' in some of his recent work has seemed to some commentators to be a retreat from his argument for the existence of a republican tradition from the fifteenth century in *Foundations*; see *Liberty Before Liberalism* (Cambridge: Cambridge University Press, 1998).

177 Worden, 'Republicanism, Regicide, and Republic', p. 311.

178 For similar arguments, see Annabel Patterson, *Early Modern Liberalism* (Cambridge: Cambridge University Press, 1997); David Zaret, *Origins of Democratic Culture: Printing, Petitions, and the Public Sphere in Early-Modern England* (Princeton: Princeton University Press, 2000).

179 Peltonen, *Classical Humanism and Republicanism*, p. 9.

180 For an overview, see Whitney R. D. Jones, *The Tree of Commonwealth, 1450–1793* (Madison: Fairleigh-Dickinson University Press, 2000).

181 Sean Kelsey, *Inventing a Republic: The Political Culture of the English Commonwealth, 1649–1653* (Manchester: Manchester University Press, 1997), p. 1. See also Sharpe, ' "An Image Doting Rabble" '. For an alternative view, see Laura Lunger Knoppers, 'The Politics of Portraiture: Oliver Cromwell and the Plain Style', *RQ* 51 (1998), 1283–1319.

182 For a later definition, see Scott, *Algernon Sidney and the English Republic*, pp. 14–30. See also Fink, *Classical Republicans*.

183 Peltonen, *Classical Humanism and Republicanism*, p. 2.

184 See Worden, 'English Republicanism'.

185 Bushnell, *Tragedies of Tyrants*; Kingdon, 'Calvinism and Resistance Theory'; J. H. Burns, *The True Law of Kingship: Concepts of Monarchy in Early-Modern Scotland* (Oxford: Clarendon Press, 1996). See also Geoffrey Whitney, *A Choice of Emblems* (1586) (ed. Henry Green [1866], rpt. New York: Verlag, 1971), pp. 1, 29, 99, *passim*.

186 See Skinner, *Foundations*, I, pt. 2; Hankins, ed., *Renaissance Civic Humanism*.

187 See Whitney, *Choice of Emblems*, A4v-B1r, pp. 109–10, *passim*; Hugh Latimer, 'The Fourth Sermon on the Lord's Prayer', in *Sermons*, ed. Canon Beeching (London: Dent, 1906), pp. 308–26, at p. 313.

188 See Pocock, *Machiavellian Moment*, chs. 7–9; Worden, 'English Republicanism', p. 446.

189 Gian Biagio Conte, *Latin Literature: A History*, trans. Joseph B. Solodow, rev. Don Fowler and Glenn W. Most (Baltimore: Johns Hopkins University Press, 1999, rpt. of 1994), p. 370.
190 See David Quint, *Epic and Empire* (Princeton: Princeton University Press, 1993), ch. 4; Norbrook, *Writing the English Republic*, ch. 1.
191 For the history of the story, see Ian Donaldson, *The Rapes of Lucrece: A Myth and its Transformations* (Oxford; Clarendon Press, 1982).
192 Spellman, *European Political Thought*, ch. 3; Kingdon, 'Calvinism and Resistance Theory'; Salmon, 'Catholic Resistance Theory; Worden, 'English Republicanism', p. 448.
193 Francisco Sansovino, *The quintesence of wit being a corrant comfort of conceites, maximies, and poleticke devises*, trans. Robert Hitchcock (London, 1590), fos.6–7, 19, *passim*. See also Peltonen, *Classical Humanism and Republicanism*, p. 103.
194 Goldie, 'Unacknowledged Republic', p. 154. See also Michael J. Braddick, *State Formation in Early Modern England, c.1550–1700* (Cambridge: Cambridge University Press, 2000).

LITERATURE AND REPUBLICANISM IN THE AGE OF SHAKESPEARE

1 Brian Cummings, *The Literary Culture of the Reformation: Grammar and Grace* (Oxford: Oxford University Press, 2002), prologue.
2 Kevin Sharpe, *Remapping Early Modern England: The Culture of Seventeenth-Century Politics* (Cambridge: Cambridge University Press, 2000), pt. 1; *Reading Revolutions: The Politics of Reading in Early Modern England* (New Haven: Yale University Press, 2000), pt. 1.
3 Livy, *The Early History of Rome*, trans. Aubrey de Sélincourt (Harmonds-worth: Penguin, 1960), pp. 80–85. T. W. Baldwin, *William Shakspere's Small Latine and Lesse Greeke*, 2 vols. (Urbana: University of Illinois Press, 1944), *passim*; Ian Donaldson, *The Rapes of Lucrece: A Myth and its Transformation* (Oxford: Clarendon Press, 1982); William Shakespeare, *The Poems*, ed. Colin Burrow (Oxford: Oxford University Press, 2002), introduction, pp. 45–55.
4 *The woorkes of Geffrey Chaucer, newly printed, with divers addicions, whiche were never in printe before* (London, 1561), fos.205–6.
5 William Painter, *The Palace of Pleasure*, ed. Joseph Jacobs, 3 vols. (London: David Nutt, 1890) I, introduction, p.xxxix. For analysis, see Andrew Hadfield, *Literature, Travel and Colonial Writing in the English Renaissance, 1545–1625* (Oxford: Clarendon Press, 1998), pp. 147–62.
6 William Shakespeare, *The Poems*, ed. F. T. Prince (London: Methuen, The Arden Shakespeare, 1960), pp. 193–96; John Webster, *The Works of John Webster, Volume 1*, ed. David Gunby, David Carnegie and Antony Hammond (Cambridge: Cambridge University Press, 1995), pp. 675–705.
7 See Annabel Patterson, *Reading Between the Lines* (Madison: University of Wisconsin Press, 1993), p. 306; Michael Platt, 'The Rape of Lucrece and the Republic for Which it Stands', *Centennial Review* 19 (1975), 59–79.

8 For a recent narrative, see Tom Holland, *Rubicon: The Triumph and Tragedy of the Roman Republic* (London: Abacus, 2003)

9 Lucan, *Civil War*, trans. Susan H. Braund (Oxford: Oxford University Press, 1992). For English Renaissance adaptations of the poem, see David Norbrook, *Writing the English Republic: Poetry, Rhetoric and Politics, 1627–1660* (Cambridge: Cambridge University Press, 1999), pp. 23–62, 83–92. See also David Quint, *Epic and Empire: Politics and Generic Form from Virgil to Milton* (Princeton: Princeton University Press, 1993), pp. 4–89, *passim*.

10 See J. A. Crook, Andrew Lintott and Elizabeth Rawson, eds., *The Cambridge Ancient History: Volume IX, The Last Age of the Roman Republic, 146–43 B.C.* (Cambridge: Cambridge University Press, 1994); Marcel Le Glay, Jean-Louis Voison, Yann Le Bohec and David Cherry, *A History of Rome* (2nd ed., Oxford: Blackwell, 2001), chs. 6–9.

11 Tacitus, *On Imperial Rome*, trans. Michael Grant (Harmondsworth: Penguin, 1956), pp. 153–221; Ben Jonson, *Sejanus His Fall*, ed. Philip J. Ayres (Manchester: Manchester University Press, 1990); Blair Worden, 'Ben Jonson Among the Historians', in Kevin Sharpe and Peter Lake, eds., *Culture and Politics in Early Stuart England* (Basingstoke: Macmillan, 1994), pp. 67–89. See also Albert H. Tricomi, *Anticourt Drama in England, 1603–1642* (Charlottesville: University Press of Virginia, 1989), pp. 72–79.

12 Sallust, *Jugurthine War and Conspiracy of Catiline*, trans. S. A. Handford (Harmondsworth: Penguin, 1963), pp. 151–233; Ben Jonson, *Catiline His Conspiracy*, ed. W. F. Bolton and J. F. Gardner (London: Arnold, 1972).

13 Suetonius, *The Twelve Caesars*, trans. Robert Graves (Harmondsworth: Penguin, 1957), pp. 209–42; Reid Barbour, *English Epicures and Stoics: Ancient Legacies in Early Stuart Culture* (Amherst: University of Massachusetts Press, 1998).

14 Plutarch, *Selected Lives*, ed. Judith Mossman (Ware: Wordsworth, 1998), pp. 563–611; Howard Jones, *Master Tully. Cicero in Tudor England* (Nieuwkoop: Bibliotheca Humanistica & Reformatorica, Vol. LVII, 1981).

15 See also Robert S. Miola, *Shakespeare's Rome* (Cambridge: Cambridge University Press, 1983); Baldwin, *William Shakspere's Small Latine passim*.

16 Aristotle, *The Politics of Aristotle*, ed. and trans. Ernest Baker (Oxford: Oxford University Press, 1946), pp. 243–50.

17 For an excellent analysis of the various ways in which the story of Caesar's assassination was later told, see Paulina Kewes, '*Julius Caesar* in Jacobean England', *The Seventeenth Century* 17 (2002), 155–86.

18 Subsequent references are to William Shakespeare, *Antony and Cleopatra*, ed. John Wilders (London: Routledge: The Arden Shakespeare, 1995).

19 On the possible dating of the play, see William Shakespeare, *Titus Andronicus*, ed. Jonathan Bate (London: Thomson: The Arden Shakespeare, 2000, rpt. of 1995), introduction, pp. 69–79; Eric Sams, *The Real Shakespeare: Retrieving the Early Years, 1564–1594* (New Haven: Yale University Press, 1995), *passim*.

20 For discussion, see Andrew Hadfield, *Shakespeare and Renaissance Politics* (London: Thomson, 2003), ch. 3; Neil Rhodes, 'Shakespeare the Barbarian', in Jennifer Richards, ed., *Early Modern Civil Discourses* (Basingstoke: Palgrave, 2003), pp. 99–104.

21 Mark A. Kishlansky, *Parliamentary Selection: Social and Political Choice in Early Modern England* (Cambridge: Cambridge University Press, 1986), ch. 1.

22 Fulke Greville, *Poems and Dramas of Fulke Greville, First Lord Brooke*, ed. Geoffrey Bullough, 2 vols. (Edinburgh: Oliver and Boyd, 1939), II, pp. 35–202.

23 See, for example, Ronald Knowles, *Shakespeare's Arguments with History* (Basingstoke: Palgrave, 2002).

24 See Patrick Cheney, *Marlowe's Counterfeit Profession: Ovid, Spenser, Counter-Nationhood* (Toronto: University of Toronto Press, 1997); Cheney, *Shakespeare, National Poet-Playwright* (Cambridge: Cambridge University Press, 2004); Stephen Greenblatt, *Renaissance Self-Fashioning: From More to Shakespeare* (Chicago: University of Chicago Press, 1980), ch. 5. Patrick Cheney is engaged on a book-length study of Marlowe and republicanism. I am very grateful to him for discussing numerous matters with me that have helped shape the following paragraphs.

25 See, for example, Harry Levin, *The Overreacher: A Study of Christopher Marlowe* (Cambridge, Mass.: Harvard University Press, 1952); Alvin Kernan, ed., *Two Renaissance Mythmakers: Christopher Marlowe and Ben Jonson* (Baltimore: Johns Hopkins University Press, 1977); Charles Nicholl, *The Reckoning: The Murder of Christopher Marlowe* (London: Cape, 1992).

26 Baldesar Castiglione, *The Courtyer of Count Baldessar Castilio*, trans. Thomas Hoby (London, 1561); *The Civile Conversation of M. Stephen Guazzo*, trans. Bartholomew Young (London, 1586). See also John Leon Livesay, *Stefano Guazzo and the English Renaissance, 1575–1675* (Chapel Hill, N.C.: University of North Carolina Press, 1961); Daniel Javitch, *Poetry and Courtliness in Renaissance England* (Princeton, N.J.: Princeton University Press. 1978).

27 Christopher Marlowe, *The Complete Plays*, ed. Mark Thornton Burnett (London: Everyman, 1999), p. 11. Subsequent references to this edition in parentheses in the text.

28 See David Scott Kastan, '"Proud Majesty Made a Subject": Representing Authority on the Early Modern Stage', in Kastan, *Shakespeare After Theory* (London: Routledge, 1999), pp. 109–27; Ann Rosalind Jones and Peter Stallybrass, *Renaissance Clothing and the Materials of Memory* (Cambridge: Cambridge University Press, 2000), pt. 3.

29 Robert Greene, *Friar Bacon and Friar Bungay*, ed. Daniel Seltzer (London: Arnold, 1963), ix, line 253.

30 See Matthew Dimmock, *New Turkes: Dramatizing Islam and the Ottomans in Early Modern England* (Aldershot: Ashgate, 2005), ch. 6. I am extremely grateful to Dr Dimmock for allowing me to see this important work in

advance of publication. See also Nabil Matar, *Islam in Britain, 1558–1685* (Cambridge: Cambridge University Press, 1998). Matar's study makes no mention of *Tamburlaine.*

31 John Skelton, *Magnificence,* ed. Paula Neuss (Manchester: Manchester University Press, 1980). On *Respublica,* see above p. 19.

32 Lacey Baldwin Smith, *Elizabeth Tudor: Portrait of a Queen* (London: Cape, 1975), pp. 186–88; John Guy, *Tudor England* (Oxford: Oxford University Press, 1988), pp. 334–37. On theatre audiences, see Andrew Gurr, *The Shakespearean Stage, 1574–1642* (3rd ed., Cambridge: Cambridge University Press, 1999), ch. 6.

33 See Julia Briggs, *This Stage-Play World: Texts and Contexts, 1580–1625* (2nd ed., Oxford: Oxford University Press, 1997), pp. 288–89.

34 See Christopher Marlowe, *Tamburlaine,* ed. J. W. Harper (London: Black, 1971), introduction, pp. xi–xvi.

35 See David Riggs, *The World of Christopher Marlowe* (London: Faber, 2004), pp. 215–19.

36 Niccolò Machiavelli, *The Prince,* ed. Quentin Skinner and Russell Price (Cambridge: Cambridge University Press, 1988), pp. 62, 77. For a recent analysis, see S. K. Roy Moulick, *Christopher Marlowe: A Study of Ovidian and Machiavellian Aspects in his Works* (Calcutta: Progressive Publishers, 1996), chs. 8–10.

37 See Paul H. Kocher, 'François Hotman and Marlowe's *The Massacre at Paris',* *PMLA* 56 (1941), 349–68; Kocher, 'Contemporary Backgrounds for Marlowe's *The Massacre at Paris',* *MLQ* 8 (1947), 151–73, 309–18; Lisa Ferraro Parmelee, *Good News From France: French Anti-League Propaganda in Late Elizabethan England* (Rochester, N.Y.: University of Rochester Press, 1996), p. 51.

38 For comment, see Hadfield, *Literature, Travel and Colonial Writing,* pp. 202–17. I have reused some passages from this earlier work in my comments here. See also Kristen Elizabeth Poole, 'Garbled Martyrdom in Christopher Marlowe's *The Massacre at Paris',* *CD* 32 (1998), 1–25.

39 As Martin Dzelzainis has recently analysed 'Marlowe's *Massacre at Paris*: Inside the "royal cabinet"', unpublished paper given at the University of York, November 2003.

40 Francisco Sansovino, *The quintesence of wit being a corrant comfort of conceites, maximies, and poleticke devises,* trans. Robert Hitchcock (London, 1590), fo.18; Sir John Fortesque, *A learned commendation of the politique lawes of Englande,* trans. Richard Mulcaster (London, 1567), ch. 37.

41 On the *Pharsalia,* see Chapter 3.

42 For analysis, see Cheney, *Shakespeare, National Poet-Playwright,* pp. 113–20; Georgia E. Brown, 'Marlowe's Poems and Classicism', in Patrick Cheney, ed., *The Cambridge Companion to Christopher Marlowe* (Cambridge: Cambridge University Press, 2004), pp. 106–26, at pp. 120–24.

43 Norbrook, *Writing the English Republic,* p. 41; *Lucans Pharsalia: Containing the Civill Warres betweene Caesar and Pompey,* trans. Arthur Gorges

(London, 1614). See also Markku Peltonen, *Classical Humanism and Republicanism in English Political Thought, 1570–1640* (Cambridge: Cambridge University Press, 1995), pp. 275, 282–3, 289; Steane, *Marlowe*, ch. 7.

44 Baldwin, *William Shakspere's Small Latine* I, pp. 103–5, *passim*.

45 Christopher Marlowe, *The First Book of Lucan Translated into English*, in *The Poems*, ed. Millar McLure (London: Methuen, 1968), pp. 219–54. Subsequent references to this edition in parentheses in the text. See J. B. Steane, *Marlowe: A Critical Study* (Cambridge: Cambridge University Press, 1970) pp. 269–70.

46 Norbrook, *Writing the English Republic*, p. 25.

47 Susan Braund renders these lines as 'if the Fates could find no other way / for Nero's coming' (Lucan, *Civil War*, p. 4.).

48 As well as the 'monarchomach' writings analysed in Chapter One, Marlowe was undoubtedly aware of more conservative French political thought such as Jean Bodin's *Les Six Livres de la République* (1576), which had a significant impact in England: see Stuart E. Prall, 'The Development of Equity in Tudor England', *AJLH* 8 (1964), 1–19; Richard Tuck, *Philosophy and Government, 1572–1651* (Cambridge: Cambridge University Press, 1993), pp. 26–9, 260–62, *passim*.

49 On this ubiquitous motif in Renaissance political theory, see W. Gordon Zeeveld, *The Temper of Shakespeare's Thought* (New Haven: Yale University Press, 1974), ch. 4. See also Aristotle, *Aristotles Politiques, Or Discourses of Government Translated out of Greeke into French . . . by Loys Le Roy* (London, 1598), bk. I.

50 For a recent overview, see Emily C. Bartels, 'Christopher Marlowe', in Arthur Kinney, ed., *A Companion to Renaissance Drama* (Oxford: Blackwell, 2002), pp. 446–63. See also David Bevington, *Tudor Drama and Politics: A Critical Approach to Topical Meaning* (Cambridge, Mass.: Harvard University Press, 1968), ch. 14.

51 See Michael Manheim, *The Weak King Dilemma in the Shakespearean History Play* (Syracuse: Syracuse University Press, 1973).

52 James Shapiro, '"Metre meete to furnish Lucans style": Reconsidering Marlowe's Lucan', in Kenneth Friedenreich, Roma Gill and Constance B. Kuriyama, eds., *'A poet and a filthy playmaker': New Essays on Christopher Marlowe* (New York: AMS, 1988), pp. 315–26.

53 See John Guy, ed., *The Reign of Elizabeth I: Court and Culture in the Last Decade* (Cambridge: Cambridge University Press, 1995); Mervyn James, *Society, Politics and Culture: Studies in Early Modern Culture* (Cambridge: Cambridge University Press, 1986), chs. 8–9; Judith Weil, *Christopher Marlowe: Merlin's Prophet* (Cambridge: Cambridge University Press, 1977).

54 Peltonen, *Classical Humanism and Republicanism*, ch. 2; Patrick Collinson, '*De Republica Anglorum*: Or, History with the Politics Put Back', in *Elizabethan Essays* (London: Hambledon Press, 1994), pp. 1–29; Riggs, *Marlowe*, chs. 3–5.

55 See Richard Helgerson, *The Elizabethan Prodigals* (Berkeley: University of California Press, 1976); Mark Thornton Burnett, *Masters and Servants in English Renaissance Drama and Culture: Authority and Obedience* (Basingstoke: Macmillan, 1997).

56 See, for example, anon., *A Breefe discourse, declaring and approving the necessarie and inviolable customes of London* (1584). For comment, see Ian W. Archer, *The Pursuit of Stability: Social Relations in Elizabethan London* (Cambridge: Cambridge University Press, 1991); Archer, 'Popular Politics in the Sixteenth and Seventeenth Centuries', in Paul Griffiths and Mark S. R. Jenner, eds., *Londinopolis: Essays in the Cultural and Social History of Early Modern London* (Manchester: Manchester University Press, 2000); Archer, 'Shakespeare's London', in Kastan, ed., *Companion to Shakespeare*, pp. 43–56; Brian Gibbons, *Jacobean City Comedies* (rev. ed., London: Methuen, 1980). Similar arguments for other 'civic' traditions were also made for other cities; see John Vowell, alias Hooker, *A pamphlet of the offices and duties of everie particular sworned officer, of the citie of Excester* (London, 1584); Peltonen, *Classical Humanism and Republicanism*, pp. 57–58.

57 Millar McLure, ed., *Marlowe: The Critical Heritage, 1588–1896* (London: Routledge, 1979), pt. 1; Ruth Lunney, *Marlowe and the Popular Tradition: Innovation in the English Drama before 1595* (Manchester: Manchester University Press, 2002).

58 David Riggs, *Ben Jonson: A Life* (Cambridge, Mass.: Harvard University Press, 1989), pp. 99–100, 176–77; Julie Sanders, *Ben Jonson's Theatrical Republics* (Basingstoke: Macmillan, 1998).

59 Thomas Lodge, *The Wounds of Civil War*, ed. J. W. Houppert (London: Arnold, 1970). Subsequent references to this edition in parentheses in the text.

60 Stuart Gillespie, *Shakespeare's Books: A Dictionary of Shakespeare Sources* (London: Athlone, 2001), pp. 285–90. On Lodge, see also C. J. Sisson, 'Thomas Lodge and His Family', in C. J. Sisson, ed., *Thomas Lodge and Other Elizabethans* (London: Cass, 1966, rpt. of 1933), pp. 1–163.

61 Appian of Alexandra, *An Auncient Historie and Exquisite Chronicle of the Romanes warres, both civile and foren*, trans. William Baker (London, 1578); Lodge, *Wounds of Civil War*, introduction, pp. xiv–xviii; Ernest Schanzer, ed., *Shakespeare's Appian: A Selection from the Tudor Translation of Appian's Civil Wars* (Liverpool: Liverpool University Press, 1956), introduction, pp. xix–xxviii; Gillespie, *Shakespeare's Books*, pp. 15–20. See also Robin Seagar, 'Sulla', in Crook et al., eds., *Cambridge Ancient History: Volume IX*, pp. 165–207.

62 Lodge, *Wounds of Civil War*, introduction, xviii–xx; Pat M. Ryan, Jr., *Thomas Lodge, Gentleman* (Hamden, Conn.: Shoe String Press, 1958), pp. 49–50; Bevington, *Tudor Drama and Politics*, p. 234.

63 For corrective views, see Charles Whitworth, '*Rosalynde: As You Like It* and As Lodge Wrote It', *ES* 58 (1977), 114–17; Robert Maslen, *Elizabethan*

Fictions: Espionage, Counter-espionage and the Duplicity of Fiction in Early Elizabethan Prose Narratives (Oxford: Clarendon Press, 1997), pp. 54–55, *passim*.

64 Lodge is actually mistaken: the Senate met in the Curia Forum (Lodge, *Wounds of Civil War*, p. 5).

65 Aristotle, *Politiques*, pp. 325–31; Aristotle, *Politics*, pp. 243–54.

66 This Brutus is only mentioned twice in Appian: see *Appian's Roman History*, trans. Horace White, 4 vols. (London: Heinemann, 1958), III, pp. 113, 431; Appian, *Auncient historie*, pp. 29–64.

67 Appian, *Appian's Roman History*, 'The Civil Wars', bk. III, p. 517–IV, p. 137.

68 Appian, *Appian's Roman History*, 'The Hannibalic War', bk. VII, I, pp. 303–99.

69 Norbrook, *Writing the English Republic*, pp. 25–26.

70 Appian, *Appian's Roman History*, 'The Civil Wars', bk. I 1, section 94, III, pp. 171–73.

71 Marcus Tullius Cicero, *Marcus Tullius Ciceroes three bookes of duties to Marcus his sonne, tourned out of Latine into English*, by Nicolas Grimald (London, 1583), fos.32–33. See also Justus Lipsius, *Two bookes of constancie*, trans. John Stradling (London, 1595), chs. 3, 6.

72 Lucan, *Civil War*, bk. IX; Crook et al., eds., *Cambridge Ancient History: Volume IX*, pp. 358–367; Baldwin, *William Shakespere's Small Latin*, I, pp. 214–7, 293–98, *passim*; Quentin Skinner, *The Foundations of Modern Political Thought*, 2 vols. (Cambridge: Cambridge University Press, 1978), I, pp. 54–55. Probably the most widely read work of contemporary Stoic philosophy in early modern Europe was Lipsius, *Two bookes of constancie*. See also Barbour, *English Epicures and Stoics*, pp. 192–9, *passim*; Norbrook, *Writing the English Republic*, pp. 29–30, *passim*.

73 On Seneca see, *Letters from a Stoic*, trans. Robin Campbell (Harmondsworth: Penguin, 1969). On Seneca's suicide, see Tacitus, *On Imperial Rome*, pp. 363–66.

74 Appian, *Appian's Roman History*, III, pp. 183–97.

75 Aristotle, *The Nicomachean Ethics*, trans. David Ross (Oxford: Oxford University Press, 1980, rpt. of 1925), pp. 261–76. See also Lipsius, *Two bookes of constancie*, pp. 66, 106–7. See also Geoffrey Miles, *Shakespeare and the Constant Romans* (Oxford: Clarendon Press, 1996).

76 The scene may well be related to one in Thomas Kyd's *The Spanish Tragedy* (*c*.1589); which came first is harder to determine. Hieronimo is so absorbed in the need to secure justice for the murder of his son, Horatio, that he fails to administer justice to the citizens who come to him asking that he sort out their cases, in his role as Knight Marshall (Thomas Kyd, *The Spanish Tragedy*, ed. Philip Edwards [Manchester: Manchester University Press, 1977, rpt. of 1959]), 3.13.45–175.

77 It is hard to accept David Bevington's judgement that Sulla's 'self-reform' is 'edifying if belated' (*Tudor Drama and Politics*, p. 236).

78 See, for example, Ryan, *Thomas Lodge*, p. 54.

79 Archer, *Pursuit of Stability*, p. 122; Lodge, 'Thomas Lodge', pp. 7–53
80 Archer, *Pursuit of Stability*, ch. 3; Archer, 'Shakespeare's London', in Kastan, ed., *Companion to Shakespeare*, pp. 43–56.
81 Anon., *Breefe discourse*, pp. 9–10.
82 Anon., *Breefe discourse*, p. 16.
83 Robert Greene and Thomas Lodge, *A Looking Glass for London and England (1594)*, ed. W. W. Greg (London: Malone Society, 1932). For comment, see Bevington, *Tudor Drama and Politics*, p. 236; Ryan, *Thomas Lodge*, pp. 54–60; Sissons, 'Thomas Lodge', pp. 151–56.
84 Greene and Lodge, *Looking Glass for London*, line 944. See also lines 1271–92, 1360–69, *passim*.
85 Thomas Lodge and George Gascoigne, *A Larum for London, or The siedge of Antwerpe With the vertuous actes and valorous deedes of the lame soldier (1602)*, ed. W. W. Greg (London: Malone Society, 1913). On Gascoigne's military career in the Netherlands, see George Gascoigne, *A Hundreth Sundrie Flowres*, ed. G. W. Pigman III (Oxford: Clarendon Press, 2000), introduction, pp. xxviii–xxxviii..
86 See also William Allen, *A True, Sincere and Modest Defence, of English Catholiques that suffer for their faith both at home and abrode* (Rouen, 1584).
87 See *DNB* entry; Sissons, 'Thomas Lodge'.
88 Thomas Lodge, *Rosalynde* (1590), ed. Brian Nellist (Keele: Keele University Press, 1995). Lodge also wrote a verse romance, *Scyllas Metamorphosis* (1589), which may have influenced Shakespeare's *Venus and Adonis*: see M. M. Reese, ed., *Elizabethan Verse Romances* (London: Routledge, 1968), pp. 58–88; Martin Seymour-Smith, *Shakespeare's Non-Dramatic Poetry* (London: Greenwich Exchange, 2000), p. 21. For discussion of exile, see Jane Kingsley-Smith, *Shakespeare's Drama of Exile* (Basingstoke: Palgrave, 2003), ch. 4.
89 A similar case has been made for prose fiction: see Constance Relihan, *Fashioning Authority: The Development of Elizabethan Novelistic Discourse* (Kent, Ohio: Kent State University Press, 1994). See also James, *Society, Politics and Culture*, chs. 8–9.
90 For a recent overview, see Annabel Patterson, 'Political Thought and the Theater, 1580–1630', in Kinney, ed., *Companion to Renaissance Drama*, 25–39.
91 See William Shakespeare, *Julius Caesar*, ed. David Daniell (London: Thomson: The Arden Shakespeare, 1998), introduction, p. 10.
92 Anon., *The Tragedy of Caesar's Revenge*, ed. F. S. Boas (Oxford: Malone Society, 1911), introduction, p.vi. Subsequent references to this edition in parentheses in the text.
93 Shakespeare, *Julius Caesar*, ed. Daniell, introduction, pp. 34, 47.
94 See Kathy Eden, *Friends Hold All Things in Common: Tradition, Intellectual Property, and the **Adages** of Erasmus* (New Haven: Yale University Press, 2001). See also Susan Brigden, *New Worlds, Lost Worlds: The Rule of the Tudors, 1485–1603* (London: Penguin, 2000), pp. 108–111.

95 For an overview, see Kewes, '*Julius Caesar* in Jacobean England'.
96 William Alexander, *The Monarchick Tragedies* (1604). For details of Alexander's eventful life, see Thomas H. McGrail, *Sir William Alexander, First Earl of Stirling* (Edinburgh: Oliver and Boyd, 1940).
97 William Alexander, *The Poetical Works of Sir William Alexander*, ed. L. E. Kastner and H. B. Charlton, 2 vols. (Manchester: Manchester University Press, 1929), II, pp. 343–442, at pp. 391, 393, 402.
98 A political interpretation that Blair Worden suggested was the norm in pre-Interregnum England: see above, pp. 50–51.
99 On the growth of an 'oppositional' culture during the reign of James, one which was centred on literary texts, see Curtis Perry, *The Making of Jacobean Culture: James I and the Renegotiation of Elizabethan Literary Practice* (Cambridge: Cambridge University Press, 1997); Michelle O'Callaghan, *The 'Shepheardes Nation': Jacobean Spenserians and Early Stuart Political Culture, 1612–1625* (Oxford: Clarendon Press, 2000). See also Jonathan Goldberg, *James I and the Politics of Literature: Jonson, Shakespeare, Donne, and their Contemporaries* (Baltimore: Johns Hopkins University Press, 1983). None of these works mentions Sir William Alexander.
100 George Chapman, *Caesar and Pompey* in *The Plays of George Chapman: The Tragedies with **Sir Gyles Goosecappe**: A Critical Edition*, ed. Allan Holaday (Cambridge: Brewer, 1987), pp. 529–615; Anon., *The Tragedie of Claudius Tiberius Nero, Romes greatest tyrant Truly represented out of the purest records of those times* (London, 1607). Subsequent references to these editions in parentheses in the text. See also *Claudius Tiberius Nero, A Critical Edition of the Play Published Anonymously in 1607*, ed. Uwe Baumann (Frankfurt am Main: Peter Lang, 1990). On the dating of Chapman's play, see also Ennis Rees, *The Tragedies of George Chapman: Renaissance Ethics in Action* (Cambridge, Mass.: Harvard University Press, 1954), pp. 126–32.
101 *Tiberius*, ed. Baumann, introduction, p. 14; Tacitus, *On Imperial Rome*, pt. 1; Suetonius, *Twelve Caesars*, ch. 3.
102 Jonson, *Sejanus His Fall*; Perry, *Making of Jacobean Culture*, p. 99; Alan T. Bradford, 'Nathaneal Richards, Jacobean Playgoer', *JDJ* 2 (1983), 63–78. More generally, see Alan T. Bradford, 'Stuart Absolutism and the "Utility" of Tacitus', *HLQ* 46 (1983), 127–55.
103 *Tiberius*, ed. Baumann, introduction, pp. 18–19, 22.
104 Blair Worden, 'English Republicanism', in J. H. Burns and Mark Goldie, eds., *The Cambridge History of Political Thought, 1450–1700*, (Cambridge: Cambridge University press, 1991), pp. 443–75; Rebecca Bushnell, *Tragedies of Tyrants: Political Thought and Theater in the English Renaissance* (Ithaca, N.Y.: Cornell University Press, 1990).
105 See Millar McLure, *George Chapman: A Critical Study* (Toronto: University of Toronto Press, 1966), p. 153; William Blissett, 'Lucan's Caesar and the Elizabethan Villain', *SP* 53 (1956), 553–75; J. E. Ingledew, 'Chapman's Use of Lucan in *Caesar and Pompey*', *RES*, ns, 13 (1962), 283–88.

106 On Chapman's representation of Stoicism in the play, see John William Wieler, *George Chapman: The Effect of Stoicism upon his Tragedies* (New York: King's Crown Press, 1949), ch. 5.

107 On Cato in the play, see Allen Bergson, 'Stoicism Achieved: Cato min Chapman's *Tragedy of Caesar and Pompey*', *SEL* 17 (1977), 295–302; Rees, *Tragedies of George Chapman*, pp. 132–36.

108 See McLure, *Chapman*, pp. 152–53.

109 Rees refers to Pompey's 'half-virtue' (*Tragedies of George Chapman*, p. 132).

110 Roman law forbade commanders to lead an army into Rome: see Duncan Cloud, 'The Constitution and the Public Criminal Law', in Crook et al., eds., *Cambridge Ancient History: Volume IX*, pp. 491–530, at p. 491; Holland, *Rubicon*, p. 73.

111 For further reflections on this problem, see Andrew Hadfield, *Literature, Politics and National Identity: Reformation to Renaissance* (Cambridge: Cambridge University Press, 1994).

112 See Hadfield, *Shakespeare and Renaissance Politics*, pp. 143–49.

113 George Chapman, *The Conspiracy of Charles Duke of Byron and The Tragedy of Charles Duke of Byron*, ed. John Margeson (Manchester: Manchester University Press, 1988), introduction, pp. 9–10; Chapman, *Tragedies*, p. 267; Katherine Duncan-Jones, *Ungentle Shakespeare: Scenes From His Life*, (London: Thomson, 2001), pp. 203–4.

114 Cyndia Clegg, *Press Censorship in Jacobean England* (Cambridge: Cambridge University Press, 2001); Leeds Barroll, 'A New History for Shakespeare and His Time', *SQ* 39 (1988), 441–64.

115 See Kishlansky, *Parliamentary Selection*; Derek Hirst, *The Representative of the People? Voters and Voting under the Early Stuarts* (Cambridge: Cambridge University Press, 1975); Conrad Russell, *The Crisis of Parliaments: English History, 1509–1660* (Oxford: Oxford University Press, 1971), pp. 256–84.

116 See James, *Society, Politics and Culture*, pp. 437, 463; McLure, *Chapman*, ch. 1; G. P. V. Akrigg, *Shakespeare and the Earl of Southampton* (London: Hamilton, 1968); Duncan-Jones, *Ungentle Shakespeare*, pp. 25, 90, 104–5, *passim*.

117 McLure, *Chapman*, pp. 60–7, 214; Duncan-Jones, *Ungentle Shakespeare*, p. 217; Ben Jonson, George Chapman, John Marston, *Eastward Ho!*, ed. C. G. Petter (London: Benn, 1973).

118 See Barbara J. Baines, *Thomas Heywood* (Boston: Twayne, 1984), for details.

119 Thomas Heywood, *The Conspiracy of Catiline and the War of Jugurtha* (1608) (London: Constable, 1924); Thomas Heywood, *The Rape of Lucrece: A true Roman Tragedy*, in *Works*, ed. A. B. Grosart (London, 1874), V, pp. 161–257.

120 See John Lyly, **Campaspe and Sappho and Phao**, ed. G. K. Hunter and David Bevington (Manchester: Manchester University Press, 1991), introduction, p. 11. Subsequent references to this edition in parentheses in the text.

121 Plutarch, 'The Lyfe of Alexander the Great', *The lives of the noble Grecians and Romanes . . . translated out of Greeke into French by James Amyot . . . ; and out of French into Englishe, by Thomas North* (London, 1579), pp. 722–63; Pliny the Elder, *Natural History*, trans. H. Rackham, W. H. S. Jones and

D. E. Eichholz, 10 vols. (London: Heinemann, 1938–62), IX, pp. 319–33; Lyly, **Campaspe** *and* **Sappho and Phao**, introduction, pp. 5–16.

122 For discussion, see Judith Mossman, '*Henry V* and Plutarch's *Alexander*', *SQ* 45 (1994), 57–73. See also Giovanni Botero, *Observations Upon the Lives of Alexander, Caesar, Scipio, newly Englished* (London, 1602).

123 For commentary, see Peter Saccio, *The Court Comedies of John Lyly: A Study in Allegorical Dramaturgy* (Princeton, N.J.: Princeton University Press, 1969), ch. 2; G. K. Hunter, *John Lyly: The Humanist as Courtier* (London: Routledge, 1962), pp. 160–66.

124 See Blair Worden, 'Republicanism, Regicide and Republic: The English Experience', in Martin van Gelderen and Quentin Skinner, eds., *Republicanism: A Shared European Heritage*, 2 vols. (Cambridge: Cambridge University Press, 2002), I, pp. 307–27, at pp. 309–10; Brendan Bradshaw, 'More on *Utopia*', *HJ* 24 (1979), 455–76; Quentin Skinner, 'Thomas More's *Utopia* and the Virtue of True Nobility', in Skinner, *Visions of Politics*, 3 vols. (Cambridge: Cambridge University Press, 2002), II, pp. 213–44.

125 Plutarch, 'Lyfe of Alexander', p. 728.

126 Botero, *Observations*, B2v–B4r, D3v, F7r.

127 Aristotle, *Politiques*, bk. 2, ch. 10; Aristotle, *Politics*, pp. 377–82; Thucydides, *History of the Peloponnesian War*, trans. Rex Warner and M. I. Finley (Harmondsworth: Penguin, 1972). Thucydides was not translated into English until 1607, but was known to all Greek speakers in sixteenth-century England: see Baldwin, *William Shakespere's Small Latin*, I, pp. 191–92, *passim*.

128 On Henry VIII's pursuit of military glory in Europe, see Guy, *Tudor England*, ch. 7; J. J. Scarisbrick, *Henry VIII* (London: Methuen, 1968), chs. 3–6. On Wyatt, Henry and Anne Boleyn, see Scarisbrick, *Henry VIII*, p. 149; Kenneth Muir, *Life and Letters of Sir Thomas Wyatt* (Liverpool: Liverpool University Press, 1963), ch. 2.

129 See, for example, Brigden, *New Worlds, Lost Worlds*, pp. 109–10; Brendan Bradshaw, 'Transalpine Humanism', in Burns and Goldie, eds., *Cambridge History of Political Thought*, pp. 95–131; Skinner, *Visions of Politics: Volume II, Renaissance Virtues, passim*. On the English tradition, see J. K. McConica, *English Humanists and Reformation Politics* (Oxford: Clarendon Press, 1965).

130 See Peter Burke, *The Fortunes of the Courtier: The European Reception of Castiglione's 'Cortegiano'* (Cambridge: Polity, 1995). See also Merryn James, 'English Politics and the Concept of Honour', in *Society, Politics and Culture*; Livesay, *Stefano Guazzo*.

131 Castiglione, *Courtyer*, trans. Hoby, OO3v–PP3v.

132 Ibid., OO4v. On liberty as a political principle in England, see David Harris Sacks, 'Parliament, Liberty, and the Commonweal', in J. H. Hexter, ed., *Parliament and Liberty: From the Reign of Elizabeth to the English Civil War* (Stanford: Stanford University Press, 1992), pp. 85–121.

133 Castiglione, *Courtyer*, trans. Hoby, PP3r.

134 See Greg Walker, *Plays of Persuasion: Drama and Politics at the Court of Henry VIII* (Cambridge: Cambridge University Press, 1991); Walker,

Persuasive Fictions: Faction, Faith and Political Culture in the Reign of Henry VIII (Aldershot: Scolar Press, 1996); Stephen Alford, *Kingship and Politics in the Reign of Edward VI* (Cambridge: Cambridge University Press, 2002), pp. 46–64, *passim*.

135 Niccolò Machiavelli, *The Prince*, ed., Quentin Skinner and Russell Price (Cambridge: Cambridge University Press, 1988), p. 31; Cicero, *Three bookes of duties*, fos. 67, 105, *passim*. See also Janet Coleman, *A History of Political Thought*, 2 vols. (Oxford: Blackwell, 2000), II, p. 259; Jones, *Master Tully*, ch. 2.

136 George Chapman, *The Conspiracie of Charles Duke of Byron*, in *Tragedies*, pp. 265–332. Subsequent references to this edition in parentheses in the text, unless otherwise stated.

137 Sallust, *Conspiracy of Catiline*, pp. 56–60.

138 Riggs, *Ben Jonson*, p. 177; Douglas Duncan, *Ben Jonson and the Lucianic Tradition* (Cambridge: Cambridge University Press, 1979), pp. 218–23.

139 George Chapman, *The Tragedie of Charles Duke of Byron*, in *Tragedies*, pp. 333–97, 3.1.1–8. Subsequent references to this edition in parentheses in the text unless otherwise stated.

140 Stephanus Junius Brutus, the Celt, *Vindiciae, Contra Tyrannos, or, concerning the legitimate power of a prince over the people, and of the people over a prince* (1579), ed. George Garnett (Cambridge: Cambridge University Press, 1994), 'The First Question', pp. 14–34.

141 Innocent Gentillet, *A Discourse Upon the Meanes of Wel Governing and Maintaining in Good Peace, a Kingdom, or other Principalitie . . . Against Nicholas Machiavell the Florentine*, trans. Simon Patericke (London, 1602). See also Felix Raab, *The English Face of Machiavelli: A Changing Interpretation, 1500–1700* (London: Routledge, 1965), pp. 56–57.

142 For the wealth of material available to English readers, see Lisa Ferraro Parmelee, *Good News From France: French Anti-League Propaganda in Late Elizabethan England* (Rochester, N.Y.: University of Rochester Press, 1996). See especially François Hotman, *A true and plaine report of the Furious outrages of France*, trans. Ernest Varamund (Striveling, Scotland, 1573); Anon., *A forme of Christain pollicie drawne out of French*, trans. Geoffrey Fenton (London, 1574).

143 Tacitus, *The Histories*, trans. W. H. Fyfe (Oxford: Oxford University Press, 1997), pp. 5, 56, *passim*.

144 George Chapman, *The Tragedie of Chabot, Admirall of France*, in *Tragedies*, pp. 627–708. For commentary, see McLure, *Chapman*, pp. 132–50; Wieler, *George Chapman*, chs. 2, 4; Rees, *Tragedies of George Chapman*, chs. 3, 6.

145 See Plutarch, 'How a Yoong Man ought to hear Poets: and how he may take profit by reading Poems', in *The Philosophie, commonlie called, The Morals, written by the learned Philosopher Plutarch*, trans. Philemon Holland (London, 1603), pp. 17–50. See also George Chapman, *The Conspiracy of Charles Duke of Byron and the Tragedy of Charles Duke of Byron*, ed. John Margeson (Manchester: Manchester University Press, 1988), introduction,

pp. 4–5; Bevington, *Tudor Drama and Politics*, pp. 25–6; Zeeveld, *Temper of Shakespeare's Thought*, p. 74; D. R. Woolf, *Reading History in Early Modern England* (Cambridge: Cambridge University Press, 2000), ch. 2.

146 Jonson, *Sejanus His Fall*, ed. Ayres, introduction, pp. 16–18; Samuel Daniel, *The Tragedy of Philotas*, in *The Complete Works in Verse and Prose of Samuel Daniel*, ed. Alexander B. Grosart (London: privately printed, 1885), X, pp. 95–181. On *Philotas*, see Richard Dutton, *Licensing, Censorship and Authorship in Early Modern England: Buggeswords* (Basingstoke: Palgrave/ Macmillan, 2000), pp. xiii–iv; Joan Rees, *Samuel Daniel: A Critical and Biographical Study* (Liverpool: Liverpool University Press, 1964), pp. 97–107; H. Gazzard, 'Samuel Daniel's *Philotas* and the Earl of Essex', *RES*, ns, 51 (2000), 423–50. On Raleigh, see Anna Beer, *Sir Walter Raleigh and his Readers in the Seventeenth Century: Speaking to the People* (Basingstoke: Macmillan, 1997).

147 For recent comment, see Bart van Es, *Spenser's Forms of History* (Oxford: Oxford University Press, 2002), ch. 6.

148 See, for example, Coleman, *History of Political Thought*, I, ch. 5; Richard Tuck, *Philosophy and Government, 1572–1651* (Cambridge: Cambridge University Press, 1993), ch. 1; Cary J. Nederman, 'Rhetoric, Reason and Republic: Republicanisms – Ancient, Medieval, and Modern', in James Hankins, ed., *Renaissance Civic Humanism* (Cambridge: Cambridge University Press, 2000), pp. 247–69.

149 John Bellamy, *The Tudor Law of Treason: An Introduction* (London: Routledge, 1979), ch. 5.

150 For discussion, see James, 'English Politics and the Concept of Honour'.

151 Sir Philip Sidney, *The Countess of Pembroke's Arcadia*, ed. Victor Skretkowicz (Oxford: Clarendon Press, 1987), introduction, pp. xxi–ii; Blair Worden, *The Sound of Virtue: Philip Sidney's **Arcadia** and Elizabethan Politics* (New Haven: Yale University Press, 1996), pt. 4.

152 James Emerson Phillips, 'George Buchanan and the Sidney Circle', *HLQ* 12 (1948–9), 23–55.

153 William Shakespeare, *King Lear*, ed. R. A. Foakes (London: Thomson: The Arden Shakespeare, 1997), introduction, pp. 100–2; Gillespie, *Shakespeare's Books*, pp. 459–65.

154 On Field, see below, p. 101. The other publisher was John Wolfe: see Parmelee, *Good News From France*, pp. 34–5. Shakespeare's relationship with Field is well documented, see Martin Dzelzainis, 'Shakespeare and Political Thought', in David Scott Kastan, ed., *A Companion to Shakespeare* (Oxford: Blackwell, 1999), pp. 100–16, at pp. 107, 111–2; Park Honan, *Shakespeare: A Life* (Oxford: Oxford University Press, 1998), pp. 61, 71, *passim*; Duncan-Jones, *Ungentle Shakespeare*, pp. 114–5, *passim*. On Shakespeare's use of French material, see William Shakespeare, *Love's Labour's Lost*, ed. H. R. Woudhuysen (London: Thomson: The Arden Shakespeare, 1998), introduction, pp. 61–74.

155 I have drawn on my discussion of the *Arcadia* in my *Literature, Politics and National Identity: Reformation to Renaissance* (Cambridge: Cambridge University Press, 1994) in the following two paragraphs.

156 See Worden, 'On Ister Bank', in *Sound of Virtue*, pp. 266–80; Annabel Patterson, *Fables of Power: Aesopian Writing and Political History* (Durham: Duke University Press, 1991), pp. 67–75.

157 See Ann Rosalind Jones and Peter Stallybrass, 'The Politics of *Astrophil and Stella*', *SEL* 24 (1984), 53–68.

158 Sidney, *Arcadia*, p. 482.

159 See David Norbrook, *Poetry and Politics in the English Renaissance* (rev. ed., Oxford: Oxford University Press, 2002), ch. 4; Richard C. McCoy, *Sir Philip Sidney: Rebellion in Arcadia* (Hassocks: Harvester, 1979); Patrick Collinson, *Elizabethans* (London: Hambledon, 2003), p. 21.

160 See, for example, Jonathan Gibson, 'Remapping Elizabethan Court Poetry', in Mike Pincombe, ed., *The Anatomy of Tudor Literature* (Aldershot: Ashgate, 2001), pp. 98–111; Michael Brennan, *Literary Patronage in the Renaissance: The Pembroke Family* (London: Routledge, 1988); Millicent V. Hay, *The Life of Robert Sidney, Earl of Leicester (1563–1626)* (Washington: Folger Shakespeare Library, 1984), ch. 9.

161 See Sams, *Real Shakespeare*, ch. 15. See also pp. 184–87. A careful study of the relationship between Spenser and Shakespeare is badly needed.

162 Sams, *Real Shakespeare*, pp. 82–4; A. Kent Hieatt, 'Shakespeare, William', in A. C. Hamilton, ed., *The Spenser Encyclopedia* (London and Toronto: Routledge/University of Toronto Press, 1990), pp. 641–3.

163 Collinson, *Elizabethans*, p. 44.

164 Edmund Spenser, *The Shepheardes Calender*, 'Maye', line 75, in *The Shorter Poems*, ed. Richard A. McCabe (Harmondsworth: Penguin, 1999), p. 75. Subsequent references to this edition in parentheses in the text. For comment, see Patrick Collinson, *Archbishop Grindal, 1519–1583: The Struggle for a Reformed Church* (London: Cape, 1979); Paul E. McLane, *Spenser's* **Shepheardes Calender***: A Study in Elizabethan Allegory* (Notre Dame, In.: Notre Dame University Press, 1961), pp. 140–57; James P. Bednarz, 'Grindal, Edmund', in Hamilton, ed., *Spenser Encyclopedia*, pp. 342–43.

165 See Thomas H. Cain, *Praise in* **The Faerie Queene** (Lincoln, Neb.: University of Nebraska Press, 1978); Andrew Hadfield, 'Spenser and Politics', in Bart van Es, ed., *The Palgrave Companion to Spenser Studies* (Basingstoke: Palgrave, forthcoming in 2006).

166 Richard A McCabe., 'The Masks of Duessa: Spenser, Mary Queen of Scots, and James VI', *ELR* 17 (1987), 224–42; Andrew Hadfield, *Shakespeare, Spenser and the Matter of Britain* (Basingstoke: Palgrave/Macmillan, 2003), ch. 8.

167 Edmund Spenser, *A View of the State of Ireland*, ed. Andrew Hadfield and Willy Maley (Oxford: Blackwell, 1997), pp. 45–46, 51, 60, 63. On James's prospects of becoming king in the 1590s, see Susan Doran, 'Revenge Her Foul and Most Unnatural Murder? The Impact of Mary Stewart's Execution on Anglo-Scottish Relations', *History* 85 (2000), 589–612.

168 Willy Maley, *A Spenser Chronology* (Basingstoke: Macmillan, 1994), p. 68.
169 Anne N. McLaren, 'Gender, Religion, and Early Modern Nationalism: Elizabeth I, Mary Queen of Scots, and the Genesis of English Anti-Catholicism', *AHR* 107 (2002), 739–67.
170 James Emerson Phillips, *Images of a Queen: Mary Stuart in Sixteenth-Century Literature* (Berkeley: University of California Press, 1964). On Malecasta, see Lauren Silberman, *Transforming Desire: Erotic Knowledge in Books III and IV of* ***The Faerie Queene*** (Berkeley: University of California Press, 1995), pp. 32–33; Andrew Hadfield, ed., *Edmund Spenser* (London: Longman, 1996), introduction, pp. 15–16.
171 For further comment, see Hadfield, *Literature, Travel and Colonial Writing*, pp. 51–3; Hadfield, 'Was Spenser a Republican?', *English* 47 (1998), 169–82, pp. 171–72.
172 Robert Lacey, *Robert, Earl of Essex: An Elizabethan Icarus* (London: Weidenfeld and Nicolson, 1970), p. 22; Paul E. J. Hammer, *The Polarisation of Elizabethan Politics: The Political Career of Robert Devereux, 2nd Earl of Essex, 1585–1597* (Cambridge: Cambridge University Press, 1997), p. 162.
173 See above, pp. 214–20. For other enthusiastic descriptions of Venice, see George Abbot, *A briefe description of the whole worlde wherein are particularly described all the monarchies, empires, and kingdomes of the same* (London, 1599), A4r; Giovanni Botero, *An historicall description of the most famous kingdomes and common-weales in the worlde* (London, 1603), pp. 117–20; Botero, *A treatise, concerning the causes of the magnificencie and greatnes of cities*, trans. Robert Peterson (London, 1606), B4r, C2r.
174 See Richard Helgerson, *Self-Crowned Laureates: Spenser, Jonson, Milton and the Literary System* (Berkeley: University of California Press, 1983); Patrick Cheney, *Spenser's Famous Flight: A Renaissance Idea of a Literary Career* (Toronto: Toronto University Press, 1993); Sir Philip Sidney, *An Apology for Poetry*, ed. Geoffrey Shepherd, rev. and expanded. R. W. Maslen (Manchester: Manchester University Press, 2002).
175 Duncan-Jones, *Ungentle Shakespeare*, pp. 35–6; Honan, *Shakespeare*, p. 175; Joan Rees, *Fulke Greville, Lord Brooke, 1554–1628: A Critical Biography* (London: Routledge, 1971), p. 42. For details of Greville's life, see Ronald A. Rebholz, *The Life of Fulke Greville, First Lord Brooke* (Oxford: Clarendon Press, 1971). A similar analysis could be made of the career of Spenser's disciple, Michael Drayton, who was also indebted to republican ideas in his poetry: see, for example, Michael Drayton, *The Barons' Wars*, in *Works*, ed. J. W. Hebel, 5 vols. (Oxford: Blackwell, 1931–41), II, pp. 1–128, at p. 29; *Mortimeriados* in *Works*, III, pp. 305–92, at p. 353.
176 Rebholz, *Life of Greville*, pp. 131–32; Rees, *Greville*, pp. 27–30.
177 Greville, *Poems and Dramas*, ed. Bullough, II. On Greville's relationship with Sidney, see Worden, *Sound of Virtue, passim*; Rebholz, *Life of Greville, passim*.
178 Greville, *Poems and Dramas*, ed. Bullough, I, introduction, p. 4; Perry, *Making of Jacobean Culture*, p. 106.

179 Greville, *Poems and Dramas*, ed. Bullough, I, introduction, pp. 14, 17. On Bacon's faith in parliaments and career as a parliamentarian, see Lisa Jardine and Alan Stewart, *Hostage to Fortune: The Troubled Life of Francis Bacon* (New York: Hill and Wang, 1998), *passim*.

180 For recent analysis of the plays, see Matthew C. Hansen, 'Gender, Power and Play: Fulke Greville's *Mustapha and Alaham*', *SJ* 19 (2001), 125–41; Perry, *Making of Jacobean Culture*, pp. 106–11.

181 See J. P. Sommerville, *Politics and Ideology in England, 1603–1640* (Harlow: Longman, 1986), chs. 1–3; Sharpe, *Remapping Early Modern England*, chs. 1–2.

182 For further discussion of this change in political emphasis, see my *Shakespeare and Renaissance Politics*.

183 Fulke Greville, *The Remains, being Poems of Monarchy and Religion*, ed. G. A. Wilkes (Oxford: Oxford University Press, 1965). Subsequent references to this edition in parentheses in the text. For recent comment, see Matthew Woodcock, '"The World is Made For Use": Theme and Form in Fulke Greville's Verse Treatises', *SJ* 19 (2001), 143–59, pp. 145–51.

184 Rebholz, *Life of Greville*, pp. 146–47.

185 For details, see J. H. Elliott, *Europe Divided, 1559–1598* (London: Collins, 1968), chs. 10–11; R. B. Wernham, *After the Armada: Elizabethan England and the Struggle for Western Europe, 1588–1595* (Oxford: Clarendon Press, 1984).

186 Howard Erskine-Hill argues that political pragmatism in favour of the monarchy such as Greville's was the dominant form of argument in Elizabethan and Jacobean England; see *Poetry and the Realm of Politics: Shakespeare to Dryden* (Oxford: Clarendon Press, 1996).

187 James VI and I, *The Trew Law of Free Monarchies*, in *The Workes* (1616) (Hildesham and New York: Verlag, 1971).

INTRODUCTION II: SHAKESPEARE'S EARLY REPUBLICAN CAREER

1 For analysis, see Lukas Erne, *Shakespeare as Literary Dramatist* (Cambridge: Cambridge University Press, 2003), ch. 2.

2 Peter Blaney, 'The Publication of Playbooks', in John D. Cox and David Scott Kastan, eds., *A New History of Early English Drama* (New York: Columbia University Press, 1997), pp. 383–422.

3 Katherine Duncan-Jones, *Ungentle Shakespeare: Scenes From His Life* (London: Thomson, 2001), ch. 3; William Shakespeare, *The Poems*, ed. Colin Burrow (Oxford: Oxford University Press, 2002), introduction, pp. 6–10, 40–45.

4 See Eric Sams, *The Real Shakespeare: Retrieving the Early Years, 1564–1594* (New Haven: Yale University Press, 1995), ch. 14.

5 *The Life and Works of George Peele*, ed. Charles Tyler, 2 vols. (New Haven: Yale University Press, 1952), I, introduction, ch. 3.

6 William Shakespeare, *Henry VI, Part One*, ed. Michael Taylor (Oxford: Oxford University Press, 2003), introduction, p. 9; E. A. J. Honigmann, *Shakespeare: The Lost Years* (Manchester: Manchester University Press, 1985).

7 For details, see Alfred Harbage, *Annals of English Drama, 975–1700: An Annotated Record of All Plays, Extant or Lost, Chronologically Arranged and Indexed by Authors, Titles, Dramatic Companies, Etc.*, rev. S. Schoenbaum (London: Routledge, 3rd ed., 1989). See also Andrew Gurr, *The Shakespearian Playing Companies* (Oxford: Clarendon Press, 1996).

8 Harold Jenkins, *The Life and Work of Henry Chettle* (London: Sidgwick and Jackson, 1934)

9 Barbara J. Baines, *Thomas Heywood* (Boston: Twayne, 1984). See above, p. 80.

10 Blaney, 'Publication of Playbooks'; Erne, *Shakespeare as Literary Dramatist*, ch. 1; David Scott Kastan, *Shakespeare and the Book* (Cambridge: Cambridge University Press, 2001), chs. 1–2.

11 Shakespeare, *Henry VI, Part One*, ed. Taylor, introduction, pp. 1–5; Henry Chettle (?), *Greene's Groatsworth of Wit: Bought with a Million of Repentance* (1592), ed. D. Allen Carroll (Binghampton, N.Y.: MRTS, 1994), pp. 131–45; Erne, *Shakespeare as Literary Dramatist*, pp. 65–70. See also William Shakespeare, *The Comedy of Errors*, ed. T. S. Dorsch, rev. Ros King (Cambridge: Cambridge University Press, 2004), introduction, pp. 38–40.

12 It is also possible that Shakespeare may have written, or partly written, the *Ur-Hamlet* which was evidently performed on the English stage in the late 1580s. For discussion, see William Shakespeare, *The First Quarto of Hamlet*, ed. Katherine O. Irace (Cambridge: Cambridge University Press, 1998); Laurie E. Maguire, *Shakespeare's Suspect Texts: The 'Bad' Quartos and Their Contexts* (Cambridge: Cambridge University Press, 1996), pp. 255–57; Sams, *Real Shakespeare*, ch. 23.

13 See Warren Boutcher, '"Rationall Knowledges" and "Knowledges . . . drenched in flesh and blood": Fulke Greville, Francis Bacon and Institutions of Humane Learning in Tudor and Stuart England', *SJ* 19 (2001), 11–40; David Harris Sacks, 'Political Culture', in Kastan, ed., *Companion to Shakespeare*, pp. 117–36; David Riggs, *The World of Christopher Marlowe* (London: Faber, 2004), chs. 3–5.

14 See Martin Wiggins, *Shakespeare and the Drama of his Time* (Oxford: Oxford University Press, 2000); Scott McMillin, 'Professional Playwrighting', in David Scott Kastan, ed., *A Companion to Shakespeare* (Oxford: Blackwell, 1999), pp. 225–38; Andrew Gurr, *The Shakespearean Stage, 1574–1642* (3rd ed., Cambridge: Cambridge University Press, 1999), ch. 3; Park Honan, *Shakespeare, A Life* (Oxford: Oxford University Press, 1998), ch. 7.

15 Michael McCanles, '*The Shepheardes Calender* as Document and Monument', *SEL* 22 (1982), 5–19.

16 William Shakespeare, *Titus Andronicus*, ed. Jonathan Bate (London: Thomson: The Arden Shakespeare, 2000, rpt. of 1995), introduction, pp. 69–83.

17 See below, pp. 156–59.

18 See Chapter 5.

19 See Chapter 4.

20 See Jonathan Bate, *Shakespeare and Ovid* (Oxford: Clarendon Press, 1993), pp. 48–67; John Roe, 'Ovid "renascent in *Venus and Adonis* and *Hero and Leander*', in A. B. Taylor, ed., *Shakespeare's Ovid*, pp. 31–46; Anthony Mortimer, *Variable Passions: A Reading of Shakespeare's **Venus and Adonis*** (New York: AMS Press, 2000).

21 See, for example, Robert S. Miola, *Shakespeare's Reading* (Oxford: Oxford University Press, 2000), pp. 140–43; James P. Bednarz, *Shakespeare & The Poets' War* (New York: Columbia University Press, 2001), pp. 124–28, *passim*.

22 Martin Dzelzainis, 'Shakespeare and Political Thought', in Kastan, ed., *Companion to Shakespeare*, pp. 100–16, at p. 107.

23 Duncan-Jones, *Ungentle Shakespeare*, p. 115.

24 Paul E. J. Hammer, *The Polarisation of Elizabethan Politics: The Political Career of Robert Devereux, 2nd Earl of Essex, 1585–1597* (Cambridge: Cambridge University Press, 1997), ch. 7; Hammer., 'The Uses of Scholarship: The Secretariat of Robert Devereux, second Earl of Essex, c.1585–1601', *EHR* 109 (1994), 26–51.

25 Dzelzainis, 'Shakespeare and Political Thought', p. 107; Margot Heinemann, 'Rebel Lords, Popular Playwrights, and Political Culture: Notes on the Jacobean Patronage of the Earl of Southampton', *YES* 21 (1991), 63–86, p. 68. See below, pp. 130–31.

26 Dzelzainis, 'Shakespeare and Political Thought', p. 107.

27 For further details, see G. P. V Akrigg, *Shakespeare and the Earl of Southampton* (London: Hamilton, 1968).

SHAKESPEARE'S PHARSALIA: THE FIRST TETRALOGY

1 William Shakespeare, *Henry VI, Part One*, ed. Michael Taylor (Oxford: Oxford University Press, 2003), 1.1.52–56. Subsequent references to this edition in parentheses in the text.

2 See, for example, Graham Holderness, *Shakespeare: The Histories* (Basingstoke: Macmillan, 2000), p. 113. See also Alexander Leggatt, *Shakespeare's Political Drama: The History Plays and the Roman Plays* (London: Routledge, 1988), pp. 1–2.

3 On forms of self-address on the early modern stage, see James Hirsh, *Shakespeare and the History of Soliloquies* (Madison: Farleigh-Dickinson University Press, 2003).

4 See Andrew Hadfield, '*Henry V*', in Richard Dutton and Jean E. Howard, eds., *A Companion to Shakespeare's Works*, 4 vols., *Volume II, The Histories* (Oxford: Blackwell, 2003), pp. 451–67.

5 See, for example, Plutarch, 'Life of Julius Caesar', in *Selected Lives*, ed. Judith Mossman (Ware: Wordsworth, 1998), pp. 467–530. An overview of Shakespeare's sources for *Julius Caesar* is provided in William Shakespeare, *Julius Caesar*, ed. David Daniell (London: Thomson: The Arden Shakespeare, 1998), introduction, pp. 79–95.

6 For details see J. A. Crook, Andrew Lintott and Elizabeth Rawson, eds., *The Cambridge Ancient History: Volume IX* (Cambridge: Cambridge University Press, 1994), chs. 10–12; Marcel Le Glay, Jean-Louis Voison, Yann Le Bohec and David Cherry, *A History of Rome* (2nd ed., Oxford: Blackwell, 2001), ch. 6.

7 As noted by Edward Burns in his edition of *King Henry VI, Part One* (London: Thompson: The Arden Shakespeare, 2000), p. 119.

8 Christopher Marlowe, *The First Book of Lucan Translated into English*, in *The Poems*, ed. Millar McLure (London: Methuen, 1968), pp. 219–54, lines 44–49.

9 *King Henry VI, Part One*, ed. Burns, introduction, pp. 3–4.

10 Cited in *Henry VI, Part One*, ed. Taylor, introduction, p. 2. See also Andrew Gurr, *The Shakespearian Playing Companies* (Oxford: Clarendon Press, 1996), pp. 261–62.

11 *King Henry VI, Part One*, ed. Burns, introduction, p. 75; Gary Taylor, 'Shakespeare and Others: The Authorship of *Henry the Sixth, Part One*', *MRDE* 7 (1995), 145–205.

12 See Nicholas Grene, *Shakespeare's Serial History Plays* (Cambridge: Cambridge University Press, 2002), p. 9.

13 William Shakespeare, *King Henry VI, Part Two*, ed. Ronald Knowles (London: Thomson: The Arden Shakespeare, 1999), introduction, pp. 111–21; William Shakespeare, *King Henry VI, Part Three*, ed. John D. Cox and Eric Rasmussen (London: Thomson: The Arden Shakespeare, 2001), introduction, pp. 44–49.

14 For analysis, see Shakespeare, *Henry VI, Part Three*, ed. Randall Martin (Oxford: Oxford University Press, 2001), introduction, pp. 96–132; Shakespeare, *Henry VI, Part Three*, ed. Cox and Rasmussen, introduction, pp. 148–76.

15 For discussion, see Laurie E. Maguire, *Shakespeare's Suspect Texts: The 'Bad' Quartos and Their Contexts* (Cambridge: Cambridge University Press, 1996), *passim*; Randall Martin, '*The True Tragedy of Richard Duke of York* and *3 Henry VI*: Report and Revision', *RES*, ns, 53 (2002), 8–30.

16 My policy in this chapter is to cite from the *Contention* and the *True Tragedie*, and then note differences with the folio texts in the endnotes, unless the example in question only occurs in the folio text.

17 See, for example, David Riggs, *Shakespeare's Heroical Histories: **Henry VI** and its Literary Tradition* (Cambridge, Mass.: Harvard University Press, 1971), chs. 1–2; Dominique Goy-Blanquet, *Shakespeare's Early History Plays: From Chronicle to Stage* (Oxford: Oxford University Press, 2003), ch. 1.

18 See, for example, Daniel Javitch, *Poetry and Courtliness in Renaissance England.* (Princeton, N.J.: Princeton University Press. 1978).

19 On Marlowe and Spenser, see Patrick Cheney, *Marlowe's Counterfeit Profession: Ovid, Spenser, Counter-Nationhood* (Toronto: University of Toronto Press, 1997). See also Cheney., *Shakespeare, National Poet-Playwright* (Cambridge: Cambridge University Press, 2004), pp. 113–20.

20 For discussion, see Grene, *Shakespeare's Serial History Plays*, pt. 1; Paulina Kewes, 'The Elizabethan History Play: A True Genre?', in Dutton and Howard, eds., *Companion to Shakespeare's Works II*, pp. 170–93.

21 See Colin Burrow, *Epic Romance: Homer to Milton* (Oxford: Clarendon Press, 1993), pp. 180–200; Clark Hulse, *Metamorphic Verse: The Elizabethan Minor Epic* (Princeton: Princeton University Press, 1981), pp. 199–205, 210–14. More generally, see David Quint, *Epic and Empire: Politics and Generic Form from Virgil to Milton* (Princeton: Princeton University Press, 1993), ch. 4. See above, p. 63.

22 Helen Estabrook Sandison, 'Arthur Gorges, Spenser's Alcyon and Ralegh's Friend', *PMLA* 43 (1928), 645–74. See also Arthur Gorges, *The Poems of Sir Arthur Gorges*, ed. Helen Estabrook Sandison (Oxford: Clarendon Press, 1953).

23 Lucan, *Lucans Pharsalia: Containing The Civill Warres betweene Caesar and Pompey*, trans. Arthur Gorges (London, 1614). See David Norbrook, *Writing the English Republic: Poetry, Rhetoric and Politics, 1627–1660* (Cambridge: Cambridge University Press, 1999), pp. 34, 41.

24 Gillian Wright, 'What Daniel Really Did with the *Pharsalia*: The *Civil Wars*, Lucan, and King James', *RES*, ns, 55 (2004), 210–32.

25 Samuel Daniel, *The Civil Wars*, ed. Laurence Michel (New Haven: Yale University Press, 1958).

26 Daniel, *Civil Wars*, ed. Michel, introduction, pp. 10–28; George M. Logan, 'Lucan – Daniel – Shakespeare: New Light on the Relation Between *The Civil Wars* and *Richard II*', *Sh. Sur.* 9 (1976), 121–40; Stuart Gillespie, *Shakespeare's Books: A Dictionary of Shakespeare Sources* (London: Athlone, 2001), pp. 122–23.

27 Logan, 'Lucan – Daniel – Shakespeare', p. 122–23.

28 See, however, the brief comments: Emrys Jones, *The Origins of Shakespeare* (Oxford: Clarendon Press, 1977), appendix B, pp. 273–77; Gillespie, *Shakespeare's Books*, p. 129; Daniel, *Civil Wars*, ed. Michel, introduction, pp. 27–28.

29 It should be noted that both Barnaby Googe and George Turbeville claimed that they had translations of Lucan ready for publication in the 1560s and 1570s (although neither version actually appeared): see James Shapiro, '"Metre meete to furnish Lucans style": Reconsidering Marlowe's Lucan', in Kenneth Friedenreich, Roma Gill and Constance B. Kuriyama, eds., *'A poet and a filthy playmaker': New Essays on Christopher Marlowe* (New York: AMS, 1988), pp. 315–26. See also Samuel Daniel, *The Collection of the History of England*, in *Complete Works in Verse and Prose*, ed. A. B. Grossart (London: privately printed, 1896), v, pp. 69–299. Daniel's history chronicles the conflicts of the Middle Ages at great length, but only reaches as far as the reign of Stephen (1612), and Edward III in the expanded edition (1618). Geoffrey Whitney refers to Lucan and Nero in his dedicatory epistle prefacing *A Choice of Emblems* (1586) (ed. Henry Green (1866), rpt. New York: Verlag, 1971), sig. A4v.

30 For a recent analysis of Richard as the 'monstrous' heir, see Mark Thornton Burnett, *Constructing 'Monsters' in Shakespearean Drama and Early Modern Culture* (Basingstoke: Palgrave, 2002), ch. 3.

31 Susan Brigden, *New Worlds, Lost Worlds: The Rule of the Tudors, 1485–1603* (London: Penguin, 2000), ch. 11; Marie Axton, *The Queen's Two Bodies: Drama and the Elizabethan Succession* (London: Royal Historical Society, 1977); John Guy, ed., *The Reign of Elizabeth I: Court and Culture in the Last Decade* (Cambridge: Cambridge University Press, 1995).

32 See Norbrook, *Writing the English Republic*, pp. 83–92, *passim*; Nigel Smith, *Literature and Revolution in England, 1640–1660* (New Haven: Yale University Press, 1994), pp. 204–7, *passim*.

33 For comment, see David Womersley, '*3 Henry VI*: Shakespeare, Tacitus, and Parricide', *N. & Q.* 280 (December 1985), 468–73; Stephen Longstaffe, '"A short report and not otherwise": Jack Cade in *2 Henry VI*', in Ronald Knowles, ed., *Shakespeare and Carnival: After Bakhtin* (Basingstoke: Palgrave, 1998), pp. 13–35; Paola Pugliatti, *Shakespeare the Historian* (Basingstoke: Macmillan, 1996), ch. 9.

34 See Michael Neill, *Issues of Death: Mortality and Identity in English Renaissance Tragedy* (Oxford: Oxford University Press, 1997).

35 Quint, *Epic and Empire*, ch. 2.

36 Ibid., p. 7.

37 Ibid., p. 9.

38 Smith, *Literature and Revolution*, p. 205.

39 Lucan, Civil War, trans. Susan H. Braund (Oxford: Oxford University Press, 1993), 3, lines 635–46. Subsequent references to this edition in parentheses in the text.

40 Virgil, *The Aeneid*, trans. David West (Harmondsworth: Penguin, 1990), p. 332.

41 See also K. J. Kesselring, *Mercy and Authority in the Tudor State* (Cambridge: Cambridge University Press, 2003), for a discussion of what such powers meant in Shakespeare's lifetime.

42 Daniel saw the battle of Towton as the English Pharsalia: see Wright, 'What Daniel Really Did with the *Pharsalia*', pp. 212–13, 226–30.

43 The speech in *Henry VI, Part Three* considerably expands the short speech Henry makes in the *True Tragedie*, leading commentators to suggest that Shakespeare revised his play, which exists as a memorial reconstruction in the earlier version: see Shakespeare, *Henry VI, Part Three*, ed. Martin, introduction, pp. 103–6; *Henry VI, Part Three*, ed. Cox and Rasmussen, introduction, pp. 148–76. For comment on this scene, see Jane Kingsley-Smith, *Shakespeare's Drama of Exile* (Basingstoke: Palgrave, 2003), p. 97.

44 Direction given in the folio; the *True Tragedie* has 'a Souldier with a dead man in his armes' enter before his speech, and then 'an other Souldier with a dead man' enter after the first – the son – has finished his first speech.

45 For general comment, see Margaret Healy, *Fictions of Disease in Early Modern England: Bodies, Plagues and Politics* (Basingstoke: Palgrave/Macmillan, 2001), ch. 6.

46 Modern productions often delete these comparisons when compressing the plays for performance: see Alan C. Dessen, *Rescripting Shakespeare: The Text, The Director, and Modern Productions* (Cambridge: Cambridge University Press, 2002), p. 169. See also Michael Hattaway, 'Shakespeare's Histories: The Politics of Recent British Productions', in Hattaway, Boika Sokolova and Derek Roper, eds., *Shakespeare in the New Europe* (Sheffield: Sheffield Academic Press, 1995), pp. 351–69.

47 Henry V also referred to himself as the 'scourge of God': see Andrew Hadfield, 'Tamburlaine as the 'Scourge of God' and *The First English Life of King Henry the Fifth*', *N. & Q.* 50, 3 (December 2003), 399–400.

48 See Shakespeare, *Henry VI, Part One*, ed. Taylor, p. 116.

49 Plutarch, *Selected Lives*, ed. Mossman, p. 503.

50 See Shakespeare, *Julius Caesar*, ed. Daniell, introduction, p. 8.

51 John Aylmer, *An harborowe for faithfull and trevve subjectes agaynst the late blowne blaste, concerninge the governme[n]t of wemen* (Strasbourg, 1559); Anne N. McLaren, *Political Culture in the Reign of Elizabeth I: Queen and Commonwealth, 1558–1585* (Cambridge: Cambridge University Press, 1999); Helen Hackett, *Virgin Mother, Maiden Queen: Elizabeth I and the Cult of the Virgin Mary* (Basingstoke: Macmillan, 1995); Amanda Shephard, *Gender and Authority in Sixteenth-Century England: The Knox Debate* (Keele: Keele University Press, 1994); Carole Levin, *The Heart and Stomach of a King: Elizabeth I and the Politics of Sex and Power* (Philadelphia: University of Pennsylvania Press, 1994).

52 Frances Yates, *Astrea: The Imperial Theme in the Sixteenth Century* (London: Routledge, 1985, rpt. of 1975), pp. 29–87. For analysis, see Leah S. Marcus, *Puzzling Shakespeare: Local Reading and its Discontents* (Berkeley: University of California Press, 1988), pp. 51–83.

53 On the Alençon match, see Susan Doran, *Monarchy and Matriarchy: The Courtships of Elizabeth I* (London: Routledge, 1996), ch. 5.

54 The lines have troubled editors: for comment, see Shakespeare, *Henry VI, Part One*, ed. Taylor, p. 129; Shakespeare, *Henry VI, Part One*, ed. Burns, p. 155.

55 Suetonius, *The Twelve Caesars*, trans. Robert Graves (Harmondsworth: Penguin, 1957), pp. 230–31. Tacitus has Nero singing of the destruction of Troy on his private stage while the city burns: see *On Imperial Rome* (*The Annals*), trans. Michael Grant (Harmondsworth: Penguin, 1956), p. 352.

56 See Georges Livet, 'France: Failure or Spiritual Heritage?', in Pierre Chanu, ed., *The Reformation* (Gloucester: Sutton, 1989), pp. 168–83.

57 Smith, *Literature and Revolution*, p. 206.

58 Lucan, *Civil War*, trans. Braund, lines 739–50.

59 Ibid., lines 773–79.

60 *Contention*, Sig. F3r.

61 For discussion, see Shakespeare, *Henry VI, Part Three*, ed. Cox and Rasmussen, pp. 340–41; Shakespeare, *Henry VI, Part Three*, ed. Martin, p. 298.

62 Suetonius, *Twelve Caesars*, p. 46.

63 On the problematic role of Brutus's Stoic 'constancy' in *Julius Caesar*, see Geoffrey Miles, *Shakespeare and the Constant Romans* (Oxford: Clarendon Press, 1996), ch. 7.

64 See G. R. Elton, ed., *The Tudor Constitution: Documents and Commentary* (Cambridge: Cambridge University Press, 1972), ch. 1; Franklin Le Van Baumer, *The Early Tudor Theory of Kingship* (New Haven: Yale University Press, 1940); Ronald Knowles, *Shakespeare's Arguments with History* (Basingstoke: Palgrave/Macmillan, 2002), chs. 1–2.

65 For relevant discussion, see Robin Headlam Wells, *Shakespeare, Politics and the State* (Basingstoke: Macmillan, 1986), ch. 6; Howard Erskine-Hill, *Poetry and the Realm of Politics: Shakespeare to Dryden* (Oxford: Clarendon Press, 1996), pt. 1.

66 See Allardyce Nicoll and Josephine Nicoll, eds., *Holinshed's **Chronicles** as Used in Shakespeare's Plays* (London: Dent, 1927), pp. 113–21; W. G. Boswell-Stone, *Shakespeare's Holinshed: The Chronicle and the Historical Plays Compared* (New York: Benjamin Blom, 1966, rpt. of 1896), pp. 205–424; Peter Saccio, *Shakespeare's English Kings: History, Chronicle, Drama* (2nd ed., Oxford: Oxford University Press, 2000), pp. 126–38.

67 The stage direction occurs in both the *Contention* and the folio text: the latter text contains far more lines.

68 Stage direction in the folio but not the *Contention*, which has 'Enter the Earles of Warwicke and Salisbury'.

69 John Lyly, *Euphues and his England* (London, 1580), fos.20–22; Charles Butler, *The Feminine Monarchie or a treatise concerning bees* (London, 1609). See also Fulke Greville, *The Remains, being Poems of Monarchy and Religion*, ed. G. A. Wilkes (Oxford: Oxford University Press, 1965), pp. 200–01.

70 The scene appears in both the *Contention* and the folio.

71 Longstaffe, '"A short report"'. See also A. L. Morton, *The English Utopia* (London: Lawrence and Wishart, 1978, rpt. of 1952), ch. 1.

72 Rodney Hilton, *Bond Men Made Free: Medieval Peasant Movements and the English Rising of 1381* (London: Methuen, 1981, rpt. of 1973), pp. 211–12; Christopher Hill, *Milton and the English Revolution* (London: Faber, 1977), p. 72.

73 See David Scott Kastan, '"Proud Majesty made a Subject": Representing Authority on the Early Modern Stage', in Kastan, *Shakespeare after Theory* (London: Routledge, 1999), pp. 109–27; Longstaffe, '"A short report"', pp. 24–27.

74 Shakespeare's characterization of Jack Cade and his representation of the rebellion can usefully be compared with that of Jack Straw and his rebellion in the anonymous play *The Life and Death of Jack Straw* (1594), ed. Kenneth

Muir (Oxford: Malone Society, 1957). Straw complains of hunger and poverty but is shown to rebel for purely selfish reasons and meets his just deserts for his transgression at the hands of the Lord Mayor of London.

75 See Michael Manheim, *The Weak King Dilemma in the Shakespearean History Play* (Syracuse: Syracuse University Press, 1973), ch. 3.

76 Logan, 'Lucan–Daniel–Shakespeare'; Logan, 'Daniel's *Civil Wars* and Lucan's *Pharsalia*', *SEL* 11 (1971), 53–68.

77 Saccio, *Shakespeare's English Kings*, ch. 7; Grene, *Shakespeare's Serial History Plays*, pp. 83–4, 105.

78 See Doran, *Monarchy and Matriarchy*, introduction.

79 *Letters of King James VI and I*, ed. G. P. V. Akrigg (Berkeley: University of California Press, 1984), *passim*; Alan Stewart, *The Cradle King: The Life of James VI and I, the First Monarch of a United Great Britain* (London: Chatto and Windus, 2003), pp. 77–92.

80 Lucan, *Civil War*, trans. Braund, lines 41–45.

81 Manheim, *Weak King Dilemma*, p. 82.

82 Of course, it is possible that the lines in *Henry VI, Part Two* were rewritten because of these in the *Contention*, but, whatever the order of composition, someone – an author or editor – made the connection between them.

83 Shakespeare, *Henry VI, Part Three*, ed. Cox and Rasmussen, introduction, p. 26; Peter Holland, 'Shakespeare Performances in England, 1993–1994', *Sh. Sur.* 48 (1995), 191–226, pp. 211–14.

84 William Shakespeare, *King Richard III*, ed. Anthony Hammond (London: Routledge: The Arden Shakespeare, 1988, rpt. of 1981), 1.3.231–36. Subsequent references to this edition in parentheses in the text.

85 See Andrew Hadfield, *Shakespeare and Renaissance Politics* (London: Thomson: Arden Critical Companions, 2003), pp. 74–76; Grene, *Shakespeare's Serial History Plays*, pp. 108–12.

86 For comment, see Hadfield, '*Henry V*', in Dutton and Howard, eds., *Companion to Shakespeare*, II, pp. 451–67.

87 On 'anaphora', see Brian Vickers, *In Defence of Rhetoric* (Oxford: Clarendon Press, 1988), p. 491.

88 For further analysis, see Chapter 6.

89 Rebecca Bushnell, *Tragedies of Tyrants: Political Thought and Theatre in the English Renaissance* (Ithaca, N.Y.: Cornell University Press, 1990), introduction; Mary Ann McGrail, *Tyranny in Shakespeare* (Lanham: Lexington Books, 2001), ch. 3. See also Leggatt, *Shakespeare's Political Drama*, p. 39.

90 See Thomas More, *The History of King Richard III and Selections from the English and Latin Poems*, ed. Richard S. Sylvester (New Haven: Yale University Press, 1976), pp. 84–89.

91 See Shakespeare, *Richard III*, ed. Hammond, introduction, pp. 99–102.

92 On the figure of the 'Vice', see Bernard Spivack, *Shakespeare and the Allegory of Evil: The History of a Metaphor in Relation to His Major Villains* (New York: Columbia University Press, 1958), ch. 10.

93 Vickers, *Defence of Rhetoric*, p. 492.

94 Shakespeare, *Richard III*, ed. Hammond, pp. 214–5; Holderness, *Shakespeare: The Histories*, pp. 97–98; Riggs, *Shakespeare's Heroical Histories*, pp. 150–51.

95 *The eyght bookes of Caius Julius Caesar conteyning his martiall exploytes in the realme of Gallia and the countries bordering uppon the same translated oute of latin into English by Arthur Goldinge* (London, 1565); *Julius Cesars commentaryes, newly translatyd owte of laten in to englysshe, as much as co [n]cernyth thys realm of England sumtyme callyd Brytayne: whych is the eld'yst hystoryer of all other that can be found, that ever wrote of thys realme of England* (London, 1530).

96 T. W. Baldwin, *William Shakspere's Small Latine and Lesse Greeke*, 2 vols. (Urbana: University of Illinois Press, 1944), I, pp. 132, 154, *passim*; Kristian Jensen, 'The Humanist Reform of Latin and Latin Teaching', in Jill Kraye, ed., *The Cambridge Companion to Renaissance Humanism* (Cambridge: Cambridge University Press), pp. 63–81, p. 74.

97 Diarmaid McCullogh, *The Boy King: Edward VI and the Protestant Reformation* (Basingstoke: Palgrave, 2001), pp. 20–22; Stephen Alford, *Kingship and Politics in the Reign of Edward VI* (Cambridge: Cambridge University Press, 2002), pp. 44–46, *passim*.

98 Eugene R. Kintgen, *Reading in Tudor England* (Pittsburgh: University of Pittsburgh Press, 1996); D. R. Woolf, *Reading History in Early Modern England* (Cambridge: Cambridge University Press, 2000), ch. 2; Kevin Sharpe, *Reading Revolutions: The Politics of Early Modern England* (New Haven: Yale University Press, 2000), pt. 1.

99 See Quentin Skinner, *Reason and Rhetoric in the Philosophy of Hobbes* (Cambridge: Cambridge University Press, 1996), ch. 4; Skinner, *Visions of Politics*, 3 vols. (Cambridge: Cambridge University Press, 2002), III, ch. 10.

100 John Roe, *Shakespeare and Machiavelli* (Cambridge: Brewer, 2002), p. 33.

101 Cicero, *On Duties*, trans. M. T. Griffin and E. M. Atkins (Cambridge: Cambridge University Press, 1991); Janet Coleman, *A History of Political Thought*, 2 vols. (Oxford: Blackwell, 2000), I, ch. 5; Cary J. Nederman, 'Rhetoric, Reason and Republic: Republicanisms – Ancient, Medieval, and Modern', in James Hankins, ed., *Renaissance Civic Humanism* (Cambridge: Cambridge University Press), pp. 247–69. See also Markku Peltonen, 'Citizenship and Republicanism in Elizabethan England', in Martin van Gelderen and Quentin Skinner, eds., *Republicanism: A Shared European Heritage*, 2 vols. (Cambridge: Cambridge University Press), I, pp. 85–106, at pp. 97–98.

102 Smith, *Literature and Revolution*, ch. 7; Roger Lejosne, 'Milton, Satan, Salmasius and Abdiel', in David Armitage, Armand Himy and Quentin Skinner, eds., *Milton and Republicanism* (Cambridge: Cambridge University Press), pp. 106–17.

103 See Kevin Sharpe, 'A Commonwealth of Meanings, Languages, Analogues, Ideas and Politics', in *Remapping Early Modern England: The Culture of Seventeenth-Century Politics* (Cambridge: Cambridge University Press, 2000), ch. 2. Glenn Burgess, *The Politics of the Ancient Constitution: An*

Introduction to English Political Thought, 1603–1642 (Basingstoke: Macmillan, 1992), pt. 1.

104 See, especially, Suetonius, *Twelve Caesars*, pp. 226–31; Tacitus, *On Imperial Rome*, ch. 12.

105 See above, pp. 19–22.

106 Mary Dewar, *Sir Thomas Smith: A Tudor Intellectual in Office* (London: Athlone, 1964), chs. 4–5; Cathy Shrank, *Writing the Nation in Reformation England, 1530–1580* (Oxford: Oxford University Press, 2004), ch. 4.

THE BEGINNING OF THE REPUBLIC: VENUS AND LUCRECE

1 Cited in E. K. Chambers, *The Elizabethan Stage*, 4 vols. (Oxford: Oxford University Press, 1923), IV, p. 310.

2 Ibid., p. 313.

3 Peter Blaney, 'The Publication of Playbooks', in John D. Cox and David Scott Kastan, eds., *A New History of English Drama* (New York: Columbia University Press, 1997), pp. 383–422

4 D. R. Woolf, *Reading History in Early Modern England* (Cambridge: Cambridge University Press, 2000); Margaret Healy, *William Shakespeare's Richard II* (Plymouth: Northcote House, 1998).

5 On Shakespeare and Pembroke's Men, see Park Honan, *Shakespeare, A Life* (Oxford: Oxford University Press, 1998), pp. 136–37, 196–97; Andrew Gurr, *The Shakespearian Playing Companies* (Oxford: Clarendon Press, 1996), ch. 15.

6 Margot Heinemann, 'Rebel Lords, Popular Playwrights, and Political Culture: Notes on the Jacobean Patronage of the Earl of Southampton', *YES* 21 (1991), 63–86; Paul E. J. Hammer, *The Polarisation of Elizabethan Politics: The Political Career of Robert Devereux, 2nd Earl of Essex, 1585–1597* (Cambridge: Cambridge University Press, 1997), ch. 7.

7 Paul E. J. Hammer, 'The Uses of Scholarship: The Secretariat of Robert Devereux, 2nd Earl of Essex, c.1585–1601', *EHR* 109 (1994), 26–51; Robert Lacey, *Robert, Earl of Essex: An Elizabethan Icarus* (London: Weidenfeld and Nicolson, 1970), pp. 265–76.

8 For recent overviews, see Anthony Mortimer, *Variable Passions: A Reading of Shakespeare's Venus and Adonis* (New York: AMS Press, 2000); Richard Rambuss, 'What It Feels Like For a Boy: Shakespeare's *Venus and Adonis*', in Richard Dutton and Jean E. Howard, eds., *A Companion to Shakespeare's Works*, 4 vols. (Oxford: Blackwell), IV, pp. 240–58.

9 See Sasha Roberts, *Reading Shakespeare's Poems in Early Modern England* (Basingstoke: Palgrave, 2003), ch. 1.

10 See G. P. V. Akrigg, *Shakespeare and the Earl of Southampton* (London: Hamilton, 1968), ch. 7.

11 William Shakespeare, *Venus and Adonis*, in *The Poems*, ed. F. T. Prince (London: Methuen: The Arden Shakespeare, 1960), lines 589–94. Subsequent references to this edition in parentheses in the text. On Elizabeth as

Venus, see Katherine Duncan-Jones, 'Much Ado with Red and White: The Earliest Readers of Shakespeare's *Venus and Adonis'*, *RES*, ns, 44 (1993), 480–501; Dympna Callaghan, '(Un)natural Loving: Swine, Pets and Flowers in *Venus and Adonis'*, in Philippa Berry and Margaret Tudeau-Clayton, eds., *Textures of Renaissance Knowledge* (Manchester: Manchester University Press, 2003), pp. 58–78.

12 On the sexuality of the poem, see Jonathan Bate, 'Sexual Perversity in *Venus and Adonis'*, *YES* 23 (1993), 80–92. On the comic ironies in the poem, see Donald G. Watson, 'The Contraries of *Venus and Adonis'*, *SP* 75 (1978), 32–63; John Klause, '*Venus and Adonis*: Can We Forgive Them?', *SP* 85 (1988), 353–77.

13 For commentary, see Mortimer, *Variable Passions*, pp. 123–24.

14 Janet Clare, *'Art Made Tongue-Tied by Authority': Elizabethan and Jacobean Dramatic Censorship* (2nd ed., Manchester: Manchester University Press, 1990), ch. 2.

15 David Norbrook, *Poetry and Politics in the English Renaissance* (rev. ed., Oxford: Oxford University Press, 2002), pp. 137–39.

16 For general analysis, see Julia M. Walker, ed., *Dissing Elizabeth: Negative Representations of Gloriana* (Durham, N.C.: Duke University Press, 1998); Helen Hackett, *Virgin Mother, Maiden Queen: Elizabeth I and the Cult of the Virgin Mary* (Basingstoke: Macmillan, 1995), ch. 6; John Guy, ed., *The Reign of Elizabeth I: Court and Culture in the Last Decade* (Cambridge: Cambridge University Press, 1995).

17 Or, as F. T. Prince suggests, Richmond's closing speech in *Richard III* (*Poems*, ed. Prince, p. 44).

18 See Edmund Spenser, *The Faerie Queene*, bk. I, canto 9, stanzas 37–51; John Donne, *Biathanatos, a declaration of that paradoxe or thesis, that selfe-homicide is not so naturally sinne* (London, 1644).

19 Ernst H. Kantorowicz, *The King's Two Bodies: A Study in Medieval Political Theology* (Princeton: Princeton University Press, 1957), introduction; Marie Axton, *The Queen's Two Bodies: Drama and the Elizabethan Succession* (London: Royal Historical Society, 1977).

20 See Ann Rosalind Jones and Peter Stallybrass, 'The Politics of *Astrophil and Stella'*, *SEL* 24 (1984), 53–68; Arthur F. Marotti, '"Love is Not Love": Elizabethan Sonnet Sequences and the Social Order', *ELH* 49 (1982), 396–428; Jonathan Gibson, 'Elizabethan Court Poetry', in Mike Pincombe, ed., *The Anatomy of Tudor Literature* (Aldershot: Ashgate, 2001), pp. 98–111.

21 For a reading of one of the sonnets along similar lines, see John Barrell, *Poetry, Language & Politics* (Manchester: Manchester University Press, 1988), ch. 1.

22 Mortimer, *Variable Passions*, p. 2; Heinemann, 'Rebel Lords'; Akrigg, *Shakespeare and the Earl of Southampton*, ch. 9.

23 On the relationship between politics and pornography in the 1590s, see Richard A. McCabe, '"Right Puisante and Terrible Priests": The Role of the Anglican Church in Elizabethan State Censorship', in Andrew Hadfield, ed.,

Literature and Censorship in Renaissance England (Basingstoke: Palgrave/ Macmillan, 2001), pp. 75–94.

24 McCabe, '"Right Puisante and Terrible Priests"', p. 75. See also Richard A. McCabe, 'Elizabethan Satire and the Bishops' Ban of 1599', *YES* 11 (1981), 188–93; Cyndia Clegg, *Press Censorship in Elizabethan England* (Cambridge: Cambridge University Press, 1997), pp. 198–217.

25 Roberts, *Reading Shakespeare's Poems*, p. 64.

26 Mortimer, *Variable Passions*, p. 3. Mortimer suggests that *The Faerie Queene* may have rivalled Shakespeare's poem in popularity, but this is unlikely.

27 See, for example, the comments contained in Colin Burrow's otherwise excellent edition: *The Poems*, ed. Colin Burrow (Oxford: Oxford University Press, 2002), introduction, pp. 53–54. Discussion of the poem as a republican work can be found in Michael Platt, *Rome and Romans According to Shakespeare* (Lanham: University Press of America, 1983), pp. 59–79; Annabel Patterson, *Reading Between the Lines* (Madison: University of Wisconsin Press, 1993), pp. 297–317. On the poem and its representation of rape, see, for example, Coppélia Kahn, 'The Rape in Shakespeare's *Lucrece*', *Sh. St.* 9 (1976), 45–72; Stephanie Jed, *Chaste Thinking: The Rape of Lucretia and the Birth of Modern Humanism* (Bloomington: Indiana University Press, 1989); Jane O. Newman, '"And Let Mild Women to Him Lose Their Mildness": Philomela, Female Violence, and Shakespeare's *The Rape of Lucrece*', *SQ* 45 (1994), 304–26. For an excellent overview, see Jocelyn Catty, *Writing Rape, Writing Women in Early Modern England: Unbridled Speech* (Basingstoke: Palgrave, 1999).

28 See Patrick Cheney, *Shakespeare, National Poet-Playwright* (Cambridge: Cambridge University Press, 2004), ch. 4.

29 Ovid, *Metamorphoses*, trans. Mary M. Innes (Harmondsworth: Penguin, 1955), p. 245. For comment, see Jonathan Bate, *Shakespeare and Ovid* (Oxford: Clarendon Press, 1993), pp. 48–67; Pauline Kiernan, '*Venus and Adonis* and Ovidian Indecorous Wit', in A. B. Taylor, ed., *Shakespeare's Ovid: The **Metamorphoses** in the Plays and Poems* (Cambridge: Cambridge Univercity Press, 2000), pp. 81–95.

30 Coppélia Kahn, 'Self and Eros in *Venus and Adonis*', *CR* 20 (1976), 351–71, at 363.

31 On the relationship between sex and tyranny, see Rebecca Bushnell, *Tragedies of Tyrants: Political Thought and Theater in the English Renaissance* (Ithaca, N.Y.: Cornell University Press, 1990), ch. 10.

32 Richard Rainolde, *A chronicle of all the noble emperours of the Romaines from Julius Caesar* (London, 1571), fos.16–17.

33 Christopher Haigh, *Elizabeth I* (London: Longman, 1988), ch. 5; Robert Lacey, *Sir Walter Ralegh* (London: Cardinal, 1975), pp. 162–66, 186–90; Agnes Latham and Joyce Younings, eds., *The Letters of Sir Walter Ralegh* (Exeter: University of Exeter Press, 1999), pp. 74–80. For another literary reference to Raleigh's marriage and imprisonment, see James P. Bednarz, 'Ralegh in Spenser's Historical Allegory', *Sp. Stud.* 4 (1983), 49–70.

34 Richard Rainolde may be one of the sources of Ulysses' famous speech on degree in *Troilus and Cressida*: see Stuart Gillespie, *Shakespeare's Books: A Dictionary of Shakespeare Sources* (London: Athlone, 2001), p. 441. If Shakespeare made use of Rainolde's *The Foundacion of rhetorike* (London, 1563), as is likely, then he may also have consulted Rainolde's work on the Roman emperors: see T. W. Baldwin, *William Shakspere's Small Latine and Lesse Greeke*, 2 vols. (Urbana: University of Illinois Press, 1944), II, pp. 43–44, *passim*.

35 A contrast central to the narrative of the first edition of Spenser's *The Faerie Queene*: see, for example, Isabel G. MacCaffrey, *Spenser's Allegory: The Anatomy of Imagination* (Princeton: Princeton University Press, 1976), pt. 3.

36 Katherine Eisman Maus, 'Taking Tropes Seriously: Language and Violence in Shakespeare's *Rape of Lucrece*', *SQ* 37 (1996), 66–82, p. 67.

37 For an overview, see Ian Donaldson, *The Rapes of Lucrece: A Myth and its Transformations* (Oxford: Clarendon Press, 1982).

38 Livy, *The Early History of Rome*, trans. Aubrey de Sélincourt (Harmondsworth: Penguin, 1960), pp. 82–83.

39 For analysis and discussion, see Constance Jordan, *Renaissance Feminism: Literary Texts and Political Methods* (Ithaca, N.Y.: Cornell University Press, 1990).

40 Livy, *Early History of Rome*, p. 84. For a study of this familiar trope, see Elisabeth Bronfen, *Over Her Dead Body: Death, Femininity and the Aesthetic* (Manchester: Manchester University Press, 1992).

41 Ovid, *Fasti*, trans. A. J. Boyle and R. D. Woodard (Harmondsworth: Penguin, 2000), fasti 2, lines 819–31.

42 Gillespie, *Shakespeare's Books*, p. 395; Shakespeare, *Poems*, ed. Burrow, introduction, pp. 48–50; Baldwin, *William Shakespere's Small Latin*, II, ch. 42.

43 St Augustine, *Concerning the City of God Against the Pagans*, trans. Henry Bettenson (Harmondsworth: Penguin, 1984, rpt. of 1972), pp. 28–31.

44 Gillespie, *Shakespeare's Books*, pp. 87–97; A. S. Miskimin, *The Renaissance Chaucer* (New Haven: Yale University Press, 1975), *passim*.

45 Antonio de Guevara, *The Diall of Princes*, trans. Thomas North (London, 1557), Sig. M6v.

46 Shakespeare, *Poems*, ed. Burrow, introduction, p. 52; Cicero, *On Duties*, trans. M. T. Griffin and E. M. Atkins (Cambridge: Cambridge University Press, 1991), pp. 70–75.

47 Livy, *Early History of Rome*, p. 85.

48 William Painter, *The Palace of Pleasure*, ed. Joseph Jacobs, 3 vols. (London: David Nutt, 1890) I, p. 25.

49 George Buchanan, *A Dialogue on the Law of Kingship among the Scots: A Critical Edition and Translation of George Buchanan's **De Jure Regni apud Scotos Dialogus***, ed. and trans. Roger A. Mason and Martin S. Smith (Aldershot: Ashgate, 2003), pp. 83, 185. See above, pp. 36–40.

50 See Livy, *Early History of Rome*, pp. 62–63; Ovid, *Fasti*, fasti 6, lines 569–610.

51 W. Gordon Zeeveld, *The Temper of Shakespeare's Thought* (New Haven: Yale University Press, 1974), pp. 101–2.

52 William Fulbecke, *An Historicall Collection of the continuall factions, tumults, and Massacres of the Romans and Italians during the space of one hundred and twentie yeares next before the peaceable Empire of Augustus Caesar* (London, 1601), p. 1. Subsequent references to this edition in parentheses in the text.

53 See, John Kerrigan, ed., *Motives of Woe: Shakespeare and 'Female Complaint', A Critical Anthology* (Oxford: Clarendon Press, 1991). Thomas Middleton's complaint, *The Ghost of Lucrece* (London, 1600), is clearly influenced by Shakespeare's poem.

54 For discussion of the possibilities, see Shakespeare, *Poems*, ed. Burrow, introduction, p. 48.

55 The earliest recorded usage of feminine rhyme in the *OED* is, however, Samuel Daniel, *A panegyrike congratulatorie delivered to the Kings most excellent Majestie at Burleigh Harrington in Rutlandshire . . . Also certaine epistles, with a defence of ryme heretofore written* (London, 1603), Sig. H3r. It is likely, given its French origin, that the concept was used much earlier. See also Brian Vickers, ed., *English Renaissance Literary Criticism* (Oxford: Clarendon Press, 1999), p. 450.

56 For a discussion of some of the legal concepts in the poem, see B. J. Sokol and Mary Sokol, *Shakespeare's Legal Language: A Dictionary* (London: Athlone, 2000).

57 John Kerrigan, 'Keats and *Lucrece*', in *On Shakespeare and Early Modern Literature: Essays* (Oxford: Oxford University Press, 2001), pp. 41–65, at p. 45.

58 J. P. Sommerville, *Politics and Ideology in England, 1603–1640* (Harlow: Longman, 1986), introduction.

59 John Bellamy, *The Tudor Law of Treason: An Introduction* (London: Routledge, 1979), p. 15. See also Lacey Baldwin Smith, *Treason in Tudor England: Politics and Paranoia* (London: Cape, 1966).

60 On the political implications of disguise in the poem, see Martin Dzelzainis, 'Shakespeare and Political Thought', in David Scott Kastan, ed., *A Companion to Shakespeare* (Oxford: Blackwell, 1999), pp. 100–16, at pp. 111–13.

61 Buchanan, *Law of Kingship*, pp. 85–87. See also Bushnell, *Tragedies of Tyrants*; Mary Ann McGrail, *Tyranny in Shakespeare* (Lanham: Lexington Books, 2001).

62 Buchanan, *Law of Kingship*, p. 3.

63 J. P. Sommerville, 'Absolutism and Royalism', in J. H. Burns and Mark Goldie, eds., *The Cambridge History of Political Thought, 1450–1700* (Cambridge : Cambridge University Press, 1991), pp. 347–73; G. R. Elton, ed., *The Tudor Constitution: Documents and Commentary* (Cambridge: Cambridge University Press, 1972), pt. 1.

64 George Buchanan, *The History of Scotland written in Latin by George Buchanan; faithfully rendered into English*, J. Fraser (London, 1690). See also

Tragedies, ed. P. Sharratt and P. G. Walsh (Edinburgh: Scottish Academic Press, 1983); *Law of Kingship*, pp. 9, 61.

65 Glenn Burgess, *The Politics of the Ancient Constitution: An Introduction to English Political Thought, 1603–1642* (Basingstoke: Macmillan, 1992), pp. 64–65, 69–71.

66 Sir John Fortesque, *A learned commendation of the politique lawes of Englande*, trans. Richard Mulcaster (London, 1567), fos.83–86.

67 Niccolò Machiavelli, *The Prince*, ed. Quentin Skinner and Russell Price (Cambridge: Cambridge University Press, 1988), p. 59. For further discussion, see John Roe, *Shakespeare and Machiavelli* (Cambridge: Brewer, 2002), ch. 3.

68 Cicero, *On Duties*, pp. 70–75; Roe, *Shakespeare and Machiavelli*, pp. 78–9.

69 Shakespeare, *Poems*, ed. Burrow, introduction, p. 52. More generally, see John Guy, 'The Rhetoric of Counsel in Early Modern England', in Dale Hoak, ed., *Tudor Political Culture* (Cambridge: Cambridge University Press, 1995), pp. 292–310.

70 Livy, *Early History of Rome*, pp. 84–85.

71 Ibid., p. 89.

72 For a related, but not identical, case, see Ciaran Brady, 'Spenser's Irish Crisis: Humanism and Experience in the 1590s', *P. & P.* 120 (1988), 17–49.

73 McGrail, *Tyranny in Shakespeare*; Bushnell, *Tragedies of Tyrants*. On the aristocratic culture of honour, see Richard C. McCoy, *The Rites of Knighthood: The Literature and Politics of Elizabethan Chivalry* (Berkeley: University of California Press, 1989); Mervyn James, *Society, Politics and Culture: Studies in Early Modern Culture* (Cambridge: Cambridge University Press, 1988), ch. 8.

74 See Sokol and Sokol, *Shakespeare's Legal Language*, pp. 376–77; James Emerson Phillips, *Images of a Queen: Mary Stuart in Sixteenth-Century Literature* (Berkeley: University of California Press, 1964).

75 Buchanan, *History of Scotland*, p. 205. See also Stephanus Junius Brutus, the Celt, *Vindiciae, Contra Tyrannos, or, concerning the legitimate power of a prince over the people, and of the people over a prince* (1579), ed. George Garnett (Cambridge: Cambridge University Press, 1994), p. 148.

76 Buchanan, *Law of Kingship*, p. 101. On the republican – or 'Neo-Roman' conception of freedom, see Quentin Skinner, *Liberty Before Liberalism* (Cambridge: Cambridge University Press, 1998).

77 For a more general discussion of the problems of inherited characteristics in early modern England, see Frank Whigham, *Seizures of the Will in Early Modern English Drama* (Cambridge: Cambridge University Press, 1996).

78 See Sommerville, *Politics and Ideology*, ch. 1.

79 Amanda Shephard, *Gender and Authority in Sixteenth-Century England: The Knox Debate* (Keele: Keele University Press, 1994), p. 25.

80 Anne N. McLaren, 'Gender, Religion, and Early Modern Nationalism: Elizabeth I, Mary Queen of Scots, and the Genesis of English Anti-

Catholicism', *AHR* 107 (2002), 739–67. See also George Buchanan, *Ane detectioun of the duinges of Marie Quene of Scottes* (1571).

81 McLaren, 'Gender, Religion, and Early Modern Nationalism', p. 765.

82 There were attempts to defend Mary from the misogynist attacks made against her: see Patrick Collinson, 'William Camden and the Anti-Myth of Elizabeth: Setting the Mould?', in Susan Doran and Thomas S. Freeman, eds., *The Myth of Elizabeth* (Basingstoke: Palgrave, 2003), pp. 79–98.

83 John F. Danby, *Shakespeare's Doctrine of Nature: A Study of **King Lear*** (London: Faber, 1961).

84 Sommerville, 'Absolutism and Royalism', pp. 363–64. See, for example, Thomas Floyd, *The Picture of a perfit Common wealth describing aswell the offices of princes and inferiour magistrates over their subjects, as also the duties of subjects towards their governours. Gathered forth of many authors, aswel humane, as divine* (London, 1600), fos.24–46; James VI and I, *The Trew Law of Free Monarchies*, in *The Workes* (1616) (Hildesham and New York: Verlag, 1971); Charles Butler, *The Feminine Monarchie or a treatise concerning bees, and the due ordering of them* (London, 1609).

85 J. G. A. Pocock, *The Machiavellian Moment: Florentine Political Thought and the Atlantic Republican Tradition* (Princeton: Princeton University Press, 1975), ch. 9; David McPherson, *Shakespeare, Jonson, and the Myth of Venice* (Newark: University of Delaware Press, 1990), chs. 1–2; Andrew Hadfield, *Literature, Travel and Colonial Writing in the English Renaissance, 1545–1625* (Oxford: Clarendon Press, 1998), pp. 46–58, 217–42.

86 The fundamental argument of Niccolò Machiavelli, *The Discourses*, trans. Leslie Walker, rev. Brian Richardson, ed. Bernard Crick (Harmondsworth: Penguin, 1970). For discussion, see Gisela Bock, Quentin Skinner and Maurizio Viroli, eds., *Machiavelli and Republicanism* (Cambridge: Cambridge University Press, 1990)

87 On the relationship between Tarquin's lust and his abuse of power, see Coppélia Kahn, *Roman Shakespeare: Warriors, Wounds, and Women* (London: Routledge, 1997), pp. 32–36.

88 J. E. Neale, *Queen Elizabeth* (London: Cape, 1934), ch. 16.

89 On slavery in Renaissance political thought, see Richard Tuck, *Philosophy and Government, 1572–1651* (Cambridge: Cambridge University Press, 1993), pp. 140, 142. See also Janet Coleman, *A History of Political Thought*, 2 vols. (Oxford: Blackwell, 2000), I, pp. 198–206, *passim.*

90 See, for example, Quentin Skinner, 'Machiavelli on *virtú* and the Maintenance of Liberty', in *Visions of Politics: Volume II, Renaissance Virtues* (Cambridge: Cambridge University Press, 2002), pp. 160–85.

91 See Pocock, *Machiavellian Moment*, p. 229.

92 See also Skinner, *Liberty Before Liberalism* (Cambridge: Cambridge University Press, 1998), pp. 66–77.

93 For a different reading of the encounter, see Kahn, *Roman Shakespeare*, ch. 2.

94 Katherine Duncan-Jones, *Ungentle Shakespeare: Scenes From His Life* (London: Thomson, 2001), pp. 50, 52. See also Philip Edwards, *Thomas Kyd and Early Elizabethan Tragedy* (London: Longman, 1966); Eugene D. Hill, 'Revenge Tragedy', in Arthur Kinney, ed., *A Companion to Renaissance Drama* (Oxford: Blackwell, 2002), pp. 326–35, at pp. 331–34.

95 Thomas Kyd, *The Spanish Tragedy*, ed. Philip Edwards (Manchester: Manchester University Press, 1977, rpt. of 1959), 3.12.63. Subsequent references to this edition in parentheses in the text.

96 The classic study is Fredson Bowers, *Elizabethan Revenge Tragedy, 1587–1642* (Princeton: Princeton University Press, 1940). See also Joel B. Altman, *The Tudor Play of Mind: Rhetorical Inquiry and the Development of Elizabethan Drama* (Berkeley: University of California Press, 1978), ch. 8.

97 See Kyd, *Spanish Tragedy*, ed. Edwards, introduction, pp. xlviii–xlxix.

98 Kyd, *Spanish Tragedy*, ed. Edwards, p. 84; Lucan, *Civil War*, trans. Susan H. Braund (Oxford: Oxford University Press, 1992), 7.818. Subsequent references to this edition in parentheses in the text.

99 See, for example, William Allen, *A True, Sincere and Modest Defence, of English Catholiques that suffer for their faith both at home and abrode* (Rouen, 1584), p. 107; Brutus, *Vindiciae, Contra Tyrannos*, pp. 67–72.

100 On Shakespeare and Troy, see Heather James, *Shakespeare's Troy: Drama, Politics, and the Translation of Empire* (Cambridge: Cambridge University Press, 1997).

101 Lisa Jardine and Anthony Grafton, '"Studied for Action": How Gabriel Harvey read his Livy', *P. & P.* 129 (1990), 30–78.

102 On the significance of the wallhangings, see Alison Thorne, *Vision and Rhetoric in Shakespeare: Looking Through Language* (Basingstoke: Palgrave, 2000), pp. 84–86.

103 Edward Hall, *Chronicles* (1548), 2 vols. (London: J. Johnson, 1809), I, p. 1. See also Paulina Kewes, 'Contemporary Europe in Elizabethan and Early Stuart Drama', in Andrew Hadfield and Paul Hammond, eds., *Shakespeare and Renaissance Europe* (London: Thomson, 2004), pp. 150–92, at pp. 153–54.

104 Raphael Holinshed, *Holinshed's Chronicles of England, Scotland and Ireland* (1587), ed. Henry Ellis, 6 vols. (London: Johnson, 1807–8), p. 1.

105 Buchanan, *Law of Kingship*, p. 13. Thomas Martland was the other character in the dialogue, a prominent Protestant politician and one of three brothers, the most important of whom, William, was secretary to Mary of Guise.

106 Ibid., p. 117.

107 For an overview, see Donald R. Kelley, 'Law', in Burns and Goldie, eds., *Cambridge History of Political Thought*, pp. 66–94.

108 On early modern readings of Lucrece as a virtuous heroine, see Roberts, *Reading Shakespeare's Poems*, pp. 103–5.

109 Kahn, 'Publishing Shame', p. 271.

110 For evidence, see Roberts, *Reading Shakespeare's Poems*, ch. 3.

111 See Anne N. McLaren, *Political Culture in the Reign of Elizabeth I: Queen and Commonwealth, 1558–1585* (Cambridge: Cambridge University Press, 1999).

112 Margaret Healy, *Fictions of Disease in Early Modern England: Bodies, Plagues and Politics* (Basingstoke: Palgrave/Macmillan, 2001), pp. 37–40, *passim*.

113 See, for example, Jed, *Chaste Thinking*; Kahn, 'Publishing Shame'; Catty, *Writing Rape*. See also Shakespeare, *Poems*, ed. Burrow, introduction, pp. 66–73.

114 Although see Lucy Hutchinson, *Order and Disorder*, ed. David Norbrook (Oxford: Blackwell, 2001); Martin van Geldern and Quentin Skinner, eds., *Republicanism: A Shared European Heritage*, 2 vols. (Cambridge: Cambridge University Press, 2002), I, pt. 2, 'The Place of Women in the Republic'.

THE END OF THE REPUBLIC: TITUS ANDRONICUS AND JULIUS CAESAR

1 For details, see William Shakespeare, *Titus Andronicus*, ed. Jonathan Bate (London: Thomson: The Arden Shakespeare, 2000, rpt. of 1995), introduction, pp. 69–70. See also *Henslowe's Diary*, ed. R. A. Foakes and R. T. Rickert (Cambridge: Cambridge University Press, 1961), p. 21. On the impact of the plague on the theatres, see F. P. Wilson, *The Plague in Shakespeare's London* (Oxford: Oxford University Press, 1999, rpt. of 1927), pp. 51–55.

2 Brian Vickers, *Shakespeare, Co-Author: A Historical Study of Five Collaborative Plays* (Oxford: Oxford University Press, 2002), ch. 3, and supported by Brian Boyd, 'Mutius: An Obstacle Removed in *Titus Andronicus*', RES, ns, 55 (2004), 196–209. See also *Titus Andronicus*, ed. Eugene M. Waith (Oxford: Clarendon Press, 1984), introduction, pp. 11–20; *Titus Andronicus*, ed. Alan Hughes (Cambridge: Cambridge University Press, 1994), introduction, pp. 10–13; Shakespeare, *Titus*, ed. Bate, introduction, pp. 80–82. All three editors assign the whole play to Shakespeare. Peele also appears to have existed within the large circle of writers who gravitated towards the earl of Essex, praising him profusely in *Anglorum Feriae* (1595). His dramatic work, especially *The Battle of Alcazar* (c.1589), owes as much to Marlowe as Shakespeare's early plays, and he may have collaborated with Shakespeare to write *Henry VI, Part Three*: see George Peele, *The Life and Works of George Peele*, ed. Charles Tyler Prouty, R. Mark Benbow, Elmer Blistein and Frank S. Hook, 2 vols. (New Haven: Yale University Press, 1952–70), and above, p. 105.

3 Shakespeare, *Titus*, ed. Bate, introduction, p. 79. For opposing judgements, see *Titus*, ed. Waith, introduction, pp. 4–11; *Titus*, ed. Hughes, introduction, pp. 1–6.

4 See Shakespeare, *Titus*, ed. Waith, pp. 195–207.

5 Katherine Duncan-Jones, *Ungentle Shakespeare: Scenes From His Life* (London: Thomson, 2001), pp. 51–53; Andrew Gurr, *The Shakespearian Playing Companies* (Oxford: Clarendon Press, 1996), *passim*.

6 On the last points, see S. P. Cerasano, ' "Borrowed Robes": Costume Prices, and the Drawing of *Titus Andronicus*', Sh. St. 22 (1994), 45–57; G. Harold Metz, 'The Early Staging of *Titus Andronicus*', Sh. St. 14 (1981), 99–109.

7 Pedro Mexia, *The Historie of all the Romane Emperors beginning with Caius Julius Caesar, and successively ending with Rodolph the second now raigning*, trans. W. T. (London, 1604). See also *Titus*, ed. Waith, introduction, pp. 34–38.

8 Herodian, *The history of Herodian, a Greeke authour treating of the Romayne emperors, after Marcus, translated oute of Greeke into Latin, by Angelus Politianus, and out of Latin into Englyshe, by Nicholas Smyth. Whereunto are annexed, the argumentes of every booke, at the begynning therof, with annotacions for the better understandynge of the same historye* (London, 1556). The work was translated again in 1629 and 1639. For comment, see Naomi Conn Liebler, *Shakespeare's Festive Tragedy: The Ritual Foundations of Genre* (London: Routledge, 1995), p. 137. On Scottish monarchs see Chapter 6.

9 Herodian, *History*, Sig. B1r.

10 Herodian, *History*, bk. I; Tacitus, *On Imperial Rome* (*The Annals*), trans. Michael Grant (Harmondsworth: Penguin, 1956), pt. 1.

11 A similar case can be made with regard to *The Tempest*, which uses names found in Italian histories such as that of Guicciardini: see Andrew Hadfield, *Shakespeare and Renaissance Politics* (London: Thomson: Arden Critical Companions, 2003), pp. 216–19.

12 Sir Philip Sidney, *An Apology for Poetry*, ed. Geoffrey Shepherd, rev. and ex. R. W. Maslen (Manchester: Manchester University Press, 2002), p. 82, *passim*.

13 For discussion, see Geraldo U. de Sousa, *Shakespeare's Cross-Cultural Encounters* (Basingstoke: Palgrave, 1999), pp. 110–13; Jonathan Bate, *Shakespeare and Ovid* (Oxford: Clarendon Press, 1993), pp. 103–5; Coppélia Kahn, *Roman Shakespeare: Warriors, Wounds, and Women* (London: Routledge, 1997), p. 70; Sid Ray, '"Rape, I fear, was root of they annoy": The Politics of Consent in *Titus Andronicus*', *SQ* 49 (1998), 22–39.

14 For further discussion, see Hadfield, *Shakespeare and Renaissance Politics*, pp. 120–37.

15 Polybius, *The Rise of the Roman Empire*, trans. Ian Scott-Kilvert (Harmondsworth: Penguin, 1979), pp. 311–18; J. G. A. Pocock, *The Machiavellian Moment: Florentine Political Thought and the Atlantic Republican Tradition* (Princeton: Princeton University Press, 1975), p. 79.

16 George Buchanan, *A Dialogue on the Law of Kingship among the Scots: A Critical Edition and Translation of George Buchanan's **De Jure Regni apud Scotos Dialogus***, ed. and trans. Roger A. Mason and Martin S. Smith (Aldershot: Ashgate, 2003). See also Markku Peltonen, 'Citizenship and Republicanism in Elizabethan England', in Martin van Gelderen and Quentin Skinner, eds., *Republicanism: A Shared European Heritage*, 2 vols. (Cambridge: Cambridge University Press, 2002), I, pp. 85–106.

17 Aristotle, *The Nicomachean Ethics*, trans. David Ross (Oxford: Oxford University Press, 1980, rpt. of 1925), bk. VII. See also Edmund Spenser, *The Faerie Queene*, ed. A. C. Hamilton (London: Routledge, 2001), bk. II; Graham Hough, *A Preface to **The Faerie Queene*** (London: Duckworth, 1962), ch. 8.

18 Herodian, *History*, bk. I. On the appeal of Marcus Aurelius in Renaissance England, see Reid Barbour, *English Epicures and Stoics: Ancient Legacies in Early Stuart Culture* (Amherst: University of Massachusetts Press, 1998), pp. 146–80, *passim*; Thomas Whythorne, *The Autobiography of Thomas Whythorne*, ed. James M. Osborn (Oxford: Clarendon Press, 1961), pp. 132–33, 142, *passim*.

19 See, especially, Quentin Skinner, 'Republican Virtues in an Age of Princes', in *Visions of Politics*, 3 vols. (Cambridge: Cambridge University Press, 2002), II, pp. 118–59; Markku Peltonen, *Classical Humanism and Republicanism in English Political Thought, 1570–1640* (Cambridge: Cambridge University Press, 1995), pp. 130–34, 150–56.

20 See Shakespeare, *Titus*, ed. Waith, p. 84.

21 Niccolò Machiavelli, *The Discourses*, trans. Leslie Walker, rev. Brian Richardson, ed. Bernard Crick (Harmondsworth: Penguin, 1970), bk. II; Quentin Skinner, 'Machiavelli on *virtù* and the Maintenance of Liberty', in *Visions of Politics*, II, pp. 160–85; Pocock, *Machiavellian Moment*, pp. 199–201, *passim*.

22 Pocock, *Machiavellian Moment*, p. 201. See also Andrew Hadfield, '*Henry V*', in Richard Dutton and Jean E. Howard, eds., *A Companion to Shakespeare's Works*, 4 vols., *Volume II, The Histories* (Oxford: Blackwell, 2003), pp. 451–67, at p. 464.

23 On the revenge cycle in the play, see Ian Smith, '*Titus Andronicus*: A Time for Race and Revenge', in Dutton and Howard, eds., *Companion to Shakespeare: Volume II, The Histories*, pp. 284–302; Frederick Kiefer, *Shakespeare's Visual Theatre: Staging the Personified Characters* (Cambridge: Cambridge University Press, 2003), ch. 2. On the 'barbarism' of Rome, see Neil Rhodes, 'Shakespeare the Barbarian', in Jennifer Richards, ed., *Early Modern Civil Discourses* (Basingstoke: Palgrave, 2003), pp. 99–104

24 On early modern elections in England, which were invariably stage-managed, see Derek Hirst, *The Representative of the People? Voters and Voting under the Early Stuarts* (Cambridge: Cambridge University Press, 1975); Mark A. Kishlansky, *Parliamentary Selection: Social and Political Choice in Early Modern England* (Cambridge: Cambridge University Press, 1986).

25 See Ania Loomba, *Shakespeare, Race, and Colonialism* (Oxford: Oxford University Press, 2002), ch. 3; John Gillies, *Shakespeare and the Geography of Difference* (Cambridge: Cambridge University Press, 1994), pp. 100–12.

26 Herodian, *History*, bk. I.

27 See Skinner, *Visions of Politics*, II, pp. 20, 289–90, *passim*.

28 Sallust, *The Conspiracy of Catiline and the War of Jugurtha*, trans. Thomas Heywood (1609), introd. Charles Whibley (London: Constable: The Tudor Translations, 1924), p. 58. Subsequent references to this edition in parentheses in the text.

29 See Peter Burke, 'Tacitism', in T. A. Dorey, ed., *Tacitus* (London: Routledge, 1969), pp. 149–71; J. H. M. Salmon, 'Seneca and Tacitus in

Jacobean England', in Linda Levy Peck, ed., *The Mental World of the Jacobean Court* (Cambridge: Cambridge University Press), pp. 169–88.

30 For details, see Andrew Lintott, 'The Roman Empire and its Problems in the Late Second Century', in J. A. Crook, Andrew Lintott and Elizabeth Rawson, eds., *The Cambridge Ancient History, Volume IX* (Cambridge: Cambridge University Press), pp. 16–39, at pp. 29–31.

31 See above, pp. 22–23.

32 Cicero, 'In Defence of Rabirius', in *The Speeches: Pro Lege Manilia, Pro Caecina, Pro Cluentio, Pro Rabirio Perduellonis*, trans. H. Grose Hodge (London: Heinemann, 1959), pp. 444–91, at p. 465. Cicero is one of the many Roman authors mentioned in the play: 4.1.14.

33 Liebler, *Shakespeare's Festive Tragedy*, p. 134; Edward Berry, *Shakespeare and the Hunt: A Cultural and Social Study* (Cambridge: Cambridge University Press, 2001), p. 86.

34 Charles Wells, *The Wide Arch: Roman Value in Shakespeare* (Bristol: Bristol Classical Press, 1993), ch. 1.

35 Berry, *Shakespeare and the Hunt*, pp. 70–86; Brian Gibbons, *Shakespeare and Multiplicity* (Cambridge: Cambridge University Press, 1993), pp. 90–95; Mervyn James, *Society, Politics and Culture: Studies in Early Modern Culture* (Cambridge: Cambridge University Press, 1988), ch. 8; Lawrence Stone, *The Crisis of the Aristocracy, 1558–1641* (Oxford: Clarendon Press, 1965).

36 See, for example, Brian Cox, '*Titus Andronicus*', in Russell Jackson and Robert Smallwood, eds., *Players of Shakespeare*, 3 vols. (Cambridge: Cambridge University Press, 1993), III, pp. 174–88. On the theme of mutilation in *Titus*, see Gillian Murray Kendall, '"Lend me thy Hand": Metaphor and Mayhem in *Titus Andronicus*', *SQ* 45 (1994), 279–303.

37 See Robert Miola, *Shakespeare's Reading* (Oxford: Oxford University Press, 2000), pp. 117–20; Bate, *Shakespeare and Ovid*, pp. 101–17; A. B. Taylor, 'Animals in "manly shape as too the outward showe": Moralizing and Metamorphosis in *Titus Andronicus*', in Taylor, ed., *Shakespeare's Ovid: The Metamorphoses in the Plays and Poems* (Cambridge: Cambridge University Press, 2000), pp. 66–80.

38 On the play's relationship with emblem books, see Kiefer, *Shakespeare's Visual Theatre*, ch. 2. Emblem books were books with pictures, which then had texts attached that explained what the pictures signified and how they should be read.

39 See Peter Burke, 'Tacitism, Scepticism, and Reason of State', in J. H. Burns and Mark Goldie, eds., *The Cambridge History of Political Thought, 1450–1700* (Cambridge: Cambridge University Press, 1991), pp. 479–98. Aaron uses the word elsewhere: see 4.2.150.

40 Christopher Marlowe, *The Jew of Malta*, ed. N. W. Bawcutt (Manchester: Manchester University Press, 1978), 1.2.273; Felix Raab, *The English Face of Machiavelli: A Changing Interpretation, 1500–1700* (London: Routledge, 1965), ch. 3.

41 See, especially, Herodian, *Historie*, bks. III–IV; Mexia, *Historie of all the Romane Emperors*.

42 For discussion, see Shakespeare, *Titus*, ed. Bate, introduction, p. 92.

43 Livy, *The Early History of Rome*, trans. Aubrey de Sélincourt (Harmondsworth: Penguin, 1960), pp. 22–24. On the Gothic savagery in *Titus*, see Taylor, 'Animals in "manly shape"', p. 76; Liebler, *Shakespeare's Festive Tragedy*, p. 146.

44 For a more positive reading of the mixed unions, see Rhodes, 'Shakespeare the Barbarian', pp. 109–10.

45 Gillies, *Shakespeare and the Geography of Difference* (Cambridge: Cambridge University Press, 1994), p. 110. See also Loomba, *Shakespeare, Race, and Colonialism*, p. 90. Other commentators see the ending as a sign of Aaron's humanity: see Leslie A. Fiedler, *The Stranger in Shakespeare* (London: Paladin, 1974), pp. 152–53.

46 See, for example, Shakespeare, *Titus*, ed. Bate, p. 274; *Titus*, ed. Waith, p. 192. Hughes preserves the attribution to Marcus, but notes that he is in the minority: 'Only Barnet agrees with me that these lines may . . . be attributed to Marcus' (*Titus*, ed. Hughes, p. 141).

47 I owe this point to James Shapiro. See also the discussion in Alan C. Dessen, *Rescripting Shakespeare: The Text, The Director, and Modern Productions* (Cambridge: Cambridge University Press, 2002), pp. 230–34.

48 For contemporary discussions on the decay of commonwealths, the signs that could be observed and the possible remedies, see William Covell, *Polimanteia, or The means lawfull and unlawfull, to judge of the fall of a common-wealth, against the frivolous and foolish conjectures of this age* (London, 1595); Richard Beacon, *Solon his Follie, or A Politique Discourse Touching the Reformation of common-weales conquered, declined or corrupted* (1594), ed. Clare Carroll and Vincent Carey (Binghampton, N.Y.: MRTS, 1996); Machiavelli, *Discourses*, bk. III.

49 Pocock, *Machiavellian Moment*, pt. 1.

50 For details, see Peltonen, *Classical Humanism*, ch. 2.

51 T. J. B. Spencer, 'Shakespeare and the Elizabethan Romans', *Sh. Sur.* 10 (1957), 27–38, p. 32. See also Kahn, *Roman Shakespeare*, pp. 46–47.

52 For discussion, see Claire Jowitt, *Voyage Drama and Gender Politics, 1589–1642: Real and Imagined Worlds* (Manchester: Manchester University Press, 2003), pp. 105–22; Andrew Hadfield, *Shakespeare, Spenser and the Matter of Britain* (Basingstoke: Palgrave/Macmillan, 2003), pp. 160–68.

53 Rhodes, 'Shakespeare the Barbarian', p. 110.

54 The following sentences are derived from my argument in *Shakespeare and Renaissance Politics*, p. 134.

55 For analysis, see Marie Axton, *The Queen's Two Bodies: Drama and the Elizabethan Succession* (London: Royal Historical Society, 1977); Susan Doran, 'Revenge Her Foul and Most Unnatural Murder? The Impact of Mary Stewart's Execution on Anglo-Scottish Relations', *History* 85 (2000), 589–612.

56 See Introduction, p. xx.

57 See Peter Thomson, *Shakespeare's Professional Career* (Cambridge: Cambridge University Press, 1992), pp. 101–3; Andrew Gurr, *The Shakespearean Stage, 1574–1642* (3rd ed., Cambridge: Cambridge University Press, 1999), pp. 142–52. See also Janette Dillon, *Theatre, Court and City, 1595–1610* (Cambridge: Cambridge University Press, 2000), *passim.*

58 A very different interpretation of the pivotal importance of *Julius Caesar* is provided in Steve Sohmer's somewhat eccentric *Shakespeare's Mystery Play: The Opening of the Globe Theatre, 1599* (Manchester: Manchester University Press, 1999).

59 Thomas Platter, *Thomas Platter's Travels in England, 1599*, trans. Claire Williams (London: Cape, 1937), p. 166. See also Richard Wilson, '"Is this a holiday?": Shakespeare's Roman Carnival', in Wilson, ed., *Julius Caesar: Contemporary Critical Essays* (Basingstoke: Palgrave, 2002), pp. 55–76, at pp. 55–56.

60 Platter, *Travels*, pp. 64, 175.

61 See, for example, A. D. Nuttall, *A New Mimesis: Shakespeare and the Representation of Reality* (London: Methuen, 1983), pp. 99–114; Alan Bloom with Harry V. Jaffa, *Shakespeare's Politics* (Chicago: University of Chicago Press, 1964), ch. 4; Wells, *Wide Arch*, ch. 3.

62 See Blair Worden, 'Shakespeare and Politics', *Sh. Sur.* 44 (1991), 1–15; Robert S. Miola, '*Julius Caesar* and the Tyrannicide Debate', *RQ* 36 (1985), 271–90; Alexander Leggatt, *Shakespeare's Political Drama: The History Plays and the Roman Plays* (London: Routledge, 1988), ch. 6.

63 Wells, *Wide Arch*, p. 15; Geoffrey Miles, *Shakespeare and the Constant Romans* (Oxford: Clarendon Press, 1996), pp. 1–2.

64 Kahn, *Roman Shakespeare*, p. 90.

65 For an example of Cicero's influence on an ordinary writer, see Haly Heron, *The Kayes of Counsaile: A New Discourse of Morall Philosophie* (1579), ed. Virgil B. Heltzel (Liverpool: Liverpool University Press, 1954), p. 3, *passim.* More generally, see Howard Jones, *Master Tully. Cicero in Tudor England* (Nieuwkoop: Bibliotheca Humanistica & Reformatorica, Vol. LVII, 1981); Jennifer Richards, *Rhetoric and Courtliness in Early Modern Literature* (Cambridge: Cambridge University Press, 2003); John O. Ward, 'Cicero and Quintillian', in Glyn P. Norton, ed., *The Cambridge History of Literary Criticism: Volume III, The Renaissance* (Cambridge: Cambridge University Press, 1999), pp. 77–87; Virginia Cox, *The Renaissance Dialogue: Literary Dialogue in its Social and Political Contexts, Castiglione to Galileo* (Cambridge: Cambridge University Press, 1993), *passim.*

66 William Shakespeare, *Julius Caesar*, ed. David Daniell (London: Thomson: The Arden Shakespeare, 1998), 1.2.185–87. Subsequent references to this edition in parentheses in the text.

67 In Plutarch's 'Life of Marcus Brutus', the conspirators do not ask Cicero to join them because 'although he was a man whom they loved dearly, and

trusted best: for they were afraid that he being a coward by nature, and age also having increased his fear, he would quite turn and alter all their purpose, and quench the heat of their enterprise, the which specially required hot and earnest execution': Plutarch, *Selected Lives*, ed. Judith Mossman (Ware: Wordsworth, 1998), p. 822. Subsequent references to this edition in parentheses in the text.

68 See Kahn, *Roman Shakespeare*, pp. 82–90.

69 Cicero, *On the Commonwealth and On the Laws*, ed. James E. G. Zetel (Cambridge: Cambridge University Press, 1999). For the speeches, see, for example, *The Speeches: Pro Lege Manilia, etc.*, trans. Hodge; *The Speeches: Pro Sestio, In Vatinium*, trans. R. Gardner (London: Heinemann, 1958).

70 Richards, *Rhetoric and Courtliness, passim*; T. W. Baldwin, *William Shakspere's Small Latine and Lesse Greeke*, 2 vols. (Urbana: University of Illinois Press, 1944), *passim*; John O. Ward, 'Renaissance Commentators on Ciceronian Rhetoric', and Paul O. Kristeller, 'Rhetoric in Medieval and Renaissance Culture', in James P. Murphy, ed., *Renaissance Rhetoric: Studies in the Theory and Practice of Renaissance Rhetoric* (Berkeley: University of California Press, 1983), pp. 126–73, and pp. 1–20, at p. 3.

71 Cicero, *On Duties*, trans. M. T. Griffin and E. M. Atkins (Cambridge: Cambridge University Press, 1991), p. 25. See also *Marcus Tullius Ciceroes three bookes of duties to Marcus his sonne, tourned out of Latine into English, by Nicolas Grimald* (London, 1583).

72 Cicero, *On Duties*, p. 36.

73 Richards, *Rhetoric and Courtliness*, p. 47.

74 Ibid., p. 3; Baldwin, *William Shakspere's Small Latine, passim*; William Shakespeare, *The Two Gentlemen of Verona*, ed. William C. Carroll (London: Thomson: The Arden Shakespeare, 2004), introduction, pp. 3–18.

75 Cicero, *Fowre Severall Treatises of M. Tullius Cicero: Conteyninge his most learned and eloquent discourses of Frendshippe, Oldage, Paradoxes: and Scipio his Dreame*, trans. Thomas Newton (London, 1577), fo.8. Subsequent references to this edition in parentheses in the text. For an image of bad friendship, see Geoffrey Whitney, *A Choice of Emblems* (1586) (ed. Henry Green [1866], rpt. New York: Verlag, 1971), p. 24.

76 Stuart Gillespie, *Shakespeare's Books: A Dictionary of Shakespeare Sources* (London: Athlone, 2001), pp. 106–12, 425–36; Robert S. Miola, *Shakespeare's Reading* (Oxford: Oxford University Press, 2000), pp. 98–109.

77 See Rebecca Bushnell, '*Julius Caesar*', in Dutton and Howard, eds., *Companion to Shakespeare's Works: Volume III The Comedies*, pp. 339–56, at p. 348.

78 See Jonathan Scott, 'Classical Republicanism in Seventeenth-Century England and the Netherlands', in van Gelderen and Skinner, eds., *Republicanism*, I, pp. 61–81; Simone Zurbuchen, 'Republicanism and Toleration', in van Gelderen and Skinner, eds., *Republicanism*, II, pp. 47–71. More generally, see Jill Kraye, 'Philologists and Philosophers', in Kraye, ed.,

The Cambridge Companion to Renaissance Humanism (Cambridge: Cambridge University Press, 1996), pp. 142–60.

79 Kahn, *Roman Shakespeare*, p. 86.

80 For comment, see Katherine Duncan-Jones, 'Did the Boy Shakespeare Kill Calves?', *RES*, ns, 55 (2004), 183–95; Edward Berry, *Shakespeare and the Hunt: A Cultural and Social Study* (Cambridge: Cambridge University Press, 2001), pp. 186–94.

81 Peltonen, *Classical Humanism*, pp. 34–35, 113–14.

82 On secrecy and spying and its relationship to literature, see Robert Maslen, *Elizabethan Fictions: Espionage, Counter-espionage and the Duplicity of Fiction in Early Elizabethan Prose Narratives* (Oxford: Clarendon Press, 1997); Curtis C. Breight, *Surveillance, Militarism and Drama in the Elizabethan Era* (Basingstoke: Palgrave, 1996); David Riggs, *The World of Christopher Marlowe* (London: Faber, 2004), chs. 7, 12–14.

83 Lucius Annaeus Seneca, *Letters from a Stoic*, trans. Robin Campbell (Harmondsworth: Penguin, 1969); Janet Coleman, *A History of Political Thought*, 2 vols. (Oxford: Blackwell, 2000), I, chs. 5–6. On the conception of Stoicism in the Renaissance, see Jill Kraye, 'Moral Philosophy', in Charles B. Schmitt and Quentin Skinner, eds., *The Cambridge History of Renaissance Philosophy* (Cambridge: Cambridge University Press, 1988), pp. 303–86, at pp. 360–75; Miles, *Shakespeare and the Constant Romans*, ch. 7.

84 Cynthia Marshall, 'Portia's Wound, Calphurnia's Dream: Reading Character in *Julius Caesar*', in Wilson, ed., *Julius Caesar*, pp. 170–87, at p. 173.

85 See the well-known analysis in G. Wilson Knight, *The Wheel of Fire: Interpretations of Shakespearean Tragedy* (London: Routledge, 1989, rpt. of 1930), ch. 6. See also Gail Kern Paster, '"In the spirit of men there is no blood": Blood as Trope of Gender in *Julius Caesar*', in Wilson, ed., *Julius Caesar*, pp. 149–69.

86 On Elizabeth, see Carole Levin, *The Heart and Stomach of a King: Elizabeth I and the Politics of Sex and Power* (Philadelphia: University of Pennsylvania Press, 1994). On tyranny, see Rebecca Bushnell, *Tragedies of Tyrants: Political Thought and Theater in the English Renaissance* (Ithaca, N.Y.: Cornell University Press, 1990).

87 Stephanus Junius Brutus, the Celt, *Vindiciae, Contra Tyrannos, or, concerning the legitimate power of a prince over the people, and of the people over a prince* (1579), ed. George Garnett (Cambridge: Cambridge University Press, 1994), pp. 63–66.

88 For analysis of the discussion of the rights and wrongs of the killing of Caesar, see Miola, '*Julius Caesar* and the Tyrannicide Debate', 271–90; Paulina Kewes, '*Julius Caesar* in Jacobean England', *The Seventeenth Century* 17 (2002), 155–86.

89 William L. Davidson, *The Stoic Creed* (Edinburgh: T. & T. Clark, 1907), p. 156; E. Vernon Arnold, *Roman Stoicism* (Cambridge: Cambridge University Press, 1911), p. 366.

90 For analysis of this notion in the Renaissance, see Wayne C. Rebhorn, *The Emperor of Men's Minds: Literature and the Renaissance Discourse of Rhetoric* (Ithaca, N.Y.: Cornell University Press, 1995), ch. 1.

91 See Michael Wood, *In Search of Shakespeare* (London: BBC, 2003), p. 52. See also Thomas Wilson, *Arte of Rhetorique*, ed. Thomas J. Derrick (New York: Garland, 1982), p. 143.

92 The treatise on eloquence, *Orator*, was also addressed to Brutus: see Cicero, *Brutus and Orator*, trans. H. M. Hendrickson and H. M. Hubbell (London: Heinemann, 1952). Shakespeare refers to this work in *Titus Andronicus*, 4.1.14: see Gillespie, *Shakespeare's Books*, p. 109.

93 Cicero, *Brutus and Orator*, pp. 53–55.

94 Brian Vickers, *In Defence of Rhetoric* (Oxford: Clarendon Press, 1988), p. 491; Wilson, *Arte of Rhetorique*, pp. 399–400.

95 For comment, see Leggatt, *Shakespeare's Political Drama*, p. 140; Miola, *Shakespeare's Rome*, pp. 81–82.

96 Kraye, 'Moral Philosophy', in Schmitt and Skinner, eds., *Cambridge History of Renaissance Philosophy*, 1988), pp. 303–86, at pp. 365–68.

97 For analysis, see Kahn, *Roman Shakespeare*, pp. 90–91.

98 Wilson, *Arte of Rhetorique*, bk. I; Cicero, *De Oratore*, trans. E. W. Sutton and H. Rackham, 2 vols. (London: Heinemann, 1959), I, p. 99.

99 Wilson, *Arte of Rhetorique*, pp. 54, 76, 184.

100 Ibid., pp. 33–34; Cicero, *De Oratore*, I, p. 99.

101 Brutus, *Vindiciae, Contra Tyrannos*, pp. 50–66; Buchanan, *Law of Kingship*, pp. 155–57, *passim*; Robert M. Kingdon, 'Calvinism and Resistance Theory, 1550–1580', in Burns and Goldie, eds., *Cambridge History of Political Thought*, pp. 193–218.

102 For discussion, see Miles, *Shakespeare and the Constant Romans*, ch. 7.

103 On Caesar's popularity, see Plutarch, 'Life of Julius Caesar', in *Selected Lives*, ed. Mossman, p. 519.

104 Plutarch, 'Life of Marcus Brutus', in *Selected Lives*, ed. Mossman p. 830.

105 See also Plutarch, 'Life of Marcus Antonius', in *Selected Lives*, ed. Mossman, pp. 677–756.

106 See Ian Donaldson, '"Misconstruing Everything": *Julius Caesar* and *Sejanus*', in Grace Ioppolo, ed., *Shakespeare Performed: Essays in Honour of R. A. Foakes* (Newark: University of Delaware Press, 2000), pp. 88–107, at p. 89. See also Wayne C. Rebbhorn, 'The Crisis of the Aristocracy in *Julius Caesar*', *RQ* 43 (1990), 78–109; Bushnell, '*Julius Caesar*'; Robin Headlam Wells, '*Julius Caesar*, Machiavelli, and the Uses of History', *Sh. Sur.* 55 (2002), 209–18, p. 211.

107 Donaldson, '"Misconstruing Everything"', pp. 90–91.

108 For discussion, see Axton, *The Queen's Two Bodies;* David Bevington, *Tudor Drama and Politics: A Critical Approach to Topical Meaning* (Cambridge, Mass.: Harvard University Press, 1968), chs. 17–18.

109 *Troilus and Cressida*, ed. David Bevington (London: Thomson: The Arden Shakespeare, 1998), 2.1.1003–4.

110 I owe this point to Jim Shapiro. On the Irish war, see Steven G. Ellis, *Tudor Ireland: Crown, Community and the Conflict of Cultures, 1470–1603* (London: Longman, 1985), ch. 9. See also Nicholas de Somogyi, *Shakespeare's Theatre of War* (Aldershot: Ashgate, 1998); Nina Taunton, *1590s Drama and Militarism: Portrayals of War in Marlowe, Chapman and Shakespeare's Henry V* (Aldershot: Ashgate, 2001).

THE RADICAL HAMLET

1 Thomas Nashe, *The Works of Thomas Nashe*, ed. Ronald B. McKerrow, corrected by F. P. Wilson, 5 vols. (Oxford: Basil Blackwell, 1966), III, p. 315.
2 Ibid., p. 316. For comment, see Katherine Duncan-Jones, 'Did the Boy Shakespeare Kill Calves?', *RES*, ns, 55 (2004), 183–95, at 188–89. Duncan-Jones speculates that Nashes's references to *Hamlet* suggest Shakespeare's authorship. Nashe seems to have a quotation from Spenser in mind, which might suggest that the reference relates to the Nashe–Harvey quarrel: see Edmund Spenser, *The Shepheardes Calender*, in *The Shorter Poems*, ed. Richard A. McCabe (Harmondsworth: Penguin, 1999), 'May' eclogue, line 276 (p. 80). On the Nashe–Harvey quarrel, see G. R. Hibbard, *Thomas Nashe: A Critical Introduction* (London: Routledge, 1962), ch. 7; Lorna Hutson, *Thomas Nashe in Context* (Oxford: Clarendon Press, 1989), ch. 10.
3 Thomas Kyd, *The Spanish Tragedy*, ed. Philip Edwards (Manchester: Manchester University Press, 1977, rpt. of 1959), introduction, p. xvii.
4 Cited in William Shakespeare, *Hamlet*, ed. Harold Jenkins (London: Routledge: The Arden Shakespeare, 1982), introduction, pp. 83–84. See also Shakespeare, *Hamlet*, ed. Philip Edwards (Cambridge: Cambridge University Press: The Cambridge Shakespeare, rev. ed., 2003), introduction, pp. 2–3; Shakespeare, *Hamlet*, ed. G. R. Hibbard (Oxford: Oxford University Press: The Oxford Shakespeare, 1987), introduction, pp. 12–14. On Newington Butts Theatre, see Andrew Gurr, *The Shakespearian Playing Companies* (Oxford: Clarendon Press, 1996), pp. 171–72, *passim*; Roslyn Lander Knutson, *Playing Companies and Commerce in Shakespeare's Time* (Cambridge: Cambridge University Press, 2001), pp. 39–40.
5 Peter Blaney, 'The Publication of Playbooks', in John D. Cox and David Scott Kastan, eds., *A New History of English Drama* (New York: Columbia University Press, 1997), pp. 383–422; Lukas Erne, *Shakespeare as Literary Dramatist* (Cambridge: Cambridge University Press, 2003), ch. 1; Alfred Harbage, *Annals of English Drama, 975–1700: An Annotated Record of all Plays, Extant or Lost, Chronologically Arranged and Indexed by Authors, Titles, Dramatic Companies, Etc.*, rev. S. Schoenbaum (London: Routledge, 3rd ed., 1989).
6 Shakespeare, *Hamlet*, ed. Edwards, introduction, pp. 7–8; *Hamlet*, ed. Hibbard, introduction, pp. 3–5; *Hamlet*, ed. Jenkins, introduction, pp. 1–13. See also Leah Marcus, *Unediting the Renaissance: Shakespeare, Marlowe, Milton* (London: Routledge, 1996), ch. 5.

7 For discussion, see William Shakespeare, *The First Quarto of Hamlet*, ed. Katherine O. Irace (Cambridge: Cambridge University Press, 1998); Laurie E. Maguire, *Shakespeare's Suspect Texts: The 'Bad' Quartos and their Contexts* (Cambridge: Cambridge University Press, 1996), pp. 255–57, *passim*.

8 Subsequent line references in parentheses in the text are to *Hamlet*, ed. Jenkins.

9 *First Quarto of Hamlet*, ed. Irace, introduction, p. 9.

10 Ibid., pp. 9–11.

11 Ibid., p. 15.

12 Ibid., p. 11.

13 See R. A. Foakes, ***Hamlet** Versus **Lear*** (Cambridge: Cambridge University Press, 1993), pp. 90–97.

14 See Erne, *Shakespeare as Literary Dramatist*. See also E. A. J. Honigmann, *The Texts of 'Othello' and Shakespearean Revision* (London: Nelson, 1996); Grace Ioppolo, *Revising Shakespeare* (Cambridge, Mass.: Harvard University Press, 1991). The first complete Shakespeare text to tackle the issue of revision was William Shakespeare, *The Complete Works*, ed. Stanley Wells and Gary Taylor (Oxford: Oxford University Press, 1988).

15 See Samuel Johnson, *Samuel Johnson on Shakespeare*, ed. H. R. Woudhuysen (Harmondsworth: Penguin, 1989), p. 243; Harley Granville-Barker, *Prefaces to Shakespeare: **Hamlet*** (London: Batsford, 1963, rpt. of 1930), p. 37. See also A. C. Bradley, *Shakespearean Tragedy: Lectures on **Hamlet**, **Othello**, **King Lear**, **Macbeth*** (London: Macmillan, 1918, rpt. of 1904), p. 89; Foakes, ***Hamlet** Versus **Lear***, ch. 2.

16 For details, see William Shakespeare, *Hamlet, Prince of Denmark*, ed. Robert Hapgood (Cambridge: Cambridge University Press: Shakespeare in Performance, 1999).

17 See, for example, William Kerrigan, *Hamlet's Perfection* (Baltimore: Johns Hopkins University Press, 1994), p. 51.

18 Shakespeare, *Hamlet*, ed. Jenkins, introduction, p. 84.

19 See Anne N. McLaren, 'Gender, Religion, and Early Modern Nationalism: Elizabeth I, Mary Queen of Scots, and the Genesis of English Anti-Catholicism', *AHR* 107 (2002), 739–67; Carol Z. Weiner, 'The Beleaguered Isle: A Study of Elizabethan and Early Jacobean Anti-Catholicism', *P. & P.* 51 (1971), 27–62.

20 See above, pp. 89–92.

21 Stuart Gillespie, *Shakespeare's Books: A Dictionary of Shakespeare Sources* (London: Athlone, 2001), pp. 36–41; Sir Israel Gollancz, *The Sources of 'Hamlet'* (London: Oxford University Press, 1926).

22 Livy, *The Early History of Rome*, trans. Aubrey de Sélincourt (Harmondsworth: Penguin, 1960), p. 80.

23 Ibid., p. 81.

24 Ibid., pp. 84–85.

25 For some relatively recent examples, which are typical of the debates about the play, see Francis Barker, *The Tremulous Private Body: Essays on Subjection*

(London: Methuen, 1984), pt. 1; Catherine Belsey, *The Subject of Tragedy: Identity and Difference in Renaissance Drama* (London: Methuen, 1985), pp. 112–16, *passim*; Ronald Knowles, 'Hamlet and Counter-Humanism', *RQ* 52 (1999), 1046–69.

26 See Shakespeare, *Hamlet*, ed. Hibbard, introduction, p. 6; Geoffrey Bullough, *Narrative and Dramatic Sources of Shakespeare*, 8 vols. (London: Routledge, 1957–75), VII (1973), p. 11.

27 Bullough, *Narrative and Dramatic Sources*, VII, p. 81.

28 Ibid., VII, pp. 82–83.

29 James Hankins, ed., *Renaissance Civic Humanism* (Cambridge: Cambridge University Press, 2000); Blair Worden, 'English Republicanism', in J. H. Burns and Mark Goldie, eds., *The Cambridge History of Political Thought, 1450–1700* (Cambridge: Cambridge University Press, 1991), pp. 443–75; J. G. A. Pocock, *The Machiavellian Moment: Florentine Political Thought and the Atlantic Republican Tradition* (Princeton: Princeton University Press, 1975), pt. 3.

30 See, especially, Lillian Winstanley, **Hamlet** *and the Scottish Succession* (Cambridge: Cambridge University Press, 1921); Stuart M. Kurland, '*Hamlet* and the Scottish Succession?', *SEL* 34 (1994), 279–300; Howard Erskine-Hill, *Poetry and the Realm of Politics: Shakespeare to Dryden* (Oxford: Clarendon Press, 1996), pp. 99–109.

31 See Andrew Hadfield, *Shakespeare, Spenser and the Matter of Britain* (Basingstoke: Palgrave/Macmillan, 2003), chs. 3, 8; Erskine-Hill, *Poetry and the Realm of Politics*, ch. 1; James Emerson Phillips, *Images of a Queen: Mary Stuart in Sixteenth-Century Literature* (Berkeley: University of California Press, 1964).

32 See Robert M. Kingdon, *Myths about the Saint Bartholomew's Day Massacres, 1572–1576* (Cambridge, Mass.: Harvard University Press, 1988).

33 Antonia Fraser, *Mary Queen of Scots* (London: Weidenfeld and Nicolson, 1969), ch.3 ; Roger A. Mason, 'George Buchanan, James VI and the Presbyterians', in Roger A. Mason, ed., *Scots and Britons: Scottish Political Thought and the Union of 1603* (Cambridge: Cambridge University Press, 1994), pp. 112–37; Hadfield, *Shakespeare, Spenser and the Matter of Britain*, ch. 3.

34 David Harris Willson, *King James VI and I* (London: Cape, 1956), pp. 42–48.

35 Subsequent references are to William Shakespeare, *Macbeth*, ed. Kenneth Muir (London: Routledge: The Arden Shakespeare, rev. ed., 1984). For a contemporary dramatic analysis of a traitor, see the anonymous play, *The Famous Historye of the life and death of Captaine Thomas Stukeley*, ed. Judith C. Levinson (Oxford: Malone Society, 1975).

36 See Shakespeare, *Macbeth*, ed. Muir, introduction, pp. xxv–xxxii.

37 Hence it is hard to read *Macbeth* as a celebration of royal power, as was once the case. See Henry N. Paul, *The Royal Play of* **Macbeth** (New York: Macmillan, 1948); Leonard Tennenhouse, *Power on Display: The Politics of Shakespeare's Genres* (London: Methuen, 1986). For the contrary argument,

see Alan Sinfield, '*Macbeth*: History, Ideology, and Intellectuals', in Sinfield, *Faultlines: Cultural Materialism and the Politics of Dissident Reading* (Oxford: Clarendon Press, 1992), pp. 95–108; David Norbrook, '*Macbeth* and the Politics of Historiography', in Kevin Sharpe and Steven N. Zwicker, eds., *Politics of Discourse: The Literature and History of Seventeenth-Century England* (Berkeley: University of California Press, 1987), pp. 78–116; David Scott Kastan, '*Macbeth* and the "Name of King"', in Kastan, *Shakespeare After Theory* (London: Routledge, 1999), pp. 165–82.

38 See above, pp. 35–39.

39 For discussion, see the important work of Anne N. McLaren, *Political Culture in the Reign of Elizabeth I: Queen and Commonwealth, 1558–1585* (Cambridge: Cambridge University Press, 1999); 'Gender, Religion, and Early Modern Nationalism', 739–67.

40 John Knox, *On Rebellion*, ed. Roger A. Mason (Cambridge: Cambridge University Press, 1994), introduction, p. xvi.

41 Ibid., p. 177.

42 Ibid., p. 9.

43 Ibid., pp. 28–29.

44 For discussion see ibid., introduction; Robert M. Kingdon, 'Calvinism and Resistance Theory, 1550–1580', in Burns and Goldie, eds., *Cambridge History of Political Thought*, pp. 193–218, at pp. 193–200.

45 Stephanus Julius Brutus, the Celt, *Vindiciae, Contra Tyrannos, or, concerning the legitimate power of a prince over the people, and the people over a prince*, ed. and trans. George Garnett (Cambridge: Cambridge University Press, 1994), p. 74.

46 See above, pp. 39–40. For analysis, see Alison Taufer, *Holinshed's **Chronicles*** (New York: Twayne, 1999), ch. 5; Norbrook, '*Macbeth* and the Politics of Historiography', pp. 81–93.

47 See the extensive narratives in *Rerum Scoticarum Historia* (1582), published as *The History of Scotland written in Latin by George Buchanan: faithfully rendered into English*, J. Fraser (London, 1690), bks. XVI–XX; *Ane Detectioun of the duinges of Marie Quene of Scottes* (1571). See above, pp. 144–46.

48 See Gillespie, *Shakespeare's Books*, pp. 71–74. Buchanan was also relying on Hector Boece's *Scotorum Historiae*, a major source of the narrative in Holinshed (Buchanan's *History* did not appear until 1582).

49 Raphael Holinshed, *Chronicle of Scotland* (Arbroath: J. Findlay, 1805), p. 301. Subsequent references to this edition in parentheses in the text.

50 See Buchanan, *History of Scotland*, bks. VI–VII; Norbrook, '*Macbeth* and the Politics of Historiography', pp. 86–88.

51 Jonathan Goldberg refers to this incident in his essay, 'Speculations: *Macbeth* and Source', in Jean E. Howard and Marion F. O'Connor, eds., *Shakespeare Reproduced: The Text in History & Ideology* (London: Routledge, 1987), pp. 242–64, at pp. 249–50.

52 See Janet Clare, *'Art Made Tongue-Tied by Authority': Elizabethan and Jacobean Dramatic Censorship* (2nd ed., Manchester: Manchester University Press, 1999), ch. 3, for the impact of this injunction on drama.

53 See Robin Headlam Wells, '"The Question of These Wars": *Hamlet* in the New Europe', in Michael Hattaway, Boika Sokolova and Derek Roper, eds., *Shakespeare in the New Europe* (Sheffield : Sheffield Acadamic Press, 1995), pp. 92–109, at p. 95.

54 Annabel Patterson, *Censorship and Interpretation: The Conditions of Writing in Early Modern England* (Madison: University of Wisconsin Press, 1984).

55 Shakespeare, *Hamlet*, ed. Jenkins, introduction, pp. 1–13.

56 For further discussion, see Andrew Hadfield, *Shakespeare and Renaissance Political Culture* (London: Thomson: Arden Critical Companions, 2003), especially ch. 2.

57 Taufer, *Holinshed's **Chronicles***, pp. 131–33.

58 Harbage, *Annals of English Drama*, pp. 54, 82.

59 For discussion, see Erskine-Hill, *Poetry and the Realm of Politics*, pp. 103–6; Winstanley, ***Hamlet** and the Scottish Succession*, ch. 2.

60 See Erskine-Hill, *Poetry and the Realm of Politics*, p. 105. On the literature written in the wake of Darnley's murder, see Phillips, *Images of a Queen*, chs. 2–3.

61 Erskine-Hill, *Poetry and the Realm of Politics*, p. 107.

62 This section draws in part on the argument in my *Shakespeare and Renaissance Politics*, ch. 2.

63 Graham Holderness sees the discussion of the nature of history as a central feature of Shakespeare's history plays: see *Shakespeare: The Histories* (Basingstoke: Macmillan, 2000), chs. 2–3.

64 For the most extensive discussion of the ghost, see Stephen Greenblatt, *Hamlet in Purgatory* (Princeton: Princeton University Press, 2001).

65 Brutus, *Vindiciae, Contra Tyrannos*, pp. 20–21.

66 Phillips, *Images of a Queen*, ch. 3. See also Sarah M. Dunnigan, *Eros and Poetry at the Courts of Mary Queen of Scots and James VI* (Basingstoke: Palgrave, 2002), pt. 1.

67 *The Tyrannous Reign of Mary Stewart: George Buchanan's Account*, trans. and ed. W. A. Gatherer (Edinburgh: The University Press, 1958), p. 169. In *The History of Scotland*, Buchanan claims that Mary's French education failed to instruct her properly so that 'the seeds of virtue, wizened by the allurements of luxury, would be prevented from reaching ripeness and fruition' (p. 54).

68 Phillips, *Images of a Queen*, p. 34.

69 See, for example, Juliet Dusinberre, *Shakespeare and the Nature of Women* (2ⁿᵈ ed., Basingstoke: Macmillan, 1996), *passim*; Kay Stanton, '"Made to write "whore" upon?': Male and Female Use of the Word "Whore" in Shakespeare's Canon', in Dympna Callaghan, ed., *A Feminist Companion to Shakespeare* (Oxford: Blackwell, 2000), pp. 80–102, at pp. 86–88.

70 Dunnigan, *Eros and Poetry*, pp. 23–27.

71 Much criticism of *Hamlet* does seek to explain the play's topical and political significance: see, for example, Robin Headlam Wells, *Shakespeare, Politics and the State* (Basingstoke: Macmillan, 1986), 101–3, 155–57; Alvin Kernan, *Shakespeare, The King's Playwright: Theater in the Stuart Court, 1603–1613*

(New Haven: Yale University Press, 1995), pp. 30–32, *passim*; Lisa Jardine, *Reading Shakespeare Historically* (London: Routledge, 1996), chs. 2, 9. Michael Neill's reading of *Hamlet* in terms of friendship, real and perverted, further underlines the republican nature of the play: '"He that thou knowest thine": Friendship and Service in *Hamlet*', in Richard Dutton and Jean E. Howard, eds., *A Companion to Shakespeare's Works*, 4 vols., *Volume I, The Tragedies* (Oxford: Blackwell, 2003), I, pp. 319–38.

72 See J. P. Sommerville, 'Absolutism and Royalism', in Burns and Goldie, eds., *Cambridge History of Political Thought*, pp. 347–73, at pp. 361–67.

73 A convenient collection of the relevant material is Elizabeth Jayne Lewis, *The Trial of Mary Queen of Scots: A Brief History with Documents* (Boston: Bedford, 1999).

74 See Robert Parsons [Doleman], *A Conference about the Next Succession to the Crowne of Ingland* (1594); Peter Wentworth, *A Pithie Exhortation to Her Majestie for Establishing her Successor to the Crowne* (1598); Marie Axton, *The Queen's Two Bodies: Drama and the Elizabethan Succession* (London: Royal Historical Society, 1977).

75 Richard A. McCabe, 'The Masks of Duessa: Spenser, Mary Queen of Scots, and James VI', *ELR* 17 (1987), 224–42.

76 See Greg Walker, *Plays of Persuasion: Drama and Politics at the Court of Henry VIII* (Cambridge: Cambridge University Press, 1991).

AFTER THE REPUBLICAN MOMENT

1 Constance Jordan, *Shakespeare's Monarchies: Ruler and Subject in the Romances* (Ithaca, N.Y.: Cornell University Press, 1997); Stuart M. Kurland, '*Henry VIII* and James I: Shakespeare and Jacobean Politics', *Sh. St.* 19 (1987), 203–17.

2 Simon Palfrey, *Late Shakespeare: A New World of Words* (Oxford: Clarendon Press, 1997), p. 48; William Shakespeare, *Pericles*, ed. Suzanne Gosset (London: Thomson: The Arden Shakespeare, 2004), introduction, pp. 121–26.

3 Mary Ann McGrail, *Tyranny in Shakespeare* (Lanham: Lexington Books, 2001); Donna B. Hamilton, *Virgil and **The Tempest**: The Politics of Imitation* (Columbus: Ohio State University Press, 1990); Edward Berry, *Shakespeare and the Hunt: A Cultural and Social Study* (Cambridge: Cambridge University Press, 2001), ch. 7.

4 Andrew Hadfield, '*Timon of Athens* and Jacobean Politics', *Sh. Sur.* 56 (2003), 215–26. On James's reign, see Robert Ashton, ed., *James I by his Contemporaries: An Account of his Career and Character as seen by Some of his Contemporaries* (London: Hutchinson, 1969).

5 On the relationship between time and republicanism, see J. G. A. Pocock, *The Machiavellian Moment: Florentine Political Thought and the Atlantic Republican Tradition* (Princeton: Princeton University Press, 1975); Pocock, *Politics, Language and Time: Essays on Political Thought and History* (London: Methuen, 1972).

6 On James's religious beliefs, see Kenneth Fincham and Peter Lake, 'The Ecclesiastical Policy of King James I', *JBS* 24 (1985), 169–207; W. B. Patterson, *King James VI and I and the Reunion of Christendom* (Cambridge: Cambridge University Press, 1997).

7 Howard Erskine-Hill, *Poetry and the Realm of Politics: Shakespeare to Dryden* (Oxford: Clarendon Press, 1996); James Emerson Phillips, *Images of a Queen: Mary Stuart in Sixteenth-Century Literature* (Berkeley: University of California Press, 1964); Arthur H. Williamson, *Scottish National Consciousness in the Age of James VI* (Edinburgh: Donald, 1979).

8 Jenny Wormald, 'Gunpowder, Treason, and Scots', *JBS* 24 (1985), 141–68; Antonia Fraser, *The Gunpowder Plot: Terror & Faith in 1605* (London: Weidenfeld and Nicolson, 1996).

9 See Patterson, *King James VI and I and the Reunion of Christendom*, chs. 9–10; D. Harris Willson, *King James VI and I* (London: Cape, 1956), ch. 15; John S. Morrill, *The Revolt of the Provinces: Conservatives and Radicals in the English Civil War 1630–1650* (London: Allen and Unwin, 1976); Curtis Perry, *The Making of Jacobean Culture: James I and the Renegotiation of Elizabethan Literary Practice* (Cambridge: Cambridge University Press, 1997).

10 For a more sustained analysis, see Andrew Hadfield, *Shakespeare and Renaissance Politics* (London: Thomson: Arden Critical Companions, 2003), ch. 5.

11 Katherine Duncan-Jones, *Ungentle Shakespeare: Scenes From His Life* (London: Thomson, 2001), pp. 169–70; William Shakespeare, *Measure for Measure*, ed. J. W. Lever (London: Routledge: The Arden Shakespeare, 1988, rpt. of 1967), introduction, pp.xxxi–v. Subsequent references to this edition in parentheses in the text.

12 For recent comment, see Peter Lake, 'Ministers, Magistrates and the Production of "Order" in *Measure for Measure*', *Sh. Sur.* 54 (2001), 165–81; Debora Kuller Shuger, *Political Theologies in Shakespeare's England: The Sacred and the State in **Measure for Measure*** (Basingstoke: Palgrave, 2001); Andrew Barnaby and Joan Wry, 'Authorized Versions: *Measure for Measure* and the Politics of Biblical Translation', *RQ* 51 (1998), 1225–54.

13 For analysis, see Paul Hammond, 'The Argument of *Measure for Measure*', *ELR* 16 (1986), 496–519.

14 On the genre of 'disguised Duke' plays, see Albert H. Tricomi, *Anticourt Drama in England, 1603–1642* (Charlottesville: University Press of Virginia, 1989), pp. 13–24.

15 Andrew Hadfield, 'Shakespeare's *Measure for Measure* (and the Homosexuality of James I)', *The Explicator* 61 (2003), 71–73; Paul Hammond, *Figuring Sex between Men from Shakespeare to Rochester* (Oxford: Oxford University Press, 2002), p. 135. See also Josephine Waters Bennett, ***Measure for Measure** as Royal Entertainment* (New York: Columbia University Press, 1966); Leah S. Marcus, *Puzzling Shakespeare: Local Reading and its Discontents* (Berkeley: University of California Press, 1988), pp. 160–202.

16 Jacques Lezra, 'The Appearance of History in *Measure for Measure*', in Lezra, *Unspeakable Subjects: The Genealogy of the Event in Early Modern Europe* (Stanford: Stanford University Press, 1997), pp. 257–96.

17 On the 'bed trick', see Marliss C. Desens, *The Bed Trick in English Renaissance Drama* (Newark: University of Delaware Press, 1994). On the plot, see Neil Rhodes, *Shakespeare and the Origins of English* (Oxford: Oxford University Press, 2004), pp. 105–10.

18 For uses of 'whoreson', see William Shakespeare, *Troilus and Cressida* ed. David Bevington (London: Thomson: The Arden Shakespeare, 1998), 2.1.39; William Shakespeare, *Hamlet*, ed. Harold Jenkins (London: Routledge: The Arden Shakespeare, 1982), 5.1.166.

19 See Margaret Healy, *Fictions of Disease in Early Modern England: Bodies, Plagues and Politics* (Basingstoke: Palgrave/Macmillan, 2001), pp. 173–78; Lawrence Manley, *Literature and Culture in Early Modern London* (Cambridge: Cambridge University Press, 1995), pp. 455–57.

20 For further discussion, see Hadfield, *Shakespeare and Renaissance Politics*, pp. 189–200.

21 *Measure for Measure*, ed. Lever, introduction, pp.xlv-xlvi; Marcus, *Puzzling Shakespeare*, pp. 160–202. On the suburbs, see John Stow, *A Survey of London* (1603), ed. Charles Lethbridge Kingsford, 2 vols. (Oxford: Clarendon Press, 2000), 'The Suburbes without the Walles', II, pp. 69–91. On the possible relationship between Stow's writings and dramatists, see Angela Stock, 'Stow's *Survey* and the London Playwrights', in Ian Gadd and Alexandra Gillespie, eds., *John Stow (1525–1605) and the Making of the English Past* (London: British Library, 2004), pp. 89–98.

22 See Rebecca Bushnell, *Tragedies of Tyrants: Political Thought and Theater in the English Renaissance* (Ithaca, N.Y.: Cornell University Press, 1990); McGrail, *Tyranny in Shakespeare*.

23 On the Elizabethan underworld, see Gamini Salgado, *The Elizabethan Underworld* (London: Dent, 1977); Salgado, ed., *Cony-Catchers and Bawdy Baskets: An Anthology of Elizabethan Low Life* (Harmondsworth: Penguin, 1972); Ian W. Archer, *The Pursuit of Stability: Social Relations in Elizabethan London* (Cambridge: Cambridge University Press, 1991), ch. 6.

24 See, especially, 2.4.170–86.

25 For comment, see B. J. Sokol and Mary Sokol, *Shakespeare's Legal Language: A Dictionary* (London: Athlone, 2000), pp. 319–24; G. R. Elton, ed., *The Tudor Constitution: Documents and Commentary* (Cambridge: Cambridge University Press, 1972), chs. 5–7.

26 See above, pp. 145–46.

27 Susan Brigden, *New Worlds, Lost Worlds: The Rule of the Tudors, 1485–1603* (London: Penguin, 2000), pp. 287–89; John Guy, *Tudor England* (Oxford: Oxford University Press, 1988), pp. 331–32.

28 Anne N. McLaren, 'Gender, Religion, and Early Modern Nationalism: Elizabeth I, Mary Queen of Scots, and the Genesis of English Anti-Catholicism', *AHR* 107 (2002), 739–67.

29 Guy, *Tudor England*, pp. 335–36; J. B. Black, *The Reign of Elizabeth, 1558–1603* (Oxford: Clarendon Press, 1959, 2nd ed.), pp. 382–88; Antonia Fraser, *Mary Queen of Scots* (London: Weidenfeld and Nicolson, 1969), chs. 25–26.

30 Fraser, *Mary Queen of Scots*, ch. 25.

31 See Paul Yachnin, 'Shakespeare's Problem Plays and the Drama of His Time: *Troilus and Cressida, All's Well That Ends Well, Measure for Measure*', in Richard Dutton and Jean E. Howard, eds., *A Companion to Shakespeare's Works*, 4 vols., *Volume IV: The Poems, Problem Comedies, Late Plays* (Oxford: Blackwell, 2003), pp. 46–68; George L. Geckle, ed., *Measure for Measure: Shakespeare: The Critical Tradition* (London: Athlone, 2001).

32 Alan C. Dessen, *Rescripting Shakespeare: The Text, The Director, and Modern Productions* (Cambridge: Cambridge University Press, 2002), pp. 133–35; Edward L. Rockin, 'Measured Endings: How Productions from 1720 to 1929 Close Shakespeare's Open Silences in *Measure for Measure*', *Sh. Sur.* 53 (2000), 213–32; Peter Holland, 'Shakespeare Performances in England, 1993–1994', *Sh. Sur.* 48 (1995), 191–226, pp. 217–22.

33 See Karen Cunningham, 'Opening Doubts Upon the Law: *Measure for Measure*', in Dutton and Howard, eds., *Companion to Shakespeare's Works*, IV, pp. 316–32.

34 See Ashton, ed., *James I by his Contemporaries, passim*.

35 See K. J. Kesselring, *Mercy and Authority in the Tudor State* (Cambridge: Cambridge University Press, 2003), ch. 1.

36 Sokol and Sokol, *Shakespeare's Legal Language*, p. 310.

37 John Bellamy, *The Tudor Law of Treason: An Introduction* (London: Routledge, 1979), pp. 25, 27; Sokol and Sokol, *Shakespeare's Legal Language*, pp. 207–12. See also M. Lindsay Kaplan, 'Slander for Slander in *Measure for Measure*', in Kaplan, *The Culture of Slander in Early Modern England* (Cambridge: Cambridge University Press, 1997), pp. 92–108.

38 Barnaby and Wry, 'Authorized Versions'.

39 Jenny Wormald, 'James VI and I, *Basilikon Doron* and *The Trew Law of Free Monarchies*: The Scottish context and the English Translation', in Linda Levy Peck, ed., *The Mental World of the Jacobean Court* (Cambridge: Cambridge University Press, 1991), pp. 36–54; Hadfield, *Shakespeare and Renaissance Politics*, ch. 5.

40 William Shakespeare, *Othello*, ed. Ernst Honigmann (London: Thomson: The Arden Shakespeare, 1997), appendices 1–3. Subsequent references to this edition in parentheses in the text.

41 Andrew Hadfield, *Literature, Travel and Colonial Writing in the English Renaissance, 1545–1625* (Oxford: Clarendon Press, 1998), pp. 49–67, *passim*; A. Lytton Sells, *The Paradise of Travellers: The Italian Influence on Englishmen in the Seventeenth Century* (London: Allen and Unwin, 1964).

42 Conti, Vittorio, 'The Mechanisation of Virtue: Republican Rituals in Italian Political Thought in the Sixteenth and Seventeenth Centuries', in Martin van Gelderen and Quentin Skinner, eds., *Republicanism: A Shared European*

Heritage, 2 vols. (Cambridge: Cambridge University Press, 2002), II, pp. 73–83, at p. 73.

43 See above, pp. 41–42.

44 R. B. Wernham, *After the Armada: Elizabethan England and the Struggle for Western Europe, 1588–1595* (Oxford: Clarendon Press, 1984), pp. 143, 194.

45 For a recent analysis, see Mark Matheson, 'Venetian Culture and the Politics of *Othello*', *Sh. Sur.* 48 (1995), 123–33. In the light of the rivalry between Jonson and Shakespeare, it is possible that Jonson's satirical analysis of Venetian justice in *Volpone* (1605) may be a response to the success of *Othello*, although this can be no more than speculation, given the lack of evidence. See David Riggs, *Ben Jonson: A Life* (Cambridge, Mass.: Harvard University Press, 1989), ch. 7; James P. Bednarz, *Shakespeare & The Poets' War* (New York: Columbia University Press, 2001).

46 Barbara Everett, '"Spanish" Othello: The Making of Shakespeare's Moor', in Catherine M. S. Alexander and Stanley Wells, eds., *Shakespeare and Race* (Cambridge: Cambridge University Press, 2000), pp. 64–81.

47 See James Shapiro, *Shakespeare and the Jews* (New York: Columbia University Press, 1996), *passim*.

48 See Virginia Mason Vaughan, *Othello: A Contextual History* (Cambridge: Cambridge University Press, 1994), ch. 1.

49 Andrew Hadfield, ed., *A Routledge Literary Sourcebook on William Shakespeare's* **Othello** (London: Routledge, 2003), pp. 44–47, *passim*.

50 For fuller analysis, see Karen Newman, '"And wash the Ethiop white": Femininity and the Monstrous in *Othello*', in Jean E. Howard and Marion F. O'Connor, eds., *Shakespeare Reproduced: The Text in History & Ideology* (London: Routledge, 1987), pp. 143–62.

51 Hadfield, ed., *Sourcebook on* **Othello**, p. 49.

52 See Lisa Jardine, '"Why should he call her whore?": Defamation and Desdemona's case', in Jardine, *Reading Shakespeare Historically* (London: Routledge, 1996), pp. 19–34.

53 Lois Potter, **Othello***: Shakespeare in Performance* (Manchester: Manchester University Press, 2002), *passim*; *Othello*, ed. Julie Hankey (Bristol: Bristol Classical Press: Plays in Performance, 1987).

54 Conti, 'Mechanisation of Virtue'; Pocock, *Machiavellian Moment*, pp. 73–6, *passim*; James M. Blythe, '"Civic Humanism" and Medieval Political Thought', in James Hankins, ed., *Renaissance Civic Humanism* (Cambridge: Cambridge University Press, 2000), pp. 30–74; John M. Najemy, 'Civic Humanism and Florentine Politics', in Hankins, ed., *Renaissance Civic Humanism*, pp. 105–43; Martin Dzelzainis, 'Milton's Classical Republicanism', in David Armitage Himy Armand and Quentin Skinner, eds., *Milton and Republicanism* (Cambridge: Cambridge University Press, 1995), pp. 3–24.

55 Gaspar Contarini, *The Commonwealth and Government of Venice*, trans. Lewis Lewkenor (London, 1599), p. 7. Subsequent references to this edition in parentheses in the text.

56 Compare Sir Philip Sidney's famous words on nature and poetry in *An Apology for Poetry*, ed. Geoffrey Shepherd, rev. and expanded R. W. Maslen (Manchester: Manchester University Press, 2002), p. 85.

57 Polybius, *The Rise of the Roman Empire*, trans. Ian Scott-Kilvert (Harmondsworth: Penguin, 1979), pp. 338–52.

58 D. G. Hale, '*Coriolanus*: The Death of a Political Metaphor', *Sh. Sur.* 22 (1971), 197–202; Anne Barton, 'Livy, Machiavelli and Shakespeare's *Coriolanus*', in Barton, *Essays, Mainly Shakespearean* (Cambridge: Cambridge University Press, 1994), pp. 136–60. See also C. C. Huffman, *Coriolanus in Context* (Lewisburg: Bucknell University Press, 1971).

59 See above, p. 198.

60 Robin Headlam Wells, *Shakespeare on Masculinity* (Cambridge: Cambridge University Press, 2000), ch. 3; Vaughan, *Othello: A Contextual History*, ch. 2.

61 Geraldo U. de Sousa, *Shakespeare's Cross-Cultural Encounters* (Basingstoke: Macmillan, 1999), pp. 113–28; Vaughan, *Othello: A Contextual History*, ch. 3.

62 William Shakespeare, *Antony and Cleopatra*, ed. John Wilders (London: Routledge: The Arden Shakespeare, 1995), introduction, p. 74. Subsequent references to this edition in parentheses in the text.

63 It is possible, as Geoffrey Bullough speculates, that Shakespeare had planned *Antony and Cleopatra* to follow *Julius Caesar* as its immediate sequel, but that the Essex coup postponed the project for some years: Geoffrey Bullough, *Narrative and Dramatic Sources of Shakespeare*, 8 vols. (London: Routledge, 1957–75), V, p. 216; Margot Heinemann, '"Let Rome in Tiber melt": Order and Disorder in *Antony and Cleopatra*', in John Drakakis, ed., *Antony and Cleopatra: Contemporary Critical Essays* (Basingstoke: Macmillan, 1994), p. 173.

64 Shakespeare's main source was undoubtedly Plutarch's 'Life of Marcus Antonius' (*Selected Lives*, ed. Judith Mossman [Ware: Wordsworth, 1998], pp. 677–56).

65 Mary Sidney Herbert, *The Collected Works of Mary Sidney Herbert, Countess of Pembroke*, ed. Margaret P. Hannay, Noel J. Kinnamon and Michael G. Brennan, 2 vols. (Oxford: Clarendon Press, 1998), I, pp. 139–207; Samuel Daniel, *The Tragedie of Cleopatra*, in *Works*, ed. Grosart, III, pp. 1–94 (subsequent references to this edition in parentheses in the text); Pascale Aebischer, 'Cleopatra in the Closet: Sexuality, Race and Royalty in Jodelle, Garnier, Pembroke, and Daniel' (unpublished paper) (I am extremely grateful to Dr Aebischer for allowing me to see this important essay before publication). See also Clifford J. Ronan, '*Caesar's Revenge* and the Roman Thoughts in *Antony and Cleopatra*', *Sh. St.* 19 (1987), 171–82.

66 Shakespeare, *Antony and Cleopatra*, ed. Wilders, introduction, pp. 61–63; Stuart Gillespie, *Shakespeare's Books: A Dictionary of Shakespeare Sources* (London: Athlone, 2001), pp. 125–27.

67 Marcel Le Glay, Jean-Louis Voison, Yann Le Bohec and David Cherry, *A History of Rome* (2nd ed., Oxford: Blackwell, 2001), ch. 8.

68 Marie Axton, *The Queen's Two Bodies: Drama and the Elizabethan Succession* (London: Royal Historical Society, 1977); David Bevington, *Tudor Drama and Politics: A Critical Approach to Topical Meaning* (Cambridge, Mass.: Harvard University Press, 1968), ch. 18.

69 Janet Clare, *'Art Made Tongue-Tied by Authority': Elizabethan and Jacobean Dramatic Censorship* (2nd ed., Manchester: Manchester University Press, 1990), pp. 148–52.

70 See, for example, Linda T. Fitz, 'Egyptian Queens and Male Reviewers: Sexist Attitudes in *Antony and Cleopatra* Criticism', *SQ* 28 (1977), 297–316; Cynthia Marshall, 'Man of Steel Got the Blues: Melancholic Subversion of Presence in *Antony and Cleopatra*', *SQ* 44 (1993), 385–408; Jonathan Gil Harris, '"Narcissus in thy face": Roman Desire and the Difference it Fakes in *Antony and Cleopatra*', *SQ* 45 (1994), 408–25.

71 Heinemann, 'Order and Disorder', pp. 166–81, at p. 175.

72 H. Neville Davies, 'Jacobean *Antony and Cleopatra*', *Sh. St.* 17 (1985), 123–58, p. 125. See also Anthony Miller, *Roman Triumphs and Early Modern English Culture* (Basingstoke: Palgrave, 2001), ch. 6.

73 Graham Parry, *The Golden Age Restor'd: The Culture of the Stuart Court, 1603–42* (Manchester: Manchester University Press, 1981), pp. 16–17; Perry, *Making of Jacobean Culture*, pp. 24–36.

74 Henry Petowe, *Englands Caesar. His Majesties most Royall Coronation* (London, 1603); Samuel Rowlands, *Ave Caesar. God save the king* (London, 1603).

75 Perry, *Making of Jacobean Culture*, pp. 93–94.

76 See above, pp. 39–40.

77 Tacitus, *On Imperial Rome (The Annals)*, trans. Michael Grant (Harmondsworth: Penguin, 1956), p. 35. Subsequent references to this edition in parentheses in the text.

78 Suetonius, *The Twelve Caesars*, trans. Robert Graves (Harmondsworth: Penguin, 1957), p. 65.

79 Davies, 'Jacobean *Antony and Cleopatra*', p. 141. For comment, see *Antony and Cleopatra*, ed. Richard Madelaine (Cambridge: Cambridge University Press: Shakespeare in Performance, 1998), pp. 203–4; Jyotsna G. Singh, 'The Politics of Empathy in *Antony and Cleopatra*: A View From Below', in Dutton and Howard, eds., *Companion to Shakespeare's Works*, I, pp. 411–29, at p. 423.

80 See Tom Holland, *Rubicon: The Triumph and Tragedy of the Roman Republic* (London: Abacus, 2003), preface.

81 For discussion – which does not mention *Antony and Cleopatra* – see Ronald Knowles, ed., *Shakespeare and Carnival: After Bakhtin* (Basingstoke: Palgrave, 1998).

82 The meeting on the galley is mentioned in Plutarch: *Antony and Cleopatra*, ed. Wilders, p. 162.

83 Mervyn James, *Society, Politics and Culture: Studies in Early Modern Culture* (Cambridge: Cambridge University Press, 1988), chs. 8–9; Gary Spear,

'Shakespeare's "Manly" Parts: Masculinity and Effeminacy in *Troilus and Cressida*', *SQ* 44 (1993), 409–22.

84 See Jonathan Dollimore, *Radical Tragedy: Religion, Ideology and Power in the Drama of Shakespeare and his Contemporaries* (Brighton: Harvester, 1984), pp. 204–17.

85 See, for example, Peggy Muñoz Simonds, '"To the Very Heart of Loss": Renaissance Iconography in Shakespeare's *Antony and Cleopatra*', *Sh. St.* 22 (1994), 220–76.

86 Ania Loomba, *Gender, Race, Renaissance Drama* (Manchester: Manchester University Press, 1989), p. 76; Singh, 'Politics of Empathy', p. 414; T. Jankowski, *Women in Power in Early Modern Drama* (Urbana: University of Illinois Press, 1992), pp. 156–57.

87 See, for example, Richard Mulcaster, *The Queen's Majesty's Passage*, in Arthur Kinney, ed., *Renaissance Drama: An Anthology of Plays and Entertainments* (Oxford: Blackwell, 1999), pp. 17–34. More comprehensively, see J. Nichols, ed., *The Progresses and Public Processions of Queen Elizabeth*, 3 vols. (New York: Franklin, rpt. of 1823). Shakespeare is developing an elaborate description already available in Plutarch: see *Antony and Cleopatra*, ed. Wilders, p. 139; Phyllis Rackin, 'Shakespeare's Boy Cleopatra, the Decorum of Nature, and the Golden World of Poetry', in Drakakis, ed., *Antony and Cleopatra*, pp. 78–100, at p. 87. On James's distaste for public ritual, see Keith M. Brown, 'The Vanishing Emperor: British Kingship and its Decline, 1603–1707', in Roger A. Mason, ed., *Scots and Britons: Scottish Political Thought and the Union of 1603* (Cambridge: Cambridge University Press, 1994), pp. 58–87, at p. 68.

88 Arthur L. Little, Jr., *Shakespeare Jungle Fever: National-Imperial Re-Visions of Race, Rape, and Sacrifice* (Stanford: Stanford University Press, 2000), chs. 3–4; John Gillies, *Shakespeare and the Geography of Difference* (Cambridge: Cambridge University Press, 1994), pp. 59–69.

89 Read one way, the surviving history of the republic was replete with similar examples of self-interested treachery: see Holland, *Rubicon*.

90 See John Russell Brown, ed., **Antony and Cleopatra**: *A Selection of Critical Essays* (London: Macmillan, 1968), pp. 25–26.

91 Holland, *Rubicon*, pp. 361–62; Plutarch, 'Life of Marcus Tullis Cicero', in *Selected Lives*, ed. Mossman, pp. 563–611, at p. 608.

92 Patterson, *King James VI and I and the Reunion of Christendom*; Ashton, ed., *James I by his Contemporaries, passim*.

93 On Shakespeare and Tacitus, see Gillespie, *Shakespeare's Books*, pp. 477–80; Martin Dzelzainis, 'Shakespeare and Political Thought', in David Scott Kastan, ed., *A Companion to Shakespeare* (Oxford: Blackwell, 1999), pp. 100–16, at pp. 108–9. Neither of these works mentions *Antony and Cleopatra*.

94 Blair Worden, 'Republicanism, Regicide and Republic: The English Experience', in Martin van Gelderen and Quentin Skinner, eds., *Republicanism: A Shared European Heritage*, 2 vols. (Cambridge: Cambridge University Press, 2002), I, pp. 307–27.

CONCLUSION

1 For comment on the political significance of *The Winter's Tale,* see Constance Jordan, *Shakespeare's Monarchies: Ruler and Subject in the Romances* (Ithaca, N.Y.: Cornell University Press, 1997), ch. 4.

2 See, for example, Quentin Skinner, *Visions of Politics,* 3 vols. (Cambridge: Cambridge University Press, 2002), I, ch. 3; II, ch. 2.

3 For relevant but widely divergent approaches, see Brian Vickers, *Shakespeare, Co-Author: A Historical Study of Five Collaborative Plays* (Oxford: Oxford University Press, 2002); Jeffrey Masten, *Textual Intercourse: Collaboration, Authorship, and Sexualities in Renaissance Drama* (Cambridge: Cambridge University Press, 1997).

4 Jonathan Scott, *Algernon Sidney and the English Republic, 1623–77* (Cambridge: Cambridge University Press, 1988); Blair Worden, 'The Commonwealth Kidney of Algernon Sidney', *JBS* 24 (1985), 1–40.

5 Markku Peltonen, 'Citizenship and Republicanism in Elizabethan England', in Martin van Gelderen and Quentin Skinner, eds., *Republicanism: A Shared European Heritage,* 2 vols. (Cambridge: Cambridge University Press, 2002), I, pp. 85–106; Andrew Hadfield, 'Was Spenser a Republican?', *English* 47 (1998), 169–82.

6 Katherine Duncan-Jones, *Ungentle Shakespeare: Scenes From His Life* (London: Thomson, 2001).

7 Anthony Munday and others, *Sir Thomas More,* ed. Vittorio Gabrieli and Giorgio Melchiori (Manchester: Manchester University Press, 1990), introduction, pp. 1–29; Park Honan, *Shakespeare, A Life* (Oxford: Oxford University Press, 1998), p. 171.

8 On the Marprelate controversy, see Cyndia Clegg, *Press Censorship in Elizabethan England* (Cambridge: Cambridge University Press, 1997), ch. 8; Jesse M. Lander, 'Martin Marprelate and the Fugitive Text', *Reformation* 7 (2002), 135–85.

9 William Shakespeare, *King Henry IV, Part One,* ed. David Scott Kastan (London: Thomson: The Arden Shakespeare, 2002), introduction, pp. 51–62; Michael Drayton et al., *The Oldcastle Controversy: **Sir John Oldcastle, Part I** and **The Famous Victories of Henry V**,* ed. Perter Corbin and Douglas Sedge (Manchester: Manchester University Press, 1991).

10 Andrew Hadfield, *Shakespeare and Renaissance Politics* (London: Thomson: Arden Critical Companions, 2003), chs. 4–5.

11 See Simon Adams, *Leicester and the Court: Essays on Elizabethan Politics* (Manchester: Manchester University Press, 2002), pt. 1.

Bibliography

PRIMARY SOURCES

Abbot, George, *A briefe description of the whole worlde wherein are particularly described all the monarchies, empires, and kingdomes of the same* (London, 1599).

Alexander, Sir William, *The Monarchick Tragedies* (1604).

The Poetical Works of Sir William Alexander, ed. L. E. Kastner and H. B. Charlton, 2 vols. (Manchester: Manchester University Press, 1929).

Allen, William, *A Treatise made in Defence of the lawful power and authoritie of Priesthod to remedie sinnes* (Louvain, 1567).

A True, Sincere and Modest Defence, of English Catholiques that suffer for their faith both at home and abrode (Rouen, 1584).

Anon., *A forme of Christain pollicie drawne out of French*, trans. Geoffrey Fenton (London, 1574).

A Breefe discourse, declaring and approving the necessarie and inviolable customes of London (1584).

The Life and Death of Jack Straw (1594), ed. Kenneth Muir (Oxford: Malone Society, 1957).

The Tragedie of Claudius Tiberius Nero, Romes greatest tyrant Truly represented out of the purest records of those times (London, 1607).

Claudius Tiberius Nero, A Critical Edition of the Play Published Anonymously in 1607, ed. Uwe Baumann (Frankfurt am Main: Peter Lang, 1990).

'An Homily against Disobedience and Wilful Rebellion', in *Certain Sermons* (1574) (Cambridge: Parker Society, 1850), pp. 551–601.

The Tragedy of Caesar's Revenge, ed. F. S. Boas (Oxford: Malone Society, 1911).

The Famous Historye of the life and death of Captaine Thomas Stukeley, ed. Judith C. Levinson (Oxford: Malone Society, 1975).

Leicester's Commonwealth: The Copy of a Letter Written by a Master of Art of Cambridge (1584) and Related Documents, ed. D. C. Peck (Athens, Ohio: Ohio University Press, 1985).

Appian of Alexandra, *An Auncient Historie and Exquisite Chronicle of the Romanes warres, both civile and foren*, trans. William Baker (London, 1578).

*Shakespeare's Appian: A Selection from the Tudor Translation of Appian's **Civil Wars***, ed. Ernest Schanzer (Liverpool: Liverpool University Press, 1956).

Appian's Roman History, trans. Horace White, 4 vols. (London: Heinemann, 1958).

Aristotle, *Aristotles Politiques, Or Discourses of Government Translated out of Greeke into French . . . by Loys Le Roy* (London, 1598).

The Nicomachean Ethics, trans. David Ross (Oxford: Oxford University Press, 1980, rpt. of 1925).

The Politics of Aristotle, ed. and trans. Ernest Baker (Oxford: Oxford University Press, 1946).

Ascham, Roger, *The Scholemaster* (1571), ed. John E. B. Mayor (London: Bell, 1934).

Ashton, Robert, ed., *James I by his Contemporaries: An Account of his Career and Character as Seen by some of his Contemporaries* (London: Hutchinson, 1969).

Augustine, Saint, *Concerning the City of God Against the Pagans*, trans. Henry Bettenson (Harmondsworth: Penguin, 1984, rpt. of 1972).

Aylmer, John, *An harborowe for faithfull and trewe subjectes agaynst the late blowne blaste, concerninge the governme[n]t of wemen* (Strasbourg, 1559).

Beacon, Richard, *Solon his Follie, or A Politique Discourse Touching the Reformation of common-weales conquered, declined or corrupted* (1594), ed. Clare Carroll and Vincent Carey (Binghampton, N.Y.: MRTS, 1996).

Bodin, Jean, *The six bookes of a common-weale*, trans. Richard Knolles (London, 1606).

Boece, Hector, *The Chronicles of Scotland*, ed. Raymond Wilson Chambers et al., 2 vols. (Edinburgh: Blackwood, 1938–41).

Botero, Giovanni, *Observations Upon the Lives of Alexander, Caesar, Scipio, newly Englished* (London, 1602).

An historicall description of the most famous kingdomes and common-weales in the worlde (London, 1603).

A treatise, concerning the causes of the magnificencie and greatnes of cities, trans. Robert Peterson (London, 1606).

Brutus, Stephanus Junius, the Celt, *Vindiciae, Contra Tyrannos, or, concerning the legitimate power of a prince over the people, and of the people over a prince* (1579), ed. George Garnett (Cambridge: Cambridge University Press, 1994).

A Short Apologie for Christian Souldiours, trans. H. P. (London, 1588).

Buchanan, George, *Ane detectioun of the duinges of Marie Quene of Scottes* (1571).

De Prosodia Libellius (Edinburgh, 1590).

The History of Scotland written in Latin by George Buchanan; faithfully rendered into English, J. Fraser (London, 1690).

De Jure Regni Apud Scotos [or a Discourse concerning the due privilege of Government in the Kingdom of Scotland] (1721).

The Tyrannous Reign of Mary Stewart: George Buchanan's Account, trans. and ed. W. A. Gatherer (Edinburgh: The University Press, 1958).

Tragedies, ed. P. Sharratt and P. G. Walsh (Edinburgh: Scottish Academic Press, 1983).

The Political Poetry, ed. and trans. Paul J. McGinnis and Arthur H. Williamson (Edinburgh: SHS, 1995).

*A Dialogue on the Law of Kingship among the Scots: A Critical Edition and Translation of George Buchanan's **De Jure Regni apud Scotos Dialogus**,* ed. and trans. Roger A. Mason and Martin S. Smith (Aldershot: Ashgate, 2003).

Butler, Charles, *The Feminine Monarchie or a treatise concerning bees, and the due ordering of them* (London, 1609).

Caesar, Julius, *Julius Cesars commentaryes, newly translatyd owte of laten in to englysshe, as much as co[n]cernyth thys realm of England sumtyme callyd Brytayne: whych is the eld'yst hystoryer of all other that can be found, that ever wrote of thys realme of England* (London, 1530).

The eyght bookes of Caius Julius Caesar conteyning his martiall exploytes in the realme of Gallia and the countries bordering uppon the same translated oute of latin into English by Arthur Goldinge (London, 1565).

Castiglione, Baldesar, *The courtyer of Count Baldessar Castilio divided into foure bookes,* trans. Thomas Hoby (London, 1561).

Chapman, George, *Caesar and Pompey* in *The Plays of George Chapman: The Tragedies with **Sir Gyles Goosecappe**: A Critical Edition,* ed. Allan Holaday (Cambridge: Brewer, 1987), pp. 529–615.

The Conspiracie of Charles Duke of Byron, in *Tragedies,* pp. 265–332.

The Tragedie of Chabot, Admirall of France in *Tragedies,* pp. 627–708.

The Tragedie of Charles Duke of Byron in *Tragedies,* pp. 333–97.

The Conspiracy of Charles Duke of Byron and The Tragedy of Charles Duke of Byron, ed. John Margeson (Manchester: Manchester University Press, 1988).

Chaucer, Geoffrey, *The woorkes of Geffrey Chaucer, newly printed, with divers addicions, whiche were never in printe before* (London, 1561).

Chettle, Henry (?), *Greene's Groatsworth of Wit: Bought with a Million of Repentance* (1592), ed. D. Allen Carroll (Binghampton, N.Y.: MRTS, 1994).

Cicero, Marcus Tullius, *Fowre Severall Treatises of M. Tullius Cicero: Conteyninge his most learned and eloquent discourses of Frendshippe, Oldage, Paradoxes: and Scipio his Dreame,* trans. Thomas Newton (London, 1577).

Marcus Tullius Ciceroes three bookes of duties to Marcus his sonne, tourned out of Latine into English, by Nicolas Grimald (London, 1583).

De Officiis, trans. Walter Miller (London: Heinemann, 1913).

Brutus and Orator, trans. H. M. Hendrickson and H. M. Hubbell (London: Heinemann, 1952).

The Speeches: Pro Sestio, In Vatinium, trans. R. Gardner (London: Heinemann, 1958).

The Speeches: Pro Lege Manilia, Pro Caecina, Pro Cluentio, Pro Rabirio Perduellonis, trans. H. Grose Hodge (London: Heinemann, 1959).

De Oratore, trans. E. W. Sutton and H. Rackham, 2 vols. (London: Heinemann, 1959–60).

De Partitione Oratoria in *Cicero,* Vol. IV, trans. H. Rackham (London: Heinemann, 1960), pp. 306–421.

On Duties, trans. M. T. Griffin and E. M. Atkins (Cambridge: Cambridge University Press, 1991).

On the Commonwealth and On the Laws, ed. James E. G. Zetel (Cambridge: Cambridge University Press, 1999).

Contarini, Gaspar, *The Commonwealth and Government of Venice*, trans. Lewis Lewkenor (London, 1599).

Coryat, Thomas, *Coryat's Crudities* (1611) (Glasgow: MacLehose, 1905), 2 vols.

Covell, William, *Polimanteia, or The means lawfull and unlawfull, to judge of the fall of a common-wealth, against the frivolous and foolish conjectures of this age* (London, 1595).

Cross, Henry, *The Schoole of Pollicie: or, the araignement of State-abuses. Directing Magistrates, adorning the Court, and beautifying, the whole Common-wealth* (London, 1605).

Daniel, Samuel, *A panegyrike congratulatorie delivered to the Kings most excellent Majestie at Burleigh Harrington in Rutlandshire . . . Also certaine epistles, with a defence of ryme heretofore written* (London, 1603).

The Collection of the History of England, in *Complete Works in Verse and Prose*, ed. A. B. Grossart (London: privately printed, 1885–96), Vol. V, pp. 69–299.

The Tragedie of Cleopatra, in *Works*, Vol. III, pp. 1–94.

The Tragedy of Philotas in *Works*, Vol. III, pp. 95–181.

The Civil Wars, ed. Laurence Michel (New Haven: Yale University Press, 1958).

Donne, John, *Biathanatos, a declaration of that paradoxe or thesis, that selfe-homicide is not so naturally sinne* (London, 1644).

Drayton, Michael, *Works*, ed. J. W. Hebel, 5 vols. (Oxford: Blackwell, 1931–41).

et al., *The Oldcastle Controversy: **Sir John Oldcastle, Part I** and **The Famous Victories of Henry V***, ed. Perter Corbin and Douglas Sedge (Manchester: Manchester University Press, 1991).

Elton, G. R., ed., *The Tudor Constitution: Documents and Commentary* (Cambridge: Cambridge University Press, 1972).

Floyd, Thomas, *The Picture of a perfit Common wealth describing aswell the offices of princes and inferiour magistrates over their subjects, as also the duties of subjects towards their governours. Gathered forth of many authors, aswel humane, as divine* (London, 1600).

God and the king. Or a dialogue wherein is treated of allegiance due to our most gracious Lord, King James, within his dominions Which (by removing all controversies, and causes of dissentions and suspitions) bindeth subjects, by an inviolable band of love and duty, to their soveraigne (Saint-Omer, 1620).

Forset, Edward, *A Comparative Discourse of the bodies natural and politique* (London, 1606).

Fortesque, Sir John, *A learned commendation of the politique lawes of Englande*, trans. Richard Mulcaster (London, 1567).

Fulbecke, William, *An Historicall Collection of the continuall factions, tumults, and Massacres of the Romans and Italians during the space of one hundred and twentie yeares next before the peaceable Empire of Augustus Caesar* (London, 1601).

Gascoigne, George, *A Hundreth Sundrie Flowres*, ed. G. W. Pigman III (Oxford: Clarendon Press, 2000).

Gentillet, Innocent, *A Discourse Upon the Meanes of Wel Governing and Maintaining in Good Peace, a Kingdom, or other Principalitie . . . Against Nicholas Machiavell the Florentine*, trans. Simon Patericke (London, 1602).

Goodman, Christopher, *How superior powers oght to be obeyd of their subjects* (Geneva, 1558).

Gorges, Arthur, *The Poems of Sir Arthur Gorges*, ed. Helen Estabrook Sandison (Oxford: Clarendon Press, 1953).

Greene, Robert, *Friar Bacon and Friar Bungay*, ed. Daniel Seltzer (London: Arnold, 1963).

and Thomas Lodge, *A Looking Glass for London and England (1594)*, ed. W. W. Greg (London: Malone Society, 1932).

Greville, Fulke, *Poems and Dramas of Fulke Greville, First Lord Brooke*, ed. Geoffrey Bullogh, 2 vols. (Edinburgh: Oliver and Boyd, 1939).

The Remains, being Poems of Monarchy and Religion, ed. G. A. Wilkes (Oxford: Oxford University Press, 1965).

Grimaldus, Laurentius, *The Counsellor: exactly portraited in two bookes*, trans. anon. (London, 1599).

Guazzo, Stephano, *The Civile Conversation of M. Stephen Guazzo*, trans. Bartholomew Young (London, 1586).

Guevara, Antonio de, *The Diall of Princes*, trans. Thomas North (London, 1557).

Hall, Edward, *Chronicle containing the History of England during the reign of Henry the Fourth and the succeeding monarchs to the End of the Reign of Henry the Eighth* (1548), 2 vols. (London: Johnson, 1809).

Hayward, John, *The First and Second Parts of John Hayward's **The Life and Raigne of King Henrie IIII***, ed. John J. Manning (London: Royal Historical Society, 1991; Camden Society, 4th series, Vol. 42).

Henslowe, Philip, *Henslowe's Diary*, ed. R. A. Foakes and R. T. Rickert (Cambridge: Cambridge University Press, 1961).

Herbert, Mary Sidney, *The Collected Works of Mary Sidney Herbert, Countess of Pembroke*, ed. Margaret P. Hannay, Noel J. Kinnamon and Michael G. Brennan, 2 vols. (Oxford: Clarendon Press, 1998).

Herodian, *The history of Herodian, a Greeke authour treating of the Romayne emperors, after Marcus, translated oute of Greeke into Latin, by Angelus Politianus, and out of Latin into Englyshe, by Nicholas Smyth. Whereunto are annexed, the argumentes of every booke, at the begynning therof, with annotacions for the better understandynge of the same historye* (London, 1556).

Heron, Haly, *The Kayes of Counsaile: A New Discourse of Morall Philosophie* (1579), ed. Virgil B. Heltzel (Liverpool: Liverpool University Press, 1954).

Heywood, Thomas, *The Conspiracy of Catiline and the War of Jugurtha* (1608) (London: Constable, 1924).

The Rape of Lucrece: A true Roman Tragedy, in *Works*, ed. A. B. Grosart (London, 1874), V, pp. 161–257.

Hobbes, Thomas, *Leviathan*, ed. C. B. McPherson (Harmondsworth: Penguin, 1981).

Holinshed, Raphael, *Chronicle of Scotland* (Arbroath: J. Findlay, 1805).

Holinshed's Chronicles of England, Scotland and Ireland (1587), ed. Henry Ellis, 6 vols. (London: Johnson, 1807–8).

Hotman, François, *A true and plaine report of the Furious outrages of France*, trans. Ernest Varamund (Striveling, Scotland, 1573).

Hume, David of Godscroft, **The British Union**: *A Critical Edition and Translation of David Hume of Godscroft's* **De Unione Insulae Britannicae**, ed. Paul J. McGinnis and Arthur H. Williamson (Aldershot: Ashgate, 2002).

Hutchinson, Lucy, *Order and Disorder*, ed. David Norbrook (Oxford: Blackwell, 2001).

James VI and I, *The Trew Law of Free Monarchies*, in *The Workes* (1616) (Hildesham and New York: Verlag, 1971).

Letters of King James VI and I, ed. G. P. V. Akrigg (Berkeley: University of California Press, 1984).

Political Writings, ed. Johann P. Sommerville (Cambridge: Cambridge University Press, 1994).

Jonson, Ben, *Catiline His Conspiracy*, ed. W. F. Bolton and J. F. Gardner (London: Arnold, 1972).

Poems, ed. Ian Donaldson (Oxford: Oxford University Press, 1975).

Sejanus His Fall, ed. Philip J. Ayres (Manchester: Manchester University Press, 1990).

Jonson, Ben, George Chapman and John Marston, *Eastward Ho!*, ed. C. G. Petter (London Benn, 1973).

Kenyon, J. P., ed., *The Stuart Constitution: Documents and Commentary* (2nd ed., Cambridge: Cambridge University Press, 1986).

Knox, John, *On Rebellion*, ed. Roger A. Mason (Cambridge: Cambridge University Press, 1994).

Kyd, Thomas, *The Spanish Tragedy*, ed. Philip Edwards (Manchester: Manchester University Press, 1977, rpt. of 1959).

Latimer, Hugh, *Sermons*, ed. Canon Beeching (London: Dent, 1906).

Lipsius, Justus, *Six Bookes of Politickes or Civil Doctrine, written in Latine by Justus Lipsius: which doe especially concerne principalitie. Done into English by William Jones* (London, 1594).

Two bookes of constancie. Written in Latine, by Justus Lipsius. Containing, principallie, A comfortable conference, in common calamities. And will serve for a singular consolation to all that are privately distressed, or afflicted, either in body or mind. Englished by John Stradling (London, 1595).

Livius (Livy), Titus, *The Early History of Rome (Books I-V of The History of Rome)*, trans. Aubrey de Sélincourt (Harmondsworth: Penguin, 1960).

Llwyd, Humphrey, *The breviary of Britayne* (London, 1573).

Lodge, Thomas, *Rosalynde* (1590), ed. Brian Nellist (Keele: Keele University Press, 1995).

The Wounds of Civil War, ed. J. W. Houppert (London: Arnold, 1970).

and George Gascoigne *A Larum for London, or The siedge of Antwerpe with the vertuous actes and valorous deedes of the lame soldier (1602)*, ed. W. W. Greg (London: Malone Society, 1913).

Lucan, *Lucans Pharsalia: Containing the Civill Warres betweene Caesar and Pompey*, trans. Arthur Gorges (London, 1614).

Civil War, trans. Susan H. Braund (Oxford: Oxford University Press, 1992).

Lyly, John, **Campaspe** and **Sappho and Phao**, ed. G. K. Hunter and David Bevington (Manchester: Manchester University Press, 1991).

Euphues and his England (London, 1580).

Machiavelli, Niccolò, *The Discourses*, trans. Leslie Walker, rev. Brian Richardson, ed. Bernard Crick (Harmondsworth: Penguin, 1970).

The Prince, ed. Quentin Skinner and Russell Price (Cambridge: Cambridge University Press, 1988).

Major, John, *A History of Greater Britain*, ed. A. Constable and A. J. G. MacKay (Edinburgh: Edinburgh University Press, 1892).

Marlowe, Christopher, *The First Book of Lucan Translated into English*, in *The Poems*, ed. Millar McLure (London: Methuen, 1968), pp. 219–54.

Tamburlaine, ed. J. W. Harper (London: Black, 1971).

The Jew of Malta, ed. N. W. Bawcutt (Manchester: Manchester University Press, 1978).

The Complete Plays, ed. Mark Thornton Burnett (London: Everyman, 1999).

Merbury, Charles, *A Briefe Discourse of Royall Monarchie, as of the best common weale wherin the subject may beholde the sacred majestie of the princes most royall estate* (London, 1581).

Mexia, Pedro, *The Historie of all the Romane Emperors beginning with Caius Julius Caesar, and successively ending with Rodolph the second now raigning*, trans. W. T. (London, 1604).

Middleton, Thomas, *The Ghost of Lucrece* (London, 1600).

More, Thomas, **The History of King Richard III** and Selections from the English and Latin Poems, ed. Richard S. Sylvester (New Haven: Yale University Press, 1976).

Moryson, Fynes, *An Itinerary Containing His Ten Yeeres Travell* (1617), 4 vols. (Glasgow: MacLehose, 1908).

Mulcaster, Richard, *The Queen's Majesty's Passage* in Arthur Kinney, ed., *Renaissance Drama: An Anthology of Plays and Entertainments* (Oxford: Blackwell, 1999), pp. 17–34.

Munday, Anthony, and others, *Sir Thomas More*, ed. Vittorio Gabrieli and Giorgio Melchiori (Manchester: Manchester University Press, 1990).

Nashe, Thomas, *The Works of Thomas Nashe*, ed. Ronald B. McKerrow, corrected by F. P. Wilson, 5 vols. (Oxford: Basil Blackwell, 1966).

Nichols, J., ed., *The Progresses and Public Processions of Queen Elizabeth*, 3 vols. (New York: Franklin, rpt. of 1823).

Ovid, *Fasti*, trans. A. J. Boyle and R. D. Woodard (Harmondsworth: Penguin, 2000).

Metamorphoses, trans. Mary M. Innes (Harmondsworth: Penguin, 1955).

Painter, William, *The Palace of Pleasure*, ed. Joseph Jacobs, 3 vols. (London: David Nutt, 1890).

Parsons [Doleman], Robert, *A Conference about the Next Succession to the Crowne of Ingland* (1594).

Peele, George, *The Life and Works of George Peele*, ed. Charles Tyler Prouty, R. Mark Benbow, Elmer Blistein and Frank S. Hook, 2 vols. (New Haven: Yale University Press, 1952–70).

Petowe, Henry, *Englands Caesar. His Majesties most Royall Coronation* (London, 1603).

Platter, Thomas, *Thomas Platter's Travels in England, 1599*, trans. Claire Williams (London: Cape, 1937).

Pliny the Elder, *Natural History*, trans. H. Rackham, W. H. S. Jones and D. E. Eichholz, 10 vols. (London: Heinemann, 1942–62).

Plutarch, *The lives of the noble Grecians and Romanes compared together by that grave learned philosopher and historiographer, Plutarke of Chaeronea; translated out of Greeke into French by James Amyot . . . ; and out of French into Englishe, by Thomas North* (London, 1579).

'How a Yoong Man ought to hear Poets: and how he may take profit by reading Poems', in *The Philosophie, commonlie called, The Morals, written by the learned Philosopher Plutarch*, trans. Philemon Holland (London, 1603), pp. 17–50.

Selected Lives, ed. Judith Mossman (Ware: Wordsworth, 1998).

Polybius, *The Hystories of the most famous and worthy Cronographer Polybius: Discoursing of the warres betwixt the Romanes & Carthaginenses, a riche and godly Worke, conteining holsome counsels & wonderfull devises against the incombrances of fickle fortune, Englished by C. W. [Christopher Warton] Whereunto is annexed an Abstract, compendiously coarcted out of the life & wothy actes, perpetrate by oure puissant Prince king Henry the fift* (London, 1568).

The Rise of the Roman Empire, trans. Ian Scott-Kilvert (Harmondsworth: Penguin, 1979).

Rainolde, Richard, *The Foundacion of rhetorike* (London, 1563).

Ralegh, Walter, *A chronicle of all the noble emperours of the Romaines from Julius Caesar* (London, 1571).

The Letters of Sir Walter Ralegh, ed. Agnes Latham and Joyce Younings (Exeter: University of Exeter Press, 1999).

Reese, M. M., ed., *Elizabethan Verse Romances* (London: Routledge, 1968).

Rowlands, Samuel, *Ave Caesar. God save the king* (London, 1603).

Salgado, Gamini, ed., *Cony-Catchers and Bawdy Baskets: An Anthology of Elizabethan Low Life* (Harmondsworth: Penguin, 1972).

Sallust, *The Conspiracy of Catiline and the War of Jugurtha*, trans. Thomas Heywood (1609), introd. Charles Whibley (London: Constable: The Tudor Translations, 1924).

Jugurthine War and Conspiracy of Catiline, trans. S. A. Handford (Harmondsworth: Penguin, 1963).

Sansovino, Francisco, *The quintesence of wit being a corrant comfort of conceites, maximies, and poleticke devises*, trans. Robert Hitchcock (London, 1590).

Seneca, Lucius Annaeus, *Letters from a Stoic*, trans. Robin Campbell (Harmondsworth: Penguin, 1969).

Shakespeare, William, *The Complete Works*, ed. Stanley Wells and Gary Taylor (Oxford: Oxford University Press, 1988).

Antony and Cleopatra, ed. John Wilders (London: Routledge: The Arden Shakespeare, 1995).

Antony and Cleopatra, ed. Richard Madelaine (Cambridge: Cambridge University Press: Shakespeare in Performance, 1998).

As You Like It, ed. Agnes Latham (London: Routledge: The Arden Shakespeare, 1989, rpt. of 1975).

The Comedy of Errors, ed. T. S. Dorsch, rev. Ros King (Cambridge: Cambridge University Press, 2004).

The first part of the contention betwixt the two famous houses of Yorke and Lancaster with the death of the good Duke Humphrey: and the banishment and death of the Duke of Suffolke, and the tragical end of the prowd Cardinall of Winchester, with the notable rebellion of Jacke Cade: and the Duke of Yorkes first clayme to the crowne (London, 1594).

Cymbeline, ed. J. M. Nosworthy (London: Thomson: The Arden Shakespeare, 2000, rpt. of 1955).

The First Quarto of Hamlet, ed. Katherine O. Irace (Cambridge: Cambridge University Press, 1998).

Hamlet, ed. Harold Jenkins (London: Routledge: The Arden Shakespeare, 1982).

Hamlet, ed. G. R. Hibbard (Oxford: Oxford University Press: The Oxford Shakespeare, 1987).

Hamlet, ed. Philip Edwards (Cambridge: Cambridge University Press: The Cambridge Shakespeare, rev. ed., 2003).

Hamlet, Prince of Denmark, ed. Robert Hapgood (Cambridge: Cambridge University Press: Shakespeare in Performance, 1999).

Henry VI, Part One, ed. Michael Taylor (Oxford: Oxford University Press, 2003).

Julius Caesar, ed. David Daniell (London: Thomson: The Arden Shakespeare, 1998).

King Henry IV, Part One, ed. David Scott Kastan (London: Thomson: The Arden Shakespeare, 2002).

King Henry VI, Part One, ed. Edward Burns (London: Thompson: The Arden Shakespeare, 2000).

King Henry VI, Part Two, ed. Ronald Knowles (London: Thomson: The Arden Shakespeare, 1999).

King Henry VI, Part Three, ed. John D. Cox and Eric Rasmussen (London: Thomson: The Arden Shakespeare, 2001).

King Henry VI, Part Three, ed. Randall Martin (Oxford: Oxford University Press, 2001).

King Lear, ed. R. A. Foakes (London: Thomson: The Arden Shakespeare, 1997).

King Richard III, ed. Anthony Hammond (London: Routledge: The Arden Shakespeare, 1988, rpt. of 1981).

Love's Labour's Lost, ed. H. R. Woudhuysen (London: Thomson: The Arden Shakespeare, 1998).

Macbeth, ed. Kenneth Muir (London: Routledge: The Arden Shakespeare, rev. ed., 1984).

Measure for Measure, ed. J. W. Lever (London: Routledge: The Arden Shakespeare, 1988, rpt. of 1967).

Othello, ed. Julie Hankey (Bristol: Bristol Classical Press: Plays in Performance, 1987).

Othello, ed. Ernst Honigmann (London: Thomson: The Arden Shakespeare, 1997).

Pericles, ed. Suzanne Gosset (London: Thomson: The Arden Shakespeare, 2004).

The Poems, ed. F. T. Prince (London: Methuen: The Arden Shakespeare, 1960).

The Poems, ed. Colin Burrow (Oxford: Oxford University Press: 2002).

Titus Andronicus, ed. Eugene M. Waith (Oxford: Clarendon Press: 1984).

Titus Andronicus, ed. Alan Hughes (Cambridge: Cambridge University Press, 1994).

Titus Andronicus, ed. Jonathan Bate (London: Thomson: The Arden Shakespeare, 2000, rpt. of 1995).

Troilus and Cressida, ed. David Bevington (London: Thomson: The Arden Shakespeare, 1998).

The true tragedie of Richarde Duke of Yorke and the death of good King Henrie the sixt: with the whole contention betweene the two houses, Lancaster and Yorke; as it was sundry times acted by the Right Honourable the Earle of Pembrooke his servantes (1595).

The Two Gentlemen of Verona, ed. William C. Carroll (London: Thomson: The Arden Shakespeare, 2004).

Mr. William Shakespeares Comedies, Histories, & Tragedies: A Facsimile of the First Folio, 1623, introduction by Doug Moston (London: Routledge, 1998).

Sidney, Sir Philip, *The Countess of Pembroke's Arcadia*, ed. Victor Skretkowicz (Oxford: Clarendon Press, 1987).

An Apology for Poetry, ed. Geoffrey Shepherd, rev. and expanded R. W. Maslen (Manchester: Manchester University Press, 2002).

Skelton, John, *Magnificence*, ed. Paula Neuss (Manchester: Manchester University Press, 1980).

Smith, Sir Thomas, *A Discourse of the Commonweal of This Realm of England, attributed to Sir Thomas Smith*, ed. Mary Dewar (Charlottesville: University of Virginia Press, 1969).

    De Republica Anglorum: A Discourse on the Commonwealth of England (1583), ed. L. Alston (Shannon: Irish University Press, 1972, rpt. of 1906).

Spenser, Edmund, *The Shorter Poems*, ed. Richard A. McCabe (Harmondsworth: Penguin, 1999).

    The Faerie Queene, ed. A. C. Hamilton (London: Routledge, 2001).

    A View of the State of Ireland, ed. Andrew Hadfield and Willy Maley (Oxford: Blackwell, 1997).

Starkey, Thomas, *A Dialogue between Pole and Lupset*, ed. T. F. Mayer (London: RHS, 1989).

Stow, John, *A Survey of London* (1603), ed. Charles Lethbridge Kingsford, 2 vols. (Oxford: Clarendon Press, 2000).

Stubbs, John, *John Stubbs's **Gaping Gulf** with Letters and Other Relevant Documents*, ed. Lloyd E. Berry (Charlottesville, Va.: University of Virginia Press, 1968).

Suetonius, *The Twelve Caesars*, trans. Robert Graves (Harmondsworth: Penguin, 1957).

Tacitus, Gaius Cornelius, *The ende of Nero and beginning of Galba Fower bookes of the Histories of Cornelius Tacitus. The life of Agricola*, trans. Henry Saville (Oxford, 1591).

    The Annales of Cornelius Tacitus. The Description of Germanie (London, 1598).

    On Britain and Germany, trans. H. Mattingly (Harmondsworth: Penguin, 1948).

    On Imperial Rome (The Annals), trans. Michael Grant (Harmondsworth: Penguin, 1956).

    The Histories, trans. W. H. Fyfe (Oxford: Oxford University Press, 1997).

Thomas, William, *Historie of Italie* (1549).

    The History of Italy, ed. George B. Parks (Ithaca, N.Y.: Cornell University Press, 1963).

Tyndale, William, *The Obedience of a Christian Man* (1528), ed. David Daniell (Harmondsworth: Penguin, 2000).

Udall, Nicholas, *Respublica: An Interlude for Christmas 1553*, ed. W. W. Greg (Oxford: Oxford University Press, 1952).

Vickers, Brian, *English Renaissance Literary Criticism* (Oxford: Clarendon Press, 1999).

Virgil, *The Aeneid*, trans. David West (Harmondsworth: Penguin, 1990).

Vowell, John, alias Hooker, *A pamphlet of the offices and duties of everie particular sworned officer, of the citie of Excester* (London, 1584).

Webster, John, *The Works of John Webster, Volume 1*, ed. David Gunby, David Carnegie and Antony Hammond (Cambridge: Cambridge University Press, 1995).

Wentworth, Peter, *A Pithie Exhortation to Her Majestie for Establishing her Successor to the Crowne* (1598).

Whitney, Geoffrey, *A Choice of Emblems* (1586) (ed. Henry Green [1866], rpt. New York: Verlag, 1971).

Whythorne, Thomas, *The Autobiography of Thomas Whythorne*, ed. James M. Osborn (Oxford: Clarendon Press, 1961).

Wilson, Thomas, *Arte of Rhetorique*, ed. Thomas J. Derrick (New York: Garland, 1982).

SECONDARY SOURCES

Adams, Simon, 'The Patronage of the Crown in Elizabethan Politics: The 1590s in Perspective', in Guy, ed., *The Reign of Elizabeth I*, pp. 20–45.
  Leicester and the Court: Essays on Elizabethan Politics (Manchester: Manchester University Press, 2002).

Aebischer, Pascale, 'Cleopatra in the Closet: Sexuality, Race and Royalty in Jodelle, Garnier, Pembroke, and Daniel' (unpublished paper).

Aers, David, 'Reflections on Current Histories of the Subject', *Literature & History*, 2nd series, 2, ii (1991), 20–34.

Aitken, James M., ed., *The Trial of George Buchanan Before the Lisbon Inquisition* (Edinburgh: Oliver and Boyd, 1939).

Akrigg, G. P. V., *Shakespeare and the Earl of Southampton* (London: Hamilton, 1968).

Alford, Stephen, *The Early Elizabethan Polity: William Cecil and the British Succession Crisis, 1558–1569* (Cambridge: Cambridge University Press, 1998).
  Kingship and Politics in the Reign of Edward VI (Cambridge: Cambridge University Press, 2002).

Altman, Joel B., *The Tudor Play of Mind: Rhetorical Inquiry and the Development of Elizabethan Drama* (Berkeley: University of California Press, 1978).

Alulis, Joseph and Vickie Sullivan, eds., *Shakespeare's Political Pageant: Essays in Literature and Politics* (Lanham: Rowman & Littlefield, 1996).

Alvis, John and Thomas G. West, eds., *Shakespeare as Political Thinker* (Wilmington, Del.: ISI Books, 2000).

Anglo, Sydney, 'A Machiavellian Solution to the Irish Problem: Richard Beacon's *Solon His Follie*', in Edward Chaney and Peter Mack, eds., *England and the Continental Renaissance: Essays in Honour of J. B. Trapp* (Woodbridge: Boydell and Brewer, 1990), pp. 153–64.

Archer, Ian W., *The Pursuit of Stability: Social Relations in Elizabethan London* (Cambridge: Cambridge University Press, 1991).
  'Shakespeare's London', in Kastan, ed., *Companion to Shakespeare*, pp. 43–56.
  'Popular Politics in the Sixteenth and Seventeenth Centuries', in Paul Griffiths and Mark S. R. Jenner, eds., *Londinopolis: Essays in the Cultural and Social History of Early Modern London* (Manchester: Manchester University Press, 2000).

Armitage, David, 'Empire and Liberty: A Republican Dilemma', in van Gelderen and Skinner, eds., *Republicanism*, II, pp. 29–46.
, Armand Himy and Quentin Skinner, eds., *Milton and Republicanism* (Cambridge: Cambridge University Press, 1995).
Arnold, E. Vernon, *Roman Stoicism* (Cambridge: Cambridge University Press, 1911).
Axton, Marie, *The Queen's Two Bodies: Drama and the Elizabethan Succession* (London: Royal Historical Society, 1977).
Baines, Barbara J., *Thomas Heywood* (Boston: Twayne, 1984).
Baker, David Weil, *Divulging Utopia: Radical Humanism in Sixteenth-Century England* (Amherst: University of Massachusetts Press, 1999).
Baldwin, T. W., *William Shakspere's Small Latine and Lesse Greeke*, 2 vols. (Urbana: University of Illinois Press, 1944).
Barbour, Reid, *English Epicures and Stoics: Ancient Legacies in Early Stuart Culture* (Amherst: University of Massachusetts Press, 1998).
Barker, Francis, *The Tremulous Private Body: Essays on Subjection* (London: Methuen, 1984).
Barnaby, Andrew and Joan Wry, 'Authorized Versions: *Measure for Measure* and the Politics of Biblical Translation', *RQ* 51 (1998), 1225–54.
Barrell, John, *Poetry, Language & Politics* (Manchester: Manchester University Press, 1988).
  Imagining the King's Death: Figurative Treason, Fantasies of Regicide, 1793–1796 (Oxford: Oxford University Press, 2000).
Barroll, Leeds, 'A New History for Shakespeare and His Time', *SQ* 39 (1988), 441–64.
Bartels, Emily C., 'Christopher Marlowe', in Arthur Kinney, ed., *A Companion to Renaissance Drama* (Oxford: Blackwell, 2002), pp. 446–63.
Barton, Anne, 'Livy, Machiavelli and Shakespeare's *Coriolanus*', in *Essays, Mainly Shakespearean* (Cambridge: Cambridge University Press, 1994).
Bate, Jonathan, *Shakespeare and Ovid* (Oxford: Clarendon Press, 1993).
  'Sexual Perversity in *Venus and Adonis*', *YES* 23 (1993), 80–92.
  'The Elizabethans in Italy', in Jean-Pierre Maquerlot and Michele Willems, eds., *Travel and Drama in Shakespeare's Time* (Cambridge: Cambridge University Press, 1996), pp. 55–74.
Baumer, Franklin Le Van, *The Early Tudor Theory of Kingship* (New Haven: Yale University Press, 1940).
Bednarz, James P., 'Ralegh in Spenser's Historical Allegory', *Sp. Stud.* 4 (1983), 49–70.
  'Grindal, Edmund', in *Hamilton*, ed., *Spenser Encyclopaedia*, pp. 342–3.
  Shakespeare & The Poets' War (New York: Columbia University Press, 2001).
Beer, Anna, *Sir Walter Raleigh and his Readers in the Seventeenth Century: Speaking to the People* (Basingstoke: Macmillan, 1997).
Bellamy, John, *The Tudor Law of Treason: An Introduction* (London: Routledge, 1979).
Belsey, Catherine, *Critical Practice* (London: Methuen, 1980).

The Subject of Tragedy: Identity and Difference in Renaissance Drama (London: Methuen, 1985).

'The Subject in Danger: A Reply to Richard Levin', *Textual Practice* 3 (1989), 77–80.

'Towards Cultural History – in Theory and Practice', *Textual Practice* 3 (1989), 159–72.

Bennett, Josephine Waters, **Measure for Measure** as *Royal Entertainment* (New York: Columbia University Press, 1966).

Bergson, Allen, 'Stoicism Achieved: Cato in Chapman's *Tragedy of Caesar and Pompey*', *SEL* 17 (1977), 295–302.

Berry, Edward, *Shakespeare and the Hunt: A Cultural and Social Study* (Cambridge: Cambridge University Press, 2001).

Bevington, David, *Tudor Drama and Politics: A Critical Approach to Topical Meaning* (Cambridge, Mass.: Harvard University Press, 1968).

Black, J. B., *The Reign of Elizabeth, 1558–1603* (2nd ed., Oxford: Clarendon Press, 1959).

Blaney, Peter, 'The Publication of Playbooks', in Cox and Kastan, eds., *New History of English Drama*, pp. 383–422.

Blissett, William, 'Lucan's Caesar and the Elizabethan Villain', *SP* 53 (1956), 553–75.

Bloom, Alan with Harry V. Jaffa, *Shakespeare's Politics* (Chicago: University of Chicago Press, 1964).

Blythe, James M., '"Civic Humanism" and Medieval Political Thought', in Hankins, ed., *Renaissance Civic Humanism*, pp. 30–74.

Bock, Gisela, Quentin Skinner and Maurizio Viroli, eds., *Machiavelli and Republicanism* (Cambridge: Cambridge University Press, 1990).

Bödeker, Hans Erich, 'Debating the *republica mixta*: German and Dutch Political Discourses around 1700', in van Gelderen and Skinner, eds., *Republicanism*, I, pp. 219–46.

Boswell-Stone, W. G., *Shakespeare's Holinshed: The Chronicle and the Historical Plays Compared* (New York: Benjamin Blom, 1966, rpt. of 1896).

Boutcher, Warren, '"Rationall Knowledges" and "Knowledges . . . drenched in flesh and blood": Fulke Greville, Francis Bacon and Institutions of Humane Learning in Tudor and Stuart England', *SJ* 19 (2001), 11–40.

Bowers, Fredson, *Elizabethan Revenge Tragedy, 1587–1642* (Princeton: Princeton University Press, 1940).

Boyd, Brian, 'Mutius: An Obstacle Removed in *Titus Andronicus*', *RES*, ns, 55 (2004), 196–209.

Braddick, Michael J., *State Formation in Early Modern England, c.1550–1700* (Cambridge: Cambridge University Press, 2000).

Bradford, Alan T., 'Stuart Absolutism and the "Utility" of Tacitus', *HLQ* 46 (1983), 127–55.

'Nathaniel Richards, Jacobean Playgoer', *JDJ* 2 (1983), 63–78.

Bradley, A. C., *Shakespearean Tragedy: Lectures on* **Hamlet, Othello, King Lear, Macbeth** (London: Macmillan, 1918, rpt. of 1904).

Bradshaw, Brendan, 'More on *Utopia*', *HJ* 24 (1979), 455–76.

Brady, Ciaran, 'Spenser's Irish Crisis: Humanism and Experience in the 1590s', *P. & P.* 120 (1988), 17–49.

Breight, Curtis C., *Surveillance, Militarism and Drama in the Elizabethan Era* (Basingstoke: Palgrave, 1996).

Brennan, Michael G., *Literary Patronage in the Renaissance: The Pembroke Family* (London: Routledge, 1988).

Brigden, Susan, *New Worlds, Lost Worlds: The Rule of the Tudors, 1485–1603* (London: Penguin, 2000).

Briggs, Julia, *This Stage-Play World: Texts and Contexts, 1580–1625* (2nd ed., Oxford: Oxford University Press, 1997).

Brink, Jean, 'Constructing *A View of the Present State of Ireland*', *Sp. Stud.* 11 (1990, published 1994), 203–28.

Bristol, Michael G., *Big-Time Shakespeare* (London: Routledge, 1996).

Bronfen, Elisabeth, *Over Her Dead Body: Death, Femininity and the Aesthetic* (Manchester: Manchester University Press, 1992).

Brooks, Douglas A., *From Playhouse to Printing House: Drama and Authorship in Early Modern England* (Cambridge: Cambridge University Press, 2000).

Brown, Georgia E., 'Marlowe's Poems and Classicism', in Patrick Cheney, ed., *The Cambridge Companion to Christopher Marlowe* (Cambridge: Cambridge University Press, 2004), pp. 106–26.

Brown, John Russell, ed., ***Antony and Cleopatra***: *A Selection of Critical Essays* (London: Macmillan, 1968).

Brown, Keith M., 'The Vanishing Emperor: British Kingship and its Decline, 1603–1707', in Mason, ed., *Scots and Britons*, pp. 58–87.

Brumbaugh, Barbara, 'Temples Defaced and Altars in the Dust: Edwardian and Elizabethan Church Reform and Sidney's "Now Was Our Heav'nly Vault Deprived of the Light"', *Sp. Stud.* 16 (2002), 197–229.

Bruster, Douglas, *Quoting Shakespeare: Form and Culture in Early Modern Drama* (Lincoln: University of Nebraska Press, 2000).

Bullough, Geoffrey, *Narrative and Dramatic Sources of Shakespeare*, 8 vols. (London: Routledge, 1957–75).

Burgess, Glenn, *The Politics of the Ancient Constitution: An Introduction to English Political Thought, 1603–1642* (Basingstoke: Macmillan, 1992).

Burke, Peter, 'Tacitism', in T. A. Dorey, ed., *Tacitus* (London: Routledge, 1969), pp. 149–71.

'Tacitism, Scepticism, and Reason Of State', in Burns and Goldie, eds., *Cambridge History of Political Thought*, pp. 479–98.

The Fortunes of the Courtier: The European Reception of Castiglione's 'Cortegiano' (Cambridge: Polity, 1995).

Burnett, Mark Thornton, *Masters and Servants in English Renaissance Drama and Culture: Authority and Obedience* (Basingstoke: Macmillan, 1997).

Constructing 'Monsters' in Shakespearean Drama and Early Modern Culture (Basingstoke: Palgrave, 2002).

Burns, J. H., 'The Political Ideas of George Buchanan', *SHR* 30 (1951), 61–68.

The True Law of Kingship: Concepts of Monarchy in Early-Modern Scotland (Oxford: Clarendon Press, 1996).

and Mark Goldie, eds., *The Cambridge History of Political Thought, 1450–1700* (Cambridge: Cambridge University Press, 1991).

Burrow, Colin, *Epic Romance: Homer to Milton* (Oxford: Clarendon Press, 1993).

Burt, Richard, *Unspeakable Shaxxxspeares: Queer Theory and American Kiddie Culture* (Basingstoke: Macmillan, 1998).

'(Un)Censoring in Detail: The Fetish of Censorship in the Early Modern Past and the Postmodern Present', in Robert C. Post, ed., *Censorship and Silencing: Practices of Cultural Regulation* (Los Angeles: Getty Research Institute, 1998), pp. 17–41.

Bushnell, Rebecca, *Tragedies of Tyrants: Political Thought and Theater in the English Renaissance* (Ithaca, N.Y.: Cornell University Press, 1990).

'George Buchanan, James VI and Neo-Classicism', in Mason, ed., *Scots and Britons*, pp. 91–111.

'*Julius Caesar*', in Dutton and Howard, eds., *Companion to Shakespeare's Works, III*, pp. 339–56.

Butler, Judith, *Gender Trouble: Feminism and the Subversion of Identity* (London: Routledge, 1990).

Butler, Martin, *Theatre and Crisis, 1632–42* (Cambridge: Cambridge University Press, 1984).

Cain, Thomas H., *Praise in* **The Faerie Queene** (Lincoln, Neb.: University of Nebraska Press, 1978).

Callaghan, Dympna, '(Un)natural Loving: Swine, Pets and Flowers in *Venus and Adonis*', in Philippa Berry and Margaret Tudeau-Clayton, eds., *Textures of Renaissance Knowledge* (Manchester: Manchester University Press, 2003), pp. 58–78.

et al., eds., *The Weyward Sisters: Shakespeare and Feminist Politics* (Oxford: Blackwell, 1994).

Cannadine, David, *Class in Britain* (New Haven: Yale University Press, 1998).

Carey, Vincent, 'The Irish Face of Machiavelli: Richard Beacon's *Solon his Follie* and Republican Ideology in the Conquest of Ireland', in Hiram Morgan, ed., *Political Ideology in Ireland, 1534–1641* (Dublin: Four Courts, 1999), pp. 83–109.

Carroll, William C., 'Theories of Kingship in Shakespeare's England', in Dutton and Howard, eds., *Companion to Shakespeare's Works, II*, pp. 125–45.

Catty, Jocelyn, *Writing Rape, Writing Women in Early Modern England: Unbridled Speech* (Basingstoke: Palgrave, 1999).

Cerasano, S. P., '"Borrowed Robes": Costume Prices, and the Drawing of *Titus Andronicus*', *Sh. St.* 22 (1994), 45–57.

Chambers, E. K., *The Elizabethan Stage*, 4 vols. (Oxford: Oxford University Press, 1923).

Cheney, Patrick, *Spenser's Famous Flight: A Renaissance Idea of a Literary Career* (Toronto: Toronto University Press, 1993).

Marlowe's Counterfeit Profession: Ovid, Spenser, Counter-Nationhood (Toronto: University of Toronto Press, 1997).

Shakespeare, National Poet-Playwright (Cambridge: Cambridge University Press, 2004).

Clare, Janet, *'Art Made Tongue-Tied by Authority': Elizabethan and Jacobean Dramatic Censorship* (2nd ed., Manchester: Manchester University Press, 1990).

'Censorship and Negotiation', in Hadfield, ed., *Literature and Censorship*, pp. 17–30.

Clegg, Cyndia, *Press Censorship in Elizabethan England* (Cambridge: Cambridge University Press, 1997).

Press Censorship in Jacobean England (Cambridge: Cambridge University Press, 2001).

Cloud, Duncan, 'The Constitution and the Public Criminal Law', in Crook et al., eds., *Cambridge Ancient History, Volume IX*, pp. 491–530.

Cohen, Derek, *The Politics of Shakespeare* (Basingstoke: Macmillan, 1993).

Coleman, Janet, *A History of Political Thought*, 2 vols. (Oxford: Blackwell, 2000).

Collinson, Patrick, *Archbishop Grindal, 1519–1583: The Struggle for a Reformed Church* (London: Cape, 1979).

'The Monarchical Republic of Queen Elizabeth I', *BJRLM* 69 (1986–7), 394–424.

'*De Republica Anglorum*: Or, History with the Politics Put Back', in Collinson, *Elizabethan Essays* (London: Hambledon Press, 1994), pp. 1–29.

Elizabethans (London: Hambledon, 2003).

'William Camden and the Anti-Myth of Elizabeth: Setting the Mould?', in Susan Doran and Thomas S. Freeman, eds., *The Myth of Elizabeth* (Basingstoke: Palgrave, 2003), pp. 79–98.

Conte, Gian Biagio, *Latin Literature: A History*, trans. Joseph B. Solodow, rev. Don Fowler and Glenn W. Most (Baltimore: Johns Hopkins University Press, 1999, rpt. of 1994).

Conti, Vittorio, 'The Mechanisation of Virtue: Republican Rituals in Italian Political Thought in the Sixteenth and Seventeenth Centuries', in van Gelderen and Skinner, eds., *Republicanism*, II, pp. 73–83.

Cox, Brian, '*Titus Andronicus*', in Russell Jackson and Robert Smallwood, eds., *Players of Shakespeare*, 3 vols. (Cambridge: Cambridge University Press, 1993), III, pp. 174–88.

Cox, John D. and David Scott Kastan, eds., *A New History of Early English Drama* (New York: Columbia University Press, 1997).

Cox, Virginia, *The Renaissance Dialogue: Literary Dialogue in its Social and Political Contexts, Castiglione to Galileo* (Cambridge: Cambridge University Press, 1993).

Craig, Hardin, Jr., 'The *Geneva Bible* as a Political Document', *PHR* 7 (1938), 40–9.

Craig, Harold, *Of Philosophers and Kings: Political Philosophy in Shakespeare's **Macbeth** and **King Lear*** (Toronto: University of Toronto Press, 2001).

Crook, J. A., Andrew Lintott and Elizabeth Rawson, eds., *The Cambridge Ancient History: Volume IX, The Last Age of the Roman Republic, 146–43 B.C.*, 14 vols. (Cambridge: Cambridge University Press, 1994).

Crupi, Charles W., *Robert Greene* (Boston: Twayne, 1986).

Cummings, Brian, *The Literary Culture of the Reformation: Grammar and Grace* (Oxford: Oxford University Press, 2002).

Cunningham, Karen, 'Opening Doubts Upon the Law: *Measure for Measure*', in Dutton and Howard, eds., *Companion to Shakespeare's Works*, IV, pp. 316–32.

Danby, John F., *Shakespeare's Doctrine of Nature: A Study of **King Lear*** (London: Faber, 1961).

Davidson, William L., *The Stoic Creed* (Edinburgh: T. & T. Clark, 1907).

Davies, H. Neville, 'Jacobean *Antony and Cleopatra*', *Sh. St.* 17 (1985), 123–58.

Dawson, Anthony B., and Paul Yachnin, *The Culture of Playgoing in Shakespeare's England: A Collaborative Debate* (Cambridge: Cambridge University Press, 2001).

Dean, David, *Law-Making and Society in Late Elizabethan England: The Parliament of England, 1584–1601* (Cambridge: Cambridge University Press, 1996).

Desens, Marliss C., *The Bed Trick in English Renaissance Drama* (Newark: University of Delaware Press, 1994).

de Sousa, Geraldo U., *Shakespeare's Cross-Cultural Encounters* (Basingstoke: Palgrave, 1999).

Dessen, Alan C., *Rescripting Shakespeare: The Text, The Director, and Modern Productions* (Cambridge: Cambridge University Press, 2002).

Dewar, Mary, *Sir Thomas Smith: A Tudor Intellectual in Office* (London: Athlone, 1964).

Dillon, Janette, *Theatre, Court and City, 1595–1610* (Cambridge: Cambridge University Press, 2000).

Dimmock, Matthew, *New Turkes: Dramatizing Islam and the Ottomans in Early Modern England* (Aldershot: Ashgate, 2005).

Dollimore, Jonathan, *Radical Tragedy: Religion, Ideology and Power in the Drama of Shakespeare and his Contemporaries* (Brighton: Harvester, 1984).

'Critical Developments: Cultural Materialism, Feminism and Gender Critique, and New Historicism', in Stanley Wells, ed., *Shakespeare: A Bibliographical Guide* (Oxford: Oxford University Press, 1990), pp. 405–28.

and Alan Sinfield, eds., *Political Shakespeare: New Essays in Cultural Materialism* (Manchester: Manchester University Press, 1985).

and Alan Sinfield, 'Culture and Textuality: Debating Cultural Materialism', *Textual Practice* 4 (1990), 91–100.

Dodds, R. and M. H., *The Pilgrimage of Grace, 1536–7, and the Exeter Conspiracy*, 2 vols. (Cambridge: Cambridge University Press, 1915).

Donaldson, Ian, *The Rapes of Lucrece: A Myth and its Transformations* (Oxford: Clarendon Press, 1982).

'"Misconstruing Everything": *Julius Caesar* and *Sejanus'*, in Grace Ioppolo, ed., *Shakespeare Performed: Essays in Honour of R. A. Foakes* (Newark: University of Delaware Press, 2000), pp. 88–107.

Doran, Susan, *Monarchy and Matriarchy: The Courtships of Elizabeth I* (London: Routledge, 1996).

England and Europe in the Sixteenth Century (Basingstoke: Macmillan, 1999).

'Revenge Her Foul and Most Unnatural Murder? The Impact of Mary Stewart's Execution on Anglo-Scottish Relations', *History* 85 (2000), 589–612.

'The Politics of Renaissance Europe', in Hadfield and Hammond, eds., *Shakespeare and Renaissance Europe*, pp. 21–52.

Drakakis, John, ed., *Alternative Shakespeares* (London: Methuen, 1985).

ed., *Antony and Cleopatra: Contemporary Critical Essays* (Basingstoke: Macmillan, 1994).

Duncan, Douglas, *Ben Jonson and the Lucianic Tradition* (Cambridge: Cambridge University Press, 1979).

Duncan-Jones, Katherine, *Sir Philip Sidney: Courtier Poet* (London: Hamish Hamilton, 1991).

'Much Ado with Red and White: The Earliest Readers of Shakespeare's *Venus and Adonis*', *RES*, ns, 44 (1993), 480–501.

Ungentle Shakespeare: Scenes From His Life (London: Thomson, 2001).

'Did the Boy Shakespeare Kill Calves?', *RES*, ns, 55 (2004), 183–95.

Dunnigan, Sarah M., *Eros and Poetry at the Courts of Mary Queen of Scots and James VI* (Basingstoke: Palgrave, 2002).

Dusinberre, Juliet, *Shakespeare and the Nature of Women* (2nd ed., Basingstoke: Macmillan, 1996).

Dutton, Richard, *Mastering the Revels: The Regulation and Censorship of English Renaissance Drama* (Basingstoke: Macmillan, 1991).

Licensing, Censorship and Authorship in Early Modern England: Buggeswords (Basingstoke: Palgrave/Macmillan, 2000).

and Jean E. Howard, eds., *A Companion to Shakespeare's Works*, 4 vols. (Oxford: Blackwell, 2003).

Dzelzainis, Martin, 'Milton's Classical Republicanism', in Armitage et al., eds., *Milton and Republicansim*, pp. 3–24.

'Shakespeare and Political Thought', in Kastan, ed., *Companion to Shakespeare*, pp. 100–16.

Eagleton, Terry, *Literary Theory: An Introduction* (Oxford: Blackwell, 1984).

Edwards, Philip, *Thomas Kyd and Early Elizabethan Tragedy* (London: Longman, 1966).

Elliott, J. H., *Europe Divided, 1559–1598* (London: Collins, 1968).

Ellis, Steven G., *Tudor Ireland: Crown, Community and the Conflict of Cultures, 1470–1603* (London: Longman, 1985).

Erne, Lukas, *Shakespeare as Literary Dramatist* (Cambridge: Cambridge University Press, 2003).

Erskine-Hill, Howard, *Poetry and the Realm of Politics: Shakespeare to Dryden* (Oxford: Clarendon Press, 1996).

Es, Bart van, *Spenser's Forms of History* (Oxford: Oxford University Press, 2002).

Everett, Barbara, '"Spanish" Othello: The Making of Shakespeare's Moor', in Catherine M. S. Alexander and Stanley Wells, eds., *Shakespeare and Race* (Cambridge: Cambridge University Press, 2000), pp. 64–81.

Ferguson, Arthur B., *The Articulate Citizen and the English Renaissance* (Durham: Duke University Press, 1965).

Fiedler, Leslie A., *The Stranger in Shakespeare* (London: Paladin, 1974).

Fincham, Kenneth and Peter Lake, 'The Ecclesiastical Policy of King James I', *JBS* 24 (1985), 169–207.

Fink, Zera S., *The Classical Republicans: An Essay in the Recovery of a Pattern of Thought in Seventeenth Century England* (Evanston: Northwestern University Press, 1962).

Firth, Katherine R., *The Apocalyptic Tradition in Reformation Britain, 1530–1645* (Oxford: Oxford University Press, 1979).

Fischlin, Daniel and Mark Fortier, eds., *Royal Subjects: Essays on the Writings of James VI and I* (Detroit: Wayne State University Press, 2002).

Fitz, Linda T., 'Egyptian Queens and Male Reviewers: Sexist Attitudes in *Antony and Cleopatra* Criticism', *SQ* 28 (1977), 297–316.

Fletcher, Anthony, *Tudor Rebellions* (3rd ed., London: Longman, 1985).

Foakes, R. A., **Hamlet** Versus **Lear** (Cambridge: Cambridge University Press, 1993).

Ford, Philip J., *George Buchanan: Prince of Poets with an Edition of Miscallaneorum Liber* (Aberdeen: Aberdeen University Press, 1982).

Fortier, Mark, 'Equity and Ideas: Coke, Ellesmere, and James I', *RQ* 51 (1998), 1255–82.

Foucault, Michel, *The Order of Things*, trans. anon. (London: Tavistock, 1970). *The History of Sexuality, Volume I*, trans. Robert Hurley (New York: Vintage Books, 1980).

Franklin, Julian H., 'Sovereignty and the Mixed Constitution: Bodin and his Critics', in Burns and Goldie, eds., *Cambridge History of Political Thought*, pp. 298–328.

Fraser, Antonia, *Mary Queen of Scots* (London: Weidenfeld and Nicolson, 1969). *The Gunpowder Plot: Terror & Faith in 1605* (London: Weidenfeld and Nicolson, 1996).

Freedman, Barbara, 'Elizabethan Protest, Plague and Plays: Rereading the "Documents of Control"', *ELR* 26 (1996), 17–45.

Garrett, Christina H., *The Marian Exiles: A Study in the Origins of Elizabethan Puritanism* (Cambridge: Cambridge University Press, 1938).

Gazzard, H., 'Samuel Daniel's *Philotas* and the Earl of Essex', *RES*, ns, 51 (2000), 423–50.

Geckle, George L., ed., **Measure for Measure**: *Shakespeare: The Critical Tradition* (London: Athlone, 2001).

Gelderen, Martin van, 'Aristotelians, Monarchomachs and Republicans: Sovereignty and *respublica mixta* in Dutch and German Political Thought, 1580–1650', in van Gelderen and Skinner, eds., *Republicanism*, I, pp. 195–217.

and Quentin Skinner, eds., *Republicanism: A Shared European Heritage*, 2 vols. (Cambridge: Cambridge University Press, 2002).

Genette, Gerard, *Paratexts: Thresholds of Interpretation*, trans. Jane E. Lewin (Cambridge: Cambridge University Press, 1997).

Gibbons, Brian, *Jacobean City Comedies* (rev. ed., London: Methuen, 1980).

Shakespeare and Multiplicity (Cambridge: Cambridge University Press, 1993).

Gibson, Jonathan, 'Elizabethan Court Poetry', in Mike Pincombe, ed., *The Anatomy of Tudor Literature* (Aldershot: Ashgate, 2001), pp. 98–111.

Gillespie, Stuart, *Shakespeare's Books: A Dictionary of Shakespeare Sources* (London: Athlone, 2001).

Gillies, John, *Shakespeare and the Geography of Difference* (Cambridge: Cambridge University Press, 1994).

Goldberg, Jonathan, 'The Politics of Renaissance Literature: A Review Essay', *ELH* 49 (1982), 514–42.

James I and the Politics of Literature: Jonson, Shakespeare, Donne, and their Contemporaries (Baltimore: Johns Hopkins University Press, 1983).

'Speculations: *Macbeth* and Source', in Jean E. Howard and Marion F. O'Connor, eds., *Shakespeare Reproduced: The Text in History & Ideology* (London: Routledge, 1987), pp. 242–64.

Goldie, Mark, 'The Unacknowledged Republic: Officeholding in Early Modern England', in Tim Harris, ed., *The Politics of the Excluded, c.1500–1850* (Basingstoke: Macmillan, 2001), pp. 153–94.

Gollancz, Sir Israel, *The Sources of Hamlet* (London: Oxford University Press, 1926).

Goy-Blanquet, Dominique, *Shakespeare's Early History Plays: From Chronicle to Stage* (Oxford: Oxford University Press, 2003).

Grady, Hugh, *Shakespeare, Machiavelli, and Montaigne: Power and Subjectivity From Richard II to Hamlet* (Oxford: Oxford University Press, 2002).

Granville-Barker, Harley, *Prefaces to Shakespeare: Hamlet* (London: Batsford, 1963, rpt. of 1930).

Graves, Michael, *Elizabethan Parliaments, 1559–1601* (2nd ed., London: Longman, 1996).

Greenblatt, Stephen, *Renaissance Self-Fashioning: From More to Shakespeare* (Chicago: University of Chicago Press, 1980).

'Invisible Bullets: Renaissance Authority and its Subversion, *Henry IV* and *Henry V*', in Dollimore and Sinfield, eds., *Political Shakespeare*, pp. 18–47.

Hamlet in Purgatory (Princeton: Princeton University Press, 2001).

Grene, Nicholas, *Shakespeare's Serial History Plays* (Cambridge: Cambridge University Press, 2002).

Gurr, Andrew, *The Shakespearian Playing Companies* (Oxford: Clarendon Press, 1996).

The Shakespearean Stage, 1574–1642 (3rd ed., Cambridge: Cambridge University Press, 1999).

Guy, J. G. A., 'The Privy Council: Revolution or Evolution?', in Christopher Coleman and David Starkey, eds., *Revolution Reassessed: Revisions in the History of Tudor Government and Administration* (Oxford: Oxford University Press, 1986), pp. 59–85.

Tudor England (Oxford: Oxford University Press, 1988).

ed., *The Reign of Elizabeth I: Court and Culture in the Last Decade* (Cambridge: Cambridge University Press, 1995).

'Introduction: The 1590s: The Second Reign of Elizabeth I?', in Guy, ed., *The Reign of Elizabeth I*, pp. 1–19.

'The Rhetoric of Counsel in Early Modern England', in Hoak, ed., *Tudor Political Culture*, pp. 292–310.

'Tudor Monarchy and its Critiques: From the Wars of the Roses to the Death of Henry VIII', in John Guy, ed., *The Tudor Monarchy* (London: Arnold, 1997), pp. 78–109.

Hackett, Helen, *Virgin Mother, Maiden Queen: Elizabeth I and the Cult of the Virgin Mary* (Basingstoke: Macmillan, 1995).

Hadfield, Andrew, *Literature, Politics and National Identity: Reformation to Renaissance* (Cambridge: Cambridge University Press, 1994).

'"We see our faults only in the English Glass": John Lyly's *Euphues* and National Identity', *Zentrum Zur Erforschung Der Fruhen Neuzeit: Mitteilungen: Nationalismus und Subjektivitat* (Johann Wolfgang Goethe-Universität Zentrum zur Erforschung der Frühen Neizeit, 1995), 260–271.

Spenser's Irish Experience: Wilde Fruyt and Salvage Soyl (Oxford: Clarendon Press, 1997).

'Sidney's "poor painter" and John Stubbs's *Gaping Gulf*', *SJ* 15.2 (Fall 1997), 45–48.

Literature, Travel and Colonial Writing in the English Renaissance, 1545–1625 (Oxford: Clarendon Press, 1998).

'Was Spenser a Republican?', *English* 47 (1998), 169–82.

The English Renaissance, 1500–1620 (Oxford: Blackwell, 2001).

'Censoring Ireland in Elizabethan England, 1580–1600', in Hadfield, ed., *Literature and Censorship*, pp. 149–64.

Shakespeare and Renaissance Politics (London: Thomson: Arden Critical Companions, 2003).

Shakespeare, Spenser and the Matter of Britain (Basingstoke: Palgrave/Macmillan, 2003).

'Was Spenser a Republican After All? A Response to David Scott Okamura-Wilson', *Sp. Stud.* 17 (2003), 275–90.

'Shakespeare and Republicanism: History and Cultural Materialism', *Textual Practice* 17 (2003), 461–83.

'*Henry V*', in Dutton and Howard, eds., *Companion to Shakespeare* II, pp. 451–67.

'*Timon of Athens* and Jacobean Politics', *Sh. Sur.* 56 (2003), 215–26.

'Shakespeare's *Measure for Measure* (and the Homosexuality of James I)', *The Explicator* 61 (2003), 71–3.

'*Tamburlaine* as the 'Scourge of God' and *The First English Life of King Henry the Fifth*', *N. & Q.* 50.3 (December 2003), 399–400.

'Spenser and Politics', in Bart van Es, ed., *The Palgrave Companion to Spenser Studies* (Basingstoke: Palgrave, forthcoming in 2006).

ed., *Edmund Spenser* (London: Longman, 1996).

ed., *Literature and Censorship in Renaissance England* (Basingstoke: Palgrave/ Macmillan, 2001).

ed., *A Routledge Literary Sourcebook on William Shakespeare's **Othello*** (London: Routledge, 2003).

ed., with Paul Hammond, *Shakespeare and Renaissance Europe* (London: Thomson, 2004).

Haigh, Christopher, *Elizabeth I* (London: Longman, 1988).

Hale, D. G., *The Body Politic: A Political Metaphor in Renaissance England* (The Hague: Mouton, 1971).

'*Coriolanus*: The Death of a Political Metaphor', *Sh. Sur.* 22 (1971), 197–202.

Hale, J. R., *Machiavelli and Renaissance Italy* (Harmondsworth: Penguin, 1961).

Hamilton, A. C., ed., *The Spenser Encyclopaedia* (London and Toronto: Routledge/University of Toronto Press, 1990).

Hamilton, Donna B., *Virgil and **The Tempest**: The Politics of Imitation* (Columbus: Ohio State University Press, 1990).

Hammer, Paul E. J., 'The Uses of Scholarship: The Secretariat of Robert Devereux, 2nd Earl of Essex, c.1585–1601', *EHR* 109 (1994), 26–51.

The Polarisation of Elizabethan Politics: The Political Career of Robert Devereux, 2nd Earl of Essex, 1585–1597 (Cambridge: Cambridge University Press, 1997).

Hammond, Paul, 'The Argument of *Measure for Measure*', *ELR* 16 (1986), 496–519.

Dryden and the Traces of Classical Rome (Oxford: Oxford University Press, 1999).

Figuring Sex between Men from Shakespeare to Rochester (Oxford: Oxford University Press, 2002).

Hankins, James, ed., *Renaissance Civic Humanism* (Cambridge: Cambridge University Press, 2000).

Hansen, Matthew C., 'Gender, Power and Play: Fulke Greville's *Mustapha* and *Alaham*', *SJ* 19 (2001), 125–41.

Harbage, Alfred, *Annals of English Drama, 975–1700: An Annotated Record of All Plays, Extant or Lost, Chronologically Arranged and Indexed by Authors, Titles, Dramatic Companies, Etc.*, rev. S. Schoenbaum (London: Routledge, 3rd ed., 1989).

Harris, Jonathan Gil, '"Narcissus in thy face": Roman Desire and the Difference it Fakes in *Antony and Cleopatra*', *SQ* 45 (1994), 408–25.

Hattaway, Michael, Boika Sokolova and Derek Roper, eds., *Shakespeare in the New Europe* (Sheffield: Sheffield Academic Press, 1995).

'Shakespeare's Histories: The Politics of Recent British Productions', in Hattaway et al., eds., *Shakespeare in the New Europe*, pp. 351–69.

Haugaard, W. P., *Elizabeth and the English Reformation* (Cambridge: Cambridge University Press, 1968).

Hawkes, Terence, *Shakespeare in the Present* (London: Routledge, 2002).

Hay, Millicent V., *The Life of Robert Sidney, Earl of Leicester (1563–1626)* (Washington: Folger Shakespeare Library, 1984).

Healy, Margaret, *William Shakespeare's **Richard II*** (Plymouth: Northcote House, 1998).

    Fictions of Disease in Early Modern England: Bodies, Plagues and Politics (Basingstoke: Palgrave/Macmillan, 2001).

Heinemann, Margot, 'Rebel Lords, Popular Playwrights, and Political Culture: Notes on the Jacobean patronage of the Earl of Southampton', *YES* 21 (1991), 63–86.

    '"Let Rome in Tiber melt": Order and Disorder in *Antony and Cleopatra*', in Drakakis, ed., *Antony and Cleopatra*, pp. 166–81.

Helgerson, Richard, *The Elizabethan Prodigals* (Berkeley: University of California Press, 1976).

    Self-Crowned Laureates: Spenser, Jonson, Milton and the Literary System (Berkeley: University of California Press, 1983).

    Forms of Nationhood: The Elizabethan Writing of England (Chicago: University of Chicago Press, 1992).

Herman, Peter C., '"O, 'tis a gallant king": Shakespeare's *Henry V* and the Crisis of the 1590s', in Hoak, ed., *Tudor Political Culture*, pp. 204–25.

Hibbard, G. R., *Thomas Nashe: A Critical Introduction* (London: Routledge, 1962).

Hieatt, A. Kent, 'Shakespeare, William', in Hamilton, ed., *Spenser Encyclopaedia*, pp. 641–43.

Hill, Christopher, *Milton and the English Revolution* (London: Faber, 1977).

Hill, Eugene D., 'Revenge Tragedy', in Kinney, ed., *Companion to Renaissance Drama*, pp. 326–35.

Hilton, Rodney, *Bond Men Made Free: Medieval Peasant Movements and the English Rising of 1381* (London: Methuen, 1981, rpt. of 1973).

Hirsh, James, *Shakespeare and the History of Soliloquies* (Madison: Farleigh-Dickinson University Press, 2003).

Hirst, Derek, *The Representative of the People? Voters and Voting under the Early Stuarts* (Cambridge: Cambridge University Press, 1975).

Hoak, Dale, ed., *Tudor Political Culture* (Cambridge: Cambridge University Press, 1995).

Holderness, Graham, *The Shakespeare Myth* (Manchester: Manchester University Press, 1988).

    Shakespeare: The Histories (Basingstoke: Macmillan, 2000).

    Cultural Shakespeare: Essays in the Shakespeare Myth (Hatfield: University of Hertfordshire Press, 2001).

Holland, Peter, 'Shakespeare Performances in England, 1993–1994', *Sh. Sur.* 48 (1995), 191–226.

Holland, Tom, *Rubicon: The Triumph and Tragedy of the Roman Republic* (London: Abacus, 2003).

Holmes, P. J., *Resistance and Compromise: The Political Thought of the Elizabethan Catholics* (Cambridge: Cambridge University Press, 1982).

Honan, Park, *Shakespeare, A Life* (Oxford: Oxford University Press, 1998).

Honigmann, E. A. J., *Shakespeare: The Lost Years* (Manchester: Manchester University Press, 1985).

*The Texts of **Othello** and Shakespearean Revision* (London: Nelson, 1996).

Hope, Jonathan, *The Authorship of Shakespeare's Plays* (Cambridge: Cambridge University Press, 1994).

Hough, Graham, *A Preface to **The Faerie Queene*** (London: Duckworth, 1962), ch. 8.

Howard, Jean E., 'The New Historicism in Renaissance Studies', *ELR* 16 (1986), 13–43.

The Stage and Social Struggle in Early Modern England (London: Routledge, 1994).

Howarth, David, *Images of Rule: Art and Politics in the English Renaissance, 1485–1649* (Basingstoke: Macmillan, 1997).

Huffman, C. C., ***Coriolanus** in Context* (Lewisburg: Bucknell University Press, 1971).

Hulse, Clark, *Metamorphic Verse: The Elizabethan Minor Epic* (Princeton: Princeton University Press, 1981).

Hume, Robert D., *Reconstructing Contexts: The Aims and Principles of Archaeo-Historicism* (Oxford: Clarendon Press, 1999).

Hunter, G. K., *John Lyly: The Humanist as Courtier* (London: Routledge, 1962).

Hutson, Lorna, *Thomas Nashe in Context* (Oxford: Clarendon Press, 1989).

Ingledew, J. E., 'Chapman's Use of Lucan in *Caesar and Pompey*', *RES*, ns, 13 (1962), 283–8.

Ioppolo, Grace, *Revising Shakespeare* (Cambridge, Mass.: Harvard University Press, 1991).

ed., *Shakespeare Performed: Essays in Honour of R. A. Foakes* (Newark: University of Delaware Press, 2000).

Jackson, MacDonald P., *Studies in Attribution: Middleton and Shakespeare* (Salzburg: Salzburg University Press, 1979).

James, Heather, *Shakespeare's Troy: Drama, Politics, and the Translation of Empire* (Cambridge: Cambridge University Press, 1997).

James, Mervyn, *Society, Politics and Culture: Studies in Early Modern Culture* (Cambridge: Cambridge University Press, 1988).

Jankowski, T., *Women in Power in Early Modern Drama* (Urbana: University of Illinois Press, 1992).

Jardine, Lisa, *From Humanism to the Humanities: Education and the Liberal Arts in Fifteenth- and Sixteenth-Century Europe* (London: Duckworth, 1986).

Reading Shakespeare Historically (London: Routledge, 1996).

and Anthony Grafton, '"Studied for Action": How Gabriel Harvey read his Livy', *P. & P.* 129 (1990), 30–78.

and Alan Stewart, *Hostage to Fortune: The Troubled Life of Francis Bacon* (New York: Hill and Wang, 1998).

Javitch, Daniel, *Poetry and Courtliness in Renaissance England.* (Princeton, N.J.: Princeton University Press. 1978).

Jed, Stephanie, *Chaste Thinking: The Rape of Lucretia and the Birth of Modern Humanism* (Bloomington: Indiana University Press, 1989).

Jenkins, Harold, *The Life and Work of Henry Chettle* (London: Sidgwick and Jackson, 1934).

Jensen, Kristian, 'The Humanist Reform of Latin and Latin teaching', in Kraye, ed., *Cambridge Companion to Renaissance Humanism*, pp. 63–81.

Johnson, Samuel, *Samuel Johnson on Shakespeare*, ed. H. R. Woudhuysen (Harmondsworth: Penguin, 1989).

Jones, Ann Rosalind and Peter Stallybrass, 'The Politics of *Astrophil and Stella*', *SEL* 24 (1984), 53–68.

Renaissance Clothing and the Materials of Memory (Cambridge: Cambridge University Press, 2000).

Jones, Emrys, *The Origins of Shakespeare* (Oxford: Clarendon Press, 1977).

Jones, Howard, *Master Tully. Cicero in Tudor England*, Vol. LVII (Nieuwkoop: Bibliotheca Humanistica & Reformatorica, 1981).

Jones, Norman, 'Parliament and the Political Society of Elizabethan England', in Hoak, ed., *Tudor Political Culture*, pp. 226–42.

Jones, Whitney R. D., *The Tree of Commonwealth, 1450–1793* (Madison: Fairleigh-Dickinson University Press, 2000).

Jordan, Constance, 'Woman's Rule in Sixteenth-Century British Political Thought', *RQ* 40 (1987), 421–51.

Renaissance Feminism: Literary Texts and Political Methods (Ithaca. N.Y.: Cornell University Press, 1990).

Shakespeare's Monarchies: Ruler and Subject in the Romances (Ithaca, N.Y.: Cornell University Press, 1997).

Joseph, Sister Miriam, *Rhetoric in Shakespeare's Time: Literary Theory of Renaissance Europe* (New York: Harcourt, Brace & World, 1962).

Jowitt, Claire, *Voyage Drama and Gender Politics, 1589–1642: Real and Imagined Worlds* (Manchester: Manchester University Press, 2003).

Kahn, Coppélia, 'The Rape in Shakespeare's *Lucrece*', *Sh. St.* 9 (1976), 45–72.

'Self and Eros in *Venus and Adonis*', *CR* 20 (1976), 351–71.

Roman Shakespeare: Warriors, Wounds, and Women (London: Routledge, 1997).

'Publishing Shame: *The Rape of Lucrece*', in Dutton and Howard, eds., *Companion to Shakespeare's Works*, IV, pp. 259–74.

Kantorowicz, Ernst H., *The King's Two Bodies: A Study in Medieval Political Theology* (Princeton: Princeton University Press, 1957).

Kaplan, M. Lindsay, *The Culture of Slander in Early Modern England* (Cambridge: Cambridge University Press, 1997).

Kastan, David Scott, *Shakespeare After Theory* (London: Routledge, 1999).

'"Proud Majesty Made a Subject": Representing Authority on the Early Modern State', in Kastan, *Shakespeare After Theory*, pp. 109–27.

Shakespeare and the Book (Cambridge: Cambridge University Press, 2001).

'Performances and Playbooks: The Closing of the Theatres and the Politics of drama', in Sharpe and Zwicker, eds., *Reading, Society and Politics*, pp. 167–84.

ed., *A Companion to Shakespeare* (Oxford: Blackwell, 1999).

Keeton, George W., *Shakespeare's Legal and Political Background* (London: Pitman, 1967).

Kelley, Donald R., 'Law', in Burns and Goldie, eds., *Cambridge History of Political Thought*, pp. 66–94.

Kelsey, Sean, *Inventing a Republic: The Political Culture of the English Commonwealth, 1649–1653* (Manchester: Manchester University Press, 1997).

Kendall, Gillian Murray, '"Lend me thy Hand": Metaphor and Mayhem in *Titus Andronicus*', *SQ* 45 (1994), 279–303.

Kendall, R. T., *Calvin and English Calvinism to 1649* (Oxford: Oxford University Press, 1979).

Kernan, Alvin, ed., *Two Renaissance Mythmakers: Christopher Marlowe and Ben Jonson* (Baltimore: Johns Hopkins University Press, 1977).

Shakespeare, The King's Playwright: Theater in the Stuart Court, 1603–1613 (New Haven: Yale University Press, 1995).

Kerrigan, John., ed., *Motives of Woe: Shakespeare and 'Female Complaint', A Critical Anthology* (Oxford: Clarendon Press, 1991).

On Shakespeare and Early Modern Literature: Essays (Oxford: Oxford University Press, 2001).

Kerrigan, William, *Hamlet's Perfection* (Baltimore: the Johns Hopkins University Press, 1994).

Kesselring, K. J., *Mercy and Authority in the Tudor State* (Cambridge: Cambridge University Press, 2003).

Kewes, Paulina, '*Julius Caesar* in Jacobean England', *The Seventeenth Century* 17 (2002), 155–86.

'The Elizabethan History Play: A True Genre?', in Dutton and Howard, eds., *Companion to Shakespeare's Works*, II, pp. 170–93.

'Contemporary Europe in Elizabethan and Early Stuart Drama', in Hadfield and Hammond, eds., *Shakespeare and Renaissance Europe*, pp. 150–92.

Kiefer, Frederick, *Shakespeare's Visual Theatre: Staging the Personified Characters* (Cambridge: Cambridge University Press, 2003).

Kiernan, Pauline, *Staging Shakespeare at the New Globe* (Basingstoke: Macmillan, 1999).

'*Venus and Adonis* and Ovidian Indecorous Wit', in Taylor, ed., *Shakespeare's Ovid*, pp. 81–95.

King, John N., *English Reformation Literature: The Tudor Origins of the Protestant Tradition* (Princeton: Princeton University Press, 1982).

Kingdon, Robert M., *Myths about the Saint Bartholomew's Day Massacres, 1572–1576* (Cambridge, Mass.: Harvard University Press, 1988).

'Calvinism and Resistance Theory, 1550–1580', in Burns and Goldie, eds., *Cambridge History of Political Thought*, pp. 193–218.

Kingsley-Smith, Jane, *Shakespeare's Drama of Exile* (Basingstoke: Palgrave, 2003).

Kinney, Arthur, ed., *A Companion to Renaissance Drama* (Oxford: Blackwell, 2002).

Kintgen, Eugene R., *Reading in Tudor England* (Pittsburgh: University of Pittsburgh Press, 1996).

Kishlansky, Mark A., *Parliamentary Selection: Social and Political Choice in Early Modern England* (Cambridge: Cambridge University Press, 1986).

Klause, John, '*Venus and Adonis*: Can We Forgive Them?', *SP* 85 (1988), 353–77

Knight, G. Wilson, *The Wheel of Fire: Interpretations of Shakespearean Tragedy* (London: Routledge, 1989, rpt. of 1930), ch. 6.

Knoppers, Laura Lunger, 'The Politics of Portraiture: Oliver Cromwell and the Plain Style', *RQ* 51 (1998), 1283–1319.

Knowles, Ronald, '*Hamlet* and Counter-Humanism', *RQ* 52 (1999), 1046–69.

Shakespeare's Arguments with History (Basingstoke: Palgrave/Macmillan, 2002).

ed., *Shakespeare and Carnival: After Bakhtin* (Basingstoke: Palgrave, 1998).

Kocher, Paul H., 'François Hotman and Marlowe's *The Massacre at Paris*', *PMLA* 56 (1941), 349–68.

'Contemporary Backgrounds for Marlowe's *The Massacre at Paris*', *MLQ* 8 (1947), 151–73, 309–18.

Knutson, Roslyn Lander, *Playing Companies and Commerce in Shakespeare's Time* (Cambridge: Cambridge University Press, 2001).

Kraye, Jill, 'Moral Philosophy', in Charles B. Schmitt and Quentin Skinner, eds., *The Cambridge History of Renaissance Philosophy* (Cambridge: Cambridge University Press, 1988), pp. 303–86.

ed., *The Cambridge Companion to Renaissance Humanism* (Cambridge: Cambridge University Press, 1996).

'Philologists and Philosophers', in Kraye, ed., *Cambridge Companion to Renaissance Humanism*, pp. 142–60.

Kristeller, Paul O., 'Rhetoric in Medieval and Renaissance Culture', in Murphy, ed., *Renaissance Rhetoric*, pp. 1–20.

Kurland, Stuart M., '*Henry VIII* and James I: Shakespeare and Jacobean Politics', *Sh. St.* 19 (1987), 203–17.

'*Hamlet* and the Scottish Succession?', *SEL* 34 (1994), 279–300.

Lacey, Robert, *Robert, Earl of Essex: An Elizabethan Icarus* (London: Weidenfeld and Nicolson, 1970).

Sir Walter Ralegh (London: Cardinal, 1975).

Lake, Peter, 'Ministers, Magistrates and the Production of "Order" in *Measure for Measure*', *Sh. Sur.* 54 (2001), 165–81.

Lander, Jesse M., 'Martin Marprelate and the Fugitive Text', *Reformation* 7 (2002), 135–85.

Leggatt, Alexander, *Shakespeare's Political Drama: The History Plays and the Roman Plays* (London: Routledge, 1988).

Le Glay, Marcel, Jean-Louis Voison, Yann Le Bohec and David Cherry, *A History of Rome* (2nd ed., Oxford: Blackwell, 2001).

Lejosne, Roger, 'Milton, Satan, Salmasius and Abdiel', in Armitage et al., eds., *Milton and Republicanism*, pp. 106–17.

Lemon, Rebecca, 'The Faculty Verdict in "The Crown v. John Hayward"', *SEL* 41 (2001), 109–32.

Lerer, Seth, 'Errata: Print, Politics and Poetry in Early Modern England', in Sharpe and Zwicker, eds., *Reading, Society and Politics*, pp. 41–71.

Levack, Brian P., *The Civil Lawyers in England, 1603–1641: A Political Study* (Oxford: Clarendon Press, 1973).

Levin, Carole, *The Heart and Stomach of a King: Elizabeth I and the Politics of Sex and Power* (Philadelphia: University of Pennsylvania Press, 1994).

Levin, Harry, *The Overreacher: A Study of Christopher Marlowe* (Cambridge, Mass.: Harvard University Press, 1952).

Levin, Richard, 'Bashing the Bourgeois Subject', *Textual Practice* 3 (1989), 76–86.
'Son of Bashing the Bourgeois Subject', *Textual Practice* 6 (1992), 264–70.

Levine, Mortimer, *The Early Elizabethan Succession Question, 1558–1568* (Stanford: Stanford University Press, 1966).
Tudor Dynastic Problems (London: Allen and Unwin, 1973).

Levine, Nina S., *Women's Matters: Politics, Gender, and Nation in Shakespeare's Early History Plays* (Newark: University of Delaware Press, 1998).

Lewis, Elizabeth Jayne, *The Trial of Mary Queen of Scots: A Brief History with Documents* (Boston: Bedford, 1999).

Lezra, Jacques, 'The Appearance of History in *Measure for Measure*', in *Unspeakable Subjects: The Genealogy of the Event in Early Modern Europe* (Stanford: Stanford University Press, 1997), pp. 257–96.

Liebler, Naomi Conn, *Shakespeare's Festive Tragedy: The Ritual Foundations of Genre* (London: Routledge, 1995).

Lindley, David, ed., *The Court Masque* (Manchester: Manchester University Press, 1984).

Lintott, Andrew, 'The Roman Empire and its Problems in the Late Second Century', in Crook et al., eds., *Cambridge Ancient History, Volume IX*, pp. 16–39.

Little, Arthur L., Jr., *Shakespeare Jungle Fever: National-Imperial Re-Visions of Race, Rape, and Sacrifice* (Stanford: Stanford University Press, 2000).

Liu, Alan, 'The Power of Formalism: The New Historicism', *ELH* 56 (1989), 721–71.

Livesay, John Leon, *Stefano Guazzo and the English Renaissance, 1575–1675* (Chapel Hill, N.C.: University of North Carolina Press, 1961).

Livet, Georges, 'France: Failure or Spiritual Heritage?', in Pierre Chanu, ed., *The Reformation* (Gloucester: Sutton, 1989), pp. 168–83.

Loach, Jennifer, *Parliament under the Tudors* (Oxford: Oxford University Press, 1991).

Loades, David, *Two Tudor Conspiracies* (Cambridge: Cambridge University Press, 1965).

The Reign of Mary Tudor: Politics, Government and Religion in England, 1553–58 (2nd ed., London: Longman, 1991).

Power in Tudor England (Basingstoke: Macmillan, 1997).

Loewenstein, David, *Representing Revolution in Milton and his Contemporaries: Religion, Politics, and Polemics in Radical Puritanism* (Cambridge: Cambridge University Press, 2001).

Logan, George M., 'Daniel's *Civil Wars* and Lucan's *Pharsalia*', *SEL* 11 (1971), 53–68.

'Lucan – Daniel – Shakespeare: New Light on the Relation Between *The Civil Wars* and *Richard II*', *Sh. St.* 9 (1976), 121–40.

Longstaffe, Stephen, '"A short report and not otherwise": Jack Cade in *2 Henry VI*', in Knowles, ed., *Shakespeare and Carnival: After Bakhtin*, pp. 13–35.

Loomba, Ania, *Gender, Race, Renaissance Drama* (Manchester: Manchester University Press, 1989).

Shakespeare, Race, and Colonialism (Oxford: Oxford University Press, 2002).

Luce, T. J., *Livy: The Composition of His History* (Princeton: Princeton University Press, 1977).

Lunney, Ruth, *Marlowe and the Popular Tradition: Innovation in the English Drama before 1595* (Manchester: Manchester University Press, 2002).

MacCaffrey, Isabel G., *Spenser's Allegory: The Anatomy of Imagination* (Princeton: Princeton University Press, 1976).

McAlindon, Tom, *Shakespeare's Tudor History: A Study of **Henry IV, Parts 1 and 2*** (Aldershot: Ashgate, 2001).

McCabe, Richard A., 'Elizabethan Satire and the Bishops' Ban of 1599', *YES* 11 (1981), 188–93.

'The Masks of Duessa: Spenser, Mary Queen of Scots, and James VI', *ELR* 17 (1987), 224–42.

'"Right Puisante and Terrible Priests": The role of the Anglican Church in Elizabethan State Censorship', in Hadfield, ed., *Literature and Censorship*, pp. 75–94.

McCanles, Michael, '*The Shepheardes Calender* as Document and Monument', *SEL* 22 (1982), 5–19.

McConica, J. K., *English Humanists and Reformation Politics* (Oxford: Clarendon Press, 1965).

McCoy, Richard C., *Sir Philip Sidney: Rebellion in Arcadia* (Hassocks: Harvester, 1979).

The Rites of Knighthood: The Literature and Politics of Elizabethan Chivalry (Berkeley: University of California Press, 1989).

McCullogh, Diarmaid, *The Boy King: Edward VI and the Protestant Reformation* (Basingstoke: Palgrave, 2001).

McFarlane, I. D., *Buchanan* (London: Duckworth, 1981).

McGrail, Mary Ann, *Tyranny in Shakespeare* (Lanham: Lexington Books, 2001).

McGrail, Thomas H., *Sir William Alexander, First Earl of Stirling* (Edinburgh: Oliver and Boyd, 1940).

McLane, Paul E., *Spenser's **Shepheardes Calender**: A Study in Elizabethan Allegory* (Notre Dame, In.: Notre Dame University Press, 1961).

McLaren, Anne N., *Political Culture in the Reign of Elizabeth I: Queen and Commonwealth, 1558–1585* (Cambridge: Cambridge University Press, 1999).

'Gender, Religion, and Early Modern Nationalism: Elizabeth I, Mary Queen of Scots, and the Genesis of English Anti-Catholicism', *AHR* 107 (2002), 739–67.

McLure, Millar, *George Chapman: A Critical Study* (Toronto: University of Toronto Press, 1966).

ed., *Marlowe: The Critical Heritage, 1588–1896* (London: Routledge, 1979).

McMillin, Scott, 'Professional Playwrighting', in Kastan, ed., *Companion to Shakespeare*, pp. 225–38.

McPherson, David, 'Lewkenor's Venice and its Sources', *RQ* 41 (1988), 459–66

Shakespeare, Jonson, and the Myth of Venice (Newark: University of Delaware Press, 1990).

Maguire, Laurie E., *Shakespeare's Suspect Texts: The 'Bad' Quartos and their Contexts* (Cambridge: Cambridge University Press, 1996).

Maley, Willy, *A Spenser Chronology* (Basingstoke: Macmillan, 1994).

Manheim, Michael, *The Weak King Dilemma in the Shakespearean History Play* (Syracuse: Syracuse University Press, 1973).

Manley, Lawrence, *Literature and Culture in Early Modern London* (Cambridge: Cambridge University Press, 1995).

Marcus, Leah S., *Puzzling Shakespeare: Local Reading and its Discontents* (Berkeley: University of California Press, 1988).

Unediting the Renaissance: Shakespeare, Marlowe, Milton (London: Routledge, 1996).

Marotti, Arthur F., '"Love is Not Love": Elizabethan Sonnet Sequences and the Social Order', *ELH* 49 (1982), 396–428.

Marshall, Cynthia, 'Man of Steel Got the Blues: Melancholic Subversion of Presence in *Antony and Cleopatra*', *SQ* 44 (1993), 385–408.

'Portia's Wound, Calpurnia's Dream: Reading Character in *Julius Caesar*', in Wilson, ed., *Julius Caesar*, pp. 170–87.

Martin, Randall, '*The True Tragedy of Richard Duke of York* and *3 Henry VI*: Report and Revision', *RES*, ns, 53 (2002), 8–30.

Maslen, Robert, *Elizabethan Fictions: Espionage, Counter-espionage and the Duplicity of Fiction in Early Elizabethan Prose Narratives* (Oxford: Clarendon Press, 1997).

Mason, Roger A., '*Rex Stoicus*: George Buchanan, James VI and the Scottish Polity', in John Dwyer, Roger A. Mason, and Alexander Murdoch, eds., *New Perspectives on the Politics and Culture of Early Modern Scotland* (Edinburgh: Donald, 1982), pp. 9–33.

'George Buchanan, James VI and the Presbyterians', in Mason, ed., *Scots and Britons*, pp. 112–37.

'James I, George Buchanan and *The Trew Law of Free Monarchies*', in Roger Mason, *Kingship and the Commonweal: Political Thought in Renaissance and Reformation Scotland* (East Lothian: Tuckwell Press, 1998), pp. 215–41.

ed., *Scots and Britons: Scottish Political Thought and the Union of 1603* (Cambridge: Cambridge University Press, 1994).

Masten, Jeffrey, *Textual Intercourse: Collaboration, Authorship, and Sexualities in Renaissance Drama* (Cambridge: Cambridge University Press, 1997).

Matar, Nabil, *Islam in Britain, 1558–1685* (Cambridge: Cambridge University Press, 1998).

Matheson, Mark, 'Venetian Culture and the Politics of *Othello*', *Sh. Sur.* 48 (1995), 123–33.

Matz, Robert, *Defending Literature in Early Modern England: Renaissance Literary Theory in Social Context* (Cambridge: Cambridge University Press, 2000).

Maus, Katharine Eisman, 'Taking Tropes Seriously: Language and Violence in Shakespeare's *Rape of Lucrece*', *SQ* 37 (1996), 66–82.

Mayer, T. F., *Thomas Starkey and the Commonweal* (Cambridge: Cambridge University Press, 1989).

Metz, G. Harold, 'The Early Staging of *Titus Andronicus*', *Sh. St.* 14 (1981), 99–109.

Miles, Geoffrey, *Shakespeare and the Constant Romans* (Oxford: Clarendon Press, 1996).

Miller, Anthony, *Roman Triumphs and Early Modern English Culture* (Basingstoke: Palgrave, 2001).

Miola, Robert S., *Shakespeare's Rome* (Cambridge: Cambridge University Press, 1983).

'*Julius Caesar* and the Tyrannicide Debate', *RQ* 36 (1985), 271–90.

Shakespeare's Reading (Oxford: Oxford University Press, 2000).

Miskimin, A. S., *The Renaissance Chaucer* (New Haven: Yale University Press, 1975).

Morrall, J. B., *Political Thought in Medieval Times* (Toronto: University of Toronto Press, 1997, rpt. of 1980).

Morrill, John S., *The Revolt of the Provinces: Conservatives and Radicals in the English Civil War 1630–1650* (London: Allen and Unwin, 1976).

Mortimer, Anthony, *Variable Passions: A Reading of Shakespeare's **Venus and Adonis*** (New York: AMS Press, 2000).

Morton, A. L., *The English Utopia* (London: Lawrence and Wishart, 1978, rpt. of 1952).

Mossman, Judith, '*Henry V* and Plutarch's *Alexander*', *SQ* 45 (1994), 57–73.

Moulick, S. K. Roy, *Christopher Marlowe: A Study of Ovidian and Machiavellian Aspects in his Works* (Calcutta: Progressive Publishers, 1996).

Muir, Kenneth, *Life and Letters of Sir Thomas Wyatt* (Liverpool: Liverpool University Press, 1963).

Murphy, James P., ed., *Renaissance Rhetoric: Studies in the Theory and Practice of Renaissance Rhetoric* (Berkeley: University of California Press, 1983).

Najemy, John M., 'Civic Humanism and Florentine Politics', in Hankins, ed., *Renaissance Civic Humanism*, pp. 105–43.

Neale, J. E., *Queen Elizabeth* (London: Cape, 1934).

Elizabeth I and her Parliaments, 2 vols. (London: Cape, 1957).

'Peter Wentworth', in E. B. Fryde and Edward Miller, eds., *Historical Studies of the English Parliament: Volume 2, 1399 to 1603* (Cambridge: Cambridge University Press, 1970), pp. 246–95.

Nederman, Cary J., 'Rhetoric, Reason and Republic: Republicanisms – Ancient, Medieval, and Modern', in Hankins, ed., *Renaissance Civic Humanism*, pp. 247–69.

Neill, Michael, *Issues of Death: Mortality and Identity in English Renaissance Tragedy* (Oxford: Oxford University Press, 1997).

'"He that thou knowest thine": Friendship and Service in *Hamlet*', in Dutton and Howard, eds., *Companion to Shakespeare's Works*, I, pp. 319–38.

Nelson, Eric, *The Greek Tradition in Republican Thought* (Cambridge: Cambridge University Press, 2004).

Newman, Jane O., '"And Let Mild Women to Him Lose Their Mildness": Philomela, Female Violence, and Shakespeare's *The Rape of Lucrece*', *SQ* 45 (1994), 304–26.

Newman, Karen, '"And wash the Ethiop white": Femininity and the Monstrous in *Othello*', in Jean E. Howard and Marion F. O'Connor, eds., *Shakespeare Reproduced: The Text in History & Ideology* (London: Routledge, 1987), pp. 143–62.

Nicholl, Charles, *The Reckoning: The Murder of Christopher Marlowe* (London: Cape, 1992).

Nicoll, Allardyce and Josephine Nicoll, eds., *Holinshed's **Chronicles** as Used in Shakespeare's Plays* (London: Dent, 1927).

Norbrook, David, '*Macbeth* and the Politics of Historiography', in Kevin Sharpe and Steven Zwicker, eds., *Politics of Discourse: The Literature and History of Seventeenth-Century England* (Berkeley: University of California Press, 1987), pp. 78–116.

'Lucan, Thomas May, and the Creation of a Republican Literary Culture', in Sharpe and Lake, eds., *Culture and Politics in Early Stuart England*, pp. 45–66.

Writing the English Republic: Poetry, Rhetoric and Politics, 1627–1660 (Cambridge: Cambridge University Press, 1999).

Poetry and Politics in the English Renaissance (rev. ed., Oxford: Oxford University Press, 2002).

Nuttall, A. D., *A New Mimesis: Shakespeare and the Representation of Reality* (London: Methuen, 1983).

Oakley, Francis, 'On the Road from Constance to 1688: The Political Thought of John Major and George Buchanan', *JBS* 2 (1962), 1–31.

O'Callaghan, Michelle, *The 'Shepheardes Nation': Jacobean Spenserians and Early Stuart Political Culture, 1612–1625* (Oxford: Clarendon Press, 2000).

Orgel, Stephen, *The Illusion of Power: Political Theatre in the English Renaissance* (Berkeley: University of California Press, 1975).

    Imagining Shakespeare: A History of Texts and Visions (Basingstoke: Palgrave, 2003).

Palfrey, Simon, *Late Shakespeare: A New World of Words* (Oxford: Clarendon Press, 1997).

Parmelee, Lisa Ferraro, *Good News From France: French Anti-League Propaganda in Late Elizabethan England* (Rochester, N.Y.: University of Rochester Press, 1996).

Parry, G. J. R., *A Protestant Vision: William Harrison and the Reformation of Elizabethan England* (Cambridge: Cambridge University Press, 1987).

Parry, Graham, *The Golden Age Restor'd: The Culture of the Stuart Court, 1603–42* (Manchester: Manchester University Press, 1981).

Paster, Gail Kern, '"In the spirit of men there is no blood": Blood as Trope of Gender in *Julius Caesar*', in Wilson, ed., *Julius Caesar*, pp. 149–69.

Patterson, Annabel, *Censorship and Interpretation: The Conditions of Writing in Early Modern England* (Madison, Wisc.: University of Wisconsin Press, 1984).

    Shakespeare and the Popular Voice (Oxford: Blackwell, 1989).

    Fables of Power: Aesopian Writing and Political History (Durham: Duke University Press, 1991).

    Reading Between the Lines (Madison: University of Wisconsin Press, 1993).

    *Reading Holinshed's **Chronicles*** (Chicago: Chicago University Press, 1994).

    Early Modern Liberalism (Cambridge: Cambridge University Press, 1997).

    'Political Thought and the Theater, 1580–1630', in Kinney, ed., *Companion to Renaissance Drama*, 25–39.

Patterson, W. B., *King James VI and I and the Reunion of Christendom* (Cambridge: Cambridge University Press, 1997).

Paul, Henry N., *The Royal Play of **Macbeth*** (New York: Macmillan, 1948).

Peck, Linda Levy, ed., *The Mental World of the Jacobean Court* (Cambridge: Cambridge University Press, 1991).

Peltonen, Markku, *Classical Humanism and Republicanism in English Political Thought, 1570–1640* (Cambridge: Cambridge University Press, 1995).

    'Citizenship and Republicanism in Elizabethan England', in van Gelderen and Skinner, eds., *Republicanism*, I, pp. 85–106.

Perry, Curtis, *The Making of Jacobean Culture: James I and the Renegotiation of Elizabethan Literary Practice* (Cambridge: Cambridge University Press, 1997).

Phillips, James Emerson, 'George Buchanan and the Sidney Circle', *HLQ* 12 (1948–9), 23–55.

    Images of a Queen: Mary Stuart in Sixteenth-Century Literature (Berkeley: University of California Press, 1964).

Platt, Michael, 'The Rape of Lucrece and the Republic for Which it Stands', *Centennial Review* 19 (1975), 59–79.

Rome and Romans according to Shakespeare (Lanham: University Press of America, 1983).

Pocock, J. G. A., *Politics, Language and Time: Essays on Political Thought and History* (London: Methuen, 1972).

The Machiavellian Moment: Florentine Political Thought and the Atlantic Republican Tradition (Princeton: Princeton University Press, 1975).

The Ancient Constitution and the Feudal Law: A Study of English Historical Thought in the Seventeenth Century (rev. ed., Cambridge: Cambridge University Press, 1987).

Poole, Kristen Elizabeth, 'Garbled Martyrdom in Christopher Marlowe's *The Massacre at Paris*', *CD* 32 (1998), 1–25.

Potter, Lois, **Othello**: *Shakespeare in Performance* (Manchester: Manchester University Press, 2002).

Prall, Stuart E., 'The Development of Equity in Tudor England', *AJLH* 8 (1964), 1–19.

Pugliatti, Paola, *Shakespeare the Historian* (Basingstoke: Macmillan, 1996).

Quint, David, *Epic and Empire: Politics and Generic Form from Virgil to Milton* (Princeton: Princeton University Press, 1993).

Raab, Felix, *The English Face of Machiavelli: A Changing Interpretation, 1500–1700* (London: Routledge, 1965).

Rackin, Phyllis, 'Shakespeare's Boy Cleopatra, the Decorum of Nature, and the Golden World of Poetry', in Drakakis, ed., *Antony and Cleopatra*, pp. 78–100.

Rahe, Paul A., 'Situating Machiavelli', in Hankins, ed., *Renaissance Civic Humanism*, pp. 270–308.

Rambuss, Richard, *Spenser's Secret Career* (Cambridge: Cambridge University Press, 1993).

'What It Feels Like For a Boy: Shakespeare's *Venus and Adonis*', in Dutton and Howard, eds., *Companion to Shakespeare's Works*, IV, pp. 240–58.

Ray, Sid, '"Rape, I fear, was root of they annoy": The Politics of Consent in *Titus Andronicus*', *SQ* 49 (1998), 22–39.

Rebholz, Ronald A., *The Life of Fulke Greville, First Lord Brooke* (Oxford: Clarendon Press, 1971).

Rebhorn, Wayne C., 'The Crisis of the Aristocracy in *Julius Caesar*', *RQ* 43 (1990), 78–109.

The Emperor of Men's Minds: Literature and the Renaissance Discourse of Rhetoric (Ithaca, N.Y.: Cornell University Press, 1995).

Rees, Ennis, *The Tragedies of George Chapman: Renaissance Ethics in Action* (Cambridge, Mass.: Harvard University Press, 1954).

Rees, Joan, *Samuel Daniel: A Critical and Biographical Study* (Liverpool: Liverpool University Press, 1964).

Fulke Greville, Lord Brooke, 1554–1628: A Critical Biography (London: Routledge, 1971).

Relihan, Constance, *Fashioning Authority: The Development of Elizabethan Novelistic Discourse* (Kent, Ohio: Kent State University Press, 1994).

Rhodes, Neil, 'Shakespeare the Barbarian', in Richards, ed., *Early Modern Civil Discourses*, pp. 99–104.

Shakespeare and the Origins of English (Oxford: Oxford University Press, 2004).

Richards, Jennifer, *Rhetoric and Courtliness in Early Modern Literature* (Cambridge: Cambridge University Press, 2003).

ed., *Early Modern Civil Discourses* (Basingstoke: Palgrave/Macmillan, 2003).

Riggs, David, *Shakespeare's Heroical Histories: **Henry VI** and its Literary Tradition* (Cambridge, Mass.: Harvard University Press, 1971).

Ben Jonson: A Life (Cambridge, Mass.: Harvard University Press, 1989).

The World of Christopher Marlowe (London: Faber, 2004).

Rist, Thomas, *Shakespeare's Romances and the Politics of Counter-Reformation* (Lampeter: Edwin Mellen Press, 1999).

Roberts, Sasha, *Reading Shakespeare's Poems in Early Modern England* (Basingstoke: Palgrave, 2003).

Rockin, Edward L., 'Measured Endings: How Productions from 1720 to 1929 Close Shakespeare's Open Silences in *Measure for Measure*', *Sh. Sur.* 53 (2000), 213–32.

Roe, John, 'Ovid "renascent" in *Venus and Adonis* and *Hero and Leander*', in A. B. Taylor, ed., *Shakespeare's Ovid*, pp. 31–46.

Shakespeare and Machiavelli (Cambridge: Brewer, 2002).

Ronan, Clifford J., '*Caesar's Revenge* and the Roman Thoughts in *Antony and Cleopatra*', *Sh. St.* 19 (1987), 171–82.

Rosenberg, Eleanor, *Leicester, Patron of Letters* (New York: Columbia University Press, 1955).

Rubenstein, Nicolai, 'Italian Political Thought, 1450–1530', in Burns and Goldie, eds., *Cambridge History of Political Thought*, pp. 30–65.

Russell, Conrad, *The Crisis of Parliaments: English History, 1509–1660* (Oxford: Oxford University Press, 1971).

Ryan, Pat M., Jr., *Thomas Lodge, Gentleman* (Hamden, Conn.: Shoe String Press, 1958).

Saccio, Peter, *The Court Comedies of John Lyly: A Study in Allegorial Dramaturgy* (Princeton, N.J.: Princeton University Press, 1969).

Shakespeare's English Kings: History, Chronicle, Drama (2nd ed., Oxford: Oxford University Press, 2000).

Sacks, David Harris, 'Parliament, Liberty, and the Commonweal', in J. H. Hexter, ed., *Parliament and Liberty: From the Reign of Elizabeth to the English Civil War* (Stanford: Stanford University Press, 1992), pp. 85–121.

'Political Culture', in Kastan, ed., *Companion to Shakespeare*, pp. 117–36.

Said, Edward, *Culture and Imperialism* (London: Chatto and Windus, 1993).

Salgado, Gamini, *The Elizabethan Underworld* (London: Dent, 1977).

Salmon, J. H. M., 'Catholic Resistance Theory, Ultramontanism, and the Royalist Response, 1580–1620', in Burns and Goldie, eds., *Cambridge History of Political Thought*, pp. 219–53.

'Seneca and Tacitus in Jacobean England', in Peck, ed., *Mental World,* pp. 169–88.

Sams, Eric, *The Real Shakespeare: Retrieving the Early Years, 1564–1594* (New Haven: Yale University Press, 1995).

Sanders, Julie, *Ben Jonson's Theatrical Republics* (Basingstoke: Macmillan, 1998).

Sandison, Helen Estabrook, 'Arthur Gorges, Spenser's Alcyon and Ralegh's Friend', *PMLA* 43 (1928), 645–74.

Scarisbrick, J. J., *Henry VIII* (London: Methuen, 1968).

Scott, Jonathan, *Algernon Sidney and the English Republic, 1623–77* (Cambridge: Cambridge University Press, 1988).

'Classical Republicanism in Seventeenth-Century England and the Netherlands', in van Gelderen and Skinner, eds., *Republicanism,* I, pp. 61–81.

Sells, A. Lytton, *The Paradise of Travellers: The Italian Influence on Englishmen in the Seventeenth Century* (London: Allen and Unwin, 1964).

Seymour-Smith, Martin, *Shakespeare's Non-Dramatic Poetry* (London: Greenwich Exchange, 2000).

Shapiro, James, *Shakespeare and the Jews* (New York: Columbia University Press, 1996).

'"Metre meete to furnish Lucans style": Reconsidering Marlowe's Lucan', in Kenneth Friedenreich, Roma Gill, and Constance B. Kuriyama, eds., *'A poet and a filthy playmaker': New Essays on Christopher Marlowe.* (New York: AMS, 1988), pp. 315–26.

Sharpe, Kevin, '"An Image Doting Rabble": The Failure of Republican Culture in Seventeenth-Century England', in Kevin Sharpe and Steven Zwicker, eds., *Refiguring Revolutions: Aesthetics and Politics from the English Revolution to the Romantic Revolution* (Berkeley: University of California Press, 1998), pp. 25–56.

Remapping Early Modern England: The Culture of Seventeenth-Century Politics (Cambridge: Cambridge University Press, 2000).

Reading Revolutions: The Politics of Early Modern England (New Haven: Yale University Press, 2000).

and Peter Lake, eds., *Culture and Politics in Early Stuart England* (Basingstoke: Macmillan, 1994).

and Steven N. Zwicker, eds., *Reading, Society and Politics in Early Modern England* (Cambridge: Cambridge University Press, 2003).

Shell, Alison, *Catholicism, Controversy and the English Literary Imagination, 1558–1660* (Cambridge: Cambridge University Press, 1999).

Shephard, Amanda, *Gender and Authority in Sixteenth-Century England: The Knox Debate* (Keele: Keele University Press, 1994).

Shrank, Cathy, *Writing the Nation in Reformation England, 1530–1580* (Oxford: Oxford University Press, 2004).

Shuger, Debora Kuller, *Political Theologies in Shakespeare's England: The Sacred and the State in **Measure for Measure*** (Basingstoke: Palgrave, 2001).

Siebert, F. S., *Freedom of the Press in England, 1476–1776: The Rise and Decline of Government Controls* (Urbana: University of Illinois Press, 1952).

Silberman, Laren, *Transforming Desire: Erotic Knowledge in Books III and IV of* **The Faerie Queene** (Berkeley: University of California Press, 1995).

Silke, J. J., *Ireland and Europe, 1559–1607* (Dundalk: Dundalgan, 1966).

Simonds, Peggy Muñoz, '"To the Very Heart of Loss": Renaissance Iconography in Shakespeare's *Antony and Cleopatra*', *Sh. St.* 22 (1994), 220–76.

Sinfield, Alan, *Faultlines: Cultural Materialism and the Politics of Dissident Reading* (Oxford: Oxford University Press, 1992).

Singh, Jyotsna G., 'The Politics of Empathy in *Antony and Cleopatra*: A View From Below', in Dutton and Howard, eds., *Companion to Shakespeare's Works*, I, pp. 411–29.

Sisson, C. J., 'Thomas Lodge and His Family', in Sisson, ed., *Thomas Lodge and other Elizabethans* (London: Cass, 1966, rpt. of 1933), pp. 1–163.

Skinner, Quentin, *The Foundations of Modern Political Thought*, 2 vols. (Cambridge: Cambridge University Press, 1978).

Machiavelli (Oxford: Oxford University Press, 1981).

Reason and Rhetoric in the Philosophy of Hobbes (Cambridge: Cambridge University Press, 1996).

Liberty Before Liberalism (Cambridge: Cambridge University Press, 1998).

Visions of Politics, 3 vols. (Cambridge: Cambridge University Press, 2002).

Smith, Ian, '*Titus Andronicus*: A Time for Race and Revenge', in Dutton and Howard, eds., *Companion to Shakespeare*, II, pp. 284–302.

Smith, Lacey Baldwin, *Treason in Tudor England: Politics and Paranoia* (London: Cape, 1966).

Elizabeth Tudor: Portrait of a Queen (London: Cape, 1975).

Smith, Molly, *Breaking Boundaries: Politics and Play in the Drama of Shakespeare and his Contemporaries* (Aldershot: Ashgate, 1998).

Smith, Nigel, *Literature and Revolution in England, 1640–1660* (New Haven: Yale University Press, 1994).

Smuts, Malcolm, 'Court-Centred Politics and the Use of Roman Historians', in Sharpe and Zwicker, eds., *Culture and Politics*, pp. 21–43.

Sohmer, Steve, *Shakespeare's Mystery Play: The Opening of the Globe Theatre, 1599* (Manchester: Manchester University Press, 1999).

Sokol, B. J. and Mary Sokol, *Shakespeare's Legal Language: A Dictionary* (London: Athlone, 2000).

Solnit, Rebecca, *A Book of Migrations: Some Passages in Ireland* (London: Verso, 1997).

Sommerville, J. P., *Politics and Ideology in England, 1603–1640* (Harlow: Longman, 1986).

'Absolutism and Royalism', in Burns and Goldie, eds., *Cambridge History of Political Thought*, pp. 347–73.

'James I and the Divine Right of Kings: English Politics and Continental Theory', in Peck, ed., *Mental World*, pp. 55–70.

Somogyi, Nicholas de, *Shakespeare's Theatre of War* (Aldershot: Ashgate, 1998).

Spear, Gary, 'Shakespeare's "Manly" Parts: Masculinity and Effeminacy in *Troilus and Cressida*', *SQ* 44 (1993), 409–22.

Spearing, A. C., *Medieval Dream Poetry* (Cambridge: Cambridge University Press, 1976).

Spellman, W. M., *European Political Thought, 1600–1700* (Basingstoke: Macmillan, 1998).

Spencer, T. J. B., 'Shakespeare and the Elizabethan Romans', *Sh. Sur.* 10 (1957), 27–38.

Spiekerman, Tim, *Shakespeare's Political Realism: The English History Plays* (Albany: State University of New York Press, 1991).

Spivack, Bernard, *Shakespeare and the Allegory of Evil: The History of a Metaphor in Relation to his Major Villains* (New York: Columbia University Press, 1958).

Steane, J. B., *Marlowe: A Critical Study* (Cambridge: Cambridge University Press, 1970).

Stanton, Kay, 'Made to write "whore" upon?: Male and Female Use of the Word "Whore" in Shakespeare's Canon', in Dympna Callaghan, ed., *A Feminist Companion to Shakespeare* (Oxford: Blackwell, 2000), pp. 80–102.

Stewart, Alan, *Close Readers: Humanism and Sodomy in Early Modern England* (Princeton: Princeton University Press, 1997).

The Cradle King: The Life of James VI and I, the First Monarch of a United Great Britain (London: Chatto and Windus, 2003).

Stock, Angela, 'Stow's *Survey* and the London Playwrights', in Ian Gadd and Alexandra Gillespie, eds., *John Stow (1525–1605) and the Making of the English Past* (London: British Library, 2004), pp. 89–98.

Stocker, Margarita, *Judith, Sexual Warrior: Women and Power in Western Culture* (New Haven: Yale University Press, 1998).

Stone, Lawrence, *The Crisis of the Aristocracy, 1558–1641* (Oxford: Clarendon Press, 1965).

Strong, Roy, *Art and Power: Renaissance Festivals, 1450–1650* (Woodbridge: Boydell, 1973).

Taufer, Alison, *Holinshed's **Chronicles*** (New York: Twayne, 1999).

Taunton, Nina, *1590s Drama and Militarism: Portrayals of War in Marlowe, Chapman and Shakespeare's **Henry V*** (Aldershot: Ashgate, 2001).

Taylor, A. B., ed., *Shakespeare's Ovid: The **Metamorphoses** in the Plays and Poems* (Cambridge: Cambridge University Press, 2000).

'Animals in "manly shape as too the outward showe": Moralizing and Metamorphosis in *Titus Andronicus*', in Taylor, ed., *Shakespeare's Ovid*, pp. 66–80.

Taylor, Gary, *Reinventing Shakespeare: A Cultural History from the Restoration to the Present* (London: Hogarth, 1989).

'Shakespeare and Others: The Authorship of *Henry VI, Part One*', *MRDE* 7 (1995), 145–205.

Tennenhouse, Leonard, 'Strategies of State and Political Plays: *A Midsummer Night's Dream, Henry IV, Henry V, Henry VIII*', in Dollimore and Sinfield, eds., *Political Shakespeare*, pp. 109–28.

Power on Display: The Politics of Shakespeare's Genres (London: Methuen, 1986).

Thomson, Peter, *Shakespeare's Professional Career* (Cambridge: Cambridge University Press, 1992).

Thorne, Alison, *Vision and Rhetoric in Shakespeare: Looking Through Language* (Basingstoke: Palgrave, 2000).

Tillyard, E. M. W., *The Elizabethan World Picture* (Harmondsworth: Penguin, 1963, rpt. of 1943).

Shakespeare's History Plays (London: Chatto and Windus, 1944).

Trevor-Roper, Hugh, 'George Buchanan and the Ancient Scottish Constitution', *EHR* Supplement 3 (1966).

Tricomi, Albert H., *Anticourt Drama in England, 1603–1642* (Charlottesville: University Press of Virginia, 1989).

Tuck, Richard, *Philosophy and Government, 1572–1651* (Cambridge: Cambridge University Press, 1993).

Vaughan, Virginia Mason, *Othello: A Contextual History* (Cambridge: Cambridge University Press, 1994).

Veeser, H. Aram, ed., *The New Historicism* (London: Routledge, 1989).

Vickers, Brian, *In Defence of Rhetoric* (Oxford: Clarendon Press, 1988).

Appropriating Shakespeare: Contemporary Critical Quarrels (New Haven: Yale University Press, 1993).

Shakespeare, Co-Author: A Historical Study of Five Collaborative Plays (Oxford: Oxford University Press, 2002).

Walker, Greg, *Plays of Persuasion: Drama and Politics at the Court of Henry VIII* (Cambridge: Cambridge University Press, 1991).

Persuasive Fictions: Faction, Faith and Political Culture in the Reign of Henry VIII (Aldershot: Scolar Press, 1996).

The Politics of Performance in Early Renaissance Drama (Cambridge: Cambridge University Press, 1998).

Walker, Julia M., ed., *Dissing Elizabeth: Negative Representations of Gloriana* (Durham, N.C.: Duke University Press, 1998).

Walsh, P. G., *Livy: His Historical Aims and Methods* (Cambridge: Cambridge University Press, 1961).

Ward, John O., 'Renaissance Commentators on Ciceronian Rhetoric', in Murphy, ed., *Renaissance Rhetoric*, pp. 126–73.

'Cicero and Quintillian', in Glyn P. Norton, ed., *The Cambridge History of Literary Criticism: Volume III, The Renaissance* (Cambridge: Cambridge University Press, 1999), pp. 77–87.

Watson, Donald G., 'The Contraries of *Venus and Adonis*', *SP* 75 (1978), 32–63

Waugh, Evelyn, *Edmund Campion: Scholar, Priest, Hero, and Martyr* (Oxford: Oxford University Press, 1980, rpt. of 1935).

Weil, Judith, *Christopher Marlowe: Merlin's Prophet* (Cambridge: Cambridge University Press, 1977).

Weiner, Carol Z., 'The Beleaguered Isle: A Study of Elizabethan and Early Jacobean Anti-Catholicism', *P. & P.* 51 (1971), 27–62.

Wells, Charles, *The Wide Arch: Roman Value in Shakespeare* (Bristol: Bristol Classical Press, 1993).

Wells, Robin Headlam, *Shakespeare, Politics and the State* (Basingstoke: Macmillan, 1986).

'"The Question of These Wars": *Hamlet* in the New Europe', in Hattaway et al., eds., *Shakespeare in the New Europe*, pp. 92–109.

Shakespeare on Masculinity (Cambridge: Cambridge University Press, 2000).

'*Julius Caesar*, Machiavelli, and the Uses of History', *Sh. Sur.* 55 (2002), 209–18.

Wernham, R. B., *After the Armada: Elizabethan England and the Struggle for Western Europe, 1588–1595* (Oxford: Clarendon Press, 1984).

Whigham, Frank, *Seizures of the Will in Early Modern English Drama* (Cambridge: Cambridge University Press, 1996).

White, Robert, 'The Cultural Impact of the Massacre of St Bartholomew's Day', in Richards, ed., *Early Modern Civil Discourses*, pp. 183–99.

Whitworth, Charles, '*Rosalynde*: As You Like It and As Lodge Wrote It', *ES* 58 (1977), 114–17.

Wieler, John William, *George Chapman: The Effect of Stoicism upon his Tragedies* (New York: King's Crown Press, 1949).

Williamson, Arthur H., *Scottish National Consciousness in the Age of James VI* (Edinburgh: Donald, 1979).

Willson, D. Harris, *King James VI and I* (London: Cape, 1956).

Wilson, F. P., *The Plague in Shakespeare's London* (Oxford: Oxford University Press, 1999, rpt. of 1927).

Wilson, Richard, 'Shakespeare and the Jesuits', *TLS*, 19 December 1997.

'"Is this a holiday?": Shakespeare's Roman Carnival', in Wilson, ed., *Julius Caesar*, pp. 55–76.

Secret Shakespeare: Studies in Theatre, Religion and Resistance (Manchester: Manchester University Press, 2004).

ed., *Julius Caesar: Contemporary Critical Essays* (Basingstoke: Palgrave, 2002).

Wilson-Okamura, David Scott, 'Spenser and the Two Queens', *ELR* 32 (2002), 62–84.

Winstanley, Lilian, ***Hamlet*** and the Scottish Succession (Cambridge: Cambridge University Press, 1921).

Wolfe, Jessica, *Humanism, Machinery and Renaissance Literature* (Cambridge: Cambridge University Press, 2004).

Womersley, David, '*3 Henry VI*: Shakespeare, Tacitus, and Parricide', *N. & Q.* 280 (December 1985), 468–73.

'Sir Henry Saville's Translation of Tacitus and the Political Interpretation of Elizabethan Texts', *RES*, ns, 42 (1991), 313–42.

Wood, Michael, *In Search of Shakespeare* (London: BBC, 2003).

Woodcock, Matthew, '"The World is Made For Use": Theme and Form in Fulke Greville's Verse Treatises', *SJ* 19 (2001), 143–59.

Woolf, D. R., *Reading History in Early Modern England* (Cambridge: Cambridge University Press, 2000).

Worden, Blair, 'The Commonwealth Kidney of Algernon Sidney', *JBS* 24 (1985), 1–40.

'English Republicanism', in Burns and Goldie, eds., *Cambridge History of Political Thought*, pp. 443–75.

'Shakespeare and Politics', *Sh. Sur.* 44 (1991), 1–15.

'Ben Jonson among the Historians', in Sharpe and Lake, eds., *Culture and Politics in Early Stuart England*, pp. 67–90.

*The Sound of Virtue: Philip Sidney's **Arcadia** and Elizabethan Politics* (New Haven: Yale University Press, 1996).

'Republicanism, Regicide and Republic: The English Experience', in van Gelderen and Skinner, eds., *Republicanism*, I, pp. 307–27.

Wormald, Jenny, *Court, Kirk, and Community: Scotland 1470–16* (London: Arnold, 1981).

'James VI and I: Two Kings or One?', *History* 68 (1983), 187–209.

'Gunpowder, Treason, and Scots', *JBS* 24 (1985), 141–68.

Mary Queen of Scots: A Study in Failure (London: George Philip, 1988).

'James VI and I, *Basilikon Doron* and *The Trew Law of Free Monarchies*: the Scottish context and the English Translation', in Peck, ed., *Mental World*, pp. 36–54.

Wraight, A. D., and Virginia F. Stern, *In Search of Christopher Marlowe: A Pictorial Biography* (Chichester: Adam Hart, 1993, rpt. of 1965).

Wright, Gillian, 'What Daniel really did with the *Pharsalia*: *The Civil Wars*, Lucan, and King James', *RES*, ns, 55 (2004), 210–32.

Wright, Johnson Kent, 'The Idea of a Republican Constitution in Old Régime France', in van Gelderen and Skinner, eds., *Republicanism*, I, pp. 288–306.

Yachnin, Paul, 'Shakespeare's Problem Plays and the Drama of His Time: *Troilus and Cressida*, *All's Well That Ends Well*, *Measure for Measure*', in Dutton and Howard, eds., *Companion to Shakespeare's Works*, IV, pp. 46–68.

Yates, Frances A., *Astrea: The Imperial Theme in the Sixteenth Century* (London: Routledge, 1985, rpt. of 1975).

Zaret, David, *Origins of Democratic Culture: Printing, Petitions, and the Public Sphere in Early-Modern England* (Princeton: Princeton University Press, 2000).

Zeeveld, W. Gordon, *The Temper of Shakespeare's Thought* (New Haven: Yale University Press, 1974).

Zurbuchen, Simone, 'Republicanism and Toleration', in van Gelderen and Skinner, eds., *Republicanism*, II, pp. 47–71.

Index